The Parliamentarians

The Parliamentarians

The History of the Commonwealth Parliamentary Association, 1911—1985

Ian Grey

Gower

Published by
Gower Publishing Company Limited
Gower House
Croft Road
Aldershot
Hants GU11 3HR
England

Gower Publishing Company
Old Post Road
Brookfield
Vermont 05036
USA

British Library Cataloguing in Publication Data
Grey, Ian
    The parliamentarians : the history of the
    Commonwealth Parliamentary Association,
    1911–1958.
    1. Commonwealth Parliamentary Association
    —History
    I. Grey, Ian
    328′.3′0601   JF501

    ISBN 0-566-05199-0

Printed in Great Britain at the University Press, Cambridge

Contents

For Robin,

Friend and Colleague

Foreword

This is an important book for all who care about parliamentary government. It is important because it is the story of the Commonwealth Parliamentary Association which has over the 75 years of its existence stood as the chief bulwark and protagonist of parliamentary democracy in the Commonwealth. It has fostered a sense of fellowship and a community of spirit among Parliamentarians. It has promoted the study and understanding of parliamentary affairs. Indeed, it has made, and continues to make, a positive contribution to the strength of the institution of Parliament which is central to our way of life.

Recent years have witnessed an alarming decline in law and order in many countries. The significance of Parliament as being at the heart of every nation has been repeatedly challenged. Military coups appear to have become endemic in some regions, while in others the spectre of anarchy has loomed. But even in those troubled parts of the Commonwealth there has remained among leaders a strong and persistent concern to re-establish a stable, democratic system in the future. It has been part of the CPA's achievement that it has kept that aspiration alive.

This history relates the fascinating story of the beginnings and the vigorous growth of the Association. At the same time it gives an insight into the progression from Empire to Commonwealth. It records also the remarkable works of Sir Howard d'Egville, a name unknown to most people but one which deserves to be remembered wherever parliamentary democracy is revered.

Bernard Weatherill
Speaker, House of Commons

Preface

The CPA is not widely known outside parliamentary circles. It is, however, a vast and influential organisation with branches in virtually all legislatures in the Commonwealth. It has well over 7000 members, all members of their respective Parliaments. It has an extensive annual programme of conferences, parliamentary seminars and study groups, as well as publications and parliamentary information services.

This history is a record of the foundation, objectives and expansion of the Empire, now Commonwealth, Parliamentary Association from its formation in 1911 up to 1985, its 75th anniversary, celebrated at the plenary conference in London in September 1986. It is a work of record, but seeks also to do more than present a bare listing of events and personalities. The Association is an important element in the Commonwealth itself, reflecting and contributing to the great constitutional changes that have taken place, especially since 1947. It is therefore presented in the context of the evolving Commonwealth.

To many during the past four decades it has seemed that the Commonwealth in action is best observed in the work of the non-governmental organisations which bring together people with professional and other common interests. Among the 200 or so organisations of this kind, examples are the Commonwealth Universities Conference, the Commonwealth Magistrates Association, the Commonwealth Broadcasting Association and, perhaps the most important of all, the Commonwealth Parliamentary Association. It is the great network of non-governmental associations which gives real meaning to the Commonwealth in times when its very existence is often threatened by conflicting political and economic interests.

The initiative in commissioning a history of the CPA was taken by Mr Peter Howson, a former Australian Minister. He played an important role in the development of the Association as Chairman of the seminal working party which met in Malta in 1967, and then as the first Chairman of the Executive Committee. He has remained a keen supporter. In 1970 Lord Gordon Walker accepted the commission to write the history. Patrick Gordon Walker had been closely involved in Commonwealth affairs throughout his long parliamentary career; and in 1962 he published *The Commonwealth*, a lengthy study, expressing his faith in its future.

Patrick Gordon Walker completed the first draft of the history in 1974. However, it proved unacceptable to the CPA Executive Committee. He had compressed the period 1960–73 into a few pages, and the Committee wished him to expand greatly his account of the major developments of these years. Gordon Walker, troubled by ill-health at this time, felt unable to undertake this further task. Subsequently, he asked me to write this second part of the history, which would then be published over our joint names. I was unable to accept this proposal. As a member of the Headquarters Secretariat, I would, I felt, have been under constraints. The production of the history then lapsed.

In 1981, Mr Peter Howson revived his initiative and proposed that I should undertake the project afresh. The Executive Committee approved, and I agreed to start work after my retirement in May 1983.

In commissioning the history, the Committee agreed that I should be free to present my own interpretation of events, policies and personalities. This was, of course, subject to the understanding that I would not necessarily express the views of the Committee or of the Association as a whole. Indeed, in an Association so complex, embracing nearly every race, culture and creed, it would be remarkable for an historian to expect agreement with his every word. It is nevertheless my hope that this history will have general approval and that it will be seen as a contribution to the understanding and further development not only of the Association but also of the Commonwealth itself.

The first part of this history might be sub-titled 'the d'Egville saga'. Howard d'Egville is the creative force, constantly at the centre of the stage, with others appearing to be no more than puppets, manipulated by him. This is a false impression. Men like Clement Attlee, Pethick Lawrence, Harold Holt, Arthur Roebuck, Donald Sangster and many others responded to d'Egville's idealism, single-mindedness and vision. The conception of a great Association promoting cooperation and understanding among MPs throughout the Commonwealth and with members of the US Congress as well as serving to strengthen parliamentary institutions exerted a strong appeal. This was d'Egville's conception and in his energetic and practical approach to making it a reality he attracted their support. He was often a tiresome man, but he was also in some degree a statesman, who contributed more to the Commonwealth than many others whose names are far better known. Thus it is inevitable that he should dominate much of this history.

I have drawn primarily on the CPA archives, on verbatim reports of conferences, General Meetings and General Assemblies. The minutes of the meetings of the General Council and of the Executive Committee as well as their reports have, of course, been indispensable. Quotations from correspondence and other unpublished papers have not been attributed since these documents are uncatalogued, but are kept in the CPA archives in the Secretariat in chronological order. References to published reports of various kinds are noted under each chapter. The memories and advice of former colleagues and of members themselves have been of great value. For the broader history of the Commonwealth I have relied mainly on the scholarly works of Sir Keith Hancock, Professor Nicholas Mansergh and Professor J.D.B. Miller.

In the period of this history many members have acquired titles. It would have been difficult to record them each time without disrupting narrative and adding further to the amount of detail. I have therefore followed the general rule of giving the title of the individual as at the time of his or her first mention. The final title is recorded in brackets in the index, thus: Braine, Bernard (Rt Hon. Sir Bernard Braine). . . .

I record my indebtedness especially to Mr Peter Howson, to Professor J.D.B. Miller of the Australian National University, to the Hon. Gerald Ottenheimer, then Minister of Justice and Attorney-General, Newfoundland and Chairman of the CPA's Executive Committee, 1981–84, to the Rt Hon. Sir Bernard Braine, MP, to Shri Subhash Kashyap, Secretary-General of the Lok Sabha, Parliament of India, to Sir Robin Vanderfelt, the present (1985) Secretary-General, to Dr John Henderson, Deputy Secretary-General (1983–85), and to Mr L.M. Fowler, formerly Assistant Secretary-General. All have kindly read the history in draft, and their comments have been most helpful and encouraging. I record my thanks to Mrs Miriam Alman, the CPA's Librarian and Information Officer, and to Mrs Susan Burchett, a former colleague, for their help and comments. I am, as always, deeply indebted to Winsome, my wife, for her constant and loving support.

IAN GREY
Chiswick, London

Introduction

The year 1911 marked the beginning of a new era in Britain. The elegance and stability of the Edwardian age had come to an end with the death of Edward VII. The new King, George V, ascended the throne in a period of troubled change. Anxieties were mounting about the dangers of war with Germany. Internally the country was torn by strikes and demands for better conditions for the workers. There was even talk of a social revolution.

At Westminster, too, there was bitter, sometimes impassioned, debate over the Parliament Bill, leading to scenes of exceptional turmoil in both Houses. The Bill was designed to limit fundamentally the powers of the Lords. The deadlock was broken only when the Prime Minister, Asquith, obtained the King's agreement to create new peers in numbers sufficient to ensure the passage of the Bill. The threat was enough: the Bill became law in August 1911.

The Empire was also a matter of concern. Disraeli had once referred to the colonies as 'wretched millstones'. Many now saw the Empire as a burden which the country could no longer afford. The great majority, however, took pride in it as a mighty achievement but all recognised that it, too, was changing and must change dramatically in the years ahead.

The coronation of George V gave a brief respite from this plague of anxieties. The Crown represented stability and the unity of the nation. The summer of 1911, the 'Coronation summer' as many were to remember it, was the hottest in living memory. On 22 June 1911 the King was crowned with customary magnificence. In the brilliant weather it was even more unforgettable. The country gave itself over to a short season of celebration.

Among the events associated with this great occasion was the formation of the Empire Parliamentary Association.

1 The Beginning

The future of the Empire was exercising many minds in Britain at the turn of the century. The general desire was to ensure its continuity by conceding the demands of the colonies of settlement while at the same time relieving Britain of the heavy financial burdens, especially for defence.

The concept of an Imperial Federation appealed to many in Britain. An Imperial Federation League had been formed in 1884. Ten years later its policies were modified and it adopted the name of the Imperial Federation (Defence) Committee. Soon after the formation of this Committee, a young barrister, Howard d'Egville, became involved in its work. By 1900 he was lecturing in London and the provinces on its objectives. On 3 December 1901 he was voted an honorarium of £20 a year and a fee of 1 guinea and expenses for each lecture he delivered. He became a member of the Committee in March 1902 and on 18 November 1903 its Honorary Secretary with an honorarium of £30 a year.

D'Egville recognised, however, that federation would never be acceptable to all the self-governing colonies, and he set about changing the Committee's policy. On 3 June 1908 he reported that he had been in contact with 'persons of influence in Canada', and that he had received letters suggesting that he visit that country for discussions. The Committee approved the visit and voted the sum of £100 to £125 for his expenses.

On his return to London he pressed for a review of its aims and organisation. The changes which he wrought were reflected in its new name, the Imperial Cooperation League. This was welcomed by the Canadians in particular, who had been strongly opposed to the concept of an Imperial Federation.

By this time d'Egville was not only running the League but dominating it. It was noteworthy that when, on 30 April 1910, thirteen new members were elected to its Executive Committee, all were nominated by him and seconded by his assistant, Lieut L.H. Hordern, RN. He was to show during his long career an impressive talent for manipulating committees and ensuring that they were supportive of his plans.

The death of Edward VII, the accession of George V, and the impending coronation precipitated new action. In a lecture, delivered in June 1910, L.S. Amery, one of the leading statesmen of the day, said:

> Why should not the coronation be made the occasion for calling together representatives of all the free Parliaments of the Empire to attend the formal inauguration of a reign destined, we all believe, to be of such momentous significance for the whole future of the Empire? The solemn ceremony of coronation, bringing deeply home to all who attend it the great ideas of imperial unity and historical continuity personified in the Crown, is one to which the members of the Empire's Parliaments might well be summoned ...[1]

This was the first public expression of an idea which had been under discussion in the Imperial Cooperation League. On 12 July 1910 the League appointed a Committee of its members who were also MPs. Its purpose was to ascertain what support the proposal to invite delegations of Dominion MPs to London for the coronation would have in the Lords and the Commons. The Committee was also to approach the government about meeting the visitors' expenses, and about the allocation of seats in Westminster Abbey.

In both Houses support for the proposal was strong. A prestigious Committee of the Lords and Commons was formed. Its first general meeting took place in November 1910 with its Deputy Chairman, W. Hayes Fisher, MP, presiding. Membership of the Committee included the Prime Minister, H.H. Asquith, the Lord Chancellor, Lord Loreburn, the Speaker of the House of Commons, J. W. Lowther, and the Leader of the Opposition, A. J. Balfour. The Earl of Rosebery was its Chairman, and the Earl of Derby, Chairman of the Invitations Committee. The Committee agreed to invite 18 members from each of the Parliaments of Australia and Canada, 14 from South Africa, 8 from New Zealand and 2 from Newfoundland.[2] It approved a draft programme for the visitors. Furthermore, it decided that the government should not be asked to defray the expenses of this parliamentary visit: members of the Committee and others at Westminster would themselves pay.

D'Egville was appointed Honorary Secretary of the Committee, whilst remaining Secretary of the Imperial Cooperation League: he needed both organisations to pursue his grand design. This emerged at a meeting of the Executive Committee of the League in June 1911, when it adopted a resolution, submitted in d'Egville's name, that:

> The work of the League had best be directed for the next few months towards the establishment of an association to be called under some such title as Empire Parliamentary Union, having branches in the United Kingdom Parliament and the Parliaments of the overseas Dominions, so that mutual intercourse and exchange of information should be facilitated between home and overseas members, and introductions, parliamentary privileges, travel facilities, meetings and information provided for members in the respective countries.

This was the true beginning of the EPA.

In the short time available, and bearing in mind the slowness of the mail and travel at the time, there must have been a fury of organisation to ensure the arrival of the 60 overseas members (most with their wives), and the arrangement of the comprehensive programme. This formidable task was carried out by d'Egville and a small team of temporary assistants.

On 19 June 1911 the visit began with a luncheon of welcome, held by special permission of the King in Westminster Hall, where the guests of honour were the visiting members, and the hosts were the Lords and Commons Committee. Between 500 and 600 people were seated in groups at circular tables which filled the vast hall. All who were of any importance in British political life at that time were present. In his speech of welcome Lord Rosebery emphasised that it was not a banquet to Leaders, Prime Ministers, or to the great peoples of the Parliaments of the Empire: it was a banquet given by the Private Members of the Parliament of the United Kingdom for the Private Members of the Dominion Parliaments.

On 22 June 1911 the coronation of King George V and Queen Mary took place in Westminster Abbey. The visiting members witnessed the ceremony. They lunched in the Harcourt Room of the House of Commons and then returned to the Abbey to watch the royal procession setting out on its tour of London.

This was the highlight of a brilliant programme, lasting a full month. Every day the visitors attended some major occasion. They were at the naval review at Spithead; they visited Windsor Castle and were received by the King; they paid two visits to Buckingham Palace; then, in July 1911, they set out on a 'country tour', visiting briefly Ireland, Scotland and Wales, and also the principal cities of England. Indeed, they could not have been more warmly received and generously entertained.

The basic purpose of the visit was not, however, overlooked. On 28 June 1911 in Committee Room 15 of the House of Commons, members of the Executive of the Lords and Commons Committee and the visitors, representing the Dominion Parliaments, met in conference. All had received in advance a paper proposing the formation of an 'Empire Parliamentary Association'. The Chairman of the conference, W. Hayes Fisher, opened the discussion in which the visiting members participated. The proposal was unanimously approved. A subcommittee of 14 members was then appointed to draft a constitution. At the final session of the conference, which took place on 18 July 1911, the conference unanimously adopted the constitution for an association, having as its objects:

> The establishment of permanent machinery to provide more ready exchange of information and to facilitate closer understanding and more frequent intercourse between those engaged in the parliamentary government of the component parts of the Empire.[3]

It was further agreed that

> An organisation shall be formed, having a branch in the United Kingdom and in each of

the self-governing Dominions of the Empire, under the title of the Empire Parliamentary Association. Whilst the Association shall be constituted upon strictly non-party lines, it is clearly understood that members making use of the facilities afforded by the Association shall not be debarred from giving the fullest expression to their political views.[4]

The constitution went on to define membership, the privileges of members, subscriptions and the appointment from each overseas delegation of representatives to act as joint Honorary Secretaries. The first Executive Committee of the United Kingdom branch was formed from the Lords and Commons Committee. The Presidents of the branch were the Lord Chancellor and the Speaker; the Chairman of the Executive Committee was Lord Grey; and d'Egville was the Honorary Secretary. In the constitution he was described as 'the founder and organizer of the Association'.

At the end of the visit Hayes Fisher paid public tribute to d'Egville's work, saying: 'the real credit must go to Mr Howard d'Egville who organised the whole of the London and provincial visits and himself conducted our guests to Ireland, Scotland and the chief centres of interest in England.' The last function was a dinner at the Waldorf Hotel, given by the delegates in honour of d'Egville and the three Assistant Secretaries. The tribute was well deserved. With amazing energy he had demonstrated his ability to organise on a grand scale while attending to the smallest detail. He had arranged for each visitor to have a personal copy of the programme, bound in leather and embossed with his own initials. All had railway passes, honorary membership of selected London clubs, and tickets for theatres and music halls, as well as parliamentary privileges. He had organised a fleet of cars for them and made special provision for the handling of their luggage on tour. But he had never lost sight of his principal purpose – the establishment of a permanent Parliamentary Association.

As soon as the visitors had departed he set to work producing a full report of the visit. It was published with lavish illustrations in a handsome binding. The whole enterprise was a considerable achievement for a man aged only 32.

Notes

1. L. S. Amery, *My Political Life* (London, 1953), vol. 1, p.350.
2. Newfoundland was regarded as a Dominion. It had had a legislature since 1832 and achieved responsible government in 1855. Its people voted against joining the Canadian confederation in 1869. Between the wars, however, Newfoundland was stricken by severe economic problems and most acutely during the world depression of the early 1930s. Threatened with bankruptcy, the legislature prayed H.M. the King to suspend the constitution and appoint Commissioners, who under the chairmanship of the Governor and under the supervision of Britain, would govern the country until it was again self-supporting. The Commissioners – three from Newfoundland and three from Britain – took office in 1934. In 1940 the people of Newfoundland voted in a referendum. The result was 78,323 in favour of confederation with Canada and

71,334 in favour of a return to reponsible government. The union of Newfoundland with Canada took effect on 31 March 1949.

3. *Parliaments of the Empire. The First Meeting of Representatives. 1911*, ed. with an introduction by Howard d'Egville (London, 1912), p.86.

4. Ibid., p.87.

2 The Association Grows

During 1912 branches of the Association were formed in the Dominions of Canada, Newfoundland, New Zealand and Australia. The South Africa branch was formed in the following year.[1] The strength of the support for the new Association at Westminster was demonstrated at its first annual general meeting, held on 30 April 1913. The membership was already some 300, including 100 peers. The Speaker took the chair, giving further evidence of Parliament's support.

At this stage the Association reflected the state of the Empire: it comprised branches in the United Kingdom and the five independent Dominions. As a matter of principle the Crown Colonies were excluded. The Dominions themselves were in fact very nearly independent. They had elected legislatures which exercised wide powers. The British government nevertheless, retained the nominal power to reserve and to disallow Dominion legislation. Foreign affairs were wholly within the 'imperial sphere'; and Britain alone could appoint ambassadors to foreign countries and negotiate and conclude treaties with them.

This British hegemony was at first taken for granted, especially at Westminster. The Dominions, however, were growing restive. They wanted a greater say in matters directly concerning their interests. Australia and New Zealand favoured the concept of an Imperial Federation; Canada and South Africa opposed any such arrangement. At this stage, however, the Dominions did not show open opposition to British predominance. They lacked the strength and the confidence to demand equality or full independence.

The Association as a whole was managed by the United Kingdom branch. None questioned its authority to do so; the arrangement simply followed the imperial pattern. But d'Egville did not think of the Association as merely a reflection of the Empire. He saw it as playing a major and independent role in the coming era of change and transformation. It should, he considered, promote discussion and new ideas and maintain a flow of information to all involved in current developments.

On 16 July 1912 the Association gave its first formal dinner, in the Harcourt

Room of the House of Commons. The guest of honour was R. L. (later Sir Robert) Borden, the Prime Minister of Canada. In a lengthy and impressive speech, he sounded a warning that 'the next ten or twenty years would be critical in the history of the Empire'. Printed in full or in extensive summary in the British press and in some Dominion newspapers, the speech provoked wide discussion. The dinner proved to be an important occasion, and it gave an indication of the role that d'Egville envisaged for the Association.

On 23 January 1913 Sir Joseph Ward, the former Prime Minister of New Zealand, was guest of honour at a luncheon in the Harcourt Room. In his speech he advocated the formation of an Empire Parliament which would include elected members from the Dominions. This speech, too, was fully reported in the press and widely discussed.

In April 1913 the United Kingdom branch accepted an invitation from Australia to send 20 members on a visit. D'Egville took charge of the organisation of this first tour and apparently met with some criticism for the way in which the delegates were chosen. On 29 June 1913 *Reynolds'* newspaper reported: 'A good deal of indignation exists among MPs on both sides of the House at the clumsy manner in which invitations were issued. . . . The result has been that no members of any standing whatever in the House will be included in the party.' The report was exaggerated. At least two of the chosen delegates – Leo Amery and Hamar Greenwood – were eminent members. Undoubtedly, however, d'Egville had been active in trying to ensure that the delegation comprised MPs who would further the interests and purposes of the Association. He could never refrain from interfering in this way, and on occasion his lobbying was to arouse strong resentment among members of the United Kingdom branch.

Travel was leisurely in those days. The delegates, accompanied by d'Egville himself, sailed for Canada on 16 July 1913 and from Vancouver on 2 August, reaching Sydney on 2 September. They returned to Britain in mid-November, having visited not only Canada and Australia, but also New Zealand and South Africa, meeting and holding discussions with MPs in all four countries.

The First World War hastened the process of change. King George V declared war on behalf of the whole Empire. The Dominions responded and made a major contribution to victory. The experience strengthened their growing sense of identity and nationhood.

In the early months of the war, however, there was mounting concern in Australia, Canada, and New Zealand about lack of consultation and of information from London. Finally the British government was moved to action. On 19 December 1916 Lloyd George, in his first speech in the House of Commons as Prime Minister, announced that the Dominions would be invited to send representatives to an imperial conference in spring 1917. Leo Amery played an important part in this conference. It was he who proposed that Ministers should be invited from the Dominions 'to join the War Cabinet itself and so assert their full equality and their right to be at the heart of things in deciding the conduct of the war'. The proposal was adopted and the Imperial War Cabinet was formed.

The Association was involved in these developments. It provided a forum in which major speeches could be delivered and a constant exchange of views could take place. Thus Sir Robert Borden addressed a meeting of the Association soon after the Imperial War Cabinet had been set up and indeed while it was actually in session. In the past Borden had strongly criticised the failure of the British government to keep the Dominions informed on matters of policy, and even more its failure to consult with them. In his speech he hailed the new Cabinet as a major advance. He stressed that Prime Ministers and other Ministers from the Dominions now sat with the British Prime Minister and others as equals, and all were responsible to their respective Parliaments. In the House of Commons, on 17 May 1917, Lloyd George also spoke warmly of the Imperial War Cabinet as an important development, and one which, all members of the British Cabinet agreed, should not be allowed to lapse.

The war imposed some restrictions on the young Association, but its activities continued and expanded. D'Egville was tireless in working to ensure that it was strongly established and at the heart of the gradual transformation that was taking place. He had introduced into the Dominion legislatures the important convention that the presiding officers of the two Chambers in each legislature should be the joint Presidents of the branch, and that the Prime Minister and the Leader of the Opposition should be the Vice-Presidents. He had also instituted the practice that the Clerk of one or other House should be the Honorary Secretary of the branch. The exception to the practice was the United Kingdom branch which had a paid Secretary (d'Egville himself) who managed the affairs of the whole Association from London.

Among d'Egville's urgent concerns in these early days was office accommodation. The Association at first shared the office of the Imperial Cooperation League. It then moved to offices of its own at 64 Victoria Street. D'Egville was determined, however, to secure offices 'in close proximity to Parliament' and preferably within the Palace of Westminster itself. This led to a long struggle with the Lord Great Chamberlain and the head of the Office of Works who controlled parliamentary accommodation at this time. It showed d'Egville at his most pertinacious. Early in 1918 rooms were allocated in the Clerk of Parliament's house in the Lords, which the Clerk no longer occupied. A few months later, however, he was told that the branch must vacate the rooms as they were needed by the department responsible for the administration of British prisoners-of-war affairs. D'Egville at once organised a campaign of protest, directed especially at the Office of Works. Finally two smaller rooms were provided in the house.

As he settled into these offices, d'Egville met with a new challenge. In January 1919 the brilliant but sybaritic F. E. Smith, created Lord Birkenhead, became Lord Chancellor. He decided to move into his official residence which included the branch rooms. D'Egville was quick to point out that no Lord Chancellor had occupied the residence before, but to no avail. As Joint President of the United Kingdom branch, however, Birkenhead wrote to the Lord Great Chamberlain expressing the strong hope that he 'would find rooms in some other part of the

Palace of Westminster'. D'Egville now mounted a new campaign with letters from the Speaker and others to the Office of Works. Finally the struggle, which might have provided the plot for a Gilbert and Sullivan opera, was won – d'Egville moved the offices of the branch into Westminster Hall, where they have remained ever since.

Another of d'Egville's initiatives was to arrange for the presentation by the United Kingdom branch to the Canadian Parliament of a Black Rod to replace the one lost in a fire in February 1916. It was the first of a number of presentations which became a feature of the branch's activities, until it was taken over by the House of Commons itself.

One of d'Egville's major achievements during the war was the holding of a conference of the Association in Britain in July 1916. Thirty-three delegates from the five Dominions attended and took part in several conference sessions with British members. They visited Birmingham, Newcastle and other centres, and special visits were made to munitions factories and military establishments. On 7 July 1916 they were received by the King at Buckingham Palace. It was an important conference which went some way to reduce the groundswell of discontent about lack of information from Westminster on the conduct of the war.

The United Kingdom branch had made a request to the Chancellor of the Exchequer for a grant, but this had been set aside on the outbreak of war. D'Egville persisted, however, and in 1916 obtained a special grant to help finance visits of Dominion members during the war. Soon afterwards the Chancellor of the Exchequer, Austen Chamberlain, approved an annual grant to the branch. The grant has continued, and the practice has been followed in all other Commonwealth countries where branches of the Association exist.

By the end of the war the Dominions were virtually sovereign and equal with the United Kingdom. This could be inferred from the facts that they had taken part in the peace negotiations at Versailles and had signed the peace treaties in 1919. They were, moreover, full members of the League of Nations. But in law they were not equal and the constitutional and political problems involved in conferring that equality exercised many men, especially General Smuts.[2]

In spite of the advances in their status and power during the war, the Dominions found that in practice Britain still controlled their relations with foreign countries. There was only the barest consultation and, apart from occasional summary reports on the international situation, there was no flow of information, with Westminster appearing scarcely to appreciate the paucity of information available in the Dominions. Britain had embassies or missions in every part of the world; its newspapers had correspondents overseas to report on news and political developments; London was a great centre for news, but such sources did not extend to the Dominions, where there was some resentment over the failure to keep them informed. D'Egville was keenly aware of the need for a flow of information. In the course of his tour in 1913 he had come to appreciate the feeling among many people in the Dominions of being remote from the centres of world affairs and of having no access to current news and information.

He had always considered that one of the basic functions of the Association must be to distribute both parliamentary and political information.

His proposals for publications to be compiled in London and sent regularly to all branches met with little enthusiasm from members of the United Kingdom branch. Among overseas members, however, he found keen support for his proposal that a quarterly journal containing summaries of proceedings in Commonwealth Parliaments be published. Indeed, the Australian, Canadian, and New Zealand branches passed resolutions in support of such a journal. The fact that the wording of each of the resolutions was remarkably similar suggests that d'Egville himself may have had a direct hand in drafting them and promoting their adoption. He was convinced that the publication was needed and he wanted to arm himself against opposition, especially on grounds of expense, within the United Kingdom branch.

In 1920 the first issues of the quarterly *Journal of the Parliaments of the Empire* appeared. Each issue contained a full summary of the main proceedings of the British and Dominion Parliaments. Reliable contributors had been enlisted in each country, and d'Egville himself carried out a scrupulous examination of each summary, checking them against the *Hansard* reports which he had also arranged to receive. He was a natural editor with a sharp eye for detail as well as the ability to maintain a broad, overall view of editorial policy.

In 1921 a second quarterly, *Report on Foreign Affairs*, was first issued. Its contents were based on information provided confidentially by the Political Intelligence Department of the Foreign Office. Its purpose was to give overseas members regular information on policies and events in foreign – that is, non-Commonwealth – countries. It took the place of, and was a great improvement on, the summary reports sent occasionally to the Dominions in the past by the British government.

The two journals were intended to be complementary. Any debate or statement on foreign affairs in Parliament was fully summarised in the *Journal of the Parliaments of the Empire*, but such proceedings could not be included in the *Report on Foreign Affairs*, and inevitably this led to omissions and imbalance. Foreign policy was not always announced and debated in Parliament, especially in the Dominion Parliaments. The policies of foreign countries were, however, regularly covered in the *Report*. The publication was nevertheless valuable in providing information which was not then available to overseas members in their press or elsewhere.

Notes

1. The imperial conference of 1907 agreed that the self-governing colonies should be called Dominions. They were then Canada, Australia, New Zealand and Newfoundland. South Africa became a Dominion after the Union in 1910 of the Cape, Natal, Transvaal and the Orange Free State.

2.   Smuts gave close thought to the further development of Empire into Commonwealth. He produced a memorandum in which he proposed that Dominion governments should become coordinate governments of the King with full equality of status. Smuts' ideas were ahead of his time, and met with strong opposition. Majority opinion at the Imperial Conference of 1921 opposed any attempts to reduce the Commonwealth to writing or to formulate what Billy Hughes, the Australian Prime Minister, scornfully dismissed as a 'flamboyant declaration of rights'. Nicholas Mansergh, *The Commonwealth Experience*, 2nd edn (London, 1982), vol. 1, pp.210–13.

3 Howard d'Egville

Howard d'Egville the man was and remains elusive. It might be expected from his incessant activity, from his extensive correspondence, and from his contact with leading politicians over nearly five decades, that information about him would be plentiful. It is, in fact, surprisingly sparse. The main reason is that he was extremely secretive about his family and his personal affairs. But also, as time passed, he came to immerse himself so completely in the work of the Association that he virtually ceased to have a private life of his own. The Association, first as the Empire Parliamentary Association, and then as the Commonwealth Parliamentary Association, of both of which he was the sole progenitor, was his life.

Howard d'Egville was born on 25 April 1879 in London. His father was a hop merchant and was apparently prosperous. Nothing is known of his background and early years – he never mentioned his parents or involved them in Association affairs. In the whole of the crowded programme of the historic visit of Dominion MPs to London in 1911 there is just a single reference in the list of the guests at the London County Council dinner on 27 June to a Mrs J. H. d'Egville, presumably his mother. One has the impression that he was an only son whose parents, like the parents of John Ruskin, the writer and art critic, cosseted him lovingly, but kept in the background.

It is believed that he did not go to school, but was educated privately. He went to St Catherine's College, Cambridge, and subsequently as a member of the Middle Temple he was called to the Bar. He practised in London and on the Midlands Circuit for a time. The future of the Empire, then on the threshold of momentous change, captured his interest, however, and soon absorbed him, drawing him away from the law.

In build he was a small, thin man with a long lean face, oval in shape, and penetrating brown eyes. It was an alert, intelligent face. By his early thirties he was going bald, which accentuated his high-domed head, giving him the look of a lively, but not invariably benign, elf.

The only glimpses of his personal life and thoughts as a young man are contained in a fairly frank diary which he kept when he accompanied the United Kingdom delegation to Canada, Australia, New Zealand and South Africa in 1913. It reveals him enjoying himself – he surfs, fishes, plays poker, performs well on the dance floor, and is accomplished on horseback. He has an eye for pretty girls and is clearly attractive to them. Miss Fuller, whom he met in Sydney on 3 September, was, he writes, 'certainly a very fine and handsome girl but a bit overdressed. However she dances well – so all the dances I had I danced with her – to the annoyance of poor [name omitted] who wanted a dance with the lovely Miss Fuller'. Then a few days later he writes, 'Miss Fuller gives me some flowers to wear in the evening from the lovely bouquet she is carrying'. On 12 September 1913, however, the diary reads: 'I sit next to Miss Jessie Tripps, the heiress.... I find she is coming to stay in Bedford Park next year, so there is still a chance for me! I'm congratulated gently by the party and told ... I shall have at least 100,000 sheep as a dowry! Like Jacob of old.'

In Melbourne on 24 September 1913 he meets two attractive sisters, the Misses Barnett, and takes them to tea: 'Gave them both boxes of chocolates.' But in the evening he has to attend an official dinner which was 'much too long. I'm intensely bored – especially as I have an alluring invitation to supper with Lucy Madden.' He thinks of leaving early, 'but I do my duty bound and miss the gentle lady'. In Pretoria, he is attracted by Frances Botha, daughter of Chris L. Botha, a member of the Legislative Assembly. On 23 October 1913 he meets her again with a Miss de Waal, 'one of the prettiest women I've seen on tour', but it is Frances he prefers. Later he had to bid 'the little girl, farewell. I feel horribly lonely.'

The diary as a whole shows a young man who, while enjoying all opportunities for pleasure, is seriously studying the places he visits and people he meets. It reflects something of the way of life in the Dominions at this time. He writes sensitively about the natural beauties of these countries, but his final comment is: 'I have been in all the Dominions now but there is no place I would gladly live in except South Africa.' Possibly he was also thinking still of the charms of Frances Botha.

Comments on the people he meets are often sharp, and usually perceptive. Lord Gladstone, the Governor-General of South Africa, infuriates him because he is so inept in his handling of leading Boers: 'I would never go near Government House if I could help it – a dull, stupid, useless lot, full of wrong ideas, pigheadedness and incompetence.' After a meeting with General Hertzog, the South African Prime Minister, he notes in the diary that 'he has a wild look in his eye which one sees in extreme radicals at home'. Field-Marshal Jan Smuts impressed him as a 'singularly able but rather shifty sort of person. Would not trust him far.'

Even as a young man he had poise and self-confidence and, without being thrusting, he made contact and held his own with the leading political figures in the countries he visited, as he did in England. His chief purpose was always to promote the ideals of the Association and to gain support for its activities, and especially its publications. He formed his own opinions and expressed them. In

1913 he was still thinking of some form of Imperial Federation and, talking with Hertzog, he argued forcefully that 'you can't run an Empire on different foreign policies'. Hertzog, a staunch Boer nationalist, was not to be persuaded. After his visit to Australia he wrote that he had become 'convinced that the White Australia policy is right though I doubted it very seriously at first'.

He believed strongly in the parliamentary system, but was often highly critical of MPs. In his own mind he divided them into two categories: there were those politicians whose only concern was to achieve personal power and prominence; then there were the parliamentarians who believed in the institution of Parliament and shared his vision of the Commonwealth and of the central role to be played by the Association. The politicians he dismissed as of no importance; he cultivated the second group. In doing so he showed remarkable perception in picking the men who would rise to the top and would be able to give valuable service to the Association. Names of influential members whom he enlisted arise in the course of this history.

D'Egville's relations with the United Kingdom branch began to deteriorate between the wars. This was inevitable, for he was clever, devious, and could be unscrupulous in the interests of 'his' Association, as he regarded it. Moreover, like many fervent democrats, he tended to be autocratic in his own field. Finally, his attitude to MPs was bound to be a source of tension. He knew that he was more perceptive and farsighted and certainly more knowledgeable about the Commonwealth than most of the branch members, and they resented this in their Secretary.

The immediate causes of his troubled relations with them were usually his attempts to have the members he had selected voted on to the Executive Committee and his efforts to fix beforehand any contentious or important issues on the Committee's agenda. His attempts to influence the composition of delegations were a major cause of annoyance. He could not abide, so he wrote at one time, 'leaving the ultimate choice of delegates to party leaders – men with no interest in the Association'. This was not merely a wilful desire to see his own friends and supporters chosen. It reflected also his deep concern for stability and continuity in the management of the Association. The problem was to prove far greater in the Commonwealth Parliamentary Association, an international organisation. In practice both in the branch and the CPA the Secretary/Secretary-General provided the continuity and the initiatives in expanding the work of the Association. But often he met with unnecessary restraints, as we shall see. Meanwhile, the problems of continuity remained unresolved.

In 1921 d'Egville received a knighthood in recognition of his services and of the importance of the Empire Parliamentary Association. But tension between the branch and its Secretary was to rise sharply during World War II. This did not apply to other branches with which his relations were unclouded, but the situation within the United Kingdom branch was to be a factor in the transformation of the Empire into the Commonwealth Parliamentary Association.

As is recounted in this history, d'Egville was to direct the affairs of the United

Kingdom branch and then of the Commonwealth Parliamentary Association as a whole until, in 1960, he retired at the age of 81. Throughout his long and dedicated service his abilities were unimpaired and continued at times to have a touch of greatness. The sadness was that the sharp and attractive young man of the diary was to become with the passing of the years a lonely, curmudgeonly old man.

4 Between the Wars

By the early 1920s the idea of an Imperial Federation was dead. Any form of centralisation was unacceptable, certainly to Canada and South Africa. The need for continuity in the process of transformation of the Empire, strongly emphasised by Leo Amery and others, did not impress those Dominions which were establishing their national identity and seeking international recognition of their sovereignty. The danger now was that the Empire would disintegrate completely. To d'Egville this threat made the Association all the more important, for it now had the special role of maintaining the links between Britain and the rest of the Empire. It would preserve that continuity which at the political level was being abandoned.

D'Egville now became concerned with the expanding of the Association. Initially, membership had been limited to Britain and the Dominions. There were, however, self-governing colonies which should also be eligible. However, this would involve amending the constitution and there was no formal machinery for doing so. D'Egville took the initiative in correspondence. A new Clause V in the constitution, enabling 'parts of the Empire under representative government' to form branches, was submitted to the 1924 conference in South Africa and approved.

Malta and Southern Rhodesia were the first of the new branches, followed by the formation of the Indian branch in 1926. Ireland, Ceylon, Bermuda, Barbados, the Bahamas, Northern Ireland, three Canadian provinces and five Australian states soon formed branches in this new category, and by the outbreak of World War II there were more than 20 branches of the Association.

Conferences continued to be an important activity. In 1924 the first full conference to be held in a Dominion took place in South Africa. Twelve delegates from the United Kingdom, eight each from Canada and Australia and four from New Zealand attended. The opening meeting was held in Maseru in September 1924. Warm approval of the publications was recorded, undoubtedly to d'Egville's satisfaction. The main business, however, was the discussion and approval of the new Clause V in the constitution. The conference was followed by a tour of Southern Africa, lasting two months.

The next full conference was held in Australia in 1926, followed by another in Canada in 1928. The conference held in London in 1935 on the occasion of King George V's Silver Jubilee was a major occasion. Forty-nine delegates came from overseas branches and no less than 103 delegates from the United Kingdom branch attended. Included among the delegations were 16 Speakers and several Prime Ministers and other Ministers. At this conference it was decided that an informal meeting of the Association should be held in London in years when there was no full conference. The first of these informal meetings took place in July 1936. A second major conference met in London in 1937 on the occasion of the coronation of King Georve VI. D'Egville arranged a special lunch in Westminster Hall and for the first time the King himself addressed the delegates. In 1938 a full conference was held in Australia; and an informal meeting was convened in London in July 1939.

From 1926 onwards Indian delegations had attended all of the full conferences of the Association. This, too, was a triumph for d'Egville. Nationalist feeling had been growing stongly in India from the start of the century. India had been loyal to the King and the Empire during World War I, and its troops had fought bravely on many fronts. However, from 1916 onwards demands for self-rule had mounted. In the face of new agitation and also out of gratitude for India's wartime services, the British government began to consider fresh reforms. In 1917 Edwin Montagu, Secretary of State for India, had announced in the House of Commons Britain's policy for the progressive advance of responsible government in India as an integral part of the British Empire. The Montagu-Chelmsford Report was published in the following year, and its recommendations enacted in the Government of India Act 1919. But while giving greater powers to Indians at the provincial level, the Act, which created a central legislature of 146 members, made no significant increase in the powers and responsibilities of Indians in the government at the centre.

Indian representatives had, however, participated in the meetings of the Imperial War Cabinet and the war conferences of 1917. Along with the Dominions, India signed the peace treaty at Versailles in 1919. Moreover, although not a 'fully self-governing' country within the terms of the covenant, India became a member of the League of Nations. But this could hardly satisfy the aspirations of the nationalists, many of whom began demanding *Swaraj* – self-rule and real independence.

It was clear that, notwithstanding the equivocations of British governments, India was on the road to independence. It was not clear, however, whether this great nation would remain within the Empire. In Britain and in India there were many who doubted whether an independent India could – or even should – so remain. D'Egville had no doubts that membership of the Association would at least encourage India to stand alongside the Dominions within the Empire.

In 1926, with the approval of the United Kingdom branch, d'Egville visited India, arriving in Delhi in February. He found a confused situation. Many Indians were deeply suspicious of British intentions. Communal problems were growing in intensity, with the Muslim League, founded in 1906, more and more strident in its demands that the British Raj should not be followed by a Hindu Raj.

D'Egville had meetings with many of the 146 members of the central legislature. He found the *Swaraj* members reluctant to join an Empire Association. Among others who sought self-government within the Empire his proposals had a better reception. He urged his case with patient, persuasive but vigorous diplomacy, aided by the fact there was a genuine rapport and respect between him and the Indians with whom he was dealing. One obstacle that he met with was the fear that, if India formed a branch, the branch and its individual members might not be considered equal with other branches and MPs in the Association. This obstacle was overcome by the addition to Clause V of a note that 'for the purpose of this clause any part of the Empire which has a representative legislature is deemed to be under representative government'. This satisfied all parties and the Indian branch was formed.

In India as in other countries there was, however, increasing restlessness over the slow pace of the transformation of the Empire into a more acceptable form. British tutelage belonged to an earlier age and had become an anachronism. In particular, South African nationalists, French Canadians and republican Irish resented being part of a British Empire. The time had come to define formally in law the constitutional status of the Dominions.

It had been agreed by the Imperial War Conference of 1917 that a post-war constitutional conference should be convened for this purpose. Bill Hughes, the ebullient and pugnacious Prime Minister of Australia at the time, opposed it. 'I am', he declared,

> totally at a loss to understand what it is that this constitutional conference proposes to do. Is it that the Dominions are seeking new powers or are desirous of using the powers they already have, or is the conference to draw up a declaration of rights, to set down in black and white the relations between Britain and the Dominions?[1]

In his opposition to what he called 'constitutional tinkering', he was supported by W. F. Massey, the New Zealand Prime Minister, and even to a degree by the Canadian Prime Minister, Arthur Meighen. The plans for the conference were abandoned. At the Imperial Conference in 1926, however, the question of the formal relationship between Britain and the Dominions was revived. Mackenzie King was now Prime Minister of Canada; General Hertzog had succeeded General Smuts as Prime Minister of South Africa; and Southern Ireland had achieved Dominion status in 1921. All wanted their constitutional position clarified beyond dispute. Australia and New Zealand reluctantly went along with the proposal. Indeed, they could hardly oppose it when the British government showed an equable readiness to cooperate.

The conference appointed an inter-imperial relations committee, with Lord Balfour, the former Prime Minister, as Chairman. Leo Amery, the first Secretary of State for the Dominions, was an active member. Its meetings were amicable and its report contained what came to be known as the 'Balfour Declaration'. This stated that the Dominions

> are autonomous communities within the British Empire, equal in status, in no way subordinate one to another in any aspect of their domestic or external affairs, though united by a common allegiance to the Crown and freely associated as members of the British Commonwealth of Nations.[2]

The Balfour Declaration adequately described the existing position, but it left outstanding a number of complex and delicate issues. Indeed, a special conference of experts was convened in 1929. Its recommendations were discussed and approved by the Imperial Conference of 1930. The Statute of Westminster enacting these changes was passed in 1931.

South Africa, Southern Ireland and to some extent Canada welcomed the Statute as doing away with many of the legal and symbolic restraints within the Commonwealth. Australia and New Zealand did not welcome or adopt it. R. G. Casey, soon to become a senior Minister and later Governor-General of Australia, observed: 'We have torn down a castle to build a row of villas.' In Britain many agreed with Winston Churchill, who dismissed the Statute as 'pedantic, painful and, to some at any rate, repellent'.[3] The changes which it brought about were, however, inevitable.

The advance of the Dominions had, in fact, been more rapid in the economic than in the political field. Many had argued for free trade within the Empire and then within the Commonwealth without fully understanding that this would mean raising a great protectionist wall around its frontiers and hampering trade with the rest of the world. At the Imperial Economic Conference, held in Ottawa in 1932, the result after much hard bargaining was a series of bilateral agreements which in effect increased Commonwealth trade. But there was no single agreement on economic policy. It was, in fact, generally realised that a policy of free trade exclusively within the Commonwealth would not be viable.

The new constitutional relationship, expressed in the Statute of Westminster, was put to the test by the abdication of King Edward VIII in 1936. The Prime Minister, Stanley Baldwin, advised the King as his 'counsellor and friend' in the early stages of the crisis. The King himself suggested that the Dominion governments should be consulted on the subject of a morganatic marriage with Mrs Wallis Simpson. Baldwin acted on this proposal and was to report that the Dominions were united in their opposition to such a marriage. The United Kingdom Abdication Act applied to Australia and New Zealand which had not yet adopted the Statute of Westminster, but their Parliaments both passed confirming resolutions. The Canadian Parliament passed its own Act in January 1937 as did the South African Parliament.

In the midst of these developments d'Egville was constantly concerned about the role of the Association in maintaining unity and continuity within the

Commonwealth. He was keenly aware of some discordant voices. The general use of the word 'Empire' offended certain branches. Moreover, there were some members who were beginning to question the role of the United Kingdom branch as director of the affairs of the whole Association.

In February 1939 d'Egville paid a hurried visit to South Africa. The immediate reason was the resignation of members of the Nationalist Party from the Union branch of the Association. Dr Malan, the Leader of the Party, then in opposition, told him that his members were incensed by the taunts of their opponents that, although staunch republicans, they were members of an 'Empire' Association. They also criticised the use of the word 'branch', arguing that the EPA should be an association of associations. Another complaint was of the bias towards Empire unity, evident in the publications and conference reports of the Association. Dr Malan told him that removal of the word 'Empire' from the title 'would be a promising line to adopt in attempting to bring the Nationalists back to the Association'. D'Egville explained that in the course of discussions held in the United Kingdom before he left, the suggestion had been made, without however securing any official support, that the difficulty involved in the word 'Empire' might be overcome by the Association having a long and a short title – the long title being 'The Parliamentary Association of the Commonwealth of Nations, India, Burma, and other legislatures of the Empire' and the short title being 'The Parliamentary Association'. This suggestion had almost certainly been made by him. At the same time, he made it clear that the Union branch alone could not change the existing title.

D'Egville undertook to raise these questions on his return to London. At the same time, he obtained an assurance that, while the resignations of the Nationalist members could not actually be withdrawn, members of the party would not be banned from joining the Association. Further, it might be considered that all who had resigned should be regarded as potential members, eager to return to the Association when conditions made this possible. Finally, he persuaded the Union branch that an *African Affairs Report*, to be edited by himself, would be a valuable contribution to wider understanding of the problems of Southern Africa. He even persuaded the South African government to make an annual grant of £1000 for this purpose![4]

Correspondence about the affairs of the South Africa branch continued after d'Egville's return to London, and was only halted by the outbreak of war.

Notes

1. Nicholas Mansergh, *The Commonwealth Experience*, 2nd edn (London, 1982), vol. 1, p.213.
2. A.B. Keith, *Speeches and Documents on the British Dominions 1918–1931* (London, 1932), p.161.
3. Ibid., p.274.
4. The Report was never produced. The grant was refunded in 1962.

5 D'Egville in Canada

The Dominions had gained their independence in the constitutional and economic spheres. It was, however, in the course of World War II that this independence became a reality. The direct experience of the war had brought them to full nationhood. They had grown in power and confidence, and they began to assert their equality with the United Kingdom. Old forms and procedures were questioned. The terms 'Dominion' and 'Empire' were heard less and less. 'Commonwealth nation or member' and 'Commonwealth' were taking their place.

D'Egville was sensitive to the growing changes in outlook within the Commonwealth. He recognised that the Empire Parliamentary Association must reflect those changes if it was to fulfil its purpose. Early in the war he set about transforming the EPA into the Commonwealth Parliamentary Association which would truly represent the new Commonwealth. In the process of making this change he virtually transferred on his own authority the headquarters of the Association from London to Ottawa.

D'Egville departed for Canada in May (or June) 1940 – the exact date is not known, but it was probably soon after the capitulation of Holland and Belgium and the British evacuation of Dunkirk. His instructions from the United Kingdom branch Executive Committee, which he probably drafted himself, were to spend two or three months in Canada, making contact with the members of the newly elected Parliament in Ottawa. His visit was timely. In a special report which he sent later to the Committee, he stated that on arriving in Canada he had found 'little interest in the Association and beyond a sparsely attended annual meeting there was practically no sign of life'. With great energy he revitalised the Ottawa branch and visiting every provincial legislature he aroused fresh interest in the Association. It was a considerable achievement at a time when the war was uppermost in the minds of the people and few were looking ahead to the possible state of the Commonwealth and of their Parliaments after the war.

Soon after his arrival in Canada d'Egville decided to remain in North America. He set up his office in Ottawa, and from there was soon editing and distributing publications to members throughout the Commonwealth. He arranged to receive material from the Ministry of Information in London for the purpose. He sent a stream of letters to members in all branches and especially to United Kingdom members, complaining at times that he had to sit up into the early hours of the morning writing or typing his own letters. He even developed his own personal war effort. He organised what he called his 'private group' in the US Congress. He claimed in a letter, dated 2 December 1940, that he had helped 'in pushing forward the supply of US destroyers'. In June 1941 he wrote that he had been instrumental in securing Roosevelt's declaration on American convoys and the freedom of the seas. A year later he was claiming that he had contributed to the enactment of the American policy of 'lend-lease'.

In his letter of 2 December 1940 to Arthur Greenwood, a friend and supporter on the United Kingdom branch Executive Committee, he wrote that he had set up 'a small informal committee in Congress to maintain contact with parliamentary bodies of the British Commonwealth through the EPA, consisting of about a dozen members of both Houses'. He added: 'I worked very quietly without the isolationists getting any wind of it.' He was planning also to forge contacts between Congress and the Canadian Parliament, but 'it has to be worked carefully so that the contacts are spontaneous on both sides'. He was also arranging to deliver a series of lectures in American universities.

D'Egville was in his element. He was a natural and at times Machiavellian organiser, adept at selecting the most influential people to further his purposes, whether to serve the British war effort or to promote the Association. He was profoundly persuasive and often acted as a catalyst in bringing together different forces to produce the action needed. This has to be borne in mind before dismissing some of his claims as far-fetched. Moreover, his work was highly valued by the British Embassy in Washington and by the High Commission in Ottawa: Lord Halifax, the Ambassador in Washington, and Malcolm Macdonald, the High Commissioner in Ottawa, both wrote letters to the United Kingdom branch, commending the work he was doing.

D'Egville was nevertheless keenly aware that in remaining in Canada he was exposing himself to criticism. German bombing of Britain mounted during July 1940 and reached a climax in September in the blitz on London. At this time he was desperately on the defensive. In a letter to Arthur Greenwood, dated 2 December 1940, he wrote: 'I feel I would like to be sharing the dangers of London, but I know and believe you will agree I could not be doing anything in England now as important or useful to the war effort as I am doing on this side.' He protested in similar terms in a great many letters. Undoubtedly he felt guilty about being away from England. He feared, too, the charge of cowardice that might be levelled at him.

On 5 December 1940 he wrote in a fury to Spencer Hess, who was working in the branch rooms, about a letter he had received from a Miss Howlett, who was clearly prompted by malice. 'She said', wrote d'Egville, that she looked into the office to find out when I was to return and was amused to find I should not be back till the *blitzkrieg* was over. Did you say anything of the kind? . . . It is not, I am sure, necessary for me to say how monstrously unfair and unjust is such a suggestion. This person is connected with several of our members and heaven knows what she may be saying to them. I would have thought that as a loyal assistant to me you would point out in general terms some of the importance of the work I am doing here. P.S. Please do not tell Miss H about this or indicate in any way at all that you have heard from me.

Spencer Hess cabled at once that he had made no such remark. On 13 June 1941 he wrote in explanation:

I am grieved that you don't have a better opinion of me. . . . It is my general attitude to defend my chief on all occasions – to avoid direct questions by referring to the useful work you are doing. My stereotyped answer to questions about your return (in whatever words they are made) is 'I don't know exactly but the fulfilment of his present programme will probably take another two or three months'.

Clearly inquiries about d'Egville's absence were frequent.

The rooms of the United Kingdom branch were destroyed by incendiary bombs on the night of 10 May 1941. Temporary accommodation was hastily arranged in the Grand Committee Room off Westminster Hall. Rebuilding was put in hand at once and by Christmas the branch was again functioning in its old rooms. After the bombing a meeting of the branch Executive Committee was finally arranged for 12 June 1941. D'Egville realised that this meeting could be critical for him. He was still Secretary of the branch, with Drummond Shiels as Acting Secretary in his absence and loyal to d'Egville in spite of the flood of often angry letters and the unending instructions. In fact, d'Egville had received a number of warnings about his continued absence. They were summed up gently in a letter from Somerville, one of his strongest supporters on the Executive Committee, who wrote that there was 'an uneasy feeling here that you ought to be at Westminster'.

In spite of this, d'Egville did not return for the meeting. He wrote lengthy letters in his own hand to members of the Executive Committee explaining and justifying his decision; and the letters to his supporters, Grenfell, Snell and Pethick-Lawrence, were phrased in similar terms. His reason for remaining in Canada was that

it is obvious beyond any question that there were such great opportunities of service that I should carry on work which might prove to be of the greatest service that the EPA could ever give to the Commonwealth. . . . I should greatly appreciate it if the Executive would indicate full confidence in my judgement as to the period of time I should deem it necessary to be here to carry through the work effectively, I am hopeful that some resolution may be passed. . . . It doesn't matter whether where one works is dangerous or safe.

The Executive Committee noted d'Egville's explanations, and in particular the commendatory letters from Lord Halifax and Malcolm Macdonald. It passed a resolution of appreciation of his work, but only after long discussion. In a letter to Snell on 21 July 1941 he wrote, somewhat plaintively:

> From what I can gather ... the Committee did not seem to be greatly impressed with the importance of the work I am carrying out here, from reading the memo which I had written, and that it was only when letters were read from Halifax and Macdonald that the necessity of my carrying on here appears to have been fully appreciated. I confess that after 30 years' work my judgement should be worth something.

Fear of the bombing may have been part of the reason for d'Egville's continued stay in Canada, but it was a very small part. As he claimed repeatedly, he was doing important work in North America which could not have been done in London. There he would have been involved in constant squabbles – some of his own making – with members who disliked him or felt that he was manipulating them. Moreover, England, bombed and severely rationed, was in the front line, and the war was foremost in the thoughts of everyone at Westminster. He would have had to struggle with small hope of success to carry through his ideas about the shape and role of the Association in the future. Another factor was that in London he was a prophet without honour, merely the Secretary of the United Kingdom branch, although recognised as influential; by many as excessively so. In Canada, where he now had many friends and supporters, he was treated with respect as a Commonwealth statesman. It was not to be wondered at that he preferred working in the congenial surroundings of Ottawa.

Some members of the United Kingdom branch had expressed the fear, so Snell informed him, that 'the Dominions might not altogether approve of the concentration of EPA activities a good deal in Canada'. D'Egville replied: 'I have kept in contact and am confident that they regard Canada not only as the senior and most important Dominion, but as occupying a key position in this war.' Again it was no idle boast. He was in constant touch with the branches by means of a voluminous correspondence. He was, in fact, managing the affairs of the whole Association from Ottawa and, in spite of wartime difficulties, organising delegations and conferences. In October/November 1941 a Canadian delegation visited London; in October 1942 a delegation of South African MPs visited Britain and Canada; and a British delegation went to Australia and New Zealand in May 1943. D'Egville was directly involved in all of these visits, and, indeed, probably initiated them.

There were, of course, failures. Late in 1942 d'Egville had taken soundings of Indian leaders, who agreed that 'a small carefully chosen delegation' from EPA branches might be invited on a visit by the India branch. Sir Stafford Cripps, then Secretary of State for India, a cold, austere man who had little understanding of the Indians, wrote expressing doubts about the wisdom of such a visit. D'Egville replied, urging that an EPA delegation could make an important contribution. 'By judicious influence one could be certain of choosing really good men', he wrote, adding: 'As regards other Dominions I think I could take steps to ensure that some of their best were available.' Cripps stood firm and the visit did not take place. Writing to Shiels, d'Egville expressed his disappointment in Cripps' attitude and reasoning. 'It is just that attitude that people criticize here. It really amounts to this: the government of India must be the sole judge as to what may be good for Indians during the war. Unless some such gesture is made during the war, we stand a very good chance of losing India when the war is over.'

Undaunted, he was already planning a conference of the Association to take place in Canada. This brought him into direct conflict with the British government and with others. The conference was due to take place in May 1943. Following his usual practice, d'Egville tried to select the United Kingdom delegation. He sent his list of delegates to be chosen to Shiels in September 1942, and so was upset to learn from a letter from Shiels that Shiels had seen Leo Amery and Clement Attlee who had proposed quite a different list. As the date of the conference drew closer, d'Egville became more disturbed. In one of his innumerable letters to Shiels he advised him on how to by-pass the Executive Committee by arranging for the Speaker's Selection Committee, which was responsible for appointing the delegation, to meet before convening the Executive Committee which would in this way be presented with a *fait accompli*. In another letter he wrote: 'I feel terrified of some nonentity pressing himself forward and getting included in the United Kingdom delegation.' He responded angrily to a suggestion from Hugh Dalton that he should return to London to explain his work in North America – 'I can't leave things in the middle just for a nice trip home,' he wrote. But he was growing desperate. In a letter on 7 April 1943 to Shiels he wrote: 'If you let me down over the personnel of our delegation, I shall never forgive you!'

His efforts were in vain. On 3 May 1943 he wrote to Shiels: 'I was, of course, terribly disappointed with the United Kingdom delegation. Apart from Wardlaw-Milne there is hardly any one of the names I dealt with so carefully.' The inclusion of a woman MP infuriated him: 'I have always set my face resolutely against women in the delegation, partly because we have no really representative women in Parliament, but also because of the difficulties in travel and general arrangements. I thought you knew,' he wrote to the unfortunate Shiels. 'I am grieved about this and with 615 members to choose a woman out of only eight or so is in itself ridiculous.'

Following on this disappointment came the threat that there might not be a delegation from Australia at the conference. Delegations from Australia and New Zealand were visiting Britain at the time, and d'Egville assumed that they would return home via Canada where they would attend the conference. In fact, he had drafted letters of invitation which the Canadian branch had sent to the Chairman of the two branches. He was therefore shocked to learn from Shiels that the Australians were unwilling to travel to Canada; and he was further incensed by the fact that some members of the United Kingdom branch supported the

Australians on the ground that they had received no notice of the conference before leaving home. D'Egville dismissed this argument as irrelevant. His somewhat arrogant attitude was expressed in letters to Shiels: 'They came as a mission of the Association and a conference is always one of our objects, and whether the conference is held in the United Kingdom or in Canada is not of the least importance.... The Commonwealth needs a visit from me.' His advice to Shiels was: 'Do please be firm with the Australians and do not put too much on the Committee, but take the responsibility yourself. I would just have told them these arrangements had been made for the return journey at a certain date and leave it at that.'

The situation was far more complex and he had more enemies in London than he himself realised. Shiels was summoned by Attlee, then Secretary of State for the Dominions, to be told that Lord Bruce, the Australian High Commissioner and a member of the War Cabinet, had informed the delegates that they should stay in London. Attlee was not in favour of the conference, 'as things might be said which were undesirable and might get out to the American and Canadian press'. He was also critical of the fact that members of the United States Congress had been invited.

On 21 May 1943 Shiels was called again to the Dominions Office, this time for a meeting with Attlee, Amery and Bruce. Reporting in detail to d'Egville, Shiels wrote: 'Bruce showed considerable personal animosity towards you.... I fancy Massey [the Canadian High Commissioner] has been hovering in the background of this controversy as he is not a friend of yours either.' In a later letter he wrote that Bruce had 'denounced the conference as only a d'Egville stunt'.

D'Egville responded with fury. Of Bruce he wrote merely, 'I wonder what I have done to incur the wrath of that great man'. He was more concerned about Attlee's misgivings over the attendance of members of Congress. After all the wrangling and heated feelings, however, the Australian delegates finally travelled to Canada. Shiels wrote that 'the delegation is taking the visit very seriously and I think you will be agreeably surprised at the impression which they make'. The resolution of this problem did something, but not a great deal, to calm d'Egville's anxieties about the success of the conference.

Soon after the arrival of the British delegation in Ottawa, he was writing to Shiels: 'They are too old and all complained of being too tired.... It was a real scandal to include Harris [Chief Liberal Whip]; he is not only too old but is universally recognised as a supreme bore. Brass is not going to add any weight. He is more interested in photography than in the future of the Empire.' D'Egville was always prone to take a pessimistic view, especially on the eve of a conference on which he had expended so much thought and nervous energy.

The Canadian conference was in fact a tremendous success. Malcolm Macdonald sent an enthusiastic telegram to London on 7 July 1943 describing it as an outstanding event in Commonwealth affairs. After the return of the British delegation Shiels sent a telegram of congratulations to d'Egville from the United Kingdom branch adding: 'Brass enthusiastic over conference. High praise of your efforts and work in Canada.'

The praise was well deserved. From its inception d'Egville had been in control of the arrangements and with his great drive he had ensured that the conference took place. He had had to battle against pusillanimous attitudes and animosities in London. It was, for example, wholly on his initiative and due to his pertinacity that for the first time members of the US Congress attended as observers and participated in the sessions on foreign affairs. In the process he made both friends and enemies at Westminster: his few friends were staunch, his enemies numerous.

Annual general meetings of the branch had been suspended from the beginning of the war. Several members were now demanding that they be resumed. One MP, Colonel Evans, was disappointed because he was not included in a delegation to Australia and pressed for a general meeting. Sir Leonard Lyle was angry about being omitted from a delegation to the West Indies: 'I do feel that things are not as they should be and this view is shared, I know, by many of my fellow members.'

The general meeting was held on 9 March 1944. D'Egville tried to have it postponed so that he could attend, but this proved impossible. He returned to London four months later. He had made a fleeting visit in June 1942 so this was only his second visit since the outbreak of the war. A special meeting of the Executive Committee was called. He was, he knew, likely to be attacked and was in a sense on trial. He gave a long report on his work in Canada, which was closely discussed.

Evidently the Committee was divided in its views, and this was reflected in its resolution, parts of which bear signs of d'Egville's drafting. The resolution expressed the view that, since d'Egville was Secretary of the branch, 'his being overseas for considerable periods might be open to criticism'. It acknowledged, however, that

> in fact, if not in constitutional theory, he was a great deal more than the Secretary of one branch and his position was more that of Secretary-General of the Association. It was undesirable that his work in Canada should be interrupted at this stage.... It was desirable for Sir Howard to return for the time being to Canada in the wider interests of the EPA and of the virility of the British Empire.

D'Egville had got what he wanted, but the resolution was in the nature of a reprieve. He was now 65 years of age. The possibility that the branch might in the near future propose his retirement was on his mind.

6 The Commonwealth and the United States

The war brought a profound change in Britain's standing in the world. The admiration and respect which the nation had commanded during the German bombing and the defiant speeches of Churchill had suggested that British power was undiminished. As the war continued, this was seen to be a myth. The belief in white supremacy, which had been damaged by the Russo-Japanese War of 1905, was destroyed by the Japanese attack on Pearl Harbor in December 1941, and most decisively by the fall of Singapore in February 1942. The sinking of the great battleships, *Prince of Wales* and *Repulse*, showed that the Royal Navy could no longer defend British power in the East. As the Japanese captured British, French, Dutch and American territories in South-East Asia and the Pacific, Australia and New Zealand began to feel increasingly vulnerable. British imperial prestige was shattered. Moreover, to those who looked ahead, it was clear that it would take decades for the British economy to recover.

Such dramatic changes affected attitudes within the Commonwealth. Australia in 1942, and two years later New Zealand, adopted the Statute of Westminster, thus proclaiming their complete independence and their equality in law with the United Kingdom. In February 1942, Australia abruptly withdrew all its troops from the Middle East. Churchill pleaded with John Curtin, the Australian Prime Minister, not to take this drastic step at such a critical stage, but to no avail. At the San Francisco conference (April–June 1945) convened to set up the United Nations Organisation, the Dominions demonstrated their independence, and on some issues, such as the veto, bitterly opposed the United Kingdom.

D'Egville closely followed the trends which would affect fundamentally the future of the Commonwealth. In Canada he was able to maintain a relative detachment from the war. He had, moreover, made repeated visits to Washington and recognised that the United States would emerge from the war as a world super-power. He set himself two tasks. One was to promote close relations between members of Commonwealth Parliaments and members of the US Congress; the other was to transform the EPA into a truly Commonwealth organisation.

D'Egville's first recorded note of the ideas which had been maturing in his mind for some time was in a letter to his friend, Duncan Hall, written from Ottawa on 7 November 1944. He asked for Hall's views

in strict confidence about a matter which I have been thinking about for some time. You know, of course, of Curtin's [Prime Minister of Australia] suggestion about an Empire Secretariat and the attitude adopted by Mackenzie King [Prime Minister of Canada] with regard to it. It has occurred to me for some time past that, though this may not be practicable for governments of the Empire, something of the kind will certainly be required after the war for the EPA. The Dominions will become more national than before and in any case it is not in the best interests in my view of all the countries of the Empire if the UK has always to take the lead in matters which should be arranged by all. Therefore it seems to me that at one centre or another of the Empire there should be some secretariat which could deal with all matters pertaining to all branches, such, for example, as to where the next conference should be held and other matters of a similar character. There would probably have to be something in the nature of a general body having a representative of each branch, meeting annually.... I have not discussed this matter at all in the UK up to the present.... I may add that I have had some private talks with Slaght, with Jackman and Coldwell, leading members of the branch, and they all think the idea a good one, and all take the view that Canada will be the right centre – at any rate to start with.

D'Egville had not mentioned his plan to the United Kingdom branch, believing that its Executive would defer all further consideration of it until the war was over, or would reject it. His strategy was to promote it among the Canadians, confident that they would adopt his plan and formally propose it to the United Kingdom. It was incidentally an achievement to gain Canadian acceptance of the idea of a central Secretariat, for of all the Dominions Canada had most vehemently opposed all moves towards centralisation of any kind.

In another letter to Duncan Hall, dated 17 November 1944, he wrote that he had discussed his plan further, 'and I think it quite possible that it may go forward in due course as a proposal of the Canadian branch.... Some of us will probably prepare a memo on the subject.' D'Egville himself wrote the memorandum, as became clear in subsequent correspondence.

The memorandum reflects well d'Egville's realism and vision. The first three paragraphs read as follows:

The Association now enters upon an important new period. Since its foundation in 1911 it has passed through several critical phases. It had to survive its difficult period of infancy; it had to weather the test of its usefulness in the First World War; it had then to adjust itself in the years between the wars to the needs and demands of a Commonwealth of equal Parliaments. The outbreak of the war was a searching test of its work in promoting a common mind within the Commonwealth Parliaments; the parliamentary decisions of September 1939 [to declare war] were unanimous in Britain, Canada, Australia and New Zealand, and there was a steady majority in South Africa.

The fourth phase on which it now enters may well be the most important and difficult of its existence. It has to make adjustments to several new factors. Within the

Commonwealth there is the changed position of Britain in the world; the increase in the relative strength and maturity of the Dominions; the prospective emergence of an independent India; and the rapid spread of parliamentary institutions in the colonial Empire. Outside the Commonwealth are two other new factors: first, the preponderance in world affairs of the USA, second, the revival of foreign Parliaments. The Parliaments of Britain and of the Dominions must lend a hand in all efforts to extend the true parliamentary principle.

In this next phase, more than in any of the previous phases, the accumulated results of the 36 years of the Association's work and its prestige are a highly important political asset to Great Britain. More than ever the Association is a vital bond of union within the Commonwealth. More than ever the Association as a whole is our most fruitful line of approach to the Congress of the United States. If we are united with America by the parliamentary principle, it is on a Commonwealth rather than a United Kingdom basis...

On 31 January 1945 the Canadian Executive Committee passed a resolution in favour of the reorganisation of the EPA on the lines proposed by d'Egville. At this stage, it decided to send the resolution and the supporting memorandum only to the United Kingdom branch.

D'Egville returned to London to attend the meeting of the United Kingdom Executive Committee on 7 June 1945. He spoke at length on the Canadian resolution and other matters. It must have been a very long meeting. Speaking to the memorandum, d'Egville referred to his discussions in Ottawa. T. W. Coldwell had emphasised that, while he agreed with Mackenzie King in opposing the idea of a common Secretariat of the governments of the Empire, he thought a common Secretariat for the Parliaments an excellent idea. A Secretariat for the governments might lead to possible interference with the foreign policy of Canada which had special relations with the United States, whereas a Secretariat for the Parliaments would serve to provide links between Parliaments and would in no way interfere with policy. He also quoted a letter, dated 5 April 1945, from Malcolm Macdonald, the British High Commissioner in Canada, which he himself had no doubt elicited. The relevant paragraph read:

Parliamentarians in this Dominion are sometimes suspected of being anxious to loosen, or even break, the Commonwealth connexion. The resolution which has been passed by the representatives of all the main political parties here indicates how untrue this conception is. I think that an acceptance of the resolution by other branches, and particularly the United Kingdom branch, would help strengthen the sentiment for Commonwealth cooperation not only here but elsewhere ...

Next, somewhat boldly, d'Egville raised the question of the location of the central Secretariat. This was, of course, a matter to be decided by all branches after they had accepted in principle the proposed reorganisation. He nevertheless advanced the suggestion that Ottawa might be a more suitable location than London. He read an extract from a letter from H. R. Jackson, MP, then Secretary to the Canadian Executive Committee:

I am venturing to express a personal view to you that Canada, perhaps along with other branches, has some peculiar advantages in the way of location. These arise partly through the recognition of the equality of Dominion status, but chiefly because of Canada's adjacency to the United States and the desirability of constant interpretation to the people of the United States of America of what the British Commonwealth and Empire is and what it stands for.... Canada's geographical position in the Empire as well as *vis-à-vis* the USA is in some respects peculiarly advantageous to accomplish the purpose of the Association ...

Finance would, d'Egville said, have to be considered later. He suggested that the grants of the branches for publications, which were the only common fund of the Association, would probably have to be increased in amounts agreed for each branch to support the expenses of the Secretariat. He added that he had been consulted by a member of the Bermuda legislature (whose identity remains unknown to the author) who was willing to make £50,000 available for an Empire project. D'Egville said that he had stopped in Bermuda to discuss this offer and had no doubt that the member would act on his advice and endow some phase of activity of the proposed Secretariat.

After lengthy discussion, the United Kingdom branch Committee passed a resolution welcoming the Canadian proposal 'of possible establishment at some centre of the Empire of a common Secretariat'. On the suggested location of the Secretariat in Canada the Committee was divided: several members insisted firmly that it must be at Westminster.

D'Egville was now impatient to return to Canada. A general election was to take place on 11 June 1945. He told the Committee that it was important for him to be in Canada before the election of the new Chairman and Secretary-Treasurer as all the work he had been doing would be materially affected by the officers chosen. He would have the resolution of the present Canadian Executive confirmed by the new Committee. He was undoubtedly anxious to be in Ottawa to influence the election of the new officers, but he was also eager to return to North America so that he could pursue his plans to promote relations between the Parliaments of the Association and the US Congress.

Following the conference in Ottawa in 1943, d'Egville had worked hard to establish an informal group in Congress. The convenors of the group would arrange for members of Commonwealth Parliaments visiting Washington to meet and possibly address members of both Houses of Congress. Several meetings had already been held. At one the Chairman of the Canadian branch (A. G. Slaght) and the Secretary (H. R. Jackman) had addressed members of Congress. He himself had attended a meeting in the Foreign Affairs Committee Room of the Senate, when Slaght, Jackman, Forde and Dr Evatt[3] had all spoken. D'Egville gave it as his opinion that at such meetings in Congress, Dominion representatives often made a greater impact than British members in explaining the Commonwealth and the links binding its members.

Among Americans, and especially in Congress, there was an abiding dislike of imperialism and colonialism in any form. Slowly after the war this antipathy diminished as communism was identified as the enemy and the Commonwealth held up a bastion against it. D'Egville was sensitive to opinion and to misconceptions in Washington. Already he was planning a conference of Commonwealth and Congress members to take place in Bermuda in 1946. He saw this as the principal way of promoting genuine understanding between the English-speaking peoples.

Meanwhile he was concerned as always about the lack of information available to Commonwealth MPs. In 1920–21 he had launched and was editor of the *Journal of the Parliaments of the Empire* and the *Report on Foreign Affairs*, which had been welcomed by members overseas, but the publications lacked information about American affairs. In 1944 he began publishing the *Summary of Congressional Proceedings, USA*, dealing especially with foreign policy. Two issues appeared in 1944 and two in 1945. In obtaining and selecting material, he was greatly helped by the informal group which he had brought together in Congress. He managed to publish the fourth issue in March 1945, well in advance of the opening of the San Francisco conference. This issue was devoted to foreign affairs, especially the Dumbarton Oaks proposals of April 1944 for post-war security and the Yalta Conference, in early February 1945, when Roosevelt, Stalin and Churchill met. He sent copies by diplomatic bag to Eden, Attlee and Lord Cranborne. He personally handed copies in Washington to Forde and the New Zealand Prime Minister, Fraser. He had also arranged for the *Summary* to be made available to the general public in Australia, New Zealand, South Africa and India. He reported that he had received letters of appreciation from newspaper editors in those countries. The editor of the *Melbourne Age* had written: 'This is a very valuable publication and should be most helpful to students of public affairs in all parts of the Empire.' Members of the Canadian and of other branches had expressed appreciation of the *Summary* and had voted money to provide for its continued publication.

D'Egville was then working on two other projects concerning Canada. The first was the International Affairs Study Group in the Federal Parliament. The second concerned his plans to stimulate the Canadian provincial branches to greater activity.

In Ottawa the study group meetings were held in a private room of the parliamentary restaurant usually during the dinner interval. Meetings were arranged whenever visiting members or others qualified to speak were in Ottawa. Before the meetings he himself circulated papers containing current information, some of it obtained from the British Information Services. He gave as one example a paper he had circulated on the situation in Greece. This had influenced debate in the House and copies had been requested by members of the informal group in Congress. He added, 'it was difficult for information of this character to be circulated to members of Parliament in any other way than through the Parliamentary Association'.

D'Egville reported that all the Canadian provincial legislatures now had branches of the Association. He had visited and addressed most of them. Each branch had also set up an International Affairs Study Group. He was, moreover, anxious to encourage them to greater activity. At an earlier meeting he had proposed that the United Kingdom branch should invite all the provincial Premiers to London. It had then been suggested that the Federal branch might not approve. On his return to Ottawa he had raised the matter and the Executive Committee there had passed a resolution in favour of the provincial branches accepting such an invitation. He had also spoken to George Drew, Premier of Ontario, who had said that he would readily go if Premier Duplessis of Quebec also accepted the invitation. At this stage, however, d'Egville considered it advisable to hold back the invitations until it was known whether New Zealand would host the conference in the near future.

On 11 December 1945 d'Egville was elected Hon. Secretary of the British–American Parliamentary Group at Westminster. Two days later at a meeting of the Executive Committee of the United Kingdom branch he reported on his plans for formalising relations between the Group and the Association, for reconstituting the informal group in the US Congress, and for organising a conference in Bermuda to be attended by delegations from Dominion Parliaments and from the US Congress. D'Egville apparently had it in mind that the British–American Parliamentary Group might become a kind of committee of the Association. Members of the Group, and especially Major Milner, its Chairman, wanted to maintain its separate identity, while seeking close relations with the Association. It was agreed that with d'Egville as Secretary of both bodies there would be close liaison and overlapping would be avoided. He himself suggested that this arrangement might provide the pattern for the similar groups which he was anxious to see established in Dominion Parliaments. He had, in fact, consulted Prime Ministers and senior members of these Parliaments. All had expressed their concern to develop their relations with Congress. He was confident that a group would soon be formed in each Parliament.

D'Egville was in North America from January until mid-April 1946, and in this period made several visits to Washington. It is not known whether he succeeded in persuading his informal group there to establish the 'British Commonwealth Congressional Group' that he had in mind. He was, however, in close contact with members of Congress concerning the conference in Bermuda. He had discussions with the President of the Senate, the Speaker of the House, and the Floor Leaders. Both Houses passed resolutions accepting the Bermudan invitation. He also consulted with the Australian Prime Minister, Ben Chifley, with the New Zealand Prime Minister, who nominated Walter Nash, his deputy, and K. J. Holyoake as delegates. Finally he discussed the conference with Field-Marshall Smuts, pressing him to attend himself. In the event, to his great disappointment, only Holyoake was able to attend. The consolation was that Holyoake himself performed with great credit.

At Westminster the Speaker's Selection Committee had a difficult task, for 114 members applied to attend the conference. A strong delegation of eight was finally appointed, with Anthony Eden as leader. Senator Fulbright was the chief representative in the congressional delegation. A crisis threatened when it was found that the sailing of the *SS Aquitania* in which the British delegation and the New Zealand representative were travelling, had been postponed. D'Egville at once got into touch with the Chairman of the Cunard Line; the departure of the liner was brought forward; and the delegates reached Bermuda on time.

The conference opened in the House of Assembly on 11 June 1946. The first subject for discussion was 'The International Security System in Relation to Defence' on which Senator Fulbright and Anthony Eden were the principal speakers. The second subject was 'British Commonwealth and United States Economic Relations' on which John Wilmot was the opening speaker. Each debate was followed by a lengthy question-and-answer session.

After the conference the delegates travelled to Washington, where the outstanding event of the visit took place on 19 June 1946 when the Commonwealth delegates were received on the Floor of the Senate during the sitting. The Floor Leader then moved the adjournment to enable Senators and delegates to be presented to each other. The delegates then returned to Ottawa via New York.

On his return to London, d'Egville raised with the Speaker the need for some reciprocal gesture in the House of Commons when a congressional delegation was received in Westminster. The Speaker said that it would be difficult to alter the rules of the House, but it might be possible to 'suspend' a sitting so that the visiting members could be received on the Floor of the House and introduced to members. He himself, however, would have to leave the Chair. D'Egville pressed for special consideration to be given to his proposal.

On his return to London John Wilmot wrote privately to the Prime Minister, Clement Attlee,

I think there is no doubt that the occasion was more than ordinarily successful. The Americans sent a team of first-rate people, including Fulbright, Green of Rhode Island, and Luther A. Johnson. They said that they had learnt much and corrected a number of misunderstandings, e.g. they were surprisingly not aware that each Dominion was quite free as to its own tariff policy.

On 4 July 1946 Attlee made a statement in the House on the success of the conference in Bermuda and of the visits to Washington and Ottawa.

Reporting to his Executive Committee d'Egville reiterated his conviction, borne out by this conference, of the value of the Commonwealth parliamentary approach to the US Congress. It was so much more important than the approach of any individual country of the Commonwealth. At this time his contention was probably valid, but profound changes in the Commonwealth were soon to make it questionable.

At all times d'Egville was on guard against intrusions by governments into what he insisted was the exclusive jurisdiction of the Association: it represented Parliaments and members of all parties, not governments and officials. In May

1945 Brendan Bracken, the influential Minister of Information and a close associate of Winston Churchill, wrote proposing that four members of the Australian delegation in San Francisco should be invited to visit England. D'Egville replied at once that parliamentary visits could be arranged only through branches of the Association. He pointed out, moreover, that during the war years a delegation from the Federal branch had come to Britain. It was now the turn of the Australian states, each of which had a branch, to be invited. In correspondence and in a personal meeting with Bracken, d'Egville stood his ground. He agreed, however, to send a telegram to Canberra, asking the Federal branch to accept an invitation. At this point a general election was called in Australia, and the visit did not take place.

For some time d'Egville had been working for a visit by a delegation of members of the United Kingdom and Dominion Parliaments to India. He had been thwarted in 1943 by Stafford Cripps and the Foreign Office. Two years later the question of a United Kingdom delegation going to India was raised. The Viceroy and the Secretary of State approved, but the agreement of the Indian branch could not be obtained until after 25 January 1946 because a general election had been called. D'Egville pressed for postponement of the visit until the Executive Committee of the Indian branch had been reconstituted and could issue an invitation under the usual Association auspices. The British government insisted on the visit taking place before the end of January 1946 and arrangements were made at government level.

A further complication which angered d'Egville was that the visit to India was announced in the House of Commons as part of a statement of government policy. To many members, he claimed, it seemed that an EPA delegation was being sent by the government, which was a regrettable confusion. Most of all, however, he deplored the fact that a parliamentary delegation was proceeding not under EPA auspices to a country of the Empire which had a branch. Finally, it was agreed that this must be regarded as a special case. For the future the position of the Association as the normal medium for arranging, receiving, and despatching of parliamentary delegations from the various parts of the Empire was confirmed.

During the mid-1940s d'Egville was closely involved with the gifts offered to the House of Commons. The Chamber, destroyed by bombs in 1941, had now been rebuilt. The Canadian branch had offered a Clerk's Table; the Australian branch or government – it was not clear which – had offered the Speaker's Chair; the gift of the New Zealand branch was despatch boxes; the South African branch offered the Clerks' chairs. Subsequently, the Southern Rhodesia branch proposed an inkpot made of Rhodesian gold. On behalf of the House the Speaker's Committee accepted these generous gifts: d'Egville served on this Committee and was involved in several minor, but delicate and time-consuming issues.

The Speakers' Chairs in the Canadian House of Commons and the Australian House of Representatives were exact replicas of the old Chair at Westminster. They had been presented by the United Kingdom branch, the cost having been met by private contributions of members of the branch. The idea now was that the three Chairs should continue to be identical. However, at a meeting of the Speaker's Committee, the architect, Sir Giles Scott, proposed making certain alterations in the design of the Chair to harmonise with the architecture of the House. He also had doubts about the ability of the Dominions to kiln the timber properly, and thought that both the kilning and the carving should be done in England. D'Egville discussed the matter with the Australian High Commissioner. He took the view that since the United Kingdom branch Executive Committee was really the only Committee of both Houses of Parliament concerned with British Commonwealth affairs, it should make the decision on the subject, having regard to the strong feelings in Australia. It was agreed that Australian wishes should be respected. The Chair must be a replica of the old Chair and must be carved in Australia.

A similar problem arose over the table to be presented by the Canadian branch. Sir Giles Scott had proposed that the timber should be kilned and the carving done in England. The Canadian branch objected that it wanted to present the table, not the wood for a table. D'Egville reported the Canadian view and it was readily agreed that the Canadian wishes should be met. Apparently no problems arose over the chairs to be presented by the South African branch.

There were so many offers of furniture from Dominion and colonial branches for the restored House of Commons that the Speaker's Committee had to rule that only one gift could be accepted from each Dominion. An exception was made in the case of the South Australian branch. It offered a piece of furniture carved from the especially beautiful local timbers, and expressed the hope that the gift could be used in the Chamber, but if this was not acceptable, the branch would welcome an alternative proposal. D'Egville suggested that the branch might present a chair for use by the Chairman at EPA meetings in place of the chair that had been destroyed. The suggestion was approved and the branch generously provided the chair.

In February 1947 the Speaker of the House of Commons, Col. Clifton Brown, wrote to the branch, suggesting that as Ceylon was on the threshold of Dominion status the gesture should be made of presenting its House of Representatives with a mace. D'Egville undertook to look into the details of cost and design and the raising of subscriptions from members of the branch to meet the cost. The mace was presented in January 1949.

Yet another activity which d'Egville was promoting at this time was the Colonial Affairs Study Group. He reported the formation of this Group to the Executive Committee on 28 May 1946. Many members had told him, he said, that opportunities for obtaining information about the colonies were few. The Colonial Office estimates provided virtually the only occasion when the subject was debated in the House. He had, therefore, written to members, proposing a study group which would meet periodically to hear addresses by the Colonial Secretary, the Parliamentary Under-Secretary, and distinguished visitors. In response to his circular nearly 200 members joined the group.

The first meeting took place on 23 May 1946 when A. Creech Jones,

Parliamentary Under-Secretary for the Colonies, spoke on 'Some Colonial Problems'. On 20 June 1946 F. W. Cavendish-Bentinck addressed the group on 'Urgent Problems in Kenya'. S. Gore-Browne spoke on 'Current Problems in Northern Rhodesia' on 10 July 1946. Films on Sarawak and Malaya were shown, with talks by L. D. Gammans and D. R. Rees-Williams at a meeting on 17 July 1946.

Apparently there had been a similar study group of the Association before the war. It had participated in meetings of the Comité Franco-Britannique d'Études Coloniales which had then existed. D'Egville told the Executive Committee on 24 July 1946 that he had recently visited Paris and had discussed the possible revival of this Franco-British committee. Parliamentary institutions in France had not, however, in his words, 'reached a sufficient stage of stability to enable members to concentrate on the study of these questions and to exchange ideas profitably with members of the Colonial Affairs Study Group, as they had done in the past'.

Major Milner, a distinguished member, often came into conflict with d'Egville on matters concerning the British–American Parliamentary Group and the Inter-Parliamentary Union. At this meeting he proposed that as the Inter-Parliamentary Union had a colonial affairs group, the Association might link up with it to restore relations with the French. This suggestion was unacceptable to d'Egville. On this occasion – as indeed usually – the Committee approved his report and agreed that a revival of exchanges with the French on colonial matters, either directly or in cooperation with the IPU, should be left in abeyance.

The IPU had been founded in Paris in 1889. Its co-founders were Frédéric Passy, a French member, and William Randal Cremer, a British member. The Union serves three broad objectives, namely, the promotion of contacts between members of all Parliaments in which it has national groups, support for the firm establishment and development of representative institutions, and the advancement of international peace and cooperation, particularly by supporting the objectives of the United Nations. The IPU has a central Secretariat in Geneva and national groups in 62 Parliaments. While basically different in character, the IPU and the CPA have much in common both in their aims and in their activities.

D'Egville had an irrational detestation of the IPU, and saw it as a rival organisation. Being international, it had groups in many countries which were, he considered, neither parliamentary nor democratic in their institutions. He would have nothing to do with de Blonay, its Secretary-General, who warmly reciprocated this antagonism. In private, d'Egville missed no opportunity to denigrate the IPU, and went to great lengths to dissuade Commonwealth countries from forming groups in their Parliaments. With the fervour of a fanatic, he maintained that there could be only one parliamentary union – the CPA.

7   EPA becomes CPA

The time was approaching for the next general conference of the Association. It was to be a crucial conference which would deal with the Canadian resolution and other matters vital to the Association's future. But the timing and the venue of the conference remained uncertain. It had been expected that it would take place in 1946 or 1947. But it was not until December 1947, just eight months before it convened, that it was decided that it should meet in London in October 1948.

New Zealand had offered to host a conference in 1940, but the war had intervened. D'Egville discussed suitable dates in 1946 and 1947 with the Prime Minister, with the Minister of Finance, and with the Leader of the Opposition. Mid-September 1948 was finally agreed. But the branch was concerned about difficulties of transport and adequacy of hotel accommodation. Finance may also have been a problem. It was the practice at this time for a main branch of the Association, acting as host to a general conference, to meet the travelling expenses for each delegate as well as providing accommodation and hospitality.

There was, moreover, a feeling in certain branches that this conference should be held in London. It was the first general conference since the end of the war and its business was of exceptional importance. D'Egville circulated to his Executive Committee on 15 July 1947 a letter he had received from Richard Thompson, a member of the New South Wales Parliament, who felt strongly on the subject. The relevant parts of the letter read:

> Whilst appreciating the value of a conference in some other part of the Empire, I am convinced that the present position calls for a gathering in London, at the heart of the Empire, of representatives from every branch not only for a discussion of Empire affairs and world relations but as evidence to the world that more than ever we are one....
>
> Many interests seek to undermine the Empire and I am convinced that one of the most spectacular and effective gestures that we of the Empire can make to the world is to have a family gathering at home...
>
> I am writing to Mr Attlee and Mr Churchill asking them to personally interest themselves in my proposal...

D'Egville reported that visiting members from Australia, Canada and other countries had expressed a similar view. D'Egville favoured London as the venue, and indeed may well have been promoting the idea. The Committee agreed in principle and showed a readiness to host the conference. At the same time, its members were anxious to do nothing that might offend the New Zealand branch and it was with that branch that the matter was left.

On 11 December 1947 d'Egville informed the Committee that the New Zealand branch had finally decided to postpone the conference from 1948 to 1950. Further, the Secretary of the branch and Fraser, the Prime Minister, in a personal letter to him, had stated that, if the United Kingdom branch decided to host the conference in 1948, New Zealand would send a strong delegation.

With only eight months in which to organise the conference, d'Egville plunged into work. He wrote to all branches enquiring about suitable dates in October. He also went to the Treasury to obtain the necessary grant. In this he had the valuable support of Glenvil Hall, then Financial Secretary to the Treasury. His industry, like his ability to organise to the smallest detail such large-scale events, was prodigious. Moreover, the conference was far from being the only business he had in hand at this time.

One difficult matter which was exercising him was the change in the Association's name of 'Empire' to 'Commonwealth'. He had informed the Executive Committee of his discussion with Malan during his visit to South Africa in February 1939. At that time the Committee had disliked the suggestion that 'Empire' should be dropped. But d'Egville had found in Canada that most members there would welcome the change of name. He mentioned this in a letter to Drummond Shiels, who commented in a letter of 29 May 1942, 'Your point about the word "Empire" ... I am inclined to think that you will find the Executive more amenable than when the matter was last brought up.'

In September 1946 d'Egville visited Eire at the suggestion of certain members of the branch there. De Valera had come to power and the annual grant for the Association's publications was withdrawn. The Irish branch was faltering and d'Egville was invited to talk to members, and in particular to De Valera himself, about the expanding activities of the Association and especially its new links with the US Congress.

On his return to London d'Egville reported that he had had a lengthy discussion with De Valera who had explained his attitude to the Commonwealth. D'Egville concluded from this meeting that De Valera wanted to maintain close relations with the Commonwealth and, while not actually conceding that Eire was a member, he did not deny that his country was part of the Commonwealth. He stated, however, that the difficulty he had concerning the Association was the use of the word 'Empire'. If this word was changed to 'Commonwealth' it would greatly encourage support for the branch in the Eire Parliament.

In March 1947 the Indian branch in the Central Legislature passed a resolution proposing that the name be changed to the Commonwealth Parliamentary Association. There were, however, still members in the United Kingdom and in the Australian and New Zealand branches who disliked this change. To d'Egville it was inevitable that the use of 'Empire' should be abandoned, and he wanted this done as soon as possible. Indeed, he was responsible for ensuring that a decision was taken by the conference in 1948 rather than later.

At this time nothing was more important to d'Egville than the need to forge close links between the US Congress and the Parliaments of the Commonwealth. Like many in Britain and elsewhere, he was somewhat awed by American economic and military power immediately after the war. The United States had become for him the guarantor of world security. He had a vision of the English-speaking world forming a union based on the Commonwealth.

Following the successful conference in Bermuda in June 1946, and the subsequent visits to Washington and Ottawa, d'Egville began planning ahead. Senator Fulbright had suggested in a speech in the Senate that such meetings should be annual. D'Egville now proposed that the next meeting should be in the Bahamas in April or May 1947, or towards the end of the year. He had already spoken with the Speaker of the Bahamas House of Assembly, then visiting England, who had confirmed that an invitation would be extended. It was finally agreed that the conference should start on 28 December 1947.

Preparations proceeded smoothly at first – the branch sent out invitations; the US Congress and the Canadian branch appointed their delegations; the United Kingdom branch was about to select its delegates. It was at this point that d'Egville received a cable that the Bahamas branch had decided reluctantly to postpone the conference indefinitely, owing to the dollar crisis and world economic conditions generally. It was already November 1947. D'Egville's first thought was to fly to Nassau immediately to persuade the branch to reverse its decision. Dalton, then Chancellor of the Exchequer, thought that all other possible steps should first be taken, bearing in mind that d'Egville would be crossing the Atlantic again in a few weeks time. He spoke by phone with the Governor and the principal officers of the branch. The Secretary of State for the Colonies sent a strongly worded letter to the Governor. All was to no avail. The Bahamas branch convened a special meeting and, in spite of the pressures brought to bear, it confirmed the decision.

D'Egville next cabled Bermuda, asking if it would be possible to hold the conference there. He received a generous reply from Sir Stanley Spurling, Speaker of the House of Assembly, that Bermuda would welcome it. He contacted the United States delegation who readily accepted the new venue. The two problems were, first, whether new arrangements could be made within a few weeks; and second, whether a strong British delegation could be chosen in that time. D'Egville himself approached all the senior Cabinet Ministers, but none could undertake to lead the delegation on the proposed dates. Finally, he consulted the Prime Minister. Attlee considered that, unless adequate representation could be ensured from all of the Dominion branches, it would be better to postpone the conference. This view prevailed and, while in North America, d'Egville obtained American and Canadian agreement to the conference taking place in Bermuda in November 1948.

On 19 December 1947 d'Egville flew to Ottawa. This visit was crucial to the success of his carefully nurtured plan to transform the Association into a truly international organisation, devoted to the promotion of closer contact and understanding among Commonwealth MPs and to the strengthening of parliamentary institutions. He had been working patiently and tenaciously for some five years towards this goal.

In 1945 the Canadian branch had passed a resolution proposing that a Secretariat, headed by a Secretary-General responsible to all branches, should be set up in some centre of the Empire, and that there should be a Council, or governing body, meeting annually. This resolution had been sent only to the United Kingdom branch, which had expressed a general welcome for the Canadian initiative. At the time it had been expected that this proposal would be considered at the conference in New Zealand in 1946 or 1947. This conference was now to be held in London in 1948. A general election had taken place in Canada and d'Egville considered it essential that the resolution should be confirmed in the new Parliament.

In a letter to Duncan Hall on 24 July 1947 d'Egville asked if he 'could think of a Liberal in the Canadian Parliament who would be useful in helping me with the secretariat proposal. I can't think of a Liberal who would be an enthusiastic supporter.' Duncan Hall was about to visit Canada and promised to keep this in mind. Between them they found as their supporter Senator Arthur W. Roebuck, KC.

D'Egville attended the meeting of the Executive Committee of the Canadian branch on 29 January 1948. Senator Roebuck proposed and John R. MacNicol, a prominent Progressive Conservative, seconded the motion. The resolution was adopted unanimously. The text was as follows:

> Whereas it is expedient to coordinate the work of all the branches of the Empire Parliamentary Association in the Parliaments of the British Commonwealth and to establish an effective link between them, it is hereby resolved: – That a General Council on which each branch should have equal representation should be established and authorized to appoint a Secretary who should also be Editor of Publications and act as a liaison officer between the branches; That the said Secretary should devote all his time to this particular work, should be responsible to the said General Council and should not be the Secretary of any of the Association's branches;
>
> And that this resolution be forwarded to all the branches of the Association with the request that it be given consideration and their views be communicated to this branch at as early a date as may be convenient.

At the annual general meeting of the Canadian branch on 5 February 1948, the resolution was unanimously approved.

Before the commencement of business at this same meeting Senator Gerald White moved and John G. Diefenbaker seconded a resolution which was supported by all the party leaders and carried unanimously. This resolution read:

That this branch of the Empire Parliamentary Association expresses its deep appreciation for the splendid services rendered to this branch by Sir Howard d'Egville and to the cause of peace by his unswerving efforts to bring into close community the Parliamentarians of the British Commonwealth and the United States of America.

While in Ottawa d'Egville discussed with the Prime Minister the arrangements for the forthcoming conference. He was guest of honour at a dinner given by Speaker Fauteux, to which all party leaders were invited. He took note of the fact that the invitation of a delegation of eight members would not allow adequate representation of all parties in the Canadian House of Commons and undertook to discuss the matter in London.

On his return d'Egville reported to his Executive Committee on his visits to Canada and the United States. He had explained to the group in the US Congress the economic reasons for the withdrawal of the Bahamas invitation to host a conference. This was readily understood and the congressional delegation already appointed would attend the conference in Bermuda in November 1948.

The Committee then considered the Canadian resolution and expressed its general support. At the same time d'Egville was asked to enquire if the other branches would support the resolution. The Committee would then consider whether any further action was necessary on the part of the United Kingdom branch before the matter came up at the conference in the autumn. The Committee approved d'Egville's proposal to ask each branch to include at least two members of its Executive Committee in its delegation in view of the matters to be worked out in the event that the resolution was adopted. The size of the delegations to be invited was left to d'Egville to decide.

Throughout this period of intensive activity d'Egville was acutely worried about his own position and his future with the Association. He was in his late sixties, but both his mental and physical energies were undiminished. Understandably, too, he was possessive about the Association which he had created, and could not bear the thought of relinquishing his control over it. But there were, he knew, members of the United Kingdom branch who would welcome his departure. He had, in fact, managed and manipulated the affairs of the branch and of its members from the beginning. His concern had been consistently to promote the growth and influence of the Association as a force for peace and stability in the world. But this did not prevent a build-up of resentment and antagonism among some members. He retained the support of the Prime Minister and of several Cabinet Ministers, but on occasion he tried even their patience.

D'Egville's immediate concern was to continue as Secretary of the branch until after the conference in October 1948 when he would, he was confident, be appointed the first Secretary-General. If, however, he was obliged to retire before the conference, there was a danger that the other appointment might not be offered to him. He could count on the support of the Dominion branches, but not of the United Kingdom branch. He, therefore, planned his campaign with great care.

The position of the Secretary and Editor of Publications was first considered at the meeting of the Executive Committee on 22 May 1947. Before this meeting d'Egville called on the Prime Minister, as Chairman of the Committee, and outlined his proposals for handing over the secretaryship in due course. Attlee was sympathetic. It was the first time, he said, that he had heard any suggestion of the Secretary's retirement. He endorsed the proposals put to him and said that the Committee should be so informed.

D'Egville also had discussions with the Speaker, Clifton Brown. He told him that he believed that the majority of members felt that his special knowledge of the work of the Association and his many contacts with members throughout the Commonwealth and in the US Congress made the question of age in his case one of minor importance and quite unlike the position in the civil service; he might have added that there was no retirement age for MPs. He was then 68. He also told the Speaker that in due course Major J. G. Lockhart would be able to take over from him. D'Egville had appointed Lockhart after the retirement of Sir Drummond Shiels. Lockhart, who had been personal assistant to Lord Halifax when Ambassador in Washington, took up his duties as Assistant Secretary in December 1946.

In presenting his proposals to the Committee, d'Egville said that since the end of the war he had had much in mind the need to train a younger man to take over from him eventually. Lockhart, whom the Committee had by this time appointed Deputy Secretary, was now being trained. He stressed, however, that adequate time must be allowed for this training and also that he had certain outstanding matters in hand which required his personal attention. These matters, which he described in some detail, were the organisation of the Bahamas conference (later postponed and to take place in Bermuda); the organisation of the New Zealand conference (later moved to London); the business arising from the Canadian resolution, if approved; and the formation of branches in colonial legislatures which had reached certain stages in self-government. After he had dealt with these matters, he said, and had completed the training of his successor, 'he would move for a time into the Commonwealth side of the work so as to place on a satisfactory basis the relations of the branches to each other and the relations of all branches with the United States Congress.' He added that the work of the United Kingdom branch and the work which might be regarded as more strictly the Commonwealth side of the Association's activities had been expanding so much that it was becoming impossible for one person to handle both. A division of functions was becoming increasingly necessary.

D'Egville was asked to withdraw while the Committee considered the matter further. There was clearly disagreement within the Committee. Only seven members were present at the meeting, however, and it was decided to leave the matter over to a later meeting when it was hoped more members would be able to attend.

The next meeting of the Committee took place on 15 July 1947. Efforts had been made (probably by d'Egville himself) to ensure that it was well attended, and the efforts were successful. The Prime Minister was in the chair. Of the 15 members present no fewer than 11 were Privy Councillors, 5 of whom were Cabinet Ministers. D'Egville reported on the preparations for the conference and other matters in hand. The main business of the meeting was, however, to decide the date of the retirement of the Secretary. D'Egville withdrew, and on his return was informed by the chairman that 'the view of the Committee was that he should remain Secretary of the United Kingdom branch until after the conclusion of the next general conference of the Association in New Zealand or the United Kingdom next year, but whether or not after that he should pass over to the Secretary-Generalship of the Association would depend on the views of all the branches of the Association'. The Finance and General Purposes Committee was empowered to recommend the name of a successor when the time came for d'Egville to leave.

This decision gave him only part of what he wanted. The date of his retirement had been fixed approximately. All would depend on his being appointed Secretary-General by the conference. There was a certain meanness of spirit in the failure of the Committee to nominate him for the office, bearing in mind his single-minded devotion to the Association over the years, and all that he had achieved.

The minutes, of course, recorded the facts and decisions, but reflected nothing of the bitter debate over the Secretaryship. In a letter to Duncan Hall, dated 24 July 1947, d'Egville wrote that the Committee's decision was 'not too bad. Yet I would have preferred if they had left the date of my going out of the branch secretaryship to the Finance Committee. As it is, one is not quite sure if the Secretariat will be set up by the end of next year.' Referring to 'the trouble over the UK Secretaryship', he wrote that 'it has been traced to three men. One of the instigators of the whole thing was Milner. The disloyalty to me of the [British–American Parliamentary] Group is almost incredible. However, he has been sat upon pretty well by Cabinet Ministers and there is no one on our Committee (with one possible exception) for turning me out.'

At the meeting of the Executive Committee on 10 March 1948, to which he reported soon after his return from Canada, the question of the Secretaryship was raised again. This happened because the General Meeting of the branch had been postponed until he could be present. A further complication was that the Executive Committee had decided not to include the Canadian proposal in the agenda for the general meeting, on the ground that replies from the Dominions would not have been received in time. This would appear to have been a questionable decision. There was no apparent reason why the members should not have been informed at their general meeting of the major developments proposed.

Lord Pethick-Lawrence, the Deputy Chairman who usually took the chair at meetings of the Committee, said that the Finance and General Purposes Committee had taken the view that Major J. G. Lockhart, the Deputy Secretary, should take over from d'Egville in due course. But, the Chairman asked, what reply should he give at the general meeting if questions were asked about the date of retirement of the present Secretary? He then invited d'Egville to speak on the matter. Unable to resist the opportunity to make a further attempt to prolong his tenure of the Secretaryship, d'Egville spoke at length. He went over the same ground that he had covered in previous meetings, which the members of the Committee present may have found tiresome, but he was always persuasive. He concluded with the statement, as recorded in the minutes of the meeting, that

> though he realised, of course, that the appointment of the Secretary to the Council must rest with the representatives of all branches of the Association, yet he felt that the Dominion branches would probably wish to see someone whom they knew and trusted as the first Secretary of the Council, and if that were so he was anxious to serve as Secretary and Editor for at any rate the first few years so as to set the whole organization, with which he had been so long connected, on the new permanent basis. Therefore he would desire that no date be fixed for his retirement from the secretaryship of the United Kingdom branch, but that the matter should be held in abeyance until the question of setting up the Council was decided.

Notwithstanding his personal anxieties, d'Egville worked out an impressive programme for the visit and conference to take place from 25 September to 26/27 October 1948. He demonstrated yet again the energy, attention to detail, and ability for organising which he had shown 37 years earlier in the coronation conference. Indeed, he followed the 1911 programme as closely as possible. Now, however, the conference was on a larger scale.

The calibre of the delegates selected was always a matter of special concern to him. He corresponded with Prime Ministers, Speakers and Premiers, impressing on them the importance of their branches and Parliaments being strongly represented. His influence was considerable. Thus he was able to report to his Executive Committee on 21 July 1948 that the Speaker and the national leaders of the political parties in the Canadian House of Commons would be delegates. He expected that seven premiers from the Canadian provinces would attend. From Australia, the Speaker of the House of Representatives, the leader of the Country Party, and Harold Holt, Deputy to Robert Menzies, then Leader of the Opposition, would be coming. The premiers and leaders of the opposition in New South Wales and Victoria would attend. From the other Australian states which were allowed only one delegate, the premiers of South Australia and Queensland had both personally accepted the invitation. New Zealand had appointed two senior members from each side of the House. He was in correspondence with the South African branch, and was hopeful that it would send a strong delegation, including two Nationalist MPs. The branch in Eire was being reconstituted, and its membership was increasing. It would, he expected, send a delegation.

Pandit Jawaharlal Nehru had written to him on 21 May 1948 and had indicated the India would probably be able to send a delegation. D'Egville also corresponded with Speaker Mavalankar. He doubted whether the branch was still in existence in the Indian Parliament. He did not agree with the Minister of

Finance, Sanmukham Chetty, who had been an active member of the branch in the Central Legislature. Chetty maintained that as the Constituent Assembly had taken over the functions of the former Central Legislature, it could be said that the branch now existed in the Assembly. D'Egville stressed that the invitation was not dependent on the formation or reconstitution of the branch. Indeed, the Indian delegation should come to the London conference before that was considered, because the change of name from Empire to Commonwealth Parliamentary Association would make it far easier to attract the support of Indian members.

In Pakistan members of the Constituent Assembly were eager to form a branch and to accept the invitation to appoint five delegates. D'Egville sent Ahmad, the Secretary of the Assembly, full information about the procedures for forming a branch. Likewise, he had advised Ralph Deraniyagala, Clerk of the House of Representatives in Ceylon, that as a Dominion Ceylon could form or reconstitute its branch without reference to the United Kingdom branch. Speaker Molamure would lead the delegation, which included the Minister of Health and Leader of the Tamil Congress Party.

In sending the invitation to Southern Rhodesia he had expressed the hope that the Prime Minister himself would be the delegate. Sir Godfrey Huggins had replied that, provided a general election was not called, he would attend. D'Egville then gave the names of the delegates appointed from Northern Ireland, the Isle of Man, Mauritius and Barbados. He reported that the delegates from the Gold Coast, Nigeria, Kenya and Northern Rhodesia would join the visit on 9 October 1948.

The amount of correspondence with the 36 branches on the appointment and travel of their delegates was massive. On top of this there was the detailed arrangement of the programme. He had secured accommodation for all of the 87 delegates expected in the Savoy Hotel. Transport had been arranged by sea or air for each delegate.

At d'Egville's suggestion a special Conference Committee of the branch was elected to which he could refer if major problems arose during the recess. Dalton was Chairman and Oliver Stanley Vice-Chairman. The members were Philip Noel-Baker (alternate, Patrick Gordon Walker), H. Butcher, D. R. Grenfell, Lord Listowel and A. C. M. Spearman.

The programme included attendance at a Buckingham Palace garden party and dinners, given by the City of London at the Guildhall, by the Drapers' Company, the London Chamber of Commerce, and by the government. Lunches were given by the Chamber of Shipping, the City Livery Companies, the Committees of Lloyds and the Baltic Exchange.

An innovation in the programme was a visit to the Continent. A few days after their arrival, delegates were divided into groups. Some 55 visited the American and British zones in Germany, the others went to Belgium and Holland. The purpose of these visits was to enable delegates to witness the operation of the Berlin airlift and to discuss the problems of post-war Germany and also the implications of the Western Union. General Clay sent his special plane to fly them from Frankfurt to Berlin, and he addressed them on the current situation. D'Egville escorted this group.

The delegates were next taken to Scotland, where they were the guests of the Lord Provosts of Edinburgh and Glasgow. In groups they then visited Manchester, Liverpool, Birmingham, Cardiff, Northern Ireland and the Universities of Oxford and Cambridge. As in 1911, it was amazing how much was packed into the programme.

The conference was officially opened on 19 October 1948 by the Prime Minister, Clement Attlee, in the Grand Committee Room, Westminster Hall. The topics discussed in the eight sessions were foreign affairs, defence, economic cooperation, migration and the future of parliamentary government.

Lord Pethick-Lawrence took the chair for the special session which dealt with the change of the name of the Association and the Canadian proposals. In the discussions representatives from Canada, India and South Africa spoke strongly in favour of the change in name to the Commonwealth Parliamentary Association. One or two delegates from other countries wanted to retain 'Empire' in the title. No one objected, however, when the motion was put to the conference, and the change of name was approved.

The proposals set out in the Canadian resolution were also adopted. There would in future be a General Council of the Association. A committee of delegates from the Executive Committees of main branches was convened. It agreed the principles and then called on d'Egville and the branch Secretaries present to draw up a detailed plan. At a subsequent meeting of delegates from branch Executive Committees this plan was approved. Many delegates, however, had the uneasy feeling that they were being kept in the dark about these developments. It was, therefore, agreed that the Chairman and delegation Secretaries should submit a report to the full conference on the proposed plan together with an estimate and a suggested allocation of the expenses of the new General Council.

The conference discussed the plan at length and finally approved it, subject to the rider that the General Council should examine the question of units of branch contributions and the number of representatives to serve on the Council from the branches. There was a consensus that the Headquarters Secretariat should be in London, while the General Council would meet annually in different countries. Its first meeting should be in Ottawa in April 1949.

The conference agreed that under the new plan Sir Howard d'Egville should become Secretary-General of the new General Council, while continuing as Editor of Publications. This appointment was, however, subject to confirmation by the Council at its first meeting. Subsequently the Executive Committee of the United Kingdom branch asked d'Egville to continue as its Secretary at least until the general meeting of the branch to be held in March or April 1949. Major J. G. Lockhart was appointed to succeed him.

At the conclusion of the conference delegates passed a resolution, expressing appreciation of the generous hospitality and the excellent arrangements made by the host branch. The second paragraph of the resolution read: 'We gratefully acknowledge the devotion of Sir Howard d'Egville to the development of the Commonwealth Parliamentary Association over the years and the debt which we owe him for the success of the present conference, and for the many acts of kindness and helpfulness which we have individually enjoyed at his hands.' The resolution also paid tribute to d'Egville's chief assistants, A. C. Spencer-Hess, Major J. G. Lockhart and Cory Williams.

D'Egville had only a few days to draw breath before setting out for Bermuda, where the second conference of members from the US Congress and Parliaments of the Commonwealth opened on 15 November 1948. Delegates attended from Britain, Canada, Australia, New Zealand and South Africa. The strong delegation of seven members from both Houses of Congress included Senators Hickenlooper and Fulbright, and Congressman Estes Kafauver. Particular interest was aroused in the session on parliamentary democracy when comparisons were made between the working of the systems in Congress and in Commonwealth Parliaments.

From Bermuda d'Egville went to Canada to discuss arrangements for the meeting of the General Council in the following spring. He met Speaker Fauteux in Montreal and called on the Premier of Quebec, Duplessis. The Quebec branch had not been represented at the London conference. D'Egville explained to Duplessis and to other members of the Cabinet the purpose and functions of the General Council and the financial implications. He also stressed the change in name of the Association, knowing how much the French-Canadians disliked the word 'Empire'. The Ministers in Quebec expressed their approval of this new era in the affairs of the Association, as did the Ministers he called on in Ottawa and Toronto. In Ottawa, too, he had lengthy discussions with Dr Arthur Beauchesne, the learned Clerk of the House of Commons and Secretary of the branch, who was a firm friend.

D'Egville then travelled on to Washington. He was anxious to discuss further development of the group in Congress, especially as there had been elections since his last visit. The result of his visit was the setting-up of an informal Commonwealth Parliamentary Committee under the chairmanship of Senator Elbert D. Thomas. At this time he was also actively promoting the formation of similar committees in Dominion branches of the Association to maintain relations with members of Congress.

By the time the General Council met in Ottawa, d'Egville had received from all branches ratification of the decisions of the London conference. The Victoria branch in Australia alone passed a resolution opposing the change of name. The United Kingdom ratified the decisions at its annual general meeting on 9 April 1949. The Prime Minister, Attlee, in the chair then commented that the changes agreed were 'a natural step ... and really parallel to what has happened in the development of the Commonwealth and Empire'. Anthony Eden, then Leader of the Opposition, said, 'the work of the Association was perhaps the strongest thing that held the whole wide family together.'

The first session of the General Council opened in Ottawa on 28 April 1949.

Sixteen members attended, representing the United Kingdom, Canada, Australia, New Zealand, South Africa, Pakistan, Malta, Bermuda and West Africa. Speaker Fauteux was elected Chairman and presided at this first session. The Canadian Parliament was, however, then dissolved, and Fauteux himself was appointed Lieut-Governor of Quebec Province. Senator Roebuck was elected in his place.

One of the first items of business was the appointment of the Secretary-General. On the proposal of Fauteux, d'Egville was unanimously elected to the office for five years with eligibility for reappointment. It was also agreed that the Headquarters Secretariat should be in London.

The Council then divided into two committees, one to consider the new constitution which d'Egville had drafted, and the other to deal with finance. Both committees reported to the full Council at its second meeting on 2 May 1949. The draft constitution was approved and adopted. One clause, however, gave rise to controversy. This was Clause IV(f) which read:

> A legislature of a country which is not part of the British Commonwealth but is closely associated with it by reason of such matters as common parliamentary practice or tradition, a common language and interests or past political relations may, on the invitation of the General Council, form an associated branch of the Association.

The clause reflected d'Egville's deep concern to maintain the close links between Commonwealth countries and the United States. Recognising that the United States could hardly become part of the Commonwealth, he nevertheless hoped to bring the US Congress into the Commonwealth Parliamentary Association, but objections were raised at the Council meeting.

Clifton Webb, the New Zealand Attorney-General and Minister of Justice, asked whether an associated branch would have a vote at a general meeting. Roebuck in the chair ruled that it would. This disturbed Clifton Webb and other members. Some argued, however, that a branch in the US Congress should have the same rights as a main branch. The two British members were wary of this principle and advised caution about the Irish Republic. The representative from Pakistan, Tamizuddin Khan, called for a distinction to be maintained between countries within the Commonwealth and those outside the Commonwealth. This was a matter to be discussed at the next meeting of the General Council.

The proposals of the Committee on financial arrangements were that payment units of £50 should be allocated to each branch, the allocation being based on the general wealth of the country, revenue, population, size of Parliament and other factors. The Council approved the recommendations for submission to the next conference. A Finance and General Purposes Committee was appointed to deal with urgent matters arising between Council meetings.

One subject to which much attention was devoted was the Association's publications programme. At this session, on 2 May 1949, d'Egville's appointment as Editor of Publications was confirmed. Tributes were paid to the *Journal of the Parliaments of the Commonwealth*,* to the *Summary of Congressional Proceedings*

USA, and to the *Report on Foreign Affairs*. There was, however, some complaint about the late arrival of the *Report* in countries overseas, where it was needed as soon as possible. The delays meant that it was used more as a source of reference than as a commentary on current affairs. The Council then approved d'Egville's proposal that a supplement to the *Report* should be prepared under his supervision and sent by airmail between issues of the *Report* to members with special interest in foreign affairs. The discussion closed with a resolution:

> That in the view of the value of the publications to the maintenance of common understanding among members of the legislatures of the Commonwealth, BE IT RESOLVED that these publications be continued by the General Council on their present basis with such improvements and extensions as may be possible from time to time.

At the third and final session on 3 May 1949, the Chairman ruled out of order the Victoria branch resolution against changing the name of the Association, since the matter had already been decided at the London conference. The next conference of the Association and the next meeting of the General Council were to take place in New Zealand in October 1950. The Council also agreed that the CPA should be deemed to have begun functioning as from 1 January 1949.

After the adjournment of the Council, the members paid official visits to Quebec and Toronto and were then flown to Washington, DC. They were received by the group in Congress, entertained by the Senate and House Foreign Relations Committees, received on the Floor of the Senate, and personally by the Speaker of the House of Representatives, Sam Rayburn. It was like a triumphal procession and was crowned by a visit to the White House where President Truman welcomed them.

D'Egville must have been deeply gratified. He had had setbacks and anxieties, but he had succeeded in creating the CPA and in forging a link with the US Congress. Patrick Gordon Walker described his triumph aptly: 'Like everything wrought by d'Egville, [it] was brought about by vision, intrigue, calculated timing, boundless energy, and a total identification of himself with the Association. . . to d'Egville almost single-handed – at the age of 70 – was due the birth of the CPA. Nor could anyone else have so well and so quickly succeeded in getting the CPA off the ground as a going concern.'

---

*The name of the *Journal* was changed to *Journal of the Parliaments of the Commonwealth* as from vol. XXX, no. 1, March 1949.

In outlook, d'Egville was suited to the office of Secretary-General. He was a Commonwealth man and even more a man of the English-speaking world. He was at home in Canada and the United States and, indeed, in most of the countries of the Commonwealth. He had no special bias towards nor loyalty to the United Kingdom branch. Rather, he regarded the branch as a source of restraint and hindrance to his great work of making the Association a powerful influence in world affairs. He saw clearly and with detachment that the hegemony of the branch belonged to the past. Many British members still did not recognise, or refused to accept, this fact, and resented his attitude. They saw him as something of a renegade because he showed indifference and even at times opposition to what they considered to be British interests. They were, moreover, inclined to regard d'Egville's initiatives as motivated by hunger for personal aggrandisement. It was a narrow view. He welcomed praise and was, in fact, very vain. He also enjoyed wielding influence over others. His purpose, however, was always to strengthen and expand the Association. Nevertheless he sometimes took too much upon himself and came into conflict not only with the United Kingdom branch but also with one or two other branches.

D'Egville did not cease to be Secretary of the United Kingdom branch until 1 May 1949, but he was looking ahead. One of his first concerns was to obtain accommodation for the new General Council Secretariat. His intention was to locate it in a room in the branch offices. Even before the first meeting of the General Council the branch Executive Committee at his instigation adopted on 9 February 1949 a resolution that 'suitable accommodation for the headquarters of the General Council should be provided within the Palace of Westminster'. It was important from the start to establish the new Secretariat as the Commonwealth headquarters of the Association, distinct and physically separate from the United Kingdom branch. Curiously, d'Egville appeared not to recognise this need at first. Later in the year he was to write in the annual report: '... it was very necessary that the Council should have its own separate offices to emphasize its identity as the headquarters of all the branches'. In the event he lost the battle to take over rooms in the branch, mainly because he himself had established the branch so firmly in Westminster Hall.

The battle for this accommodation involved both the Speaker and the Prime Minister. On 19 April 1949, while d'Egville was in Ottawa, Attlee wrote to Lockhart, then Secretary-Designate, that the Speaker's view was 'that there would be real difficulty in carrying out the resolution of 9 February. On consideration I am satisfied that he is right about this and that it would be a mistake for the Executive Committee to press this demand.' Subsequently, the Speaker informed Attlee that he would have no objection to the Secretariat occupying 24 Abingdon Street. Technically this was part of the Palace of Westminster, although physically it was across the road from the Palace and to the south of Old Palace Yard. The house was part of a terrace, much of which had been badly damaged by flying bombs towards the end of the war.

On 27 April 1949 Attlee wrote to Lockhart: 'I have heard from Mr Speaker and it is understood that the United Kingdom branch should re-occupy its present offices when these are reconditioned and that this will remain at its exclusive disposal.' On the following day Lockhart wrote to d'Egville in Ottawa, but somehow d'Egville had already heard of the decision. On 28 April 1949 (the date on which Lockhart wrote) Wilmot, one of the British representatives on the General Council, wrote to Lockhart, emphasising how important it was 'that d'Egville should have a *pied-à-terre* in the United Kingdom offices'. On the same day d'Egville drafted a resolution, which the General Council approved, expressing 'its strong sense of the value and importance of the headquarters being located in the building which for many centuries has been the home of the Mother of Parliaments ... and requests the appropriate authorities to provide such accommodation in the Palace of Westminster'.

On his return from Ottawa d'Egville acknowledged defeat and moved his Secretariat into 24 Abingdon Street 'on a temporary basis' taking with him Spencer Hess as his assistant, Mrs Blattner, the assistant editor, and secretarial staff. It was some compensation that after a struggle he prevailed on the Treasury to meet the cost of these offices. This generous contribution to the CPA by the British government continued after the Secretariat moved in March 1960 to 7 Old Palace Yard, also technically within the Palace of Westminster.*

The years 1949–50 were exceptionally busy for the new Secretariat. The formation of a branch in India; correspondence about the constitution; organisation of the conference in New Zealand in November 1950, and a further conference in Canberra in December 1950; the opening of the rebuilt House of Commons in August 1949, visits to branches, publications, and other matters all made their claims on d'Egville's time.

The draft constitution, which was to be ratified by the general meeting of the Association in New Zealand in November 1950, was sent to all branches so that

---

*The houses in Abingdon Street were demolished in 1960. In their place an underground car park was built and a lawn laid over it.

they would have ample time to consider it and table amendments. Clause IV(f), providing for a special relationship of the United States and the Republic of Ireland with the Association, remained a cause of concern.

The British government was especially anxious that representatives of the Irish Republic should not be able to use the CPA as a forum to promote their policies. In the past, Irish members had been active in the Association. A branch had been established in the Dáil Éireann of the Irish Free State in 1926. This had followed soon after the agreement in December 1925, fixing the borders between the 26 southern counties and the six counties in the north. The constitutional links between Britain and the Irish Free State were defined by the British External Relations Act 1936. Gradually, however, these links were removed by the Dáil and Ireland's formal association with Britain and the Commonwealth was finally severed by the Republic of Ireland Act 1948. The CPA branch in what became known as Ireland or Eire in 1937 was active until 1934, but continued to pay a token grant until 1948.

On 7 October 1950 Patrick Gordon Walker, who was then Under-Secretary of State at the Commonwealth Relations Office, had a meeting with d'Egville. He told him that both the Prime Minister and the Secretary of State were

> very worried about the provision in the constitution for associated membership by countries outside the Commonwealth and that in their view membership of the CPA should be limited to the Parliaments of the Commonwealth and not therefore include countries like the United States and the Irish Republic. It might be possible to have *ad hoc* relations with such countries, but it was essential to make it clear in the constitution that only members of the Commonwealth could aspire to membership.

According to Gordon Walker, d'Egville replied that his own view was similar. In fact, he wanted not possible '*ad hoc* relations', but provision in the constitution for regular participation in conferences and greater contacts between members of CPA branches and members of Congress and of the Dáil. He said that changes would have to be made in Clause IV(f). He had in mind calling them associated groups rather than branches. The constitution should also make clear that such groups would have no vote and would play no part in the management of the CPA.

On 11 October 1949 d'Egville visited Northern Ireland to discuss these proposed changes. He addressed members of the branch and appeared to have secured their general agreement, provided such groups had no voice in the running of the Association, but any attempts to involve the Irish Republic aroused fierce suspicions among members at Stormont. Indeed on 19 October 1949, soon after his return to London, he received a letter from Major George Thomson, Secretary of the Northern Ireland branch, which reflected the mood there. Thomson wrote:

> The matter of Southern Ireland and its relations to the CPA has been discussed by some

of our people who were in London last week and I have received a straight hint that neither the Prime Minister on your side nor the Commonwealth Relations people look favourably on any approach being made to Southern Ireland regarding its association with the CPA. I would advise you very strongly not to get in touch with Southern Ireland until the situation has been considerably clarified.

D'Egville did not accept dictation from the United Kingdom nor from Northern Ireland. He was now Secretary-General, answerable to all branches of the Association. Moreover, he understood the Commonwealth attitude to the withdrawal of the Irish Republic, as distinct from the British and Northern Ireland attitudes. At the meeting of Commonwealth Prime Ministers in October 1948, representatives of the British, Canadian, Australian and New Zealand governments had discussions with Southern Irish representatives. It emerged clearly at these discussions that the 'old Dominions' were united in the view that Ireland's withdrawal should not be allowed to impair relations between Ireland and the other countries of the Commonwealth.[1] The Republic of Ireland was proclaimed on 18 April 1949.

A few weeks after his talk with Gordon Walker and his visit to Northern Ireland, d'Egville was in Dublin. He had kept in touch with friends in the Dáil, the Irish Parliament, who had been members of the Irish branch when the Irish Free State was still within the Commonwealth. On 9 August 1949 Senator O'Sullivan had written to him that J. A. Costello, the Prime Minister, and Sean MacBridge, the Minister for External Affairs, were both keen for Ireland to take part in Commonwealth activities. D'Egville had discussions in Dublin with O'Sullivan and also with Senator Douglas. They agreed that countries outside the Commonwealth should be able to have ties with the CPA without accepting responsibility for its policies. On 16 December 1949 Douglas wrote that he had consulted several prominent members of the Dáil. All had agreed that the Irish Republic should have no vote in the CPA. An associated group was formed in the Dáil in 1952.

The Irish Republic withdrew from the Commonwealth on 18 April 1949: on 26 January 1950 India became a republic but resolved to remain in the Commonwealth. In the months leading up to midnight on 14–15 August 1947, the fateful date for the transfer of power, it was far from clear whether India would remain a member of the Commonwealth. Many Indians believed that the ending of British rule should also put an end to all formal relations with Britain and the West: 'Asia for the Asians' was the slogan. Independent India should turn to Asia and perhaps form a neutral Asian block. In London, too, many held the view that republican India as a member of the Commonwealth would prove to be a disruptive force, especially in such issues as race relations in South Africa, colonialism and neutrality.

On 16 June 1947 the Burmese leader, Aung San, had moved a resolution in his Constituent Assembly that Burma should become an independent sovereign republic outside the Commonwealth, and it was adopted. In taking this step he had no doubt that this was the step that India was bound to take. He was mistaken.

India and Pakistan became independent states simultaneously. The Indian leaders were then faced by a number of factors in deciding whether India should be a member of the Commonwealth. One was that Mohammed Ali Jinnah had maintained consistently that Pakistan would remain a member after independence. In Delhi it was feared that, if India withdrew, Pakistan would be able to count on British and Commonwealth support in the various post-partition disputes, especially over Kashmir. Another factor was that India needed to foster good relations with Britain and the West in its own economic and political interests. It was also notable that among the Indian leaders there remained a fund of goodwill towards Britain.

On the British side it was earnestly hoped that India would become one of the leading members of the Commonwealth. Speaking in the House of Commons on 15 March 1946, the Prime Minister, Clement Attlee, said:

> I hope that the Indian people may elect to remain within the British Commonwealth. I am certain that she will find great advantages in doing so. In these days demand for complete, isolated nationhood apart from the rest of the world, is really outdated. Unity may come through the United Nations, or through the Commonwealth, but no great nation can stand alone without sharing in what is happening in the world. But if she does so elect, it must be by her own free will. The British Commonwealth and Empire is not bound together by chains of external compulsion. It is a free association of free peoples.[2]

In private talks and messages to Nehru and other Indian leaders Attlee expressed forcefully the British concern and hope on this score.

The fact that India finally decided to remain in the Commonwealth as an independent nation was in the main the work of three statesmen – Jawaharlal Nehru, Clement Attlee and Lord Mountbatten, the last Viceroy. Nehru himself favoured Commonwealth membership and he overcame the doubts of many members of Congress. The outcome was the Jaipur Resolution of 18 December 1948, declaring that Congress would welcome India's 'free association with independent nations of the Commonwealth for their common welfare and the promotion of peace'.[3] At the conference of Commonwealth Prime Ministers held in London on 21–28 April 1949, agreement was reached that India, although becoming a sovereign independent republic, would remain a member of the Commonwealth. The one problem remaining was the modification of the King's title to make acceptable the membership of a republic without offending the member nations which remained loyal to the Crown. Finally it was decided that the King should be designated 'Head of the Commonwealth' and as such the symbol of the free association of the independent member nations.

The continued membership of India, the world's most populous parliamentary democracy, was received with general acclaim. Further, this agreement opened the way for other republics to retain their membership of the Commonwealth, and republics were soon to form the great majority among the member nations. The London declaration read as follows:

The Governments of the United Kingdom, Canada, Australia, New Zealand, South Africa, India, Pakistan and Ceylon, whose countries are united as members of the British Commonwealth of Nations and owe a common allegiance to the Crown, which is also the symbol of their free association, have considered the impending constitutional changes in India.

The Government of India have informed the other governments of the Commonwealth of the intention of the Indian people that under the new constitution which is about to be adopted India shall become a sovereign independent republic.

The Government of India have, however, declared and affirmed India's desire to continue her full membership of the Commonwealth of Nations and her acceptance of The King as the symbol of the free association of its independent member nations and as such Head of the Commonwealth.

The governments of the other countries of the Commonwealth the basis of whose membership of the Commonwealth is not hereby changed, accept and recognize India's continuing membership in accordance with the terms of this declaration.

Accordingly the United Kingdom, Canada, Australia, New Zealand, South Africa, India, Pakistan, and Ceylon hereby declare that they remain united as free and equal members of the Commonwealth of Nations, freely cooperating in the pursuit of peace, liberty and progress.[4]

Another factor which, indirectly but in some degree, influenced Nehru and other Indians against severing links with Britain and the Commonwealth was their determination to adopt the British parliamentary system. From its first meeting in Bombay in 1885 the Indian National Congress had demanded the extension of British parliamentary institutions to India. At no stage during the long struggle to independence were the Indian leaders ever deflected from this determination. The paradox was that at Westminster the opinion, firmly held, was that the system would not suit India. 'It would be a western importation uncongenial to eastern tastes.'[5] The Simon Commission in its report, published in 1929, made the comment that 'The British parliamentary system ... has been fitted like a well-worn garment to the figure of the wearer, but it does not follow that it will suit everybody ...'.[6]

In Whitehall studies were made of the American presidential, the Swiss, and the old Austro-Hungarian systems which, it was thought, might better suit Indian conditions. In 1917, however, British policy was declared to be one of increasing association of Indians in every branch of the administration and the gradual development of self-governing institutions. This development, more and more in Indian hands, was to lead to parliamentary democracy. Since independence the Parliament of India, comprising the Lok Sabha (House of the People) and the Rajya Sabha (Council of the States), has proved to be a strong and innovative institution at the heart of the nation.

The Indian branch of the Association, formed in February 1926, had lapsed on independence. D'Egville, eager for it to be reconstituted, was in regular correspondence with G. V. Mavalankar, Speaker of the Constituent Assembly (Legislative), with M. N. Kaul, the distinguished Secretary to the Assembly, and with Indian Ministers. On 21 March 1949 he wrote to Mavalankar, asking if he could arrange for an Indian observer to attend the General Council meeting in Ottawa. Mavalankar replied on 1 April that the time was too short. The real reason was that 'I do not want it to be said that by any action on my part I tried to force the hands of the members one way or the other with reference to the question of India's constitutional position vis-a-vis the Commonwealth.'

D'Egville's pleasure was great when he received a letter from Mavalankar, dated 18 July 1949, stating that he would be 'glad to form a branch of the CPA'. It was a prompt response after the Commonwealth Prime Ministers meeting in London in April 1949. D'Egville replied that the Parliament should pass a resolution to form a branch, which he hoped Nehru would propose. Mavalankar wrote a letter of agreement. The Indian branch was formed in August 1950. It has always given strong support to and has participated actively in the work of the Association. Moreover, branches have been formed over the years in all but one of the Indian state legislatures.

A further development at this time was the attendance as observers of Commonwealth MPs at sessions of the Consultative Assembly of the Council of Europe. Mr Julian Amery, a member of the British delegation, suggested such visits. D'Egville acted promptly. In August 1949 he arranged for four members to travel to Strasbourg. They were P. C. Spender (soon to become Minister for External Affairs, Australia), J.M. Macdonald (Canada), and Dr Henry Gluckman and R. S. Brooke (South Africa). The visit was a success.

In August 1950 the Consultative Assembly passed a resolution to invite Parliaments of Commonwealth countries having links with certain member states of the Council of Europe, to send observers to the next session. The President of the Assembly, Henri Spaak, then wrote to the Speakers in Canada, Australia, New Zealand, South Africa, India, Pakistan and Ceylon. This annoyed d'Egville. He had advised that the proper channels for such invitations were the branches of the Association. However, the branches apparently did not respond. Nothing further seems to have happened.

An important event in October 1950 was the opening of the new House of Commons. On behalf of the House, Speaker Clifton Brown invited the Speakers and Presiding Officers of Commonwealth Parliaments to be present as his guests. D'Egville proposed to his Finance and General Purposes Committee that, since the Speakers and Presiding Officers were all *ex officio* Presidents of their respective branches, it would be fitting for the General Council to give a dinner for them. The occasion would provide an opportunity not only for thanking the British Speaker and government but also for explaining the new constitution and the expansion of the work of the Association. This was agreed. The members of the General Council, chosen to act as hosts at the dinner were Senator Roebuck, Chairman of the General Council, Lord Wilmot, the Deputy Chairman, W. Glenvil Hall, Tamizuddin Khan, Sir Francis Molamure and E. O. Asafu-Adjaye.

The dinner, held on 27 October 1950 in the members' dining-room of the House of Commons, was an impressive occasion. Clement Attlee and Anthony Eden sat on either side of the Chairman. The Speaker and eight British Cabinet Ministers, including Patrick Gordon Walker, were present. The speeches dwelt on the CPA and the value of its work. Herbert Morrison, Lord President of the Council, said that the dinner presented 'a striking evidence of the real parliamentary comradeship which exists within the Commonwealth'.[7]

During 1949–50 d'Egville was involved in heavy correspondence with the New Zealand and other branches concerning the conference to be held in Wellington. Clifton Webb, the Attorney-General, had been appointed Chairman of a Cabinet Subcommittee, responsible for the arrangements for the visit and the conference. C. M. Bothamley, the Clerk of the Parliaments and Secretary of the New Zealand branch, was not experienced in organising an international conference on this scale. He turned constantly to d'Egville for guidance.* Moreover, at this time d'Egville was also organising a second conference. This was to take place in Canberra, immediately after the New Zealand conference. It was to provide for a delegation from the US Congress to meet delegates from the main branches of the Association.

Long before the New Zealand conference d'Egville was, as usual, attempting to ensure that certain members were chosen as delegates. He was well aware that this involved interfering in the affairs of autonomous branches. He considered, however, that it was of overriding importance to secure some continuity of membership in the Council and the General Meeting. It was especially important in New Zealand. The conference and the General Meeting were the first such meetings of the CPA. The constitution was to be ratified, plans for the future approved, financial arrangements agreed.

Letters about the delegates to be chosen show d'Egville at his most devious. His machinations failed in many cases, but he was gratified by the attendance of Harold Holt, Diefenbaker, Tamizuddin Khan and Malik, who although now ambassador to Indonesia, continued as a member of the Pakistan Constituent Assembly and so of the Pakistan branch. While d'Egville agonised over continuity in the affairs of the Association, most members were unconcerned. They wanted their share of trips overseas and were quick to resent any member who appeared to be favoured, especially if that member belonged to a rival party.

The General Council, appointed for the year 1950–51, met in Auckland on 6–7 November 1950. Roebuck took the chair and it was agreed that he should hold office until his successor was elected at the next meeting. Clifton Webb was elected Vice-Chairman. The Council agreed on amendments to Clause IV(f) and to the creation of a category of subsidiary branches. The United Kingdom representatives proposed a cut in the contribution of their branch to the CPA budget. This aroused such strong disapproval that the proposal was hurriedly withdrawn. On behalf of the Prime Minister of Ceylon, Sir Francis Molamure

*In fact, Bothamley was to retire in June 1951 when he was succeeded by H. N. Dollimore.

extended an invitation to the Council to meet next in Colombo. It was agreed provisionally that this meeting should not be until January 1952, because elections were expected in India in December 1951.

The first General Meeting of the Association took place in Wellington on 24 November 1950. Roebuck in the chair welcomed the delegations from the newly formed branches in India, the Federation of Malaya, Singapore and British Honduras. He extended a special welcome to Newfoundland, which had recently become Canada's tenth province and had sent as its delegate, R. S. Sparkes, Speaker of the House of Assembly.

The conference took place in Wellington from 27 November–1 December 1950. Eighty delegates attended from 48 branches.[8] The verbatim report of the conference, published by the Secretariat in London, showed that the standard of the speeches was high. Delegates returned to their home countries fired with enthusiasm for the conference and for the Association.

Reporting to the United Kingdom branch, Lord Llewellin said:

> This was really the first phase in a new stage in the Commonwealth Parliamentary Association in which we have passed from being as it were the father and general centre of the whole Association to being the elder brother in a meeting of brother bodies such as the one in New Zealand. That new relationship has gone extremely smoothly as I think it always will.[9]

The elder brother was to be prone on occasions, however, to act as Big Brother.

The Speaker of the New Zealand House of Representatives, M. H. Oram, expressed the view that

> The important thing was not that the conference should pass resolutions, but that the Parliamentarians representing each country comprising the Commonwealth should understand the difficulties and problems and the circumstances of the other countries of the Commonwealth. The conference has been of tremendous value from that point of view.[10]

This comment, together with the following extract from the report of G. J. Bowden to the General Meeting of the Australian branch, probably expressed the feelings of all of the delegates. Bowden wrote:

> It is misleading to attempt to summarise speeches which were themselves by time necessarily condensed. They have to be heard or, next best, read to give the great stimulus and inspiration and information which delegates derived from them. It is placed on record the conviction of the Australian delegation that the conference was a great education as well as a grand experience to mould understanding and goodwill between Commonwealth members. It is suggested that branches regard future conferences with the utmost respect and importance so that delegates of the greatest usefulness for the conference purposes will be elected to go.[11]

From New Zealand the delegates from the main branches in the United

Kingdom, Canada, Australia, New Zealand, India, Pakistan and Ceylon travelled to Australia for the conference with representatives from the US Congress. The Australian Prime Minister, Robert Menzies, welcomed them in Canberra. Four Congressmen had been chosen, but pressure of business in Washington had reduced the delegation to two – Senator Theodore F. Green and Senator Homer Ferguson.

The conference was opened on 10 December 1950. Menzies himself led the discussion on 'Foreign Relations and Defence' which was the subject of all the sessions. The conference, rated by Lord Alexander 'an outstanding success', was the subject of a full and glowing report by Senators Green and Ferguson to the US Senate on their return.

On the way to New Zealand, d'Egville had flown to Canada and had visited the branches in Quebec, Ontario, Manitoba, Saskatchewan and British Columbia. On the conclusion of the conference in Canberra he visited and addressed members of the branches in New South Wales, Tasmania, Victoria, South Australia and Western Australia. He returned to London by sea, stopping over in Ceylon to visit the branch there. All of these branches provided him with an office and secretarial assistance. In this way he kept in touch with branches throughout the Commonwealth and maintained the momentum of his obsessive work for the Association.

Although he was now over 70, his energies remained prodigious. On top of his multifarious activities he had a steady flow of visitors when he was in London. Prime Ministers, Speakers, Ministers and Senior Clerks of Parliament figured among those who called on him. In the period from May 1949 to September 1950, 85 overseas members signed the visitors' book at 24 Abingdon Street. The number was 148 in the period from October 1950 to October 1951. The numbers increased further in subsequent years. D'Egville received them all personally. He talked at length about their branches and CPA affairs, and he had a detailed knowledge of their countries. Usually he entertained them to lunch or dinner; at weekends he took the more important visitors to the Hurlingham Club where he was a member. The annual reports of the Council list the names of these visiting members. It is notable how many were eminent in the political life of their countries and how many were to attain even greater eminence. He counted on the support of these people for the Association.

Notes

1. N. Mansergh, *The Commonwealth Experience* (London, 1982), vol. II, p.143.
2. House of Commons Debates, vol. 420, col. 1421.
3. Mansergh, *op. cit.*, vol. II, p. 154.
4. Ibid., p.157.
5. Ibid., p.45.
6. Ibid., p.46.
7. Report of General Council, 1950–51, p.24.
8. **Agenda and Opening Speakers, Wellington, 1950**

Economic Relations (Trade and Finance) – Walter Nash, Leader of the Opposition (New Zealand) and Lord Llewellin (United Kingdom)

Parliamentary Government – J. G. Diefenbaker (Canada) and O. H. Malik (Pakistan)

Migration – Harold Holt, Minister for Immigration (Australia) and W. S. Morrison (United Kingdom)

Defence and Pacific Relations – Viscount Alexander, Chancellor of the Duchy of Lancaster (United Kingdom) and Dev Kanta Borooah (India)

Foreign Affairs – F. W. Doidge, Minister for External Affairs (New Zealand) and J. Duthie (South Africa)

9. Report of General Council, 1950–51, p.11.
10. *Loc. cit.*
11. Ibid., p.12.

9 The Troubled Years, 1951–53

From the beginning d'Egville saw the publications and the information service as lying at the heart of the Association's activities. The three main quarterlies – *Journal of the Parliaments of the Commonwealth, Report on Foreign Affairs,* and the *Summary of Congressional Proceedings USA* – appeared regularly. The monthly *Commentary on Foreign Affairs,* sent by airmail to all members who requested it, was especially welcomed.

The information service had expanded. In response to queries about the Public Accounts Committee at Westminster, d'Egville had commissioned Hugh Farmer, Clerk to the Committee, to write a memorandum which was widely distributed. Another development was the agreement with the Commonwealth Economic Committee, whereby some 2000 copies of each of its up-to-date commodity reports were sent by the General Council Secretariat to members overseas. A list of books suitable for parliamentary libraries was prepared in the Secretariat for the Barbados, Northern Rhodesia and other branches.

Receiving many requests for information about the payments and privileges of Commonwealth MPs, d'Egville sent a questionnaire to all branches. He embodied the information received in a 32-page memorandum which was much in demand. It remained in demand and a new up-to-date version had to be produced. Requests for information on procedural matters were frequent. D'Egville wrote to each of the branches, asking for two copies of the standing orders of its legislature, one copy to be kept in the reference library of the Secretariat, the other to be available on loan to members or branches requesting it.

The annual reports of the General Council contained full statements on the publications and information services. Usually tributes by Prime Ministers, members and Clerks were included. At the General Meetings of the Association the publications and information service were always strongly supported. Certain United Kingdom members alleged that this support was elicited by d'Egville. He certainly promoted the publications. It is, however, difficult to credit that so many senior members and Clerks paid their tributes to the value of the publications without meaning them and solely at the behest of d'Egville.

The problem was the attitude of the United Kingdom branch. Its Executive Committee had not been enthusiastic when d'Egville launched the publications. Overseas branches, however, had welcomed them and continued to do so. It was exclusively from the United Kingdom branch that criticism of the publications and proposals for curtailing them emanated. Glenvil Hall, a friend of d'Egville and of the Association, several times suggested a reduction in their distribution on grounds of cost. On this subject the views of the United Kingdom branch were, however, contradictory.

At the General Meeting in Wellington on 24 November 1950, Lord Wilmot, in seconding the adoption of the report of the General Council, spoke with enthusiasm about the publications as an essential part of the Association's activities. He went on to quote statements by Lester Pearson, Secretary of State for External Affairs, Canada, by Ben Chifley, Leader of the Opposition, Australia, and by Campbell Calder, a prominent member from Ontario. All asserted the value of the publications, especially the *Commentary on Foreign Affairs*. At the same meeting Lord Alexander, the leader of the United Kingdom delegation, said: 'I doubt whether any document has existed in the world, in democratic circles, which has contained between its covers such an efficient summary of British parliamentary proceedings and other Commonwealth parliamentary proceedings throughout the whole Commonwealth, as the *Journal of the Parliaments of the Commonwealth*. There is nothing quite like it in the rest of the world'.[1] Another United Kingdom delegate, Gilbert McAllister, said at this meeting:

> I am sure that those of us who take the trouble – and it is no trouble – to read them find them of infinite value in all our deliberations. *The Journal of the Parliaments of the Commonwealth*, the *Report on Foreign Affairs*, and the *Summary of Congressional Proceedings USA* are now standard, and we all have appreciated them over several years. But I would like, if I might, to pay special tribute to Sir Howard d'Egville and his staff for the really brilliant editing of the monthly *Commentary on Foreign Affairs*. It is almost impossible to be objective in these matters, but I think that if any complete degree of objectivity can be realised then it has been reached in this monthly report on foreign affairs, and I hope that the Council will go on and extend the scope of these publications.[2]

Even allowing for the hyperbole which afflicts most MPs on such occasions, there could be no doubt that the British delegates had expressed strong support. Notwithstanding this support, some three months later the Executive Committee of the United Kingdom branch passed a resolution directed at cutting expenditure on publications.

On the journey from Australia d'Egville received a letter from Spencer Hess, informing him that the Treasury wanted to cut the United Kingdom contribution to the General Council. On 2 February 1951 Spencer Hess wrote again, reporting that the Treasury had agreed to keep the annual contribution at £8400 for a further year, after which it would be cut to £7000. He wrote, too, that the branch

Executive Committee had debated whether to cut immediately the United Kingdom contribution to the General Council and spend the remainder in other ways. James Griffiths argued that parliamentary visits to the colonies were more important than contributions to the Council. Another member asked: 'What is the Council anyway?' The proposal might have been carried but for Glenvil Hall's strong defence of the Council and the need to support it.

In London again d'Egville learnt that Pethick-Lawrence intended to move a resolution at the next meeting of the branch Executive Committee 'for a reduction in total expenditure' of the General Council. On 9 March 1951 he wrote to Pethick-Lawrence that it would be 'very unfortunate if this resolution were passed'. This was a matter for the General Council and 'different from the reduction of a contribution of a branch'. Knowing that the reduction was intended to fall on publications, d'Egville mentioned that in Wellington a British delegate had suggested reducing the distribution of publications and 'This met with a chorus of disapproval'. He wrote in similar terms to Lord Llewellin and three other members of the Executive Committee.

On 15 March 1951 Llewellin informed d'Egville that, although he had moved an amendment, Pethick-Lawrence's resolution had been carried. He added: 'Many seemed to think that too much is spent – especially on the *Report on Foreign Affairs*, which is a bit out of date.' On 15 March 1951 Pethick-Lawrence sent d'Egville a copy of his resolution with a note explaining that: 'The resolution is in no sense hostile to yourself. It could only become so were you to exercise your unrivalled powers of persuasion in opposition to it.' Here was a warning and an expression of the suspicion, felt strongly in the branch, that d'Egville lined up the General Council against its views. Members of the branch did not recognise that, despite the influence which he wielded, d'Egville was, in fact, representing the views of all the branches – and, indeed, of the Commonwealth – as distinct from the British view. The elder brother among brother bodies still on occasion had the outlook of Big Brother.

D'Egville himself, however, was now to learn the full significance of the autonomy of branches. He was used to getting his way in most major matters, but he was rebuffed over the chairmanship of the General Council. At the first meeting of the Council in Ottawa on 28 April 1949, Senator Roebuck had been elected Chairman. In New Zealand in November 1950 Roebuck was unanimously re-elected, and he indicated that he would retire at the following Council meeting.

In a letter to the Speaker of the Canadian House of Commons, dated 13 January 1951, d'Egville wrote that shortly after the arrival of the Canadian delegates in New Zealand,

I was informed by Mr Beaudoin, a Canadian member, that the Prime Minister [Louis St Laurent] had asked him to take Senator Roebuck's place on the Council for the ensuing term, which presumably meant 1951.... I feel sure your Committee will unanimously request Senator Roebuck to continue on the Council. In all the circumstances I believe you will give your full support to him in the interests of the Association.

D'Egville was uneasy about the situation in Ottawa. On 15 March 1951 he wrote reassuringly to Roebuck, 'It seems to me certain that the committee in your Parliament can hardly do otherwise than elect you.... I am most anxious to hear from you.' He added that he might fly to Ottawa for the branch meeting.

The annual meeting of the branch took place on 7 June 1951. Roebuck had cabled d'Egville in advance: 'Your presence essential. Annual meeting will elect an Executive which will appoint Chairman and Councillor.' D'Egville, recognising that if present in Ottawa he would become too involved, replied that he could not get away from London. He wrote to Coldwell and Diefenbaker, seeking their support for Roebuck.

The decision of the meeting came as a profound shock. Beaudoin was nominated to be Chairman and also the Canadian member of the General Council.

Roebuck in letters to d'Egville explained the reasons for this *coup*. 'It is never difficult', he wrote, 'to work up a campaign in one House against the other.... I have held office for too long ... Beaudoin has been working continuously in the Commons.' Then on 28 June 1951, he wrote again giving the basic reason. 'There is prevalent the idea that attendance at the General Council and, I suppose, the Executive as well, is a joyride and a plum which should be handed around. Beaudoin pointed out that I had enjoyed certain favours since 1948 and that it was now his turn to enjoy the candy-sucker.'

This was a fact of political life which d'Egville was never able to accept. He campaigned against it with fervour, but without real effect. In a letter dated 9 July 1951 to Clifton Webb, the Vice-Chairman, he expressed his indignation. 'It is absolutely intolerable', he wrote, 'that a General Council Chairman should be subjected to attack from the rear.... He should not be subject to being hauled off the chair by some group with an axe to grind in his local branch.... You have automatically become Chairman.' This was in accordance with the constitution which provided that the Vice-Chairman became Chairman in the event of a vacancy in that office.

On 19 July 1951 Clifton Webb replied that in his view there was no vacancy. Roebuck remained under Clause XII of the constitution Chairman 'until his successor was appointed'. D'Egville was now concerned that he would be placed in a difficult position of criticising by implication the Canadian branch for appointing Beaudoin as its representative. Writing to Clifton Webb on 31 July 1951 he suggested that 'The best way is that you should write a letter which I can circulate to all members of the Council. It will be important for my protection as Secretary-General to receive a letter signed by you, typed of course on your own paper.... I enclose a draft. Send cable whether you approve the draft.' Clifton Webb did not approve it. He informed d'Egville that it would be illogical to state, as in the draft, that Roebuck was still Chairman and then propose that the Council should pass a formal resolution, requesting him to attend. He amended the draft letter.

On 24 August 1951 d'Egville sent Webb's letter to all members of the General Council. Writing to Roebuck 'in strict confidence' he explained that he had 'framed the covering letter slightly differently to Beaudoin and Bandaranaike of Ceylon'. He added, 'I am sure representatives of the United Kingdom, Australia, New Zealand, India, Pakistan, Southern Rhodesia, Nigeria, Mauritius, the West Indies, and Singapore will be for Webb's argument; South Africa and Ceylon probably so. I do not think that Mr Beaudoin could have any objection.'

D'Egville was able to inform Clifton Webb on 26 September 1951 that replies from members of the Council showed that thirteen agreed with his view, while five disagreed, and one was neutral. Thus Roebuck remained Chairman. In the event neither he nor Clifton Webb were able to attend the meeting in Colombo. The argument nevertheless continued.

The General Council met in Colombo in January 1952. Harold Holt, Minister of Labour and National Service and for Immigration, Australia, was unanimously elected Chairman. Sir John Kotelawala, Minister of Transport and Works and Leader of the House of Representatives, Ceylon, was elected Vice-Chairman.

One of the main items on the agenda came under the heading of 'The Vacancy in the Chair'. Amendments to Clause XII were discussed at length. D'Egville presented the view that a Chairman remained in office 'until his successor was appointed'. Beaudoin argued that the Chairman should vacate his office if he was no longer a member of the General Council. The amendment to Clause XII finally agreed was that the Chairman as well as the Vice-Chairman should 'normally be elected at the intermediate meetings of the Council', thus serving for two years. This was, however, subject to the provision, which Beaudoin had argued so persuasively, namely: 'provided that he retains the nomination of his branch and his seat in Parliament'.

The Council at this meeting gratefully accepted the offer of the Canadian branch to host the general conference in 1952. D'Egville reported that he had visited Canada in October 1951 to discuss this possibility. He had had meetings with the Prime Minister (Louis St Laurent), the Speaker (W. Ross Macdonald), and the Leaders of the Opposition parties, and had submitted estimates of the expenditure involved. The matter had been approved by the Cabinet. The Prime Minister had then called on the Speaker and had asked him to inform the Executive Committee of the branch that the government and Opposition parties were in favour of hosting the conference for which finance would be voted.

Another of d'Egville's initiatives, which the Council approved, was to invite Secretaries of main branches, most of whom were Clerks of Parliament, to visit the Headquarters Secretariat in London as guests of the Council. The purpose was to exchange views on the work and development of the Association. The visiting Clerks would also be able to meet colleagues at Westminster and discuss parliamentary matters with them. D'Egville was always keenly aware of the key role of the Clerks in the efficient running of their Parliaments and especially in the effectiveness of their branches of the Association. He cultivated the Clerks as assiduously as he cultivated Ministers and members.

On his return to London d'Egville wrote to Roebuck about the proposed amendment to Clause XII. He had to admit that his view had been rejected. 'But', he added, 'in Colombo there was not quite the same spirit as at Ottawa and Wellington.' In sending Roebuck a copy of the amended Clause XII on 3 March 1952, he commented that 'personally I do not like the words starting "provided that"'!

Roebuck sent an irascible reply. He rejected the amended clause and enclosed a new draft of his own. This provided that the Chairman could not be removed if his branch did not re-elect him or even if he lost his seat. This was the logic of Webb's argument, but it went too far. D'Egville replied that a member of the General Council must retain his seat.

Roebuck was now unsure whether his branch would choose him as a delegate to the conference to be held in Ottawa in September 1952. On 31 March 1952 d'Egville was advising him to approach Coldwell and Diefenbaker. Roebuck replied that such an approach would be 'most inappropriate'. He wrote again on 3 April 1952, asking d'Egville to come to Canada long enough before the conference 'to save the day'. In the end to his bitter disappointment Roebuck was not a member of the Canadian delegation.

Always concerned about continuity in the Council, d'Egville wrote to the branches during March and April, asking them to ensure that their General Council members were included in their delegations to the conference. His appeal had some effect. All but one of the Councillors were in Ottawa.

There were, however, moments of anxiety on this score. On 20 February 1952 Harold Holt wrote asking d'Egville to send him a separate invitation to the conference as Chairman of the General Council. On 30 May 1952 Holt informed d'Egville that the Australian branch had decided to leave the selection of its delegation to a ballot. In the event Holt was chosen to lead the Australian delegation. The South African branch had replied that it was 'unable to comply with the request' to include its two Council members, but in the end did so.

In the midst of all the correspondence concerning the conference, and it included arrangements for the travel of delegates to Ottawa, d'Egville had other matters in hand. In Colombo he had obtained the Council's approval for senior Clerks to visit the Secretariat in London. He had discussed with Ralph Deraniyagala, Clerk of the House of Representatives and Secretary of the Ceylon branch, his plan for the visit to take place in June 1952. Deraniyagala could not accept the invitation because a general election was expected in Ceylon a few months earlier and he would have a new Parliament to serve. D'Egville then sent invitations to Leon Raymond, Clerk of the Canadian House of Commons, to H. N. Dollimore, Clerk of the House of Representatives in New Zealand, and to W. T. Wood, Clerk of the South African Senate. All were Secretaries of their branches. The visit was to start on 23 June and was to link with the course for colonial legislators at Westminster. Unfortunately, parliamentary business prevented Raymond and Dollimore from coming.

The course for colonial legislators was first discussed in 1951. A Committee of the United Kingdom branch was set up to consider the possibility of inviting to London some 25 or 30 selected members from colonial legislatures to attend a course of lectures on parliamentary practice and procedure. At this time, however, the British Treasury was cutting down on all grants and the branch was unable to finance a visit of even twelve overseas members in 1952.

At this stage d'Egville was invited to attend a meeting of the Committee. He was asked whether he thought that the Finance and General Purposes Committee of the General Council would favour a contribution from Council funds towards the expenses of such a course. D'Egville made it clear that, while the project was of primary interest to the United Kingdom, he was concerned with the interests of all branches. He recognised, however, that the course would benefit branches in colonial legislatures, which contributed to Council funds. He said that he believed that the Finance and General Purposes Committee and the Council as a whole would be in favour of supporting this project.

Without delay he sent to all members of his Committee a paper explaining the project, and obtained authority to contribute from Council funds. This contribution was to be on the basis of meeting the cost of the accommodation 'in a reasonable hotel' of six or eight of the visiting members. The invitations were sent out jointly by the Secretary-General and the Secretary of the branch.

The eight members from colonial legislatures were joined by a number of overseas members who happened to be in London and were invited. Alan Tregear, Clerk Assistant of the Australian House of Representatives, and W. T. Wood, Clerk of the Senate in South Africa, also attended.

As part of the programme the visiting members travelled to Northern Ireland, accompanied by Lockhart, Secretary of the United Kingdom branch. They attended several sessions at Stormont when the practices of smaller legislatures were discussed.

This first course on parliamentary practice and procedure was a resounding success. It set the pattern for what was to become an annual event and one of the most valuable and rewarding of the Association's activities. Future courses were to include visits also to Jersey and the Isle of Man. The further development of the courses into seminars will be recorded later in this history.

As the Canadian conference drew nearer, d'Egville found himself involved in a dispute about representation of the Australian states on the General Council. He had acted in the interests of the Association, but he had interfered in a minor way in the procedure laid down in the constitution. This provided that where branches were grouped in an area or federation, like the Australian states, the right to appoint the states' representative on the General Council should rotate according to the seniority of all branches.

Some months after the conference d'Egville explained what had happened in a letter, dated 22 December 1952, to the Secretary of the South Australian branch. 'Realising that Queensland was next in seniority', he wrote,

I was aware that it was necessary to invite Queensland to appoint the next representative to the General Council. I found Mr Brosnan had been appointed. He had been in Parliament only twelve months. As I understood that Sir Robert Nicholls was coming from your branch and there was only a very slight difference between the seniority of South Australia and Queensland, I cabled Queensland and received a reply that it was agreeable to the Queensland branch that Sir Robert should be the Council representative on the understanding that the next Councillor should come from Queensland.

On 13 August 1952 d'Egville wrote to Sir Robert Nicholls that 'as Queensland has selected a delegate who is a very new MP and knows little about the Association, they have agreed that on this occasion South Australia should send a representative to Council. I am very pleased about this as you have taken so much interest in the Association for a great many years.'

D'Egville was clearly gratified by what appeared to be a satisfactory and amicable arrangement. But then he received a belligerent letter, dated 11 August 1952, from H. Robbins, the Secretary of the New South Wales branch: 'Neither you, the Queensland branch, the South Australia branch ... have any right to vary the express provision of the constitution.... I sincerely hope that the Queensland delegate will represent our state branches at the forthcoming Council meeting.' On the following day, 12 August 1952, Robbins learnt that the Queensland branch had agreed the arrangement. Robbins, a zealous constitutionalist, was still not satisfied. He wrote at once to d'Egville that 'What has been agreed to is nothing more or less than an abrogation of the constitution, a course of action of which I strongly disapprove.' D'Egville replied on 28 August 1952:

Of course there is no question that what you say is correct re the rotation by seniority.... I am all in favour of a strict interpretation of the constitution. At the same time one has to look at the interests of the Association ... and it is sometimes wise to allow a little latitude in the strict interpretation of a clause.... It was obvious that the representative from Queensland would not be likely to help the Association very much.... The course taken should not be regarded as a precedent.

This mild reply probably incensed Robbins further. He rallied the state branches. On 7 September 1952, the day before the meeting of the Council in Ottawa, delegates from the Australian states met and passed a resolution affirming 'the principle of group representation by rotation. As Queensland is at present the state entitled to such representation its delegate shall be the representative of the group on the General Council'.

In his account of this 'somewhat unfortunate and embarrassing situation', d'Egville wrote in his letter of 22 December 1952 to the Secretary of the South Australian branch:

I was greatly surprised just before the first meeting of the Council when I was informed by Brosnan that a meeting of representatives of the Australian state branches had decided that Brosnan must attend the council meetings. The whole matter has apparently been discussed on the initiative of Robbins.... I informed Brosnan that I did not think delegates representing states had any authority to over-ride a decision of the Queensland branch. Holt and I agreed to Brosnan being the representative mainly because Sir Robert had not turned up in consequence of the decision of the state delegates.

The third conference of the Commonwealth Parliamentary Association took place in Canada in September 1952. Over 100 delegates, and Secretaries from 47 branches, arrived in Montreal early in September. They were taken on a tour of Quebec, Nova Scotia, New Brunswick and Prince Edward Island. They travelled then to Ottawa for the conference and the General Meeting. At the end of the conference they visited Ontario and then in a special train they toured the western provinces. Canadian members joined them at various stops on this tour. D'Egville made special reference in his report to the work done by René Beaudoin in the planning of these admirable tours. They had evidently made their peace after the earlier dispute. The conference, the tours, the excellent arrangements and the boundless hospitality made a deep impression on all the delegates.

The associated group, formed on d'Egville's instigation in the Congress of the USA, was active. It responded to the invitation of the Canadian branch to send a delegation of eight Congressmen to take part in the sessions on foreign affairs. A strong delegation was chosen, four from the Senate and four from the House of Representatives. Senator Theodore F. Green was designated leader of the delegation. An invitation to the group in the Irish Republic to send four delegates was also accepted. The conference was opened in Ottawa by Harold Holt, the Chairman of the General Council, on 10 September 1952.[3]

In January 1953 the US delegates presented a report to the Senate on the conference and specifically on the sessions which they had attended. Their conclusion is summed up in the following extract from that report:

> The United States delegation feels very strongly that both the formal meetings and the informal conversations were extremely informative and valuable as a means of gaining better first-hand knowledge of the problems and attitudes of the people of the countries concerned, and also as a means of making the other delegates better aware of the problems and attitudes of the people of the United States.
>
> No resolutions were adopted or other formal actions taken by the Association, but the United States delegation is convinced that the intangible results of the exchange of views will prove very much worthwhile.

The Irish representatives caused a stir when they insisted on raising the subject of the partition of Ireland. Lord Llewellin at once objected on the ground that they were violating the resolution, passed by the General Meeting in Wellington in 1950, which precluded representatives of associated groups from raising controversial intra-Commonwealth subjects in conference. The Irish leader made it clear that the problem would be raised at every international conference at which an Irish delegation was present. The incident was discussed at length by the General Council which emphasised both the importance of the Wellington resolution and the value of having representatives from the US Congress present.

Finally it was decided to refer the question to the Council meeting to be held in London in May 1953.

The General Council had a heavy agenda. It met in Ottawa on 8 September and adjourned to meet again in Toronto on 15 September 1952. The subject of regional or area conferences was discussed in the light of the successful conference hosted by the Tasmania branch in August 1951. Two delegates from each of the Australian state branches together with their branch Secretaries had attended. L. W. Galvin from the Victoria branch, who was a member of the Council at the meeting in Wellington in November 1950, had spoken with enthusiasm about the value of such conferences. Regional conferences had also been held in Singapore with the branches in Malaya, and in Jamaica with the other branches in the West Indies.

All three conferences had taken place on initiatives within the regions and there had been no reference to the General Council. In a letter dated 22 May 1952, however, Donald Sangster from Jamaica, who was a representative of the West Indies on the Council, informed d'Egville that he proposed to invite the United Kingdom branch to send a delegation to the next West Indian regional conference. On 10 June 1952 H. Robbins, the Secretary of the New South Wales branch, wrote to inform him that his branch proposed to invite the New Zealand branch to send a delegation to the second Australian area conference to be held in Sydney in April 1953.

To both Sangster and Robbins, d'Egville wrote that a conference of branches within an area or region was acceptable, and it was necessary only to inform him as Secretary-General. If, however, branches outside the region were invited, it became a matter for the General Council. The Chairman and the Secretary-General should be consulted and their approval obtained in advance. He made this firm ruling wholly on his own authority. In Ottawa, however, the Council endorsed it. The Council also stressed the importance of holding these conferences. It added that the copies of the records of their proceedings should be sent to the Secretary-General for circulation to other branches.

Incidentally, it was this exchange and d'Egville's exercise of his authority as Secretary-General that affronted Robbins and led to his aggressive stand over the Australian states representative on the Council. This affront rather than the sanctity of the constitution would seem to have stirred him to action 'to get his own back'.

A matter which took up much of the Council's time and was later to lead to a blazing row with the United Kingdom branch concerned the coronation of Queen Elizabeth II. Lord Llewellin on behalf of his branch extended an invitation to the Council to meet in London at the time of the coronation. An invitation had already been extended by Sangster to meet in Jamaica. He said that Jamaica would readily host the Council in 1955. The British invitation was warmly accepted.

Holt, the Chairman, then said that he had been in correspondence with the Secretary-General about the steps the Council should take to mark this occasion.

He proposed a coronation luncheon on the lines of the Empire Parliamentary Association luncheon to the monarch in 1937. At that time the Secretary-General had been Secretary of the United Kingdom branch, which had acted as host, and had organised the function. Now, however, there was a General Council. He considered that all branches of the Association should combine through the Council to act as hosts in entertaining the Queen to a luncheon in honour of her coronation. However, Lord Llewellin stated that the matter had been discussed at several meetings of his branch Executive Committee in London. The Committee had decided that the United Kingdom branch would host the luncheon. This announcement produced a stunned silence in the Council meeting.

Llewellin went on to explain the view of his Committee. The luncheon would take place in their Parliament building and the majority of those present would be members of the United Kingdom branch. It was therefore logical that his branch should act as hosts on behalf of the Council. He added, however, that 'it was indicated that if there was a strong wish on the part of the Council to be the hosts, he and his fellow councillor would put the matter again to the branch Executive Committee'.

The attitude of the United Kingdom branch Committee amounted to ignoring the existence of the General Council of the Association. Holt now reminded them. The function was, he said,

> one of tremendous symbolic meaning for all nations of the Commonwealth. The Queen was not only Queen of the United Kingdom. Surely it would be an occasion of far greater significance if the hosts of Her Majesty were representatives of fifty branches in fifty Parliaments, who would be demonstrating their loyalty and unity, than if the host were merely one branch – important though it undoubtedly was.... An important question of principle is involved – whether on such an historic and unique occasion the CPA as such should do nothing and leave it to one branch to represent it, or whether, while being delighted to accept the kind invitation of the United Kingdom to be their guests in London, they should not act for all branches at a function of their own in a matter which fundamentally affects them all and in which they are all equally interested.

Noting the strong reaction of the Chairman and the Council, the United Kingdom members undertook to report back to their Executive Committee the wish of the Council to be host and to be responsible for the expenses. Then they suggested that the United Kingdom branch should make the actual arrangements for the luncheon. Holt on behalf of the Council readily accepted this proposal. No attempt was made to define precisely what was meant by 'actual arrangements'. It was to give rise to angry disputes and, in the words of Gordon Walker, to the United Kingdom branch 'usurping the functions of the Council and of the Secretary-General'.

Llewellin next informed the Council that the United Kingdom branch intended to invite the Presiding Officers of the two Houses in each national Parliament to be their guests for the coronation. This was in addition to the invitation to members of the General Council. It would also extend to those who were 'alternate' members of the Council. This meant the inclusion of an 'alternate' member from the branches in Southern Rhodesia, the Bahamas, the West Indies, Nigeria, Kenya and Singapore. The Council was to meet the travel expenses of councillors and 'alternate' members.

D'Egville requested that the Secretary of each main branch should also be invited. All were Clerks of Parliament and they made a major contribution to the work of the Association. This proposal was considered at the next meeting of the Council. It was agreed that, if the United Kingdom branch decided to invite the main branch Secretaries, the cost of their fares would be a charge on Council funds.

The adjourned meeting of the Council was held in the Parliament buildings in Toronto on 15 September 1952. The first business was to consider the place and dates of the next conference. Major F. W. Cavendish-Bentinck was present by invitation. He conveyed an invitation from the Kenya branch to host the 1954 Commonwealth Parliamentary Conference in Nairobi. He said that the conference had not yet been held in Africa and he was sure that the branches in South Africa and in Northern and Southern Rhodesia would support the Kenyan offer and be prepared to act as joint hosts. On the motion of Llewellin and Mavalankar, the invitation was unanimously accepted. It was agreed that the Secretary-General should, if possible, visit the four African branches in advance of the conference.

The Council also agreed at this meeting that the presentation to the Queen at the CPA luncheon should take the form of a richly-bound volume, containing a picture signed by the presiding officers of the Parliament House of every legislature in which a branch existed. The Secretary-General was asked to produce the volume.

The second General Meeting of the Association was held in the Senate Chamber in Ottawa on 10 September 1952. In the discussion on the adoption of the annual report of the General Council, a delegate sought to raise the question of Commonwealth intervention in the troubled relations between India and Pakistan. The Chairman, Harold Holt, firmly ruled him out of order.

Several delegates spoke in praise of the publications. W. Glenvil Hall, a United Kingdom representative on the Council, said that the publications were costing nearly £10,000 a year and that among members of his branch there was criticism of the excessive cost of the *Journal of the Parliaments of the Commonwealth* and other journals. The Council would be conducting a review of the matter. He added, however, '. . . although the cost is a mounting one and, as far as we can see will continue to increase, we must through the General Council, see to it that our main periodicals at any rate, instead of being diminished or cut off entirely, are made of increasing value to every part of the Commonwealth'.

Donald Sangster (Jamaica) made a persuasive speech on the need to increase the representation of the West Indies on the General Council. He was supported by African delegates. It was pointed out, however, that the Council should not be allowed to become too large and unmanageable. Finally it was agreed that the subject of branch representation should be reviewed by the Council.

On his return to London d'Egville set about producing the official report of the conference and of the General Meeting, as well as the minutes of the Council. Much of his time was taken up by the disputes, provoked by the United Kingdom branch, over the coronation lunch.

Lord Llewellin had succeeded Lord Pethick-Lawrence as Deputy Chairman of the United Kingdom branch in May 1952. In effect he was Chairman, since the Prime Minister, who held this office, was rarely free to take the chair. On their return from Ottawa both Llewellin and Glenvil Hall had had difficulty in persuading their Executive Committee to agree that the Council should host the luncheon. On 15 October 1952, Llewellin wrote to d'Egville stating that prompt decisions were needed for the guidance of the Coronation Committee of the branch. He posed two questions 'having in view what transpired in Ottawa'. The first was: 'Should all invitations be issued by the United Kingdom branch and all general arrangements made through the branch?' And the second: 'Should the luncheon in Westminster Hall, while designated a CPA luncheon, be arranged by the United Kingdom branch?' The questions suggested that the branch was seeking quietly to disregard the wishes of the Council so strongly expressed in Ottawa. On 7 November 1952 d'Egville wrote to Holt that the United Kingdom branch had decided that

the CPA will act as host and will pay, whilst the UK will make all the arrangements.... In strict confidence I have seen the minutes of the UK branch meeting. One member put forward the astonishing proposal that the UK would be acting for all the branches. Gordon Walker said that all the arrangements would be through the Association. I have told Lockhart that I cannot accept the view that has been put forward.... The Council must act on behalf of the Association.

He listed some of the matters which were for decision by the Council, such as arrangements for the Queen's reception and who would preside at the lunch. He suggested that Holt should write directly to Llewellin, and also enclosed a draft letter which, if Holt approved it, he would send to all members of the Council.

Holt wrote to d'Egville on 19 November 1952. He agreed that the United Kingdom view was 'untenable' and that the CPA Chairman should preside at the luncheon. He had written to Llewellin, and enclosed a copy, which expressed fully all of d'Egville's arguments. In this letter Holt wrote that he was not sure what was meant by the words 'all the arrangements should be made by the United Kingdom branch'. He was sure, however, that it was not the desire of the branch to exclude the views and decisions of the Council 'on some important questions on which there are no precedents'.

At this time Llewellin was at the United Nations in New York. He replied briefly to Holt on 3 December 1952. The branch had no intention, he stated, of excluding the views of the Council, but he rejected all the other points which Holt had raised. In particular he laid down, somewhat arrogantly, that the Queen should preside and there should be one speech by the United Kingdom and one from 'someone from one of the Dominions'.

On 1 January 1953, as soon as he learnt about Llewellin's letter to Holt, d'Egville cabled Holt advising him not to reply until he had heard further from him. On 7 January he wrote, enclosing an amended draft of the letter to all members of the Council. The draft stated that the United Kingdom executive had 'reversed its previous decision'. The draft continued,

> It was more or less agreed at the Council meeting that probably the most convenient course would be for the United Kingdom branch to carry out the details of the arrangements.... But nevertheless the Chairman has taken the view that Councillors should decide on some of the main points.

He listed these points in the form of a questionnaire, and added: 'It would appear that if there is to be a Chairman at the luncheon it should be the Chairman of the Council. The Chairman and the Speakers of the United Kingdom and Canadian (or Indian) Parliaments should make speeches.'

Holt cabled d'Egville that he approved the draft letter and agreed that it should be circulated. It was sent to all members of the Council, including the two United Kingdom representatives.

Llewellin was furious. He saw d'Egville on 28 January 1953 and expressed himself forcefully, and wrote on 4 February: 'I take the greatest possible exception to your going back on the condition on which alone I got the United Kingdom branch to agree' that the CPA should act as host. 'I am afraid that the action you have taken may cause friction within the United Kingdom branch, and between the United Kingdom branch and yourself.' D'Egville replied at once to Llewellin's letter. 'I do not think I have in any way gone back on any condition. The difference was probably due to different interpretation of words. I have interpreted this in the light of the Chairman's observations in his letter to you.... The Chairman took the view that I should consult the members.'

Llewellin called a special meeting of the United Kingdom Executive on 10 February 1953. He wrote on the following day to Holt, giving the Executive's decisions. He stated that the arrangements for the luncheon had been made by the branch before the receipt of the questionnaire. 'I am sorry if members of the Council should express different views in answer to the questionnaire, but we have made these arrangements in complete accord with the agreement ... I regret this cannot be altered now.'

On 13 February 1953 Llewellin informed d'Egville of the decisions of the special meeting.

> In the unanimous view of the Executive Committee, the issue of the letter and question-naire was most unfortunate.... I must emphasise beyond any possibility of further mis-understanding that the arrangements for the luncheon are the responsibility of the United Kingdom branch ... I have written to Holt and to members of the Council to outline the arrangements we have made.'

On 24 February 1953 d'Egville wrote to Holt, asking him to rebuke Llewellin for usurping the functions of the Council. On the same day d'Egville received a letter from Llewellin which revealed the main source of the antagonism of the branch towards him personally. 'Of course', he wrote, 'the Chairman could not have put in all these detailed points without the suggestions coming from you.'

It was an extraordinary rebuke. It was surely the Secretary-General's function to brief and advise his Chairman. Indeed, there can be no doubt that Lockhart was performing the same function for his Deputy-Chairman. D'Egville replied on 27 February 1953: 'Of course the Chairman did not draft the details of the circular letter, but he wanted me to draft something with as much explanation as possible and he subsequently approved the draft.'

In a letter to Roy Welensky, who represented Northern Rhodesia and Kenya on the Council, d'Egville gave some explanation of the reasons for the conflict.

> I think the real basis of all this was the belief of Lord Clydesmuir (who is an ex-Indian provincial governor under the old regime and who never played any part in the Association's activities during my secretaryship of the United Kingdom branch, but is a great friend of the present United Kingdom Secretary) that I wanted to run the lunch and so interfere with Lockhart's work.... The only complaint is that I was wrong in saying that the Executive Committee of the United Kingdom branch 'reversed' its previous decision. The matter was left a little vague at our Council meeting.... It is necessary for me to consult those who are like-minded in order to establish the Council's activities and those of the Secretary-General as an essential link in Commonwealth affairs.

This conflict certainly involved personal animosities and rivalries. D'Egville himself in his single-minded pursuit of the Association's interests was prone to provoke antagonism. The United Kingdom branch Secretary, Lockhart, always kept in the background, but his dislike of d'Egville was intense. He played an active role in advising Llewellin and Clydesmuir. Fundamentally and underlying these events, was the difficulty many United Kingdom members found in adjusting to and accepting the changed position of their branch in the Association. Only five years earlier it had been the dominant branch. Now it was no longer dominant. D'Egville who had been their Secretary appeared to be the leader of a Commonwealth revolt against them, and this was hard for them to stomach. Time and perhaps a new generation of members were needed before the changed role was understood and accepted. In the end, however, good counsels prevailed. The innate sense of the dignity and decorum at an occasion when the Sovereign is present, which is so strong in Britain, rose above personality conflicts. The arrangements were discussed and agreed with the Palace and the government, and carried out effectively by the branch.

The coronation luncheon in Westminster Hall on 27 May 1953 was a grand and highly successful occasion. The Prime Ministers of six Commonwealth countries attended and of the 750 guests nearly all were members of Commonwealth legislatures, about half of them from overseas. It was, moreover, a Commonwealth occasion. Harold Holt, as Chairman of the General Council, sat on the Queen's right hand and Winston Churchill on her left. On the arrival of the Queen at St Stephen's Porch, Harold Holt was presented by the Lord Great Chamberlain, Lord Cholmondeley. The Chairman then presented the Prime Ministers and Presiding Officers and their wives, and also the Secretary-General. At the garden party on the following day, d'Egville was able to present the members of the Council.

Harold Holt delivered the opening speech and proposed the toast to Her Majesty. He presented the volume of pictures of the parliamentary buildings of the Commonwealth. Sir John Kotelawala, the Vice-Chairman of the Council, spoke in support. The Queen in her reply said:

> On the eve of his own coronation sixteen years ago, my dear father also met in Westminster Hall those who represent the legislatures of the Commonwealth. I am indeed glad to follow his example. It is a stirring thought that all legislatures are descended from the assembly which first met under this roof nearly seven centuries ago.
>
> We stand here in the Palace of Westminster which is the home of the Mother of Parliaments. Of the many ties linking this family of nations not the least is that system of parliamentary government which is common to us all. . . . To this great Association I offer my best wishes for the success of their coming deliberations.

Sir Winston Churchill and then Louis St Laurent expressed their thanks to the Queen for her gracious address.

D'Egville had reason to be gratified. He had proposed this luncheon with the previous grand occasions in Westminster Hall in mind. He had wanted it to be a CPA, not a United Kingdom branch function, which it was. But, as with so many of his initiatives in the past, he had achieved his aim only after a struggle with the branch.

The General Council met on 29 May 1953 in the ministerial conference room in the House of Commons, Westminster. Before starting on the agenda, Holt raised the question of the chairmanship of the Council. He said that his understanding was that the Chairman was elected for a minimum period of two years and that rotation at reasonable intervals was to the advantage of the Association. He did not want to give the slightest impression of seeking to prolong his term, and would welcome a frank discussion.

Harold Holt had undoubtedly been an outstanding Chairman. He behaved with dignity, had shown impartiality and firmness in the chair, but had always been sensitive to the views of others. He had demonstrated these qualities during the Canadian conference and on other occasions. Councillors were unanimous in agreeing that his term of office should be continued, and that at the next meeting of the Council a Chairman should be elected or re-elected for the following two years. The Council also extended its congratulation to Holt on his appointment to the Privy Council.

The Chairman expressed appreciation of the way in which the United Kingdom branch had fallen in with the wishes of the Council in its desire to make the coronation luncheon a Commonwealth occasion. D'Egville undertook to produce an account of the luncheon with illustrations, the text of all speeches, and an historical note.

A memorandum on the publications, submitted by d'Egville and containing replies to a questionnaire sent to branches was noted. The Chairman commented that the replies showed that the branches set a high value on the publications. The need to speed up their issue and their despatch by air mail in certain cases was considered.

At the conference in Ottawa in September 1952, representatives of the associated group in the Dáil had sought to raise the matter of partition in Ireland, but had been ruled out of order. The leader of the Irish delegation, John Lynch, had then sent a letter to all delegates protesting against this ruling. The Council had agreed unanimously that it was its responsibility to decide which associated groups should be invited to a conference. Further it was agreed that associated groups had to abide by the rule that no matter of a controversial intra-Commonwealth nature could be raised by them at a conference. At its meeting in London, after much discussion, the Council endorsed this decision.

The Council also set up a subcommittee to consider 'the changing political structure of many countries of the Commonwealth in relation to their representation on the Council and to frame a long-term scheme so that adequate representation could be given to branches as they attained certain degrees of constitutional status'. The subcommittee met several times and drafted amendments to the constitution for submission to the General Meeting in Nairobi.

There was preliminary discussion about the African conference to be held in Kenya in 1954. A Conference Arrangements Committee was appointed with representatives from the branches which would be hosts in Africa, and the Committee held its first meeting.

In December 1953 d'Egville sailed for Africa. He had been invited to attend the second meeting of the Conference Arrangements Committee in Nairobi in mid-January 1954. In the course of several sessions the Committee worked out detailed arrangements for the conference tours and the conference itself, including the agenda. D'Egville had discussions with E. A. Vasey, Minister of Finance, a member of the Legislative Council who was also Secretary of the Kenya branch, and also with A. W. Purvis, Clerk of the Legislative Council. He addressed members of the branch on new developments in the work of the Association.

D'Egville now flew to Salisbury, Southern Rhodesia. He had been invited to attend on 3 February 1954 the opening of the first Parliament of the Federation of Rhodesia and Nyasaland. He later addressed a meeting of Federal members. The Speaker, Ian Wilson, was in the chair. Some of the Federal members were well informed about the Association previously having been members of the branches in Southern and Northern Rhodesia. There were, however, a number who had been elected to the Parliament for the first time. D'Egville talked in detail about the purposes and activities of the Association, and made suggestions for the formation and working of a new branch. He also held discussions with the Federal Prime Minister, Sir Godfrey Huggins, with Speaker Wilson, Sir Roy Welensky, and with Colonel G. E. Wells, the Clerk of the Federal Assembly.

For part of his stay in Salisbury, d'Egville was the guest of the Governor-General at Government House. The new Governor-General was none other than Lord Llewellin. One cannot but wonder if the two men reminisced over the coronation luncheon.

D'Egville then flew to Cape Town, South Africa. He had discussions with the Prime Minister, Dr D. F. Malan, and with Ministers. Fifteen years had passed since his last visit to South Africa and yet he knew so many from the Governor-General, G. E. Jansen, and the Prime Minister, to Ministers and Members of the Parliament. He addressed a meeting of the branch and met each Member at private functions. Invitations poured upon him. He was, indeed, fêted as an elder statesman.

Notes

1. Report of General Council, 1950–51, p.18.
2. Report of General Meeting, 24 November 1950.
3. **Agenda and Opening Speakers, Ottawa, 1952**
   The subjects discussed and the opening speakers at each session were as follows:
   Migration – W. H. Fortune, Minister of Police and Minister Assistant to the Prime Minister (New Zealand) and G. V. Mavalankar, Speaker of the Lok Sabha (India)
   Economic and Financial Relations of the Commonwealth – P. Heathcoat-Amory, Minister of Pensions (United Kingdom) and G. G. Ponnambalam, Minister of Industries and Fisheries (Ceylon)
   International Affairs and Defence – four sessions were devoted to this subject. Delegates were joined in these sessions by representatives from the associated groups in the US Congress and the Parliament of the Irish Republic
   The opening speakers in each of these sessions were Brooke Claxton, Minister of National Defence and Acting Secretary of State for External Affairs (Canada), Senator Theodore F. Green (USA) and also John Lynch (Irish Republic), Senator Leverett Saltonstall (USA) and J. S. Labushchagne (South Africa).

10 The Momentous Years, 1954–59

Conferences had been held successfully in the United Kingdom and in the 'old' Dominions of New Zealand and Canada. It was always d'Egville's vision, however, that conferences should take place in the 'new' Commonwealth. Only in this way would the international and multi-racial character of the Association and its role in the Commonwealth and the world be clearly established.

In the years 1954–57 conferences were held for the first time in Africa and for the first time in Asia, while the General Council had its first meeting in the West Indies. These developments owed a great deal to the farsightedness and the patient but forceful diplomacy of the Secretary-General.

For the General Meeting of the Association to be held in Nairobi in August 1954, d'Egville produced a review of the developments during the first five years of the General Council. It was an impressive record. Conferences had been held at two-yearly intervals. The Council had met five times in different cities of the Commonwealth. Twenty new branches had been formed. Publications had appeared regularly, and the information service was in demand. The courses on parliamentary practice and procedure at Westminster had become an annual event; with a fourth course due to take place in May 1955. The African conference would crown five years of dynamic growth.

D'Egville was, in fact, anxious about this conference. On 30 October 1953 he wrote to W. T. Wood, Secretary of the South African branch, 'As regards any of the delegates visiting the Union, your people might want to confine any visitors to the white representatives.' Wood, who apparently did not share this concern, replied: 'As regards inviting only white delegates I seem to remember your view was that this might be considered so invidious by the non-white representatives as possibly to have serious repercussions upon the future solidarity of the membership of the Association.' D'Egville's anxiety was not assuaged. On 8 December 1953 he wrote to Welensky: 'It is recognised, of course, that there would be difficulties with any but white people in the Union.'

The planning went ahead. The Conference Arrangements Committee had seven meetings, the first in London on 4 June 1953, the others in Nairobi, the

Victoria Falls and in Johannesburg. All were chaired by J. W. Higgerty, the Vice-Chairman of the Council, who was Chief Opposition Whip in the South African Parliament. D'Egville attended each of these meetings, except one in Johannesburg on 2 November 1953.

He was responsible for two innovations. The first was the introduction of an official opening of the conference as for the formal opening of Parliament. In this the precedent set in Nairobi was followed at all subsequent General Conferences of the Association. The second was the designing and issue to each delegate of a special badge. It took the form of an enamelled shield, half coloured in the red of the Upper House and the other half in the green of the Lower House. The shield was crossed by representations of the Mace and Black Rod. The badge had a metal attachment to hold the delegate's name.

The visit and conference – the first to be hosted jointly by several branches – extended over nearly two months. For the tours, the delegates were divided into groups because of difficulties with transport. They travelled extensively in Kenya, Uganda, Tanganyika, Zanzibar and Northern and Southern Rhodesia. After the conference, delegates from the United Kingdom, Canada, Australia, New Zealand, Pakistan, Ceylon and Bermuda spent two weeks touring South Africa. It was a highly successful tour and not marred by incidents or problems of any kind.

The conference was opened on 21 August 1954 by the Governor of Kenya, Sir Evelyn Baring. He drove in state to the Legislative Building in Nairobi. He took the royal salute and inspected the guard of honour. He was then received by the Chairman of the Council, Harold Holt, by the Vice-Chairman, J. W. Higgerty, by representatives of the host branches, and by the Secretary-General. He entered the Chamber to a trumpet fanfare. In his speech he referred to 'this great Association ... one of the most powerful unifying forces among nations in the troubled and distracted world of today'. He then invited Harold Holt to take the Speaker's Chair. Leaders of delegations spoke, after which the Governor left the Chamber.[1]

In January 1955 d'Egville travelled to Ceylon and from there to India. During February and March he carried out an extensive programme in India, which would have taxed the strength of men half his age. He was now 76.

In Ceylon he had talks with J. R. Jayewardene, then Minister of Agriculture, Leader of the House, and acting Prime Minister, and also with Ralph Deraniyagala, Clerk of the House of Representatives. He addressed members and attended a meeting of the branch Executive Committee, chaired by the Speaker, Sir Albert Peries. At this meeting he put forward tentatively the suggestion that the next conference might be held in an Asian country. The idea was welcomed. The Ceylon branch expressed readiness to be a joint host with India and Pakistan.

Arriving in Madras, d'Egville found a full programme prepared for him. It included meetings with the Chief Minister, the Speaker, the Leader of the Opposition as well as a luncheon in his honour given by the Governor, a garden party, and a tour of places of interest. He addressed a packed meeting of members of the Legislature, explaining the purpose and activities of the Association. The same full programme of meetings, speeches and social occasions was followed in West Bengal, Bihar, Uttar Pradesh, Madhya Bharat, Madhya Pradesh and Bombay.

The highlight of this Indian tour was his stay in New Delhi. On 24 February 1955 he was met at the airport by M. N. Kaul and S. L. Shakdher, Secretary and Joint Secretary of Lok Sabha and of the Indian branch, the two learned and able officers of the Indian Parliament. Next morning he laid a wreath on the *Samadhi* (cremation place) of Mahatma Ghandi, whom he had visited at the Ashram near Ahmedabad more than 20 years earlier. In the following days he was entertained by the Vice-President of India, Dr Radhakrishnan, by Speaker Mavalankar and by Jawaharlal Nehru. As long ago as 1926 when he had visited India, he had established close relations with Motilal Nehru, then leader of the *Swaraj* Party, and with his son, who was now Prime Minister. In discussions with Kaul and Shakdher he promoted the idea that when a sufficient number of branches had been formed in state legislatures, regional conferences should be held regularly, as had been done by the Australian states with great success.

At tea with Nehru he broached the idea of India and Ceylon jointly hosting the next conference. He discussed it also with Mavalankar, Kaul and Shakdher. The idea was well received. The Indian leaders, who were generous and statesmanlike in their concern to heal the wounds of partition, were even receptive to the idea of Pakistan joining as the third host branch.

The time was indeed ripe for such a conference in Asia. At the fifth Unofficial Commonwealth Relations Conference in Lahore in 1954, 'much emphasis was placed rightly and inevitably on the Asian viewpoint on Commonwealth and world affairs'.[2] The CPA conference would provide a forum for the Asian viewpoint.

While in Delhi, d'Egville spoke by phone with Tamizuddin Khan, President of the Constituent Assembly of Pakistan, whom he knew well, and with Dr Shuja-ud-din, Speaker of the Punjab Legislative Assembly. He was intending to visit Karachi and Lahore. It was decided, however, to postpone this visit. Probably in his telephone conversation with Tamizuddin Khan he first mentioned that Pakistan might join India and Ceylon in hosting the Asian conference. It was a bold idea. Relations between Pakistan and India were very strained at this time, primarily over Kashmir. He had nevertheless sown the seed.

Both Shri Kaul and Shri Shakdher told the writer of this history in 1975 that they remembered clearly d'Egville's visit to India in 1955, and that it was like a royal procession. He talked with the highest in the land and endeavoured to meet every member of the Indian Parliament. He followed the same course in the Indian states. He was indefatigable. At all times his subject of discussion was the importance of the Association and of each branch in promoting understanding among MPs and strengthening parliamentary institutions.

As a direct result of this visit new branches were formed in the legislatures of Madhya Pradesh and Madhya Bharat, in addition to the branches already existing in Delhi, Bombay and West Bengal. In the near future branches were to be formed in the states of Bihar, Uttar Pradesh, Madras and the Punjab. He had, moreover, secured the agreement of the Indian and Ceylon leaders that the next conference would be held in India. He had greatly stimulated among members at the centre and in the states a new interest in the Association. At the next meeting of the Council A. Casely-Hayford, representing the Gold Coast, and R. A. Njoku, representing the Federation of Nigeria, expressed the hope that he would make a similar tour of West Africa.

On 28 March 1955, while d'Egville was returning by sea to London, Mrs Hilda Blattner died. She had been d'Egville's closest colleague from the beginning. She had joined him as his private secretary in 1910 when he was appointed Secretary of the Committee of the Lords and Commons. He came to rely heavily on her in the editing of the publications. She shared also in other activities, such as organising overseas parliamentary delegations. In 1932 she was awarded the OBE in recognition of her work. In the Silver Jubilee Celebrations of 1935 and the coronation of 1937 she had heavy responsibilities, especially in organising the luncheon in Westminster Hall. During the war years, when d'Egville was in Canada, she carried on the editing and was responsible for the printing and distribution of the publications. In 1949 she was appointed Assistant Secretary and Assistant Editor. Subsequently her work was acknowledged by the award of the CBE.

For d'Egville her death was a grave loss. He had always been able to rely on her completely. She had accepted him, his tantrums, his times of acute anxiety and nervous stress. Between them over the long years of working together, there had grown a close understanding. D'Egville wrote a generous tribute to her which was published as an obituary in *The Times*. He wrote a fuller tribute which appeared in the annual report of the General Council, 1954–55.

In 1952, when Mrs Blattner's health was already beginning to fail, Sidney Arnold Pakeman joined the Secretariat. He had had a distinguished career from 1921 to 1942 as Professor of Modern History in the University College and then the University of Ceylon. He had commanded the Ceylon Defence Force from 1932 to 1938. Moreover from 1947 until 1952 he was an appointed member of the Ceylon House of Representatives and a member of the Ceylon branch of the Association. Indeed, he had a deep love of Ceylon and its people, and on retiring from his University Chair he returned to England only because of his wife's ill-health.

Although in his late sixties when he joined the staff, Pakeman was energetic, conscientious and reliable. Gradually he took over from Mrs Blattner the burden of the work on the publications, while at the same time acting as Assistant Secretary-General. He quickly earned the trust of d'Egville who came to rely very much upon him. A genial personality, courtly in his manners, Pakeman was to serve the Association with distinction as Editor of Publications and as acting and then full Secretary-General for a short period reverting to Deputy Secretary-General until his retirement in 1964.

In this period three other members of staff, who were to give long service to the

Association were engaged by d'Egville. They were Ian Grey, the writer of this history, as Assistant Editor and Assistant Secretary-General, L. M. Fowler, as d'Egville's personal assistant, and Miss Betty May as his personal secretary.

During these months in 1955 the chairmanship had been on the minds of councillors. At the Council meeting at the Victoria Falls in August 1954, Holt had announced that his term of office would come to an end at that meeting. This was, as d'Egville stated, 'an event vitally affecting the interests and activities of the Association'. Indeed, the Association had been fortunate in having Roebuck and Holt as its Chairmen in the first years of the Council. Both men had been outstanding. Difficult problems for which there were no precedents had arisen. Holt in particular had always been firm but understanding, and had kept the interests of the Association foremost in his mind. At the same time he had, as Chairman, imparted a human warmth which was felt by all who met him. The tributes paid to him at the meeting at the Victoria Falls were far more than formalities.

The Council had reached an understanding at its previous meeting in Nairobi that the next Chairman should come from an Asian country. Holt had agreed to continue in office until, by letters to India and Pakistan and in consultations by d'Egville in Delhi, the Secretary-General had established who should be nominated for the office. It was a delicate situation. In May 1953 d'Egville had written to persuade Holt to stay in office for the African conference. In a letter to him before the conference he had written: 'Tamizuddin Khan of Pakistan has claims to the chairmanship. There is supposed to be no colour bar in Nairobi, but in practice there is. There would be considerable difficulties if there is a tour of Northern and Southern Rhodesia or South Africa. It is therefore of real importance that you should be in office for this rather critical conference.' Holt, who had been Chairman for only 16 months and who understood d'Egville's anxiety about the conference and his concern for continuity, agreed. In the event the colour bar problem did not arise, but without any doubt Holt himself contributed greatly to the harmony and success of the occasion.

D'Egville was forthright in his views about the United Kingdom branch as expressed in another letter to Holt. 'The South African branch', he wrote,

has suggested a United Kingdom chairman. At the present time this is out of the question if the Association is to continue and develop. It was only when the Council came into being that overseas branches became a real part of the show. To put any more influence into the United Kingdom would be the very worst that could happen at the present moment. Now is the formative period and we must get all the branches in full working order before the chairmanship comes to the United Kingdom ... I am sure you realize how extremely difficult it is going to be for the Secretary-General if the Chairman changes every two years.

Holt was not prepared, however, to serve a second two-year term as d'Egville wished.

On receiving d'Egville's report that the Indian Speaker, Mavalankar, would serve as Chairman, if elected, Holt wrote to all members of the Council in July 1955 proposing that he should succeed him. The proposal was readily approved. On 24 January 1956 in Kingston, Jamaica, the Council at its first meeting unanimously elected Mavalankar as Chairman. Higgerty proposed and Abdul Wahid Khan from Pakistan seconded the motion. Sadly, Mavalankar died on 27 February 1956. It was a great loss to the Association and a disappointment for d'Egville. He had known Mavalankar for many years and liked and respected him. A quiet, dignified and learned man, he would have served admirably as the first Asian Chairman of the Association.

The Council meeting was formally opened at Headquarters House in Kingston by the Governor, Sir Hugh Foot, on 14 January 1956 with the formality which attended the opening of Parliament. As at the opening of the conference in Nairobi in the previous year, this set a precedent which was to be followed at all the succeeding meetings of the Council between conferences. J. W. Higgerty, as Vice-Chairman, became Chairman on the death of Mavalankar and held office until the Council meeting in Delhi on 30 November 1957.

The principal business of the Council at this meeting was to appoint a Conference Arrangements Committee, representative of the host branches. The Committee had a heavy and complex task. It included the allocation of cost between the host branches, the agenda for the conference, the numbers of delegates to be invited from each branch and their division into groups for the extensive tours, and the invitations to the associated groups. It was of interest that provision was made for an invitation to the Parliament of Burma, to send a delegation, if its members formed an associated group in time.

The decision of the Pakistan branch about its participation as a joint host had not yet been made. D'Egville reported to the Council that he would be in Karachi in February 1957. He would be meeting the Prime Minister, the Speaker and others. If no communication about the conference had been received before his visit, he would raise the matter with them. Tentative arrangements were made to change the dates of the tours and the conference if Pakistan decided to take part.

At the Council meeting in Jamaica in January 1956, a subcommittee, of which Patrick Gordon Walker was a member, was set up to draft an amendment to the constitution. This concerned the position of the Vice-Chairman. It was proposed that, like the Chairman, he should not represent his branch on the Council and should not be a member of the delegation of his branch at conferences. This meant that the branch would appoint an extra councillor and an extra delegate. The Council approved the subcommittee's draft. Later it was unanimously adopted at the General Meeting in Delhi.

The constitution, drafted at the first meeting of the Council in Ottawa in 1949, had, in fact, been subject to many amendments. It was not until 1954 that it was printed and available to all members. The reason for the amendments was mainly the rapid constitutional evolution of the colonies towards self-government and then independence and the consequential changes in the status of their branches.

Another factor was the policy of seeking to embrace within the Association all Commonwealth legislatures.

The categories of branches were defined in Clause IV of the 1954 constitution. Representation on the Council, divided into permanent and non-permanent members, was set out in Clause XI. At every meeting the Council had to consider applications from branches to move to a higher category and to decide to which category a new branch properly belonged. It was a complex situation but probably unavoidable at this stage of the development of the Commonwealth.[3]

From Jamaica, on 5 February 1956 d'Egville travelled to Washington to meet Senator Theodore F. Green, Chairman of the associated group. He had two purposes. The first was the reconstitution of the group since the recent elections, and the appointment of a Secretary. The second was to ensure the attendance of representatives at the conference in India. This was of special importance, since no representative of the group had attended the African conference.

A strong Committee was appointed. The Chairman was again Senator Theodore F. Green, who was Chairman of the Senate Foreign Relations Committee. The Deputy-Chairman was Congressman James P. Richards, Chairman of the Foreign Relations Committee of the House of Representatives. The membership comprised eight Senators and eight Congressmen. Dr George B. Galloway of the Legislative Reference Service of the Library of Congress was appointed Secretary of the group. He was to prove active and helpful in keeping the group in touch with the Association.

At a meeting on 15 February 1956, which d'Egville attended, it was agreed that November–December 1957 would be a suitable time for a congressional delegation to visit India, Pakistan and Ceylon, and also to take part in the final sessions of the conference in Delhi.

D'Egville went on to Ottawa, arriving on 21 February 1956. He was keen to organise a conference of the Canadian provincial branches. Saskatchewan responded to the idea. The other provinces showed no enthusiasm. In part this was due to the fear in certain quarters that a CPA conference might detract from the conferences of premiers. In June 1956 d'Egville returned to Canada and made some progress. Writing to Roebuck on 10 July 1956, he stated that the branches in Saskatchewan, Alberta and Nova Scotia were now keen to hold such a conference, but he was 'not so sanguine about Manitoba and Ontario'. He did not give up and his persistence was to be rewarded.

In 1956 the Suez crisis shattered many of the accepted ideas about the Commonwealth. The crisis had arisen following the announcement by President Nasser of Egypt on 26 July 1956 that the Suez Canal had been nationalised. The British government reacted strongly. It was concerned to maintain British influence in the Middle East. It was also concerned that the existing Soviet support for Egypt in arms and in other ways would lead to the extension of Soviet influence and the eventual Soviet domination of the canal and the oil resources of the region. Furthermore, the protection of the sea link by way of the canal was seen as vital to the interests of Britain, Australia, New Zealand, India, Pakistan,

Ceylon, Singapore and Malaya.

The Anglo-French attack on Egypt in October 1956, nevertheless, provoked a storm of protest in Britain and in many Commonwealth countries. Relations between the United Kingdom and the United States were severely strained. In discussions before the attack the American attitude, as expressed particularly by John Foster Dulles, had been equivocal and misleading. The British government was taken aback by American refusal of support of any kind and by its condemnation of the attack. Canada, having no interest in the canal, felt un-involved. The Canadian Minister for External Affairs, Lester Pearson, however, exercised a profound influence as intermediary between Britain and the United States, thus fulfilling what many Canadians considered to be Canada's role of providing a bridge between the two nations.

Australia and New Zealand supported Britain's action. India and Ceylon joined with Burma and Indonesia in issuing a statement in New Delhi on 14 November 1956 directed against the Soviet use of force in Hungary and the Anglo-French attack on Egypt. In India and Pakistan there were popular demonstrations in support of their quitting the Commonwealth. Nehru in India and Suhrawady in Pakistan rejected all suggestions of withdrawal.

By the time of the Commonwealth Prime Ministers' meeting in London in July 1957, the storm over Suez seemed to have passed. It had, however, made a deep impact. It had brought home to many people certain basic facts, obscured by idealistic conceptions of the Commonwealth. It demonstrated that Common-wealth solidarity was a myth. Throughout the crisis each country had shown concern not with Commonwealth but with its own national interests. At the same time there was some resentment that Britain had not consulted with the Commonwealth before embarking on the Egyptian campaign. The second important effect of the Suez crisis was that it made many people recognise that Britain was no longer an imperial power. It had neither the military nor the economic strength to bear alone the burdens of the colonies and their defence.

Two consequences flowing from this were, first, an undercurrent in Britain of resentment towards the United Nations and the United States, and a growing doubt about the real value of the Commonwealth to Britain. The second consequence was its contribution to Macmillan's 'wind of change' policy and the determination to shed the colonies by giving them independence as early as possible, especially in Africa.

Against this background d'Egville, who was a realist, saw that Commonwealth solidarity, a goal which he had once pursued, was no longer possible. This did not mean, however, that the Commonwealth had no function to perform and no contribution to make: it should provide machinery for consultation and cooperation. In this field the Association had a special role not only in bringing MPs together on a regular basis but also in the promotion of parliamentary institutions. He concentrated on the immediate practical measures to be taken if the Commonwealth was to be held together.

The year 1957 was exceptionally busy for d'Egville and the Association. In

January he was in Ceylon, attending the meetings of the Conference Arrangements Committee. He also proposed to members of the branch the formation of a study group on foreign affairs, and a group was duly formed. It functioned on the same lines as the groups in Canada.

From Colombo, he flew to Madras. The Prime Minister, Jawaharlal Nehru, happened to be there at the time, and d'Egville discussed the coming conference with him. He also met his old friend, Sri Hanumanthappa, Secretary of the Madras branch, who arranged for him to address a meeting of members. In Madras d'Egville probably influenced the choice of Dr P. V. Cherian, Chairman of the Legislative Council, as the member to attend the next course on parliamentary practice and procedure at Westminster.

In Bombay he again carried out a busy programme of meetings, social occasions and tours, arranged by Shri S. H. Belavadi, Clerk of the Legislative Assembly, another old friend. He enjoyed visiting India. Indeed, India and Canada appear to have been his favourite countries of the Commonwealth, and he was well known in both.

D'Egville's visit to Karachi was something of a triumph. From the airport in Karachi he was taken at once to a meeting of members. The Prime Minister, H. S. Suhrawardy, and the Speaker, Abdul Wahab Khan, welcomed him. He spoke at length on the work of the Association and in particular about the conference to be held in Delhi. This was the main purpose of his visit. No reply had yet been received to his suggestion that Pakistan might join with the other two host branches. The matter had been widely discussed in Karachi. Disputes with India were, however, the chief concern of Pakistan at this time, and there was reluctance to join with India in this way. It took the presence and persuasion of d'Egville to force a decision. He talked at length about the conference with the Prime Minister, with Syed Amjad Ali, Minister of Finance, and with M. B. Ahmad, Secretary of the National Assembly. Towards the end of his visit he was informed that Pakistan would join with India and Ceylon in hosting the conference.

In Canada the Progressive Conservative Party won the general election in June 1957. Diefenbaker became Prime Minister. An orator and a staunch champion of the Commonwealth, he had, soon after becoming Prime Minister, made two pronouncements about it. In the first he stated that 'Canada's membership of the Commonwealth is fundamental to our destiny'; in the second he declared: 'The Commonwealth, which has no rules or regulations and no constitution, has, nevertheless, a unity forged in the sharing of the heritage of common ideals and a love of freedom under the law.'

D'Egville knew Diefenbaker well and could count on his support. In September 1957 he flew to Ottawa to meet as many of the newly elected members as possible and to ensure that the branch was active in the new Parliament. The House elected as its Speaker Roland Michener, who became *ex officio* Chairman of the Canadian branch. He believed strongly in the value and importance of the Association, and became one of d'Egville's closest confidents.

On 23 October 1957 d'Egville wrote to Michener, asking that George Stephen,

Clerk of the Saskatchewan legislature, should attend the coming conference as Secretary to the Canadian delegation, adding, 'This would be of greater value to the Association and to me personally.' Stephen was appointed. He was one of the most active and able Clerks in Canada at this time, and later became a valued contributor to the Association's publications.

On 17 November 1957 d'Egville flew to India to prepare for the Council meetings and the conference in Delhi. One of the first matters to be settled was the chairmanship. J. W. Higgerty, elected Vice-Chairman in 1954, had become Chairman on the death of G. V. Mavalankar in February 1956 and had held office since then. He considered, however, that the Council's intention, as expressed at its meeting in Jamaica in 1956, was that a Chairman from Asia should be elected to preside over the conference in India. At the Council meeting in Delhi on 30 November 1957 he nominated M. Ananthasayanam Ayyangar, who had succeeded Mavalankar as Speaker of the Lok Sabha. Ayyangar was unanimously elected.

The re-election of J. W. Higgerty as Vice-Chairman at this meeting was a considerable accolade for him personally, and also an example of the Commonwealth spirit as it existed at the time. Higgerty, although not a nationalist, was a South African. India in particular was strongly critical of the policy of apartheid as applied to people of Asian race in the Union. Nehru raised the matter at the United Nations, but never at Commonwealth meetings. He respected the convention, then observed, that a member of the Commonwealth does not attack or criticise another member. Delegates from Pakistan several times in conferences tried to raise its dispute with India over Kashmir, but were ruled out of order. When in New Delhi on 30 November 1957 the election of the Vice-Chairman arose, Gordon Walker proposed and A. Casely-Hayford of Ghana seconded the nomination of Higgerty. The Chairman, M. A. Ayyangar, asked to be associated with the motion and paid a warm tribute to Higgerty, who was elected unanimously.

The conference, jointly hosted by India, Pakistan and Ceylon, was one of the most successful of all the conferences of the Association. Delegates – 109 in number together with 16 Secretaries to delegations – arrived in Karachi on 11/12 November 1957. They were taken on an extensive tour of West Pakistan. Next, they were divided into two parties, one of which toured South India and Ceylon, while the other toured Bombay and Calcutta. The post-conference tours reversed this order. All delegates departed shortly before Christmas.

The delegations included some of the outstanding political leaders of the time. Jawaharlal Nehru, India's Prime Minister, led his delegation. He was supported by the Minister of Finance, T. T. Krishnamachari, by the Deputy Chairman of the Rajya Sabha, S. V. Krishnamoorthy Rao, and by the Deputy Speaker of the Lok Sabha, Sardar Hukam Singh. The Pakistan delegation had as its leader the Minister of Finance, Syed Amjad Ali, supported by the Speaker of the National Assembly, Abdul Wahab Khan. A. P. Jayasuria, Minister of Home Affairs, led the Ceylon delegation which included S. W. R. D. Bandaranaike, the Prime Minister.

The United Kingdom delegation was, in the words of Gordon Walker, 'one of the most distinguished ever appointed to attend an overseas conference'. Led by D. Heathcoat-Amery, Minister of Agriculture, Fisheries and Food, and soon to become Chancellor of the Exchequer, it included Hugh Gaitskell, Leader of the Opposition, Douglas Houghton, Peter Smithers and George Thomson. Gordon Walker himself was also a member. The Australian delegation was led by William MacMahon, Minister for Primary Industries, later to be Prime Minister. Among the 16 Secretaries to delegations were some of the most distinguished Clerks ever to serve their Parliaments and to act as Honorary Secretaries of their branches.[4]

The opening of the conference on 2 December 1957 was an occasion of notable splendour. The President of India, Dr Rajendra Prasad, drove to Parliament House in his state coach, escorted by his bodyguard of mounted lancers. He was received by the Chairman of the General Council, Ananthasayanam Ayyangar, and by the Secretary-General. He was met also by the Vice-President, Dr Sarvapalli Radhakrishnan, by the Prime Minister, Jawaharlal Nehru, by the Prime Minister of Ceylon, S. W. R. D. Bandaranaike, by the recently appointed Minister of Finance and Law of Pakistan, Abdus Pirzada Sattar, deputising for his Prime Minister. D'Egville then presented J. W. Higgerty, the Vice-Chairman, and the leaders of the main branch delegations. All then moved into the Central Hall in procession, where the arrival of the President was heralded by a trumpet fanfare.

International affairs and defence were discussed in the last two days of the conference, when the three Senators from the associated group in the US Congress participated. These were Senators Wayne L. Morse, Thurston B. Morton and Frank Carlson. The three members appointed to the delegation by the House of Representatives were unable to attend. It was, however, the report to the Senate, made after their return to Washington, which perhaps best summed up the feelings of all delegates about the value of the conference and of the Association. The main paragraphs read as follows:

The conference provided the delegates of the countries concerned with a forum to espouse their divergent views on current problems and share experiences with those who have similar problems. It served as a clearing house for ideas and gave them an opportunity to explore fresh avenues of approach. Because a vital part of the Commonwealth is an affinity of ideas, any organization that stimulates a frank interchange of views and opinions among citizens of member countries is doing worthwhile work. This is especially true when it makes possible discussion among legislators, since they are in a position to influence their governments and peoples for peace and prosperity and mutual understanding of the world....

The Commonwealth Parliamentary Association is a practical, glowing example of co-operation on the basis of mutual understanding and respect. Its conference in New Delhi made a contribution toward strengthening the Commonwealth as a great influence for peace, freedom, and the rule of law. It brought delegates in friendly contact with people from all parts of the world who shared a common dedication to free parliamentary democracy. There was no formalism, no rigid agenda, no parade of delegates with prepared speeches and decided attitudes who had to refer to their respective capitals for every little thing. A 'temper of democracy' prevailed in the gatherings and discussions at the conference, in the assembly room as much as without. There was regard for public opinion, a tolerance of the minority point of view, and respect for the dignity of the individual. It brought about relationships which are ultimately the most valuable part of the proceedings because their effects carry down through the years and extend the spirit of democracy beyond the Commonwealth itself and to the world as a whole.

The United States Senate delegation deems it an honour and a privilege to have attended the conference in New Delhi. We wish to express our sincere appreciation to the joint host governments of India, Pakistan and Ceylon for their hospitality and the facilities they placed at our disposal, and to all the delegates for their many courtesies and friendly assistance. We departed from the conference convinced that the Association is one of the most constructive and fruitful organizations in the free world today.... It is our unanimous recommendation to the Senate that on those occasions that host countries for Commonwealth Parliamentary Association meetings invite the Congress to designate members to participate in those meetings, timely and appropriate arrangements should be made for such participation.

During these busy years d'Egville had to devote time to defending the publications against attacks from the United Kingdom branch. He sent a questionnaire to all branches on 16 April 1953 asking whether their members found the publication to be of value. On 23 April he wrote to his Chairman, Holt, that he had received 'good replies'. Again in March 1956 he sent a circular to all members who received the *Report on Foreign Affairs*, asking if they found it useful and wished to continue receiving it. In a letter to Michener in Ottawa on 3 April 1959 he wrote: 'I have gone to a great deal of trouble in trying to discover from the various branches those members who find our publications of value.' At this time, too, he sent a memorandum on publications to the Executive Committee of the United Kingdom branch, in which he wrote that he was 'gratified by the number of appreciative comments made by representatives in various branches throughout the Commonwealth'. The attacks continued.

It was a curious situation. Individual British members apparently valued the *Journal*. Hugh Gaitskell, Leader of the Opposition, wrote to d'Egville on 13 July 1956 commending the July issue. He had made use of the summary of a government statement in the Australian Parliament on parliamentary salaries and allowances in his speech in the House of Commons on the previous day. The Secretary of State for the Colonies, Alan Lennox-Boyd, also expressed appreciation of the *Journal* at this time. He welcomed in particular the summary of the debates in the Gold Coast Parliament on new constitutional proposals. There was ample evidence that many members at Westminster, as in other Parliaments, made use of the publications. The smaller their legislatures and the greater their distance from London the greater was their appreciation. D'Egville himself took pride in the fact that requests for the *Journal* received from members of the group in the US Congress had steadily increased.

The attacks on publications emanated from the Executive Committee of the United Kingdom branch, usually on the ground of their cost. The suspicion lingers, however, that another factor, albeit a minor one, namely the antagonism towards d'Egville personally on the part of Lockhart, the branch Secretary, and certain other members of the Committee, played a part.

The *Journal* had been growing in size. One reason for this was that the sittings of many Commonwealth Parliaments were longer than in the past and the summaries of their proceedings were lengthier as a consequence. Another reason was the need to publish full summaries of important constitutional developments. The new constitution in Ghana (formerly the Gold Coast) and the constitutions of the Federation of Malaya and the Federation of the West Indies required extra space. This growth was soon to be checked.

The information work of the Secretariat – or General Council Office, as d'Egville called it – was expanding. In 1957 a memorandum was produced and issued to branches entitled *Mr Speaker: The Position, Powers and Privileges of Speakers in Parliaments of the Commonwealth*. In 1958 another memorandum, dealing with the composition, functions and powers of Second Chambers in sovereign Parliaments of the Commonwealth, was published. The value of Second Chambers was especially topical and under discussion following the abolition of New Zealand's Second Chamber on 1 January 1951. Also in 1958 a revised edition of *Payments and Privileges of Commonwealth Members of Parliament* was issued to all branches.

In the case of each memorandum a first draft was produced under d'Egville's active supervision. The relevant sections of the draft were then sent to the Clerk of each Parliament for correction and approval. The cooperation of the Clerks was usually prompt and generous. The memoranda were an achievement, too, for the Secretariat's information section with its staff of only two, or sometimes three.

D'Egville was also working on a new project. This was the production of a booklet on the basic principles and working of parliamentary democracy, written in simple language and readily translatable, designed for people in the new democracies, especially in India and Africa. The idea had first emerged at the General Meeting of the Association in Canada in 1952. During his visit to India and Ceylon in 1955, d'Egville was pressed to give priority to this booklet, which was urgently needed in Indian villages, not only to explain parliamentary democracy but also to counter communist propaganda then circulating in India. The General Council meeting in Jamaica in 1956 approved it as a priority project. The production of such a booklet, adaptable to the needs of each territory was, however, a task of extraordinary difficulty. D'Egville gave much thought to it and it was still on his agenda when he retired.

The General Council met in Barbados in January 1959. At the ceremonial opening Sir Grantley Adams, Prime Minister of the new Federation of the West Indies, welcomed the councillors to his homeland. The Premier of Barbados, Dr H. G. H. Cummins, speaking in support, also expressed the hope that the full conference of the Association would be held in the West Indies in the near future.

At its meetings the Council agreed on three major matters of policy. The first concerned area and regional conferences which had become an important CPA activity. The Tasmanian branch had first taken the initiative when it hosted a conference of branches in the Australian states. It had proved a success and such conferences had since been held in Sydney, Melbourne, Brisbane and Adelaide. In 1952 the Singapore branch had hosted the first conference of its region, embracing branches in the Federation of Malaya, Sarawak and North Borneo. Each of these branches had subsequently hosted a conference. The North Borneo branch in hosting the sixth conference had gone beyond South-East Asia and had invited observers from Australia and New Zealand. In 1958 Jamaica hosted the first conference of branches in the Caribbean area.

The Canadian area held its first conference in Halifax, Nova Scotia, in September 1958. D'Egville had worked hard to persuade the Canadian branches to take this step. He was gratified by the success of the Halifax meeting, which agreed that such conferences should be held regularly in future. At this stage it was envisaged that area conferences would be held in years when the biennial conferences of the Association did not take place. In Halifax it was also agreed to set up an Area Council, comprising the Speakers of the Canadian House of Commons and Senate and of the provincial legislatures, together with one extra member from each legislature. During his visit to Ottawa in July 1958, d'Egville found that the extension of the conference to include members from the United Kingdom and the West Indies was under discussion.

The growth of area and regional conferences had been a spontaneous development, and d'Egville had been active in promoting it. It also gave witness to the dynamism of the Association and the need felt by members in all parts of the Commonwealth for consultation and cooperation. In the Council, however, some feared that these conferences might prove divisive and damaging to Commonwealth unity. At its meeting in New Delhi in December 1957, the Council laid down certain principles, which were reconsidered and approved at its Barbados meeting. It agreed that area and regional conferences were to be encouraged, but, while area conferences should be held regularly, regional conferences should be held only on an *ad hoc* basis. A clear distinction was drawn between an area, like the federation of Canada and of Australia, and a region, and the Secretary-General was asked to draw up a scheme defining the regions of the Commonwealth geographically. Further in these conferences, which were to be conducted on the same lines as the full biennial conferences and without resolutions, the discussion should be concerned with matters of direct relevance to the area or region. Care should be taken not to detract from the work of the full conference.

In Barbados the discussion on area and regional conferences was in some degree overshadowed by another proposal. This was that the full conferences of the Association should in future be held not biennially but annually. The Council agreed in principle, but asked the Finance and General Purposes Committee to examine the financial implications. The Vice-Chairman, J. W. Higgerty, reporting on behalf of the Committee, stated that if the conferences were held annually, host branches should be asked to meet only the cost of delegates' accommodation and hospitality, and not their travelling expenses, as in the past. It would be necessary to create an annual central fund of some £60,000 for delegates' travel, the fund to be administered by the Secretary-General. The Council would at a future meeting decide on the contributions to be made by each branch. This report was to be considered further by the Council in Canberra in November 1959.

The Finance and General Purposes Committee examined the accounts for 1958 and the estimates for 1959, noting that there would be a deficit. This arose mainly from non-payment of certain branch contributions. To reduce this deficit the Committee recommended that expenditure on publications should be limited to £4000 in 1959. D'Egville argued strongly against this proposal in the Council meeting. He pointed out that one of the privileges of members under the constitution was to receive the *Journal* and the other publications were available on request. The *Journal* provided a direct link with the membership – now over 5000 – but only a small proportion of members would be able to attend even annual conferences. The ceiling proposed would entail a drastic reduction in the size and effectiveness of the *Journal* and the *Report on Foreign Affairs*. It would probably mean closing down the *Summary of Congressional Proceedings USA* and the *Commentary on Foreign Affairs*. This would come at a time when the demand for the information they contained was mounting. He urged that the ceiling be raised to £5000, observing that even this figure would involve severe economies. After long discussion the Council agreed the figure of £5000 for 1959.

This decision was a setback for d'Egville. He had always set great store on the publications. The *Journal* and the *Report* had, however, remained unchanged since their first publication nearly 30 years earlier. He was always so prescient about the rapid developments within the Commonwealth that it was perhaps surprising that he did not see the need for the publications to change to meet new demands. The fact nevertheless remained that in all the countries of the Commonwealth, except perhaps the United Kingdom, there was, and there continues to be, a paucity of information about Commonwealth parliamentary and other affairs, unless some disaster, scandal or dramatic crisis claims international media headlines. His purpose was to give information and create greater understanding among members in all parts of the Commonwealth. Initially the publications were effective. After the war, however, increasing postal delays meant that many members received them up to three months after issue by which time they seemed out-of-date. Several times he looked into the possibility of sending them by airmail, but the extra cost was prohibitive. The *Commentary on Foreign Affairs* which was well-written, up-to-date and sent by airmail, was unfortunately the first to be abandoned. The debate on publications was to continue.

From Barbados, d'Egville flew to Trinidad, his first visit to the island. He met all members of the Federal Parliament and had several meetings with Erskine L. Ward, Speaker of the Federal House of Representatives. He established close relations with Dr Eric Williams, then Premier of Trinidad and Tobago. Williams was keen to hold a regional conference which would include West Indian representatives and also members from the United Kingdom and Canada. He considered that such a regional conference would be of greater value to West Indian members than attendance at the full conference. The Cabinet system of government, then evolving in the West Indies, was not fully understood by their members. They needed to discuss this topic as well as parliamentary control of statutory bodies and kindred matters with British and Canadian members. Subsequently, d'Egville discussed this proposal with Sir Grantley Adams, then in London. The Federal branch took the initiative. The conference of the North Atlantic region took place in Port of Spain in April 1960. Dr Arnott Cato, President of the Senate of the Federal Parliament, was elected Chairman of the conference. Erskine L. Ward and Sir Roland Robinson, then Vice-Chairman of the Council, were elected the Vice-Chairmen.

From Trinidad, d'Egville flew to Bermuda to discuss the possibility of a conference of representatives from the United Kingdom, Canada, and from the associated group in the US Congress. Next he visited Washington to pursue this proposal further. He was also eager to ensure that a congressional delegation attended the conference in Canberra later in the year. He constantly emphasised the need to develop contacts between Commonwealth Parliaments and Congress. In this he was strongly supported by Howard Beale, the Australian ambassador in Washington, who at d'Egville's request was able to attend some of his meetings with Congressmen.

D'Egville also cultivated his special relationship with Carl Marcy, the Chief of Staff of the Senate Committee on Foreign Relations, and with Dr George B. Galloway, the Secretary of the associated group. Over the years he had, indeed, built up a special position in Congress. He had access to the Speakers, to senior Congressmen, and to the chief executive officers on the staff of Congress. In fact, it may be doubted whether the United Kingdom or any other Commonwealth embassy had succeeded in establishing such a close relationship with Congress, as distinct from the presidency, as he had.

From Washington, d'Egville flew to Ottawa for talks with John G. Diefenbaker, with Mark R. Drouin, Speaker of the Senate, and with Roland Michener, Speaker of the House of Commons. He was well known in Ottawa and always welcomed.

Notes

1. **Agenda and Opening Speakers, Nairobi, 1954**
   Relationship between Parliament and the Executive – Donald Fleming (Canada) and Derek Walker-Smith (United Kingdom)
   Cooperation within the Commonwealth – J. W. Higgerty, Chief Opposition Whip (South Africa) and Vice-Chairman of the General Council, and Khan Abdul Qaiyum, Minister of Industries, Food and Agriculture (Pakistan) and Victor T. Bryan, Minister of Agriculture and Lands (Trinidad)
   Development Programmes and Planning in Commonwealth Countries – E. A. Vasey, Minister for Finance and Development (Kenya) and R. S. Garfield Todd, Prime

Minister (Southern Rhodesia)

International Affairs and Defence – Earl de la Warr, Postmaster General (United Kingdom) and Duncan McF. Rae (New Zealand) and B. H. Aluwihare (Ceylon)

2. N. Mansergh, *The Multi-Racial Commonwealth* (London, 1955), p.137.

3. Appendix A, this volume, pp.300–302, sets out the dates of the formation of branches and changes in status of branches.

4. **Agenda and Opening Speakers, Delhi, 1957**

The subjects of discussion and opening speakers in each session of the conference, which took place from 2–10 December 1957, were as follows:

Economic Relations in the Commonwealth – Derick Heathcoat-Amery, Minister of Agriculture, Fisheries and Food (United Kingdom) and T.T. Krishnamachari, Minister of Finance (India)

The Problem of the Underdeveloped Territories of the Commonwealth – Syed Amjad Ali, Minister of Finance and Development (Kenya)

The Working of the Party System in Parliament – S. W. R. D. Bandanaraike, Prime Minister (Ceylon)

Social Services in the Commonwealth – F. D. Shaw (Canada)

The Future of the Smaller States of the Commonwealth – Dr Glendon Logan, Minister of Local Government and Housing (Jamaica)

The Role of the English Language in the Commonwealth – Patrick Gordon Walker (United Kingdom)

International Affairs and Defence – Hugh Gaitskell, Leader of the Opposition (United Kingdom) and Wayne Morse, US Senator (Oregon, USA) and Jawaharlal Nehru, Prime Minister (India).

11 D'Egville Departs, 1959–60

In 1959 d'Egville was 80 years old. His mental faculties were unimpaired. Physically he had suffered some decline after a prostate operation a few years earlier, but he had still a firm overall grip on the affairs of the Association. He knew, however, that it was time for him to retire. The manner of his going can nevertheless be recorded only with regret.

After his return to London from the Council meetings in Barbados in January 1959 and his subsequent visits to Trinidad and to North America, d'Egville was busy with the Council minutes and report, with publications, and especially with the arrangements for the Council meetings and conference in Canberra to be held in November of that year. A Conference Arrangements Committee had been appointed in Barbados, with M.A. Ayyangar as Chairman, J.W. Higgerty as Vice-Chairman, the Secretary-General, and the two Australian representatives on the Council, Sir Alister McMullin and B. D. Snider from Victoria. Its meetings were attended by Alan G. Turner and H. K. McLachlan, Secretaries respectively of the Australian Federal and Victoria branches of the Association, and also by S. A. Pakeman, the Assistant Secretary-General.

At its meetings in Barbados, the Committee approved the arrangements provisionally made for delegates to tour in Australia. It agreed the numbers of delegates to be invited from each branch. It made important recommendations concerning the attendance of branch Secretaries, which the Council approved. For the next conference, and in future, each main branch – that is, a branch in a country which was fully self-governing – would appoint a Secretary to accompany its delegation. A Secretary to delegations from auxiliary branches in legislatures, which had responsible government but were not fully self-governing, would be chosen from such branches in order of branch seniority. In Federations, the Secretary would be chosen from the main branch in one conference year and from the state or provincial branches in order of seniority in the following conference year, and alternating thereafter.

Working on the heavy correspondence which the conference always involved, d'Egville had no inkling of the plot which was hatching across the road from his office in the rooms of the United Kingdom branch, where a cabal had formed. Its members were Sir Roland Robinson and Alfred Robens the United Kingdom representatives on the Council, and Lockhart, the branch Secretary. Its purpose was to remove d'Egville.[1]

The members of the cabal kept their plan secret: Patrick Gordon Walker knew nothing about it. D'Egville held him in high regard and he was seen as one of d'Egville's men. Robens had deputised for Gordon Walker at the meetings in Barbados in January 1959. He was now the second councillor appointed by the United Kingdom branch to serve on the Council in Canberra. It was d'Egville's attempt to secure the reappointment of Gordon Walker in place of Robens that finally made Robens his enemy.

In a letter to Michener, written in January 1960, long after the events presently recorded, d'Egville wrote:

> I am puzzled about Mr Robens who had worked cordially with me for many years, but I think he had got the idea that a letter that was written by the former Vice-Chairman of the Council to the United Kingdom branch, asking if they could continue Gordon Walker as councillor for one more meeting as he had special knowledge and had been most helpful, was due to my influence.... The Vice-Chairman, Mr Higgerty, did mention to me that he intended writing, but he assured me that he would suggest nothing that would in any way affect the normal term of office of Mr Robens as councillor.

D'Egville must have realised that the proposal would involve Gordon Walker taking Robens' place on the Council. The branch rigidly followed the rule that if one of its two councillors was a Conservative, the other must be a Labour member. There would be no question of Gordon Walker, a Labour member, taking the place of Sir Roland Robinson, a Conservative.

Robens was a powerful and influential Labour member and, in the words of Gordon Walker, he 'arrived at the conference in a mood of unrelenting hostility towards d'Egville'. During the tours in Australia and in Canberra he campaigned actively for support among the councillors and delegates for the removal of d'Egville. In this he had the full backing of Sir Roland Robinson.

In Canberra in November 1959 d'Egville was in poor health. He had travelled to Australia against medical advice. He was, however, something of a hypochondriac, and always had at hand his black bag, containing an assortment of pills, medicines and placebos. He was a man of tremendous nervous energy, but as he grew old he could no longer replace this energy as quickly as he had done in the past. His recent operation had weakened him. He was prone now to depressions, to heart trouble, and other real or imagined ailments. In Canberra where the tensions, especially in the Council, were high he was vulnerable.

The campaign which the two United Kingdom councillors were waging against him was complicated by another struggle within the Council concerning the Chairmanship. M. A. Ayyangar's term of office came to an end in Canberra. D'Egville had promoted as his successor the Speaker of the Canadian House of

Commons, Roland Michener. Ayyangar himself was ready to nominate him, and d'Egville had secured the promise of Sir Roland Robinson to second the motion. Michener's election seemed certain.

There was, however, another contender for the office, Sir Alister McMullin, President of the Australian Senate. D'Egville made the mistake of not taking McMullin's candidacy seriously. His reason was that both the Australian Prime Minister, Robert Menzies, and the leader of the Australian delegation, Harold Holt, were emphatic that it would be a mistake to elect another Australian as Chairman so soon after Holt's term of nearly four years in this office. McMullin himself told d'Egville that he would support Michener's election.

Alister McMullin, a rugged individualist and shrewd politician, nevertheless wanted to be Chairman. He had served on the Council for two years. He believed in the work and purposes of the Association, and he valued the fellowship which it provided. He continued to campaign, while Michener stood back, presumably reassured by d'Egville that he would be the next Chairman. At some point, however, Robens and Robinson promised McMullin their votes for the chairmanship if he in turn would support them in ousting d'Egville.

'On Sunday November 1st, the day before the conference opened', d'Egville recorded in his long letter of 18 January 1960 to Michener,

> I received a phone call from the United Kingdom representatives asking for a meeting of the Council for that evening in order that Sir Alister McMullin could be elected Chairman of the Council. I replied that I doubted whether Shri Ayyangar would agree to this, but I would, of course, consult him. Shri Ayyangar said that, as he had been invited to attend the conference as Chairman and to preside over the opening ceremony before handing over the duties to his successor, he would regard any replacement of his chairmanship at the opening as a slight to India and, if persisted in, he would return to India the next day. This would lead almost certainly to the withdrawal of the branches in India and possibly Ceylon. I told the United Kingdom representatives that the Chairman would not agree to calling a meeting that night.

The haste was unseemly. Ayyangar was known to be very sensitive about his personal dignity and the dignity of his country. It was evident, however, that Robens and Robinson were impatient to finalise the election of the Chairman and the Vice-Chairman so that they could proceed without delay to the task of ousting d'Egville. In the event, at the Council meeting on Monday, 2 November 1959, the elections to both offices went forward smoothly. With grace Michener proposed and S. V. K. Rao of India seconded the election of Sir Alistair McMullin and it was carried unanimously. The election of Sir Roland Robinson as Vice-Chairman was also unanimous.

Robens proposed at this meeting that for the future there should be a recognised convention that the Chairman should, if possible, be a national of the country which was to host the next conference and the Vice-Chairman a national of the succeeding host country. The Council placed on record that this was a desirable convention. In advancing this proposal Robens was making it virtually certain that Sir Roland Robinson, the Vice-Chairman, would be the next Chairman. The reason for this certainty was that the leader of the United Kingdom delegation had a letter from the British Prime Minister inviting the Association to hold its next conference at Westminster in September–October 1961. The invitation was reported to the Council at its meeting on the following day, 3 November 1959, and accepted with acclamation.

D'Egville was indisposed and unable to attend the Council meeting on 2 November 1959. He was distressed by the results of the elections. He believed it to be wrong for the Association at this time. He saw, too, that the results were not auspicious for himself. 'There is, I think, no doubt that the present Chairman and Vice-Chairman have regarded my work as Secretary-General as inclining too much to the encouragement of the Afro-Asian elements in the Association,' he wrote to Michener.

The mood of a General Meeting, Council and even a Committee, like the mood on the Floor of the House, cannot always be anticipated. It may be even-tempered, when suddenly a wrong word or a behind-the-scenes lobby inflames it, turning it to anger, concentrated on one member or group. In the ten years of its existence the Council had always been supportive and appreciative of d'Egville's work. In Barbados and in Canberra for the first time he met with a degree of veiled hostility. This was clear at the first meeting of the Council on 2 November from which he was absent. Robens and Robinson, abetted by the Chairman, Alister McMullin, led the attack and some councillors began to support them. They were motivated not only by antagonism towards d'Egville personally, but also by the conviction that for far too long he had managed and directed the Association. It was time for the Council to play a more active part. This had been discussed in Barbados. In Canberra it was minuted baldly: 'visits to overseas branches should, when possible, be made by the Chairman and Vice-Chairman, or, by agreement with them, by the Secretary-General', and 'That the Chairman and Vice-Chairman should play a more active part than hitherto in guiding the affairs of the Association'. D'Egville, who had travelled so widely in the past, would have to obtain permission to visit an overseas branch in future; he would also come under the direct control of the Chairman and Vice-Chairman, and no longer be free to act on his own initiative.

Robens and Robinson's campaign was not yet over. They were still not sure that they had the necessary majority of votes in the Council to get rid of d'Egville. They had gained McMullin's vote, but their approaches to Harold Holt were firmly rebuffed. Holt believed in loyalty to old friends. It is not known how all members of the Council responded. It is evident, however, that they managed to scrape together a majority, but to the end it was a close-run thing. If d'Egville had not been ill at this time, the moves against him would probably have failed.

At some time between the Council's meetings on 2 and 6 November d'Egville was summoned to a meeting with the new Chairman and Vice-Chairman. Robens was also present, for he had led the campaign and was ready to deliver the *coup de grâce*. It must have been a difficult meeting, marked by acrimony and a complete lack of generosity. D'Egville was told that, since he was well past retiring age, he had had the considerable benefit of receiving full pay since the age of 65. In fact, his salary had always been low and his tireless work for the Association had deserved higher rewards. Then, evidently, it was put to him that he should write a letter expressing his intention of retiring. The alternative would be a motion to the Council, expressly retiring him from office. He was left in no doubt that such a motion would be passed.

In his letter of 18 January 1960 to Michener, d'Egville wrote:

In the state of health I was in on Friday night [6 November 1959] being tired, dispirited, and intensely disappointed at the turn events had taken and being, moreover, in constant fear that the anxiety and strains might cause a recurrence of the heart trouble at any moment, it seemed to me that the only thing I could do was to keep to the promise I had made to the Chairman, Vice-Chairman, and Mr Robens. But, of course, I was not capable of exercising sound judgement.

The Council met at 8 p.m. on 6 November 1959 in the Senate committee room of the Parliament. The Chairman, Sir Alister McMullin, called on d'Egville who stated that for some time he had been considering his retirement on the grounds that the strenuous nature of the work had affected his health. In Canberra, moreover, he had sensed a feeling that a change was desirable. He was therefore prepared to go into retirement as from 1 July 1960 on certain conditions, which he read to the meeting.

A number of councillors felt disquiet over the position of the Secretary-General. They suspected that pressure had been brought to bear on him and objected to this having been done without prior consultation with the Council. There was considerable discussion, but this was not recorded in the minutes of the meeting. Indeed, the Chairman stated that the minutes would 'be as short as possible and would include essential matters only, such as the record of decisions taken. . . . A more detailed record of the proceedings would be kept for reference.' Unfortunately, this 'more detailed' record is hardly fuller than the bare minutes sent out to all branches. A draft of the fuller record has survived. It shows excisions, marked in Lockhart's hand. One lengthy excision concerned a motion, moved by Stanley de Zoysa, the councillor from Ceylon, and seconded by Ashford Sinanan, deputising for Sir Grantley Adams, as councillor from the Federation of the West Indies, which requested d'Egville to withdraw the conditions he had read out, and by implication withdraw his intention to retire. The Vice-Chairman, Sir Roland Robinson, insisted that if he was going to retire, the matter should be decided before the Council dispersed.

In response to the de Zoysa–Sinanan motion, d'Egville said that he found himself in a difficult position. His original idea was to remain in office until after the next Council meeting or even after the next conference. He had a good deal of energy and capacity left, and could have done everything required at the conference and Council meetings if he had not left England before he was thoroughly fit. He felt he would like to have some freedom left to him to decide the precise date of his retirement.

The Chairman assured the Council that, when he did retire, he would do so on handsome terms, and if his pension would not amount to two-thirds of his present salary, it would be made up to that figure out of Council funds. He said that d'Egville would always remain a part of the Association, which would assist him, if he decided, as they hoped he would, to undertake the writing of the history of the CPA.

At this point d'Egville asked leave to withdraw for a short time to consult on the matter. He faced a difficult decision. He knew that the time for him to retire was close, but he did not want to retire yet. The Association had been and was still his whole life. On the other hand, if he decided to hold on it would probably mean a bitter debate, led by Robens, which would split the Council and possibly the Association. It would also be extremely difficult for him to work with Sir Roland Robinson, the next Chairman. Clearly if he decided to fight, the Association itself would suffer most damage. He consulted with Casely-Hayford and de Zoysa, two of his closest supporters, and made his decision. Returning to the meeting he read out his letter of resignation, as follows:

Dear Mr Chairman,
For reasons of health, I wish to retire as Secretary-General of the Commonwealth Parliamentary Association effective as from the 1st July 1960.
In the meanwhile I should be glad if the Council would give me leave of absence from work for a period of six months as from 1st January 1960 on full pay.
Between January and March 1960, I shall be prepared, however, to give full attention to clearing up all my papers and documents in the office at the central headquarters, preparatory to the move to new headquarters.
I shall also be glad to assist in any direction within my power any person whom the Council may appoint to carry on my duties until I give up my functions and authority on 1st July next.
I will gladly consider undertaking the preparation and publication of a history of the Commonwealth Parliamentary Association since its inception, on a mutually satisfactory basis.
Yours sincerely [sgd]
Howard d'Egville, Secretary-General

The resignation was accepted with a formal expression of regret. Robens at once moved that the question of d'Egville's successor be considered immediately. He proposed that a letter, outlining the qualifications and requirements of the post, be sent to all branches and that the post should be advertised. In the meantime an Acting Secretary-General should be appointed, taking up his duties on 1 January 1960 and holding the post until 31 December 1961. The Council agreed.

Robens then proposed that J. G. Lockhart, Secretary to the United Kingdom branch who was in Canberra as Secretary to the delegation, should be invited to accept the post. The Council agreed. It also appointed S. A. Pakeman to be Deputy Secretary-General and Editor-in-Chief of Publications, thus separating the two offices which d'Egville had held.

In the closing session of the conference tributes were paid to d'Egville, Sir Alister McMullin, the Chairman, spoke of his great contribution to the goodwill between the countries of the Commonwealth and in welding the newly independent countries into the Association. Sir Roland Robinson, the Vice-Chairman said of d'Egville: 'He had nurtured us and seen us grow, and I think we can truthfully say that he can regard the Commonwealth Parliamentary Association as his child. . . . When we take leave of him now, we say with truth that we hope to see you often, old friend, and we will remember you with the affection and respect that is always given by the son to the father . . .'.[2]

The tributes which truly merit recording were from Ashford Sinanan, Harold Holt and M. A. Ayyangar. Sinanan stated:

It is my conviction that if it were not for Sir Howard d'Egville the separate colonies of this great Commonwealth might have gone their separate ways. Although we had the concept of the Commonwealth developing, one body that kept us in this loose association, yet rigidly held to the centre, was the Commonwealth Parliamentary Association to which Sir Howard has dedicated the major part of his very useful life. I am sure that I speak for the entire West Indies when I say that we will miss him particularly because whenever we visited London, he spared the time to tender advice to us and to inspire us so that in the West Indies there was this very strong growth of the parliamentary way of life.[3]

Harold Holt, who had worked closely with him during his four years as Chairman, spoke warmly of his achievements.

When the history of the Association is written, and I understand that he is to play a part and perhaps a major part in the writing of it, it will be found to have been very considerably a biography of Sir Howard d'Egville himself. Indeed he needs no oral testimony nor written record of the contribution that he has made to the development of the Association which, as we see it around us now, is the testimony of his work. It has grown during the period of his office from six branches, made up of people of British blood and British stock, to seventy branches representing just on a quarter of the world's population, and including some 500 million diverse people, not only of British blood and stock, but representing virtually all sections of the world's communities at this time. That is a remarkable achievement in the lifetime of any man.

History will record this contribution to the ideals which mankind has treasured through the centuries. As has been so rightly stated in the course of this conference, much of the hope of the world for the attainment of the objectives of peaceful coexistence, racial equality, prosperous development and the brotherhood of man depends upon the success we make of this experiment in which we are all engaged.

Along the course of the years there has been occasion after occasion when all that has been achieved could have been split asunder had there not been the wise and intelligent guidance of the affairs of the Association by the man who was necessarily at the core of all its activities. We have not had a regular executive, able to meet frequently. Geography, time and circumstance have defeated that otherwise very desirable objective and have prevented us from providing the kind of machinery necessary. In these circumstances there was need for a man who could hold the threads together and see that the Association should progress in the orderly way that it has done.[4]

And M. A. Ayyangar spoke of his work in India:

Except for the central branch of the Commonwealth Parliamentary Association in India, all the other branches that have been formed in the legislatures have come into existence through the efforts of Sir Howard. During the last conference that we had in Delhi in 1957 he was mainly responsible for bringing the various countries together. He helped enormously in organizing the conference, and I want to pay a humble tribute to him for the excellent work he has done, and the interest he has taken in the affairs of the Association and all its branches.[5]

D'Egville made a dignified and restrained reply to these tributes. He laid emphasis on one principle, stating: 'The one great thing I have tried to do during the time I have been with the General Council has been to pursue the policy which has been laid down by most of the leading statesmen of the Commonwealth, that is, equality of status amongst the nations of the Commonwealth'.[6]

There was, however, an aftermath to this farewell ceremony. Lockhart took up his duties as Acting Secretary-General on his return from Australia. He held office officially from 1 January 1960. Five days later, on 6 January 1960, he unexpectedly died. Pakeman took over as Acting Secetary-General the next day, 7 January 1960. D'Egville was greatly troubled by these events. The Association seemed to him to be in jeopardy.

In his long letter of 18 January 1960 to Michener, reporting on what had happened in Canberra, passages from which have been quoted already, he made a desperate appeal for help to resume charge temporarily as Secretary-General:

Our Association should have an experienced hand at the helm and one known and trusted by political leaders throughout the Commonwealth for the next few months. Irreparable damage could be done in a few days or even hours. . . . Representatives of the United Kingdom have been put in charge of certain matters at the office of the H.Q. The matter is extremely urgent as some action may be taken soon after Parliament meets in London.

You are the only member of Council who can deal with the present emergency. . . . I do not suggest the possibility of going on after the conference of 1961 if some good man can be found for training as a successor. . . . I hope you can sign the circular letter, on the lines of the enclosed draft, to members of the Council. . . . I feel that the proposed resolution would meet with almost unanimous approval except by the Chairman and the two United Kingdom representatives.

The draft circular letter read as follows:

On 6 November Sir Howard d'Egville was called on by the Chairman at a late hour to read a statement indicating his desire to resign as Secretary-General from 1 July 1960.

From his reference to having had an interview with the newly elected Chairman and Vice-Chairman and having sensed a desire for change, some members of the Council concluded that pressure had been exercised upon Sir Howard to resign and a protest was made that this should have been done without prior consultation with the Council. However, although the Council decided that the statement should be withdrawn and the matter left to Sir Howard to consider afresh, Sir Howard decided to keep to the promise he had made to the Chairman and Vice-Chairman and wrote a letter of resignation. Sir Howard attended the Canberra conference against medical advice.... Sir Howard d'Egville is Secretary-General till 1 July 1960 and any alteration in this can only be made by a decision of the Council as a whole under the constitution.... Sir Howard is most anxious to serve the Association in the present emergency in any way that is likely to be most effective.

The lamented death of Major Lockhart has afforded us, I submit, another chance of getting Sir Howard's full help and co-operation in the following matters, namely:

The place of the next meeting of the Council.

Suggestions for revising certain clauses of the constitution.

Raising of funds to establish a special pool to meet the cost of travel to annual conferences.

Consideration of the qualification required for the post of Secretary-General and the best methods of ascertaining the names of those likely to be suitable and available.

Therefore in the light of the observations in this letter, I ask for your support of the following resolutions of the General Council:

> That in the special circumstances arising from the sudden death of Major Lockhart who had just commenced his duties as Acting Secretary-General of the CPA, Sir Howard d'Egville, in view of his improved physical condition, be invited to withdraw his resignation from the post of Secretary-General at least until after the next Council meeting and possibly, if so determined at the next meeting of the Council, until the next conference in 1961, when a younger man will be appointed.... I shall be grateful, in the event of the resolution receiving your support, if you will kindly sign the form below and send it to me.

The letter to Michener closed with the words: 'As the Association means everything to me, I shall, of course, await an airmail reply from you with great anxiety.' Michener was slow to reply. D'Egville wrote again on 20 February 1960, commenting, 'Pakeman has more than enough to do in editing the publications and there is no other member of the small staff capable of handling the administrative side. I am prepared to terminate my so-called "leave" at any time and take charge of the administrative side ... but a move must be made by the Council to bring this about.'

Michener's reply, dated 22 February 1960, was a short and firm rejection. 'Although I have a high regard for your merits and a great appreciation of what the Association owes to you, I do not feel that I, as a member of the Council, should undertake a campaign with individual council members to alter the collective decisions which were taken at Canberra. However, I shall discuss the matter with associates in the Canadian branch to see whether we can offer any suggestions to the officers which might be useful in the circumstances.'

D'Egville's long career with the Association, extending over nearly 50 years, had ended. From the beginning he had pursued his vision of a united Commonwealth with, as part of its strong foundations, the Parliamentary Association, dedicated to promoting understanding and cooperation among MPs and to strengthening parliamentary institutions. As he recognised the extent of the economic power and influence of the United States after the war, he sought also to involve members of the US Congress. At one stage he envisaged the Association at the centre of the whole English-speaking world.

His great fear was that the United Kingdom branch might establish its dominance within the Association and obstruct his plans. To British members this dominance or leadership was seen as an historical right. Britain was the senior member of the Commonwealth and had far greater experience and maturity than the others. Moreover, it made by far the largest contribution to the Association's funds. It followed for them that their branch should have a special role in policy direction and management. D'Egville had no patience with this attitude. He had a wholly Commonwealth outlook. As he had stressed in his farewell speech in Canberra, his goal had always been a united Commonwealth of equal nations.

This fundamental difference lay at the root of the hostility of the United Kingdom branch towards d'Egville. Britain was passing through a difficult time of adjustment after the war. Decades of wielding imperial power had inculcated habits and an outlook which could not be changed in one generation. Not until the Suez crisis was the diminished power and prestige of their country fully acknowledged by political leaders in Britain. D'Egville was ahead of most members at Westminster in understanding and accepting the changed circumstances, and in his vision of the role that the Commonwealth might play.

From the time when the General Council was set up in 1949, d'Egville considered himself to be free from the dictates and influence of the United Kingdom government and branch. He treated the branch as equal with other branches, and firmly resisted attempts by the branch to play a paternalistic role and to act as Big Brother. This was shown in many major and minor incidents – most strikingly in 1953 when the branch insisted that it should host the Association's coronation lunch in honour of the Queen. D'Egville, strongly supported by his Chairman, Harold Holt, opposed this presumption, and the General Council was properly the host on this significant occasion. He was always on guard against any attempts by the branch to resume its pre-1949 position and ignore or by-pass the Council.

The Commonwealth was evolving rapidly and he had an unrivalled knowledge of its member countries. He had travelled widely and had friendly and long-standing relations with their political leaders and members. He was thus uniquely qualified to represent their collective views, and not merely adept at persuading them to oppose the United Kingdom branch on matters like publications, as so many of its members believed.

At the same time d'Egville may have gone too far in his determination to prevent the United Kingdom branch wielding special influence within the Association. Westminster, the 'Mother of Parliaments', commanded great respect and affection in all countries of the Commonwealth. It was a dynamic and innovative Parliament to which members in other countries looked for precedents and example. Erskine May's *Parliamentary Practice and Procedure* was an essential handbook. The course on practice and procedure had become an annual event at Westminster, with requests from branches invariably exceeding the number of places available. There were requests for a second course to be arranged each year.

The principle of the equality of branches was an ideal which d'Egville stoutly defended. In practice, however, there was need for members with the experience and background, which Westminster, Ottawa and Canberra could best provide. Westminster and its branch in fact held a senior position in the Association as in the Commonwealth. Nor did other branches deny or resent this fact. They acknowledged in the full conferences that the United Kingdom delegation was usually the most outstanding in performance.

D'Egville's attitude was no doubt coloured by memories of the difficulties he had had to overcome in establishing the Association and then the General Council. But he had become too rigid in his assertion of the equality of branches and his opposition to the United Kingdom branch. In Canberra at the time of his retiring, however, he had to recognise that the branch had now gained a degree of dominance which might well increase.

It was d'Egville's practice of seeking to influence the appointment to the Council of members whom he considered to have most to contribute that often incurred the hostility of the United Kingdom branch. This anger came to a head in 1959. Undoubtedly Gordon Walker was better informed and more involved in the Commonwealth than Robens, and it was understandable that d'Egville wanted him on the Council. But Robens, an able and dynamic politician, felt personally affronted. He went to Canberra determined to humble and oust d'Egville. He succeeded in his task, but he came very close to failure. Many councillors and delegates had a deep respect and affection for d'Egville and his achievement.

D'Egville should have retired earlier. But he found it impossible to stand down and hand over to another this great organisation which he had built up and to which he had devoted his life. It was all the more difficult for him at this time when the Association was still growing strongly under his direction, and despite his age he was fully in charge. In the opinion of many members he should have been allowed to remain in office until time took its final toll.

As Harold Holt said in his valedictory speech, d'Egville's achievement was the Association which had grown under his direction from 6 to 70 branches with members representing some 500 million people in the Commonwealth. It was to continue its steady expansion, but in its purposes and activities it has followed along the lines which he laid down. Indeed, his spirit continues to permeate the Association.

It is far more difficult to define or quantify the contribution of d'Egville and of the Association to the Commonwealth and to world affairs. He certainly exercised a strong influence in keeping some countries in the Commonwealth. He knew most of the political leaders and was a persuasive advocate of Commonwealth unity. In India, Pakistan and Ceylon he inspired new enthusiasm and assuaged the fears of many Indian members before 1947 that they might not have full equality in the Association. He had a passionate belief in the Commonwealth and its role in the world. But he could not have foreseen the developments after 1960 which have changed the nature of the Commonwealth and have inevitably had an impact on the Association. These matters will be considered in subsequent chapters of this history.

D'Egville was a lonely man. In London he lived in a room in the Goring Hotel near Victoria railway station. He had a flat in Hove, Sussex, to which he retreated on weekends if he was not entertaining visiting members. In later years he had as a companion a distant cousin, Mrs Colville Halls, who accompanied him on several conferences. He was very fond of his Boston terrier, Dagwood, a dog of unpredictable temper, who once in the office caused a drama by biting Mrs Colville Halls' nose. He dreaded holidays when he was often alone. He used to say that he hated Christmas, and it was probably then that he felt his loneliness most acutely. Such was the price he paid for his dedication to the Association, which was so single-minded as to have excluded marriage, family and a home.

He had a lively mind, a retentive memory, and was widely read. In his late seventies he could still recite from memory page after page of certain of the novels of Charles Dickens. Here again his exclusive interest in the Association limited his reading in later years to newspapers and parliamentary affairs. Duncan Hall, a friend of long standing, noted that in company he took part actively in the conversation when the Commonwealth and the CPA were under discussion, but quickly lost interest when the subject changed. In his habits he was austere, spending little on himself, and eating and drinking sparingly.

Within the Secretariat he could be a petty tyrant. He was selfish, inconsiderate and demanding. His own practice was to work on CPA matters in his hotel room from early morning, sitting up in bed. He would occasionally phone members at their homes at this time, a practice which was unpopular. He would arrive in the office at about 11 a.m. and work through the day until 7 or 8 p.m., unless he was giving lunch or dinner to visiting members. He expected the staff to be available at all times, holding that their personal lives must be subordinate to the work of the Association. Thwarted in his wishes he became bad-tempered.

Times of sheer exasperation among the small staff were offset by their respect for his ability and tireless activity. Moreover, he was capable on occasions of showing appreciation of their work. He had great respect for Mrs Blattner who as Assistant Editor worked long hours sub-editing and proof-reading the publications. He recommended the award to her of the OBE, and later the CBE, in the honours list, and ensured each time that the recommendation was not overlooked. He took some pleasure in bullying Sidney Pakeman, a mild and elderly man. He nevertheless respected his views and even had some affection for him. To others who incurred his dislike he could be ruthless and their term of service would be cut short.

D'Egville remained Secretary of the British–American parliamentary group, after retiring from the CPA. He had a small office in the basement of 7 Old Palace Yard, and quite separate from the CPA Secretariat. He did not visit the Secretariat and indeed was rarely seen in the building. Except when he made an appearance at the General Meeting in London in September 1961 to receive the testimonial fund, to which reference is made below, he seemed to be isolated, even ostracised. No honours came to acknowledge his years of dedicated service and his achievements. He said that he should have received a peerage, but such awards were for other men. On 9 January 1965 he died in Hove at the age of 86.

Notes

1. On 10 January 1960, in the process of clearing Lockhart's desk, then still in the Abingdon Street office, a typewritten foolscap sheet was found, amended in his handwriting, setting out the plan of campaign for the removal of d'Egville in Canberra. It also had the admonition to Robens and Robinson that once embarked on the campaign they must pursue it relentlessly or else d'Egville would contrive to stay on. At the bottom of the page Lockhart had written a quotation from *Macbeth*, which read, 'If it were done when 'tis done, then 'twere well it were done quickly'. The paper was seen by Ian Grey, Betty May and Jack Fowler. It was handed to Robens.
2. Report of Conference (Canberra, 1959), p.241.
3. *Loc. cit.*
4. Ibid., p.242.
5. Ibid., p.243.
6. Ibid., p.245.

12　Canberra and Kampala, 1959–60

The General Council meetings in Canberra and Kampala made decisions of far-reaching importance for the Association.

In Canberra at the first Council meeting on 2 November 1959 it was established beyond question that the rule of the Secretary-General was ended. In future the Chairman and Vice-Chairman would play an active part in conducting the affairs of the Association. They would visit branches overseas; the Secretary-General would continue to travel but only 'by agreement with them'. At the General Meeting, moreover, amendments to the constitution, proposed and circulated in advance by the United Kingdom branch, struck at the publications. Clause VIII stated that every member of the Association was entitled to receive the *Journal of the Parliaments of the Commonwealth*, and on request the *Report on Foreign Affairs* and the *Summary of Congressional Proceedings USA* and any other periodical publications, authorised and published by the General Council. The amendment removed the specific reference to the *Report* and the *Summary*.

In Clause XIV, defining the responsibilities of the Secretary-General as Editor, the names of all of the publications were deleted. The reason for the two amendments was that in Barbados in January 1959, when severe cuts in the publications budget were proposed, d'Egville advanced as one argument against the cuts the fact that the three periodicals were entrenched by name in the constitution.

The two amendments were passed. There was, however, some uneasiness among councillors about the intentions of the United Kingdom branch. A few were aware that for years the Executive Committee of the branch had been trying to cut back publications drastically. In part this was to save money, but it was also directed against d'Egville and, one strongly suspects, instigated by Lockhart.

In supporting the two amendments Roland Robinson stated, 'It is the desire of the Council that the publications should continue'. This assurance did not prevent Harold Holt rising at once to ask, 'Would you give some indication as to the future of the *Report on Foreign Affairs*?' In his reply Robinson said, rather ominously, 'We do not wish to kill the *Report on Foreign Affairs*, but we want to do the job at less expense.'[1]

In Barbados, and again in Canberra in November 1959, the proposal that the conferences of the Association should in future be held annually was discussed at length. On 6 November the Council accepted the report of its subcommittee, set up to consider the finance involved in this major development. It was recognised that the existing system whereby the host branch paid all expenses of the delegates, including the cost of their travel, could not continue if conferences were held annually. The subcommittee's solution was to establish a central pool of £50,000 per annum. This would involve an additional contribution from each branch, equal approximately to $1\frac{1}{6}$ times the amount of its existing annual contribution.

The Secretary-General was instructed to explain this proposal to all branches, asking them to discuss the suggested increase in their contributions with the financial authorities in their countries. He was also to advise that contributions should be sent to the Treasurer (an office which did not then exist) by 31 December 1961. Roland Robinson announced that the new arrangement would not apply to the conference to be held in London in 1961. The United Kingdom branch would be responsible for all expenses on the old basis.

The General Meeting on 4 November 1959 debated the subject at length. Finally, on the motion of Alfred Robens, it agreed in principle the proposal for annual conferences, 'subject to confirmation by the respective branches and governments of the additional sum so required'.[2]

Harold Holt then moved an interesting motion. He had referred earlier to the meeting of Commonwealth Prime Ministers due to take place in London in 1960. He suggested that there should be some link between these meetings and the conferences of the Association. In effect this was a partial revival of the ideas, set out in a memorandum by Jan Smuts on the eve of the Imperial Conference of 1921. Holt's motion read:

> That this General Meeting of the Commonwealth Parliamentary Association, meeting at Canberra in the course of the sixth post-war conference of the Commonwealth Parliamentary Association, expresses the view that it would welcome a discussion by the Prime Ministers of the Commonwealth, when next they meet in conference, on the question of how the Commonwealth Parliamentary Association can most effectively serve the cause of parliamentary democracy within the Commonwealth and, by its activities, further promote our Commonwealth objectives.[3]

Robinson seconded the motion which was adopted. (Similar proposals were to arise later and will be recorded together with the outcome in a subsequent chapter.)

Consideration of a re-draft of the constitution was referred to M. E. Currie, the councillor from the Southern Rhodesia branch and a practising lawyer. He was asked to obtain by correspondence the views of other councillors who were skilled in legal matters. At the same time the Secretary-General was instructed to write to Secretaries, inviting them to submit the views of their branches and any amendments they wished to move. In fact, Currie himself produced a substantial re-draft of the constitution. This was discussed in detail by the Council at its next meeting and recommended for adoption by the General Meeting of the Association in London in 1961. It was a long and cumbersome process but, at least in theory, democratic.

The Commonwealth and state branches of Australia were joint hosts to the Sixth Commonwealth Parliamentary Conference, held in Canberra in November 1959. It was attended by 105 delegates from 49 branches. A delegation of four Senators, accompanied by Dr George B. Galloway, from the associated group in the US Congress, came to take part in the sessions on 'International Affairs and Defence'. The delegations included a number of distinguished members. Lord Mills, the Paymaster-General, was leader, and Earl Attlee, the former Prime Minister, was deputy leader of the United Kingdom delegation, which included Alfred Robens and W. Glenvil Hall. Roland Michener, Speaker of the Canadian House of Commons, led his delegation. The Australian delegation was especially strong. Harold Holt, then Treasurer and Leader of the House of Representatives, was its leader. He was supported by Dr H. V. Evatt, Leader of the Opposition, and one of the foremost international jurists of the day. Dato'Ong Yoke Lin, Minister of Labour and Social Welfare, led the Federation of Malaya delegation. Ian Smith, Chief Government Whip, led the delegation from the Federation of Rhodesia and Nyasaland. Most of the other delegations were led by Speakers or Ministers.

The delegates assembled in Perth on 24 September 1959. They toured the six Australian states in the course of the following weeks, seeing sights of interest, meeting the local people, and enjoying unstinted hospitality. The tours in Australia, as in other countries, had a dual purpose. They enabled delegates to gain some insight – albeit often superficial – into the country, while witnessing its problems and achievements. They also gave the delegates, coming from every part of the Commonwealth, the opportunity to mingle closely, and to learn something of each others' attitudes and concerns. On such tours it has always been noteworthy and even moving to see how delegates, who have never been away from their own country or even their state, have opened their eyes with wonder as they have experienced a totally new environment, and so often at the same time have found common problems and different approaches to dealing with them. This has always been the special value of pre-conference tours. Moreover, they have usually developed a comradeship, even a community spirit, from which many friendships have sprung. They have also fostered during the conference itself a warmth and familiarity which are important in the discussions, and even more so away from the floor of the conference.

By the beginning of November 1959 all delegates were gathered in Canberra. On the morning of 2 November the Governor-General, Field-Marshal Sir William Slim, opened the conference. The President of the Australian Senate, Sir Alister McMullin, and the Assistant Secretary-General, S. A. Pakeman, Sir Howard d'Egville being indisposed, presented to him the leaders of delegations as well as the Prime Minister of the Federation of Malaya, Tunku Abdul Rahman al-Haj, who was in Australia on an official visit at this time, and M. A. Ayyangar, the Chairman of the General Council, who then invited the Governor-General to declare the conference open. The Prime Minister of Australia, Sir Robert Menzies, the leader of the United Kingdom delegation, Lord Mills, the leader of the delegation from the Federation of Rhodesia and Nyasaland, Ian Smith, and Sir John Cox, Speaker of the House of Assembly, Bermuda, also delivered speeches. Finally, by invitation the Prime Minister of the Federation of Malaya, addressed the conference.

The subjects of discussion and opening speakers in the conference, which took place from 2 to 7 November 1959 in the chamber of the House of Representatives, are set out in the notes to this chapter.[4]

The General Council next met in Kampala on 13–16 September 1960, almost a year after its meetings in Canberra. Sir Alister McMullin was still Chairman and Roland Robinson Vice-Chairman. There were, however, certain important changes in membership. Peter Howson was the new councillor from the Commonwealth of Australia branch. The two United Kingdom councillors were unable to attend; Bernard Braine deputised for Sir Herbert Butcher, and Arthur Creech Jones deputised for Alfred Robens.

The Council meetings were formally opened on 13 September by the Hon. R. L. Dreschfield, Attorney-General of Uganda, on behalf of the Governor, Sir Frederick Crawford, whose wife had died on the day before the councillors arrived. This formal opening took place in the Town Hall, Kampala, where the Legislative Council used to meet. The sittings of the Council were in the Long Committee Room of the new Parliament Building by special permission of the Speaker, Sir John Griffin. It was a concession, for the building had not yet been formally opened for the Legislative Council.

On 19 September members of the Council attended the formal opening of the new building, performed by the Rt Hon. Iain Macleod, Secretary of State for the Colonies. On behalf of the CPA, Roland Robinson presented to the Uganda Legislative Council a specially bound copy of *Erskine May*. Representing the United Kingdom branch he also presented two despatch boxes for the table in the Legislative Council.

On the question of annual conferences the Chairman reported that 38 branches had given their full support. Indications from Canada and the provincial branches and from Ceylon that they favoured annual conferences would bring the total to 49 branches. In fact, with the exception of India, the branches of the Association were unanimous that the conference should be convened annually.

The two Indian councillors, Krishnamoorthy Rao and Sardar Kapoor Singh, argued that, taking place annually, the discussions would become repetitious and interest in the conferences would diminish. Rao said that India's need to conserve foreign currency was no longer a factor, since the Association had now opened a rupee bank account in New Delhi. He suggested, however, that the Indian branch might decide to send delegates to annual conferences at its own expense without contributing the full membership fee to the central fund.

The Chairman pointed out that a number of Commonwealth countries which were members of the Inter-Parliamentary Union, paid far more to the Union than they were now asked to contribute to the Association. He stressed that the CPA was the more important organisation. Indeed, he believed that it should become the Parliament of the Commonwealth to which the Prime Ministers would refer matters for discussion. The Indian councillors undertook to ask their main branch to reconsider the question. Subsequently the Indian branch agreed to send delegations to the annual conferences, but it met their travel expenses.

Publications were the subject of a lengthy, somewhat confused discussion on the basis of a paper submitted by the Assistant Editor. It was decided that articles of a controversial nature should not be published in the *Journal*, but that one or two articles 'of a not too controversial nature' might be included in each issue, together with notes on important rulings of presiding officers.[5] Illustrations might also help to make the publication more interesting. Consideration of changes in the *Report on Foreign Affairs* was deferred.

Certain branches were still uneasy about the treatment of d'Egville in Canberra. The Council now had on its agenda a motion from the Australia branch: 'That it be recommended to the General Council that suitable recognition be made of the long period of devoted and valuable service given by Sir Howard d'Egville as Secretary-General of this Association and to its development and that the General Council consider the most suitable and satisfactory way in which this could be done.'[6] The motion was referred to the Finance and General Purposes Committee. One suggestion was that a plaque, recording d'Egville's service to the Association, be put up within the Palace of Westminster. Roland Robinson explained that the rule in Parliament was that nothing could go on the walls nor could a statue be erected in honour of anyone associated with the House of Commons until ten years after his death. He then reported that he had discussed the matter in London. D'Egville had stated firmly that he would like a testimonial in cash. He had rejected all other suggestions, including one that his portrait be painted and hung in the offices of the General Council. Krishnamoorthy Rao objected strongly to a cash testimonial in view of the 'liberal pension' he was already receiving. Finally it was agreed, Rao dissenting, that the Chairman should sign a letter to all branches, inviting them to contribute to a testimonial fund.

The proposal that d'Egville should write the history of the Association was also referred to this Committee. Roland Robinson reported that d'Egville had asked for £2500 a year for two years to carry out this work. The Committee was incensed by this demand, although £2500 was no more than the annual salary of the Secretary-General at this time. The Council decided that the project should be reconsidered by the Salaries and Management Committee in London.

A full session of the Council was devoted to the new draft of the constitution, ably prepared by M. E. Currie, assisted by Betty May. It was, he said, primarily a work of clarification and contained no fundamental changes. There were, however, several important changes. The first was that the Chairman and Vice-

Chairman should be elected annually, thus embodying in the constitution the convention approved in Canberra in 1959. The second was that the immediate past Chairman should remain a member of the Council for the year following the completion of his term of office. The third change was the addition of three members to the Council, one to be elected each year and to hold office for three years. The Council itself would elect these members from among those who had experience and understanding of the Association. Their election would not affect the representation on the Council of the branches to which the three members belonged.

The addition to the Council of the 'three wise men', as they came to be called, was important. It indicated that the Council was awakening to the need for stability and continuity in the affairs of the Association. It was, however, and still is extremely difficult to ensure continuity in a parliamentary organisation. The appointment of the three new councillors was an advance. The Association was, moreover, fortunate in the members who were elected and who served it well.

The fact that the immediate past Chairman would in future serve for one year after completing his term of office was a further advance. It meant that as Vice-Chairman, Chairman and immediate past Chairman he would serve for three years. The new provisions, approved by the Council, for submission to the General Meeting in London in the following year, nevertheless presented dangers. Roland Robinson had served for two years as Vice-Chairman. He was elected Chairman at the end of the meetings in Kampala. He served for a further year after the London conference in 1961. He then became eligible for election as one of the 'three wise men' and was, in fact, elected. Thus he served for seven years. Roland Robinson was an able Chairman and councillor, and he made a considerable contribution to the work of the Association. The danger arose when a member less able and devoted to the Association was nominated by his branch for the chairmanship. The Council itself was obliged to accept the nomination. Indeed, mainly for this reason the provision that the immediate past Chairman remained on the Council for a year was subsequently rescinded.

Another innovation in the constitution was the creation of the office of Honorary Treasurer. The Council agreed that he should be the councillor or one of the councillors from the branch in the country in which the headquarters office was situated. This meant another United Kingdom branch member on the Council. The Treasurer would be able to countersign cheques and keep a watching brief on expenditures. The Secretary-General had always been Treasurer, as in the Inter-Parliamentary Union, where this arrangement still holds. In the mood of the Council in 1959–60, when it was asserting a new control over the Association, the election of an Honorary Treasurer as financial watchdog, had a strong appeal. In practice over the years the members nominated by the United Kingdom branch, and elected to this office, with a few notable exceptions, have lacked financial expertise and have tended to regard the office as a formality.

The Salaries and Management Subcommittee, to which several matters were referred, was, it was stated in Kampala, set up by the Council in Canberra in

1959. This is not clear from the minutes. The Subcommittee was formally established in Kampala. It comprised the Chairman and Vice-Chairman, the Treasurer, the United Kingdom councillor, and any other councillor who happened to be in London at the time of a meeting.

In effect, the United Kingdom branch was now in charge of the Association's affairs. It had been brought about by the skill of Alfred Robens, the powerful Labour politician, by Roland Robinson, the wealthy Conservative backbencher, and by Lockhart, the branch Secretary, in managing the Council. There were other factors, like the fall of d'Egville and the invitation of the branch to host the conference in London in 1961, which had been envisaged and embodied in their plan of campaign.

The dominance of the branch, which d'Egville had feared and had warded off for so many years, was now a fact. It proved to be a stabilising and on the whole beneficial control, but it was to be short-lived. The Association, like the Commonwealth itself, was evolving and a new system of managing its affairs was soon to be introduced.

The Council meetings in Kampala during four days, often with evening sessions, were busy and productive. Consideration was given to arrangements for the conference in London in the following year and a conference agenda was drafted. Certain branches were advanced in status. Salaries of headquarters staff were reviewed. The finances of the Association were closely examined.

Another important matter which the Council dealt with in Kampala was the appointment of the new Secretary-General.

Notes

1. Conference Report (Canberra, 1959), pp.25–6.
2. Ibid., p.21.
3. Ibid., pp.21–2.
4. **Agenda and Opening Speakers, Canberra, 1959**
   Economic Cooperation within the Commonwealth – Rt Hon. Harold Holt, Treasurer and Leader of the House of Representatives (Commonwealth of Australia) and Rt Hon. Lord Mills, Paymaster-General (United Kingdom)
   Problems of the Underdeveloped Countries of the Commonwealth – A. S. Sinanan, Leader of the Opposition (Federation of the West Indies) and Hon. Roland Michener, Speaker of the House of Commons (Canada)
   Technical and Educational Development and Cooperation within the Commonwealth – Hon. P. O. S. Skoglund, Minister of Education (New Zealand)
   Parliamentary Control of Statutory Bodies – Shri S. V. Krishnamoorthy Rao, Deputy Chairman of the Rajya Sabha (India)
   International Affairs and Defence – Rt Hon. Robert Menzies, Prime Minister (Commonwealth of Australia) and Hon. J. Allen Frear, US Senator (Delaware, USA).
5. Minutes of General Council Meeting, 14 September 1960.
6. Ibid.

13 Into the 1960s, 1960–63

At the meeting of the Council in Kampala on 14 September 1960, the Chairman, Sir Alister McMullin, reported that the post of Secretary-General had been advertised in British and Commonwealth newspapers. The Vice-Chairman, Sir Roland Robinson, had also written to the Presidents of all branches about the post. There had been 146 applicants. Many were senior officers, recently retired from the armed forces. A number were former members of the British foreign and colonial services, who had had distinguished careers. The acting Secretary-General, S. A. Pakeman, had read all applications and had compiled a shortlist of 19 names.

The Chairman proposed that, before appointing a subcommittee to consider the applications in detail, councillors should discuss the qualifications which they looked for in the new Secretary-General. As stated in the minutes of this meeting,

> In the ensuing discussion it appeared that the overwhelming preference was for a man young enough to give many years' service to the Commonwealth Parliamentary Association. It was felt that he should not be a retired colonial civil servant or a retired senior officer of the armed forces. It was desired to find somebody who could mix well with all members of the Association, who understood the work of the Association and believed in its ideals and principles, and who was prepared to function in accordance with the wishes of the General Council.[1]

Most of the councillors, in particular those from the United Kingdom, were determined that the new Secretary-General should not direct or manage the Association. The Council's chief executive officer must be its servant. In future the Council would be in charge, giving explicit instructions to the Secretary-General and his staff. Thus a senior officer from the armed forces, accustomed to exercising authority, was unacceptable.

This policy appeared sound. In fact, it ignored the transient nature of the membership of the Council and the General Meeting. At its London meeting in 1961 the Council had 31 members of whom 21 were new members. It was unrealistic to expect a Council of this size, comprising mostly new members who would serve for only one year, to be able to manage the affairs of a vigorously growing international organisation. It was even more unrealistic to expect the General Meeting, the final authority in the Association, to function effectively. All of the delegates, appointed by their branches to attend the conference, were the members of the General Meeting. The great majority were new to the CPA and in no position to exercise authority over its affairs.

In 1960–61 there was an inner group which had the confidence of the Council and was virtually in control. Roland Robinson and his supporters could expect to be on the Council for some time. The problem of continuity had apparently been resolved. This was, however, a shortsighted view. Seven years later further constitutional changes were made in an attempt to get greater efficiency and continuity in the management of the Association. Hostile memories of d'Egville, whose achievement was to have created the CPA, inhibited recognition of the fact that the Secretary-General and the Secretariat alone could provide the stability and continuity essential to the Association.

The Council, having agreed on the qualities it was looking for in its new chief executive officer, then set up a subcommittee to consider the applications and recommend the most suitable candidate for appointment. The members of this subcommittee were the Chairman and Vice-Chairman, both *ex officio*, Krishnamoorthy Rao (India), Casely Hayford (Ghana), Arthur Creech Jones (United Kingdom), V. T. Joyce (Federation of Rhodesia and Nyasaland), Peter Howson (Australia) and Ong Yoke Lin (Federation of Malaya). The subcommittee met in the evening of 14 September 1960. It quickly reached the conclusion that none of the candidates satisfied the requirements laid down by the Council. It then considered the names of three men, mentioned to them, who had not applied, but who might be interested. Recalling the meeting of the subcommittee and later of the Council, one of its members felt that it had all been in the nature of a charade. The decision had already been made by the Chairman and the Vice-Chairman that Robin Vanderfelt should be appointed Secretary-General. Indeed, the Chairman was so confident about the outcome that he had cabled Vanderfelt on the day before the subcommittee and Council meetings, telling him to stand by for a telephone call on the following morning.

Vanderfelt fully satisfied the qualifications required by the Council. He was 39 years of age. He had been educated at Haileybury – a school which had produced many distinguished men in British public life, including the former Prime Minister, Attlee – and Peterhouse, Cambridge where he read history. He had been a captain and adjutant in the Royal Berkshire Regiment, serving in India and Burma from 1941 to 1945. He was Assistant Secretary of the United Kingdom branch, 1949–59. The ten-year period had given ample opportunity for him to show his talent for getting on well with members both at Westminster and from the Commonwealth. He was also a competent and dependable administrator. It was, moreover, clear that he was not a man to take matters into his own hands. He was always punctilious in referring all decisions to his seniors. Robinson and the Council could be confident that he would never follow the example of d'Egville or assume any authority which was not explicitly granted to him. His great caution and keenness to be at all times the servant of the Council and the Association were factors of special importance at this time.

Lockhart, as Secretary of the branch and his chief, had undoubtedly had it in mind that Vanderfelt might become Secretary-General, and had begun grooming him for the job. Instead of himself attending the memorable conference in India in 1957 as Secretary to the United Kingdom delegation, he had insisted that his assistant should go, especially as he had spent three years in India during the war. It gave Vanderfelt the opportunity to meet many of the most prominent members of the Association at this time. He made an excellent impression and earned for himself a fund of goodwill. At the same time Lockhart was protective towards his protégé. He was careful not to involve him in the plans to oust d'Egville, and Vanderfelt, who was always discreet, did not seek to know. Thus he appeared to be the ideal man for the office. In Kampala none opposed his appointment. Roland Robinson offered him the post by telephone, as he had arranged, and the offer was readily accepted. He took up his duties on 15 May 1961.

The Council also advanced S. A. Pakeman to the post of Secretary-General from 1 July 1960, when d'Egville retired. On 7 January 1961 he would be 70 and would retire. The Council requested, however, that on retirement he should continue as Editor of Publications and also have the title of Deputy Secretary-General.

Early in 1960 the Association's Secretariat had moved from 24 Abingdon Street, which it had occupied for some ten years, to the second floor of 7 Old Palace Yard. The new accommodation was conveniently situated and pleasant, but far from spacious and indeed was inadequate. It was, however, generously provided by the British government free of all charges for rent, rates and maintenance. It was into this accommodation that the Secretary-General and the Secretariat moved. The new offices seemed to emphasise the break with the past. But as Gordon Walker observed, with d'Egville's departure 'a certain dash and drama went out of the Association's record'.[2]

The major CPA event in 1961 was the 7th Commonwealth Parliamentary Conference, held in London from 25–30 September. Following the decision of the Council, confirmed by the General Meeting on 26 September 1961, this was the first of the annual conferences of the Association. Sir Roland Robinson was Chairman. In the absence of an invitation from a branch to host the conference in 1962, the office of Vice-Chairman was vacant. Sir Alister McMullin acted as Vice-Chairman. In July 1961 an offer came from the Federation of Nigeria branch to host the 1962 conference. The name of R. A. Njoku, Minister of Transport and Aviation, was put forward for the office. It was circulated to the Council and approved.

The Council met on 22 and 23 September 1961. The Vice-Chairman, R. A. Njoku, confirmed the invitation of the Nigerian branch. Next, Dato'Ong Yoke Lin extended an invitation from the Federation of Malaya branch to host the 1963 conference. It was accepted with acclamation. The Council conducted its routine business, appointing the new Finance and General Purposes Committee and reappointing the Salaries and Management Subcommittee. On the proposal of the South Australian branch, it approved the attendance at its meetings of branch Secretaries as observers, both in the interest of continuity and also to enable them to assist the councillors from their own branches. It admitted new branches and advanced others in status.[3] The Salaries and Management Subcommittee had been empowered to give interim approval of new branches and changes in status, and this authority was confirmed and extended. It also approved a suggestion from the Southern Rhodesia branch that a CPA tie should be produced for members with the same design of Mace and Black Rod crossed as in the Association's badge.

The General Meeting of the Association took place in the Royal Gallery of the House of Lords on 26 September 1961. An early item of business was the presentation of the testimonial fund to Sir Howard d'Egville. The sum donated amounted to £2027 12s 9d. In a dignified speech d'Egville expressed his thanks. He then spoke of the importance of close relations with the US Congress, which exercised great influence on American foreign policy. He recalled the conference in Canada in 1943, attended by members of Commonwealth Parliaments and of the US Congress. He had been delighted to learn in February 1961 that a plaque had been put up in Room 16 of the Canadian House of Commons to commemorate this meeting. As Honorary Secretary of the British-American Group, an office he still held, he had organised a conference in Bermuda in February 1961, and planned to make it an annual event. He concluded: 'Although now we have only the United Kingdom and Canada with this particular liaison with the Congress, yet we hope that other countries will come in later on. It should then form not only an Atlantic Community but a community of the free parliamentary democracies of the English-speaking world with a background of common institutions and common language.'[4] Although in his eighties he still had breadth of vision. Sadly this particular vision was to fade, and the links which he had forged between the Association and Congress were to weaken.

The General Meeting devoted much of its time to the re-draft of the constitution, produced by M. E. Currie, and already examined by the Council in Kampala in 1960. With only minor amendments this constitution was approved. The Council met again on 28 September 1961 to take action on the basis of the new constitution. Clause 24 provided for the appointment of the three new councillors. Sir Alister McMullin was appointed for the three-year term; Sardar Hukam Singh was appointed for the two-year term; Roland Michener was appointed for the one-year term. Roland Robinson, the retiring Chairman, would serve for a further year as immediate past Chairman. In his place R. A. Njoku was elected Chairman and Dato' Ong Yoke Lin Vice-Chairman.

The delegates – 125 in number and representing 64 branches, together with 17 branch Secretaries – arrived in London on 2/3 September 1961. They included a large number of Speakers and Ministers. Among the most eminent was the leader of the Federation of Nigeria delegation, Alhaji Shehu Shagari, who was to be elected President of the Federation in 1979 and re-elected President in 1983, but deposed in a military *coup* on 31 December 1983. The United Kingdom delegation, which included eight Privy Councillors, was led by Rt Hon. Duncan Sandys, Secretary of State for Commonwealth Relations. The Secretary of State for the Colonies, Rt Hon. Iain Macleod, was also a member of the delegation. From the associated group in the US Congress, four Senators attended the conference. Senator J. William Fulbright, Chairman of the Senate Foreign Relations Committee, was the leader of this delegation. Dr George B. Galloway was its Secretary.

All delegates were accommodated in the Savoy Hotel in London. They spent the weekend in London attending various functions. At an informal meeting summoned in the hotel on 5 September 1961, the delegates approved by a large majority the admission of the press to the conference. It was a significant departure from the previous practice of excluding the media. On 6 September 1961 the delegates were divided into two groups. One visited Jersey, Cardiff, Bristol, Edinburgh, York or Bury St Edmonds and Birmingham. The other group visited Coventry, Blackpool, Glasgow, Edinburgh and Northern Ireland. Delegates reassembled in London on 21 September. On the following evening they attended a reception at St James's Palace, given by all the Commonwealth High Commissioners in London.

On 25 September 1961 H.M. the Queen opened the conference in an impressive ceremony in Westminster Hall. Some 2000 guests were present. The BBC televised and broadcast the proceedings. On entering Westminster Hall the Queen and the Duke of Edinburgh were received by the Chairman and Vice-Chairman of the General Council, who presented the leading members of the Association attending the conference. In his speech, inviting the Queen to open the conference, Roland Robinson reminded all present that this was the Association's jubilee year. In her address the Queen recalled that she had been the guest of the Association in Westminster Hall eight years earlier on the eve of her coronation. She then declared the conference open.

The Prime Minister, the Rt Hon. Harold Macmillan, expressed thanks to Her Majesty. He welcomed the delegates on behalf of the government and people of the United Kingdom. Speaking of the Commonwealth he said:

> The form and composition of our association may change. For the Commonwealth is an organic structure, bound by no rigid constitutional frame. But the spirit remains the same. The Commonwealth depends for its vitality and usefulness on cross-fertilization of ideas through personal exchanges. Sometimes these take the form of ministerial meetings – Prime Ministers, Finance Ministers, and so forth. But Ministers, even Prime Ministers, are, happily, but transient figures – like phantoms they flit across the stage, and with few exceptions are soon forgotten. Even Parliamentarians come and go. Nevertheless, while we enjoy our brief authority, it is of the greatest value that we should constantly meet and discuss our common problems.[5]

The Vice-Chairman, R.A. Njoku, spoke. The Queen and the Duke of Edinburgh then proceeded down the central aisle of the Hall. They later attended a reception at Lancaster House to which all delegates and Secretaries to delegations were invited.

The nine sessions of the conference took place in the Royal Gallery of the House of Lords. The subjects discussed and the opening speaker in each session are set out in the notes to this chapter.[6]

The General Council next met in Lagos, Federation of Nigeria, on 3 November 1962. At this meeting it discussed at some length a resolution from the Society of Clerks-at-the-Table. The Society was founded in 1932. Its purpose is to enable parliamentary officials throughout the Commonwealth to meet and discuss parliamentary practices and to foster interest in their duties, rights and privileges. Membership of the Society is open to Clerks and other parliamentary officials in Commonwealth legislatures. Since its foundation the Society has published an annual volume, *The Table,* containing articles and notes on parliamentary privilege, on constitutional law in relation to Parliament, and on other matters of professional interest to Clerks of Parliament. The officials of the Society are appointed by the Clerks of the Parliament at Westminster. The management of the Society is the responsibility of the Clerk of the Overseas Office under the direction of the Clerks of the two Houses.

The Society's resolution, dated 25 September 1961, proposed that the CPA should facilitate and finance meetings of its members annually, biennially or triennially, and further that they, together with those present as Secretaries of delegations, should be able to hold a meeting during the conference period.

Members of the Society were keenly aware of the arrangements for Clerks and parliamentary officials in the Inter-Parliamentary Union. The Association of Secretaries-General of Parliaments is an autonomous section of the Union. Its purposes are similar to those of the Society, and it publishes a quarterly bulletin entitled *Constitutional and Parliamentary Information.* Its meetings take place at the same time as meetings of the Union which finances its activities.

The Council recognised the need to foster close relations with the Society of Clerks-at-the-Table. With the exception of the Canadian and United Kingdom branches, the Clerks of legislatures are the Honorary Secretaries of their branches. Their work has always been of vital importance to the Association. The efficiency and level of activity of branches have been to a large extent dependent upon them. The Society's resolution presented the opportunity to strengthen the position of Clerks and parliamentary officials while at the same time promoting the study and understanding of parliamentary institutions, a key purpose of the CPA itself.

At its Lagos meeting the Council readily confirmed the need for close cooperation with the Society. It also approved the idea that the Society should be able to organise a meeting of its members, present as Secretaries to delegations. On grounds of finance, however, it declined the proposal that the Association should provide for the attendance of Clerks, who would not otherwise be present at conferences.

Relations between the Association's Secretariat and individual Clerks throughout the Commonwealth have always been close, and cooperation between them could hardly be improved. This factor is of the greatest importance in providing continuity in the work and in maintaining the spirit of community and friendship within the Association.

The Clerk of the Overseas Office at Westminster, known until 1968 as the Fourth Clerk-at-the-Table, plays a special role in this relationship. This senior Clerk has the main function of liaising with other Parliaments and in particular of providing paliamentary information and responding to requests for assistance from Commonwealth and other legislatures. His services are in constant demand, a fact which reflects the great respect which other countries have for the Parliament at Westminster. Indeed, it may be stated that this office makes an important contribution to the maintenance of parliamentary government in many parts of the Commonwealth.

Since 1965 meetings of the Society have regularly taken place at the time of the annual conferences of the Association. The Clerks of the Houses of Commons at Westminster and in Ottawa are invited as guests of the host branch. The Clerk of the Overseas Office also attends to arrange the Society's meeting, his travelling expenses being met from the budget of the Clerk of the House.

In Lagos the Council received confirmation from Dato' Haji Mohamed Noah bin Omar, Speaker of the House of Representatives, Federation of Malaya, that his branch would host the conference in 1963. The Council accepted two further invitations, one extended by Donald Sangster, Deputy Prime Minister and Minister of Finance, Jamaica, to host the conference in 1964, and another from the New Zealand branch to host it in 1965. The flow of invitations was an indication of the vigour of the Association and the strength of support for it.

At the conclusion of its meeting the Council elected Dato' Noah Chairman and Donald Sangster Vice-Chairman of the Association. It also re-elected the Rt Hon. Arthur Creech Jones to be Treasurer. Shortly after his return to Kuala Lumpur, however, Dato' Noah suffered a heart attack and on medical advice he gave up the chairmanship. (He subsequently made a complete recovery.) The Federation of Malaya branch nominated Dr Lim Swee Aun, Minister of Commerce and Industry, to succeed him. In January 1963 Arthur Creech Jones' two-year term on the Council ended. He was succeeded by G. M. Thomson. Bernard Braine, the other United Kingdom councillor, became Treasurer.

The General Meeting of the Association took place on 6 November 1962 in the Chamber of the House of Representatives in the National Hall, Lagos. The report of the Finance and General Purposes Committee that the Association would have a deficit of £30,000 in the next two years was a matter of concern. The delegate from Tasmania, L. Costello, argued strongly that in future the Association should provide only economy class travel for delegates, not first class as had always been the practice. Considerable savings would be made if members were prepared to travel economy class. Objections to this proposal were that delegates as a rule had to travel great distances to the conference venue, and further that in most countries Ministers and senior civil servants travelled first class. The Salaries and

Management Subcommittee was asked to consider this proposal in making a survey of probable expenditure over the next five years.

For the 8th Commonwealth Parliamentary Conference, the delegates, 104 in number, with 21 Secretaries from 53 branches of the Association, assembled in Lagos on 14 October 1962. After a three-day programme in Lagos they were formed into three groups for a 15-day tour of the three regions into which Nigeria was then divided. A delegation of three Senators from the associated group in the US Congress and also two Deputies from the Irish Republic arrived to take part in the sessions on international affairs and defence.

The conference was formally opened on 5 November 1962 by the Governor-General, H. E. Dr the Rt Hon. Nnamdi Azikiwe. A guard of honour was mounted by the Federal Guard of the Royal Nigerian Army. He was received at the entrance to the National Hall by the Chairman, who presented to him the Vice-Chairman, immediate past Chairman, leaders of the main branch delegations, and representatives of other delegations. In their speeches in this opening ceremony both the Governor-General and the Prime Minister, Alhaji the Rt Hon. Sir Abubakar Tafawa Balewa, stressed the importance to Nigeria of the Commonwealth and the common heritage of parliamentary democracy and respect for the rule of law. They welcomed the fact that the first three conference sessions were to be devoted to the subject of 'The Role of the Commonwealth in the Modern World'.

The subjects discussed and the opening speakers in the nine sessions of the conference are set out in the notes to this chapter.[7]

The speeches in the three sessions on the role of the Commonwealth were of a high standard and showed a deep commitment. Several speeches were outstanding, especially those of the Hon. Paul Hasluck, Dr the Rt Hon. Charles Hill, Alhaji the Hon. Shehu Shagari, Maharaja P. K. Deo and Harold Winch from Canada. All of the speakers agreed that the strength of the Commonwealth derived from the devotion of its members to the principles of parliamentary democracy and the rule of law. It came also from the freedom, tolerance and the 'sense of family' which characterised the Commonwealth. There was, however, a reluctant recognition of the fact that a common defence or economic policy was no longer possible. The discussion, extending over some nine hours, revealed a strong idealism and at the same time a sense of frustration because the Commonwealth was apparently powerless to tackle problems facing the world and especially the underdeveloped world.

The Rt Hon. Sir John Vaughan-Morgan, United Kingdom, made the final speech at the end of the third session. He perhaps summed up the mood of the delegates, when he concluded: 'After listening to all the discussions, I am somewhat confused as to what the role of the Commonwealth is. But surely we are all agreed that, even though we do not know what that role is, we are all of us certain that the Commonwealth has a great role to play in the modern world.' This statement received loud applause.[8]

In the last session of the conference, when the subject was 'The Character,

Role, and Potentialities of the Commonwealth Parliamentary Association', Sir Roland Robinson purported to relate the history of the CPA from the coronation luncheon in 1911 without once mentioning Sir Howard d'Egville. He spoke, too, of the decision implemented in this conference to allow controversy. As Dr Hill later stated, 'This is the very first conference not stultified by being limited to non-controversial topics.'[9] In fact, the agenda was similar to earlier ones. Controversial issues might have been raised as readily at previous conferences. In Lagos there was, however, a greater frankness and readiness to criticise, and the criticism was directed at the United Kingdom. A new mood was discernible. Britain's declared intention of joining the European Economic Community meant for many delegates that the Commonwealth would be weakened and, indeed, that Britain was turning its back on the Commonwealth. British denials were not credited.

A statement by the British Prime Minister, the Rt Hon. Harold Macmillan, was seized upon by the leader of the Nigerian delegation. The statement was as quoted: 'The Commonwealth can no longer be described as a family, but with the constitutional process of growth from dependence to independence of member countries so largely accomplished, the Commonwealth is perhaps best regarded as a group of friends and relations...'. This was interpreted to mean, in the words of the Nigerian leader, that 'Britain apparently regrets the emancipation of her former colonies and resents the presence of what may be called hybrids in her family'.[10] Among delegates, especially African delegates, there seemed to be a feeling that having achieved independence and sovereignty they must now criticise and even attack the country which had ruled over them. This tendency was to be more pronounced in future conferences.

In this final session several delegates voiced their concern about the future of the Association. In the main they were expressing frustration. They had taken part in the previous sessions when the major problems facing the Commonwealth and the world were discussed. The Association, like the Commonwealth, seemed to them to be impotent. It had no machinery to debate resolutions and still less to implement them. They were rebelling against the fact that the CPA had been established and maintained as a deliberative, not an executive, organisation.

The Chairman and others pointed out that, in educating and promoting understanding among MPs, the Association was a major influence in Commonwealth affairs. Most of the delegates were visiting Nigeria for the first time. All that they had seen in Nigeria had made a profound impact upon them. This was not something that could be evaluated in terms of direct results, but it was undeniably of the greatest importance. The New South Wales delegate, C. B. Cutler, after making suggestions for the better running of the conference, concluded: 'Broadly speaking the future of the Commonwealth Parliamentary Association will continue to be limited to increasing the understanding between member nations of the Commonwealth...'.[11]

In seeking a constructive future for the Association, A. Casely Hayford from Ghana proposed that it should explore the possibility of setting up a

Commonwealth University with branches in the various regions, and also a Commonwealth Bank. Ideas of this kind were to arise from time to time in the future, but were outside the Association's terms of reference.

One of the most forthright expressions of frustration came in the speech of V. K. Joshi, the delegate from the Aden branch. He could not accept that the Association was merely a debating society, as another delegate had described it. It was not justified, he said, that so much money, 'taxpayers' money from the whole of the Commonwealth', should be spent on conferences which provided 'some sort of deliberation and consultation and nothing more'.[12] He proposed that

> a committee be appointed to investigate and report to the General Council of the Association the best method in which mutual understanding and cooperation between the various Commonwealth countries can be better assured, the way in which the Commonwealth can be strengthened and maintained as a world force, and whether for this purpose an organisation such as a Commonwealth Cooperation Organisation can be established; and, if so, what its form and main functions should be.[13]

Another suggestion made by Joshi concerned the perennial problem of continuity. His solution might have gained wider support, but for the cost involved. He expressed himself clearly.

> I come from a small country, and naturally I am the only one who has come from there, and in the past there was also only one member. From other countries also I hear that some delegates have attended this time for the first time. Imagine what happens to a man in this position. He comes to an august assembly of this kind; he does not know the level of the debates; he does not know very much about the procedure of this conference; he gets to the General Council; he does not know what happened in the past; therefore more often than not he is lost in all this. I therefore suggest that each branch should send not less than two members and that at least one of the members must be a person who has attended the previous year's conference. If there are four members, then 50 per cent of the members should be those who have attended the previous year's conference so that continuity would be kept.[14]

The Aden resolution was discussed and then referred to the General Meeting which was to meet in Kuala Lumpur in November 1963. There it was debated at length. Finally, on the suggestion of Sir Roland Robinson and with the concurrence of the delegate from Aden, it was agreed that the resolution should provide the theme for a session in the full conference to be held in Jamaica in November 1964.

The new Secretary-General, Robin Vanderfelt, was quickly swept up by the work of the Association. He and his colleagues were directly involved in the arrangements for the London conference in 1961. At the end of May 1962 he accompanied the Chairman, R. A. Njoku, on an extensive Commonwealth tour, visiting 16 branches of the Association in 14 countries. In April 1963 he went to Geneva to meet the Secretary of the Bureau of the Inter-Parliamentary Union, M.

de Blonay. In one brief visit he was able to demolish the barrier, erected mainly but not entirely by both d'Egville and de Blonay, which had separated the two parliamentary organisations for decades. In June 1963 he visited Kuala Lumpur to discuss arrangements for the conference to be held there in November 1963. On his return journey he called on Sir George Oehlers, President of the Singapore branch. In New Delhi he had talks with Shri S. V. Krishnamoorthy Rao, Sardar Hukam Singh, and others. In Malta he called on the Speaker, the Prime Minister and the Leader of the Opposition. In August 1963 he flew to Ottawa and from there to Regina, Saskatchewan, to attend the Fifth Canadian Area Conference. From Regina he went to Toronto and then on to Jamaica for preliminary discussions with the Vice-Chairman, Donald Sangster, about the 1964 conference.

The General Council met in the Senate Chamber of the old Parliamentary Building in Kuala Lumpur on 24 October 1963, when 34 members attended. It had a lengthy agenda and a second meeting proved necessary. This took place on 4 November, when 44 councillors were present. The Chairman, Dr Lim Swee Aun, presided at both meetings.

Among the councillors present a larger number than in the past had attended previous meetings. They were well informed about the Association's work and enthusiastic in their support. The office-holders and the three councillors, appointed under Clause 24 of the constitution were, of course, experienced. Others, like Sardar Hukam Singh and Shri S. V. Krishnamoorthy Rao from India, Bernard Braine (United Kingdom), Senator T.P. de Zoysa (Ceylon), Alhaji the Hon. Shehu Shagari (Nigeria), Al-Haj Chief A. S. Fundikira (Tanganyika) had attended two or three conferences and Council meetings and were able to make informed contributions.

The question of delegates and councillors travelling economy class, raised at the General Meeting in Lagos, had been referred to the Salaries and Management Subcommittee. Its report was now before the Council. The Subcommittee recognised that the change from first to economy class travel would achieve substantial savings. It recommended, however, that the threatened deficit in the Association's finances should be met by a 20 per cent increase in branch contributions to CPA funds. This would produce a small surplus, while enabling delegates to continue to travel first class. The Council adopted this proposal.

The Subcommittee had also made recommendations on the conduct of conference proceedings, which the Council approved. The appointment of a Conference Steering Committee was the main innovation. The three office-holders and the three Clause 24 councillors would be the members of this Committee, which would be responsible for the running of the sessions and the resolution of any procedural problems that arose.

A number of suggestions from the Secretariat concerning publications had been referred to the Finance and General Purposes Committee. It had agreed that the circulation of the Secretary-General's *Newsletter* should be expanded to include branch Presidents, Executive Committees and delegates to conferences. In March

1963 Robin Vanderfelt had issued to councillors and branch Secretaries the first *Newsletter*, intended to keep them and through them the members of their branches informed about current and future CPA activities. The *Newsletter* had been widely welcomed.

The Committee also agreed that the revised and expanded memorandum on *Payments and Privileges of Commonwealth Members of Parliament* should be printed, not mimeographed. It welcomed a new leaflet, entitled *Aims, Constitution, and Activities of the CPA*, which had been produced in the Secretariat. It was designed to publicise the Association and to aid branch Secretaries in recruiting new members. The Committee, however, rejected two proposals. One was for the production in the Secretariat of a handbook of practices and procedures in Commonwealth Parliaments. The other was for the expansion of the contents of the *Report on Foreign Affairs* to include the countries of the Commonwealth.

One subject, recorded regularly in the annual reports of the Association and closely followed by the Council, was the holding of regional and area conferences. The Seventh Australian Area Conference took place in Canberra in June 1963. Every branch in the area had thus hosted an area conference. Since they had been initiated by the Tasmania branch in 1951, these conferences had demonstrated the vitality of the Australian branches and had attracted full support. There was now, however, a move to reach beyond Australia and to embrace branches in the South-East Asian and Pacific regions. The proposal agreed in Canberra for discussion was that biennial conferences should take the place of area conferences and that they should be held alternately in Australia and in a member country in the South-East Asian and Pacific regions.

Another proposal considered by the conference in Canberra was that each year a selected overseas branch or group of branches should be invited to send a small delegation and a Secretary to Australia as the guests of the Federal and state branches. This proposal would complement the valuable practice, initiated by the Victoria branch in 1960, thanks to the farsighted attitude of the Premier, Sir Henry Bolte. This practice was to fund three members, one from each of the political parties represented in the legislature, to make Commonwealth tours each year. The Premier stipulated only that they should visit the United Kingdom and as many other branches as possible. This practice has since been adopted in South Australia and New South Wales.

In Canada, too, the area conferences have become a regular event. The Fifth Canadian Area Conference took place in Saskatchewan from 11–17 August 1963, and was attended by 41 members, including 9 Speakers, together with branch Secretaries. Special guests were the Speaker of the House of Representatives, Trinidad and Tobago, Arnold Thomasos, and from Jamaica, Roy McNeill, Minister of Home Affairs.

In federations as vast in area as Canada and Australia, these conferences have undoubtedly fostered a sense of unity and nationhood. In South-East Asia the branches had held a series of regional conferences since 1952. In the early 1960s it was felt that the conferences had contributed directly to the formation of the

Federation of Malaysia. The Prime Minister of the Federation of Malaya, Tunku Abdul Rahman, had first publicly mentioned the idea of a broader federation at a luncheon in Singapore on 27 May 1961, given by the Foreign Correspondents Association. Two months later, in July 1961, delegates from the Malaya–Borneo group of the Association met in Singapore at the Eighth Regional Conference. The broader federation was the chief subject of discussion. A Malaysia Solidarity Consultative Committee was set up. This Committee and the branches in the region were in part responsible for the formation on 16 September 1963 of the Federation of Malaysia.

At the General Meeting of the Association, held in Kuala Lumpur on 7 November 1963, the delegate from Singapore, the Hon. Yong Nyuk Lin, spoke with enthusiasm about the value of regional conferences and expressed the hope that similar conferences would be held in Africa and the Caribbean. Indeed, arrangements were already in hand for a conference of the Caribbean region to be held in Barbados. The first African regional conference was hosted by Zambia in 1969.

The 9th Commonwealth Parliamentary Conference took place in Kuala Lumpur from 4–9 November 1963. Delegates, numbering 121, together with 17 Secretaries, representing 66 branches, assembled in the capital earlier. They were taken on extensive tours of Malaysia, including the new states of Sabah and Sarawak, and Singapore. The associated groups in the US Congress and in the Irish Republic were not represented. The US Senate had appointed a delegation to be led by Senator Fulbright, but the business of Congress, especially concerning the passage of the Foreign Aid Bill, prevented their attendance.

The formal opening of the conference took place on 4 November 1963, when H.M. the Yang Di-Pertuan Agong, King of Malaysia, officiated in the banquet hall of the spacious new Parliament Building. It was an occasion of great and colourful splendour. The Yang Di-Pertuan Agong, accompanied by his consort, H.M. the Raja Permaisuri Agong, were heralded by a fanfare of trumpets on reaching the ceremonial entrance. The Chairman of the Association, Dr Lim Swee Aun, received them and presented the Vice-Chairman, Donald Sangster.

On entering the building Their Majesties were greeted by the Prime Minister and Deputy Prime Minister of Malaysia, by the President of the Senate and the Speaker of the House of Representatives. The Chairman then presented the members of the General Council, the leaders of main branch delegations, and representatives of other branches.

On the invitation of the Chairman, H.M. the King declared the conference open. The Prime Minister of Malaysia then spoke on the history of his country and the forging of the federation. He referred also to the current tension and difficulties caused by the confrontation, provoked by Indonesia. The Vice-Chairman, Donald Sangster, expressed thanks on behalf of the delegates to Their Majesties, to the Prime Minister, and to the Malaysian branch.

The three broad subjects on the conference agenda, which were discussed in eight sessions, and the names of the opening speakers are set out in the notes to this chapter.[15]

Throughout the conference discussions the earnest concern of delegates for cooperation in resolving the problems of the underdeveloped countries and raising their living standards was strongly expressed. It was acknowledged that the great disparities between the 'haves' and the 'have nots' were a source of suspicion and antagonism. At the same time there was recognition and appreciation of the contributions which Britain and other more developed countries were making. The note of acerbity and even of hostility towards Britain, which had been discernible in Lagos a year earlier, nevertheless became more pronounced in Kuala Lumpur.

The leader of the United Kingdom delegation, the Rt Hon. Robert Carr, MP in opening the session on 'Technical and Educational Cooperation' gave a wide-ranging account of all that Britain was contributing in this field. Bernard Braine, then Joint Parliamentary Secretary at the Ministry of Health, United Kingdom, spoke on the needs of many countries for trained doctors and nurses, and health services. He gave figures illustrating the extent of British endeavours to meet these needs. Canadian, Australian and New Zealand delegates spoke of the educational and general aid programmes maintained by their countries.

The demand of delegates from many of the underdeveloped countries was for greater assistance and capital investment. 'After years of colonial exploitation', it was said, the United Kingdom had 'a great moral obligation' to give more and more.[16] The Kenyan delegate, C. M. G. Argwings-Kodhek, and the two delegates from Singapore, Yong Nyuk Lin and Enche A. Rahim Ishak, spoke provocatively about British colonial exploitation. They drew a vigorous response from the Rt Hon. Viscount Boyd of Merton, who as Alan Lennox Boyd had been Colonial Secretary. 'I would say to the Hon. Delegate, Mr Argwings-Kodhek, from Kenya', Lord Boyd declared, 'that Kenya's great potential wealth – the product mainly of European enterprise and agricultural skill – is at the service of the nation, but it is endangered not in any way by the consequences of colonialism or by any dispute between the old colonial powers and the peoples of Kenya, but by the deep tribal divisions and suspicions in Kenya itself which we must all hope will prove groundless and will disappear.'[17]

'As to the two delegates from Singapore', he continued,

I should just like to say this – Exploitation indeed! Stamford Raffles landed in Singapore in 1819. In six months the population of Singapore had grown from 154 to 5000 people; in two more months it was 10,000; in four years it was a great port, and in seven years it was second only to Calcutta as a great port in the Far East. People of many races flocked there – voting with their feet – flocked there to seek and find in that island the rule of law and religious toleration. [Hear! Hear!] And generations of colonial officers, with the ungrudging help of all races in Singapore, have made the development of that great city state – in education, health, housing and trade – one of the greatest achievements in Asia. [*Applause*] There was Dr Ridley, whom I had the honour of saluting on his 100th birthday, who, as a young Director of Kew Gardens in London, by maintaining the fertility of the Brazil rubber plant in charcoal and bringing it out here to Singapore, may be said to be the father of the rubber industry of Singapore and Malaya.[18]

The sessions on Commonwealth trade were opened in a masterly speech by Tun Tan Siew Sin, the Minister of Finance, Malaysia. He reviewed the possibilities of expanding trade, especially in primary products. He spoke highly of the surveys of Commonwealth production and trade, and of the commodity reports, produced by the Commonwealth Economic Committee. He suggested that the Committee should extend its analytical work into the future by examining trade and production patterns and also the problems implied in the economic policies and developments in member countries. This suggestion drew support from a number of delegates.

The leader of the Nigerian delegation, Alhaji Shehu Shagari, spoke of the instability of commodity prices as the greatest threat to the primary-producing countries. He again expressed 'resentment' of Britain's decision to seek entry into the EEC. Gerard Montano, leader of the delegation from Trinidad and Tobago, also spoke impressively on commodity prices. He commended arrangements like the Commonwealth Sugar Agreement.[19] Several African delegates were critical of Britain's trade with South Africa.

The final sessions on 'International Affairs and Defence' were opened by the Rt Hon. Walter Nash, a former Prime Minister of New Zealand. He presented the subject in broad terms, speaking of the East–West conflict, Soviet Russia and the People's Republic of China, South Africa, and the conflict between India and Pakistan. A wide-ranging discussion might have followed. The African delegates were intent, however, on discussing South Africa and on condemning Britain for maintaining relations with and supplying arms to the Republic.

At one stage arguments broke out between delegates from India and Pakistan, not only over Kashmir but also India's relations with the USSR. The delegate from Kenya, C. M. G. Argwings-Kodhek, rose on a point of order to complain that the conference had heard enough about the 'family matters' of India and Pakistan.[20] Senator Magnus Cormack from Australia said that he supported the Chairman's decision to allow the delegate from Uganda to speak on South Africa and his decision to allow Pakistan to raise the Kashmir issue and to allow India to reply. He suggested, however, that enough time had already been given to these problems. He reminded the conference, 'We are here to try to defend the institutions of Parliament and not to line up faction against faction.'[21] The appeal was ignored.

The leader of the Nigerian delegation, Alhaji Shehu Shagari, in a dignified speech, referred to the new Organisation of African States and its purpose. He also condemned the regime in South Africa. Another delegate alleged that in the break-up of the Central African Federation, Southern Rhodesia had been favoured in the sharing out of the armed forces. Bernard Braine, the United Kingdom delegate, in a forceful speech, rejected these allegations and also the criticisms of Britain. The speeches continued, reaching an angry level with a provocative speech by C. M. G. Argwings-Kodhek of Kenya.

Incensed by this and other speeches, the leader of the New Zealand delegation, W. J. Scott, rose to state, in his words,

How concerned I am that this conference appears to be developing into a medium for an attack on Great Britain.... A few minutes ago, when Pakistan and India got into an argument, the general consensus of opinion seemed to be that this was a domestic matter between two member countries which should not be raised publicly – and I completely agree with it – I hope it does not rise again.... But as soon as that was ended we find a lot of other delegates are quite happy to get up and kick at the United Kingdom, and nobody seems to worry about it at all. ... This is the first conference that I have attended and I have been concerned to find this state of affairs. I do not know whether this has happened before and I do hope that this would be the last conference that I would attend if this state of affairs is going to develop further...[22]

The rancour which marked some speeches was, however, confined to the conference sessions. Away from these sessions cordial relations between delegates continued. There were, of course, some exceptions, but in general this applied in Kuala Lumpur and in subsequent conferences. In the tours, at receptions, and over meals in hotels delegates mingled and talked together. Indeed many have taken the view that these informal meetings gave real opportunities for exchanges and mutual understanding and were far more valuable than the formal sessions in conference for which speeches were often prepared with a far wider audience in mind. Such informal meetings perhaps illustrate the sense of community – that indefinable quality which sets Commonwealth meetings apart from the conferences and meetings of the United Nations, the Inter-Parliamentary Union and other international organisations, and which is of the essence of the Commonwealth.

Notes

1. Minutes of General Council Meeting, 14 September 1960.
2. P. Gordon Walker, *History of the CPA*, p.72.
3. Appendix A, this volume, pp.300–302, lists all branches with the dates of their formation or reformation and their advances in status.
4. Reports of General Meeting, 26 September 1961, pp.6–7.
5. Conference Report (London, 1961), p.4.
6. **Agenda and Opening Speakers, London, 1961**
   The Place and Functions of the Commonwealth in the World – Rt Hon. Duncan Sandys, Secretary of State for Commonwealth Relations (United Kingdom)
   Economic Cooperation in the Commonwealth and Economic and Social Development in the Underdeveloped Countries of the Commonwealth – L. H. E. Bury (Commonwealth of Australia); Alhaji the Hon. Shehu Shagari, Minister of Establishments (Federation of Nigeria); J. J. M. Nyagah, Deputy Speaker of the Legislative Council (Kenya); Rt Hon. Edward Heath, Lord Privy Seal (United Kingdom)
   Constitutional and Parliamentary Practice in the Commonwealth – Hon. Shri M. Ananthasayanam Ayyangar, Speaker of the Lok Sabha (India); Sir George Oehlers, Speaker of the Legislative Assembly (Singapore)
   International Affairs and Defence – Hon. Dato'Ong Yoke Lin, Minister of Health and Social Welfare (Federation of Malaya); Senator J. W. Fulbright, Chairman of the Senate Foreign Relations Committee (USA).

7. **Agenda and Opening Speakers, Lagos, 1962**
   The Role of the Commonwealth in the Modern World – Hon. Al-Haj Chief Abdullah Saidi Fundikira, Minister of Justice (Tanganyika); Dr the Rt Hon. Charles Hill (United Kingdom); Dr H. M. Horner (Canada)
   Regional Cooperation within the Commonwealth – Alhaji Shehu Shagari, Minister of Establishments (Federation of Nigeria); C. G. E. Harker (New Zealand); Tuan Haji Abdul Khalid bin Awang Osman, Assistant Minister of Rural Development (Federation of Malaya)
   International Affairs and Defence – Paul M. C. Hasluck, Minister for Territories (Commonwealth of Australia); Amirali Habib Jamal, Minister of Communications, Power and Works (Tanganyika)
   The Character, Role, and Potentialities of the Commonwealth Parliamentary Association – Rt Hon. Sir Roland Robinson (United Kingdom).
8. Conference Report (Lagos, 1962), p.71.
9. Ibid., p.220.
10. Ibid., p.72.
11. Ibid., p.222.
12. Ibid., pp.228–9.
13. *Loc. cit.*
14. *Loc. cit.*
15. **Agenda and Opening Speakers, Kuala Lumpur, 1963**
   Technical and Educational Co-operation – Rt Hon. Robert Carr, Secretary for Technical Cooperation (United Kingdom)
   Promotion and Expansion of Trade between Commonwealth Countries – Enche' Tan Siew Sin, Minister of Finance (Malaysia)
   International Affairs and Defence – Rt Hon. Walter Nash (New Zealand) and Sardar Hukam Singh, Speaker of the Lok Sabha (India).
16. Conference Report (Kuala Lumpur, 1963), pp.43, 45, 48–9 and *passim*.
17. Ibid., p.100.
18. *Loc. cit.*
19. Ibid., pp.129–30.
20. Ibid., p.187.
21. Ibid., p.190.
22. Ibid., pp.199–200.

14 The Changing Commonwealth, 1964–66

During the 1960s the Commonwealth expanded in membership and changed in character. The expansion was dramatic. In 1956 at the time of the Suez crisis, the Commonwealth comprised eight member countries;[1] in 1965 the number was 22; in 1969 it was 28; and in 1970 it was 32.[2]

The increase in membership was only one of the factors bringing profound change in the Commonwealth. Among other factors were the growth in the number of international and regional organisations in which the new nations could participate; the spread of multilateralism in the economic field; the rivalries of the super-powers as they began to take an interest in Africa; and the increasing orientation of Britain towards Europe. Most important of all at this time, however, was the emergence of the African bloc of nations, and its impact on the Commonwealth.

In 1956 the eight member countries accepted certain principles as fundamental to membership of the Commonwealth. These principles were: respect for the rule of law, for parliamentary democracy and for the rights of minorities, and loyalty to the Crown or, in the case of the Indian Republic, acknowledgement of the Monarch as Head of the Commonwealth. Another important principle was that of non-interference in the domestic affairs of member countries. This applied not only within the Commonwealth, but had also been embodied in Article 2(7) of the Charter of the United Nations.

Multi-racialism or racial equality in the Commonwealth was a new principle. It was much debated, although as Professor Bruce Miller observed, 'The full implications of this protean term were rarely considered...'.[3] At their meeting in 1964 the Prime Ministers accepted multi-racialism as 'an objective of policy'.[4]

During the decade the old principles were shown to be less and less relevant to membership of the Commonwealth. This was due primarily to the assertiveness of the newly independent African states. Indeed in 1960, which has been called 'Africa's Year',[5] the practice of non-intervention came under severe strain in the discussion of South Africa's membership.

A referendum was to be held in October 1960 to decide whether South Africa should become a republic. The Prime Minister, Dr H. F. Verwoerd, had stated that as a republic the country would remain in the Commonwealth, subject to the formal approval of the other member countries. In the 1960s, however, with the changing attitudes, reflected in Macmillan's 'wind of change' speech, the racial policies of the South African government raised acute problems. Other member countries found apartheid repugnant. At the same time they were bound by the principle of non-intervention. The Sharpeville incident in March 1960, when police fired on a demonstration, killing 67 Africans, inflamed world opinion; within the Commonwealth it provoked a crisis.

Addressing Parliament in Kuala Lumpur on 26 April 1960, the Prime Minister, Tunku Abdul Rahman, declared: 'Those who rule South Africa today ... do not conform to our Commonwealth ideas and ideals of human rights and justice, and I am beginning to think whether a country like South Africa has any right to be within this family of nations...'. In the same speech he was careful to distinguish between the Sharpeville shooting, which he condemned, and the policy of apartheid which was 'purely a domestic and internal affair of South Africa.[6]

The Australian Prime Minister, Robert Menzies, strongly upheld this distinction. Speaking in the House of Representatives on 29 March 1960, he said: 'I should offer a word of warning against the danger of abandoning certain principles which are of very great importance not only in the British Commonwealth of Nations but also in the world at large.... The greatest of these principles is that one government ... does not interfere in matters which are within the domestic jurisdiction of another ...'.[7]

At Westminster on 8 April 1960 a strongly worded resolution was debated. It deplored racialist policies in South Africa and called on the government to impress upon the South African Prime Minister at the Commonwealth Heads of Government meeting in May 1960 British abhorrence of these policies. In an outstanding speech Bernard Braine reminded the House that at the United Nations Britain had consistently abstained in votes on resolutions condemning racialist policies in South Africa. The reason was that such resolutions were contrary to the Charter, and not because Britain approved or condoned such policies. The dilemma was whether, holding such views, Britain should seek to drive South Africa from the Commonwealth. This would, he argued, be totally wrong. 'But', he said, 'we cannot balk the issue as to whether what is going on in South Africa is consistent with the spirit and letter of the Commonwealth relationship ... however we approach this problem, we cannot be silent about it.'[8]

At the meetings of Heads of Government in May 1960 and in March 1961 the principle of non-interference was nevertheless observed to the extent that no one demanded the expulsion of South Africa. But there was mounting pressure from among the Africans and Asians for the exclusion of South Africa. Several countries threatened to leave the Commonwealth if South Africa remained a member. Indeed, the future of the Commonwealth was placed in jeopardy over this issue. It was resolved by the decision of Dr Verwoerd to withdraw the application of South Africa to continue as a member after becoming a republic.

The withdrawal took effect on 31 May 1961.

The next major crisis arose in Central Africa. The Federation of Rhodesia and Nyasaland had been established in 1953. The Africans in Northern Rhodesia and Nyasaland were opposed to it. They were the responsibility of the British Colonial Office. Southern Rhodesia had had self-government since 1923 and came under the Commonwealth Relations Office. In the United Kingdom the general elections in 1959 confirmed Macmillan's Conservative government in power. He and his new Colonial Secretary, Iain Macleod, were determined to hasten the pace of decolonisation, especially in Africa. In December 1963 both Nyasaland and Northern Rhodesia seceded from the Federation. Malawi (Nyasaland) and Zambia (Northern Rhodesia) became independent in 1964. Southern Rhodesia under its white-settler regime demanded independence. The British government refused to concede independence until there were guarantees of eventual 'majority rule'. In November 1965 the Southern Rhodesian government, led by Ian Smith, made a unilateral declaration of independence.

The rebellion of the Southern Rhodesian regime threatened to break up the Commonwealth. It gave rise to bitter exchanges between the African states and the United Kingdom, which had to endure much intemperate abuse. At one stage Ghana and Tanzania broke off diplomatic relations with Britain, because they were dissatisfied with British handling of the crisis. Civil war ensued in Southern Rhodesia, but still the Smith regime remained in power.

In August 1979 the Heads of Government meeting in Lusaka managed to find a formula acceptable to all parties. It was an achievement for all who took part in the meeting. In the following eight months a cease-fire was followed by a constitutional conference and elections, and finally the independent republic of Zimbabwe emerged. It was a striking demonstration of the value of the Commonwealth in providing machinery for close consultation, and it restored some of its lost prestige.

The withdrawal of South Africa from the Commonwealth and the independence of Zambia, Malawi and Zimbabwe were seen as African victories. In achieving them the African states demonstrated their attitude towards the Commonwealth. They acknowledged the principles of parliamentary democracy and rule of law, but did not accept the convention of non-interference in the domestic affairs of member countries, whenever African interests were involved. Moreover, they insisted that, no matter what other principles might have been established, racial equality should be the predominent principle of Commonwealth membership. By racial equality they meant in practical terms African equality with, indeed dominance over, white communities in Africa. Under their influence the Commonwealth lost something of its flexibility and privacy, and was in danger of splitting into racial groups on some topics.

The CPA was affected by these and other major developments. At times during the 1960s it seemed that the Association itself was threatened. On each occasion the threat faded away. All branches, including those in Africa, showed a deep reluctance to do anything that might damage or diminish the Association.

Nevertheless the Africans were determined to play a leading role in its activities and to make changes that would further their objectives. While all countries sought to use the Commonwealth to further their national interests, the African approach was at times arrogant and aggressive. Their mood was expressed by many African delegates to the Jamaica conference in 1964, and perhaps most baldly by the Attorney-General of Uganda, Mr G.L. Binaisa, who said: 'Mr Chairman, these conferences must realise that Africa is on the go; that Africa is not going to be taught by other nations how to govern itself, that Africa knows where Africa is going . . .'.[9]

The force of African feeling over South Africa and Rhodesia was felt during the conferences of the Association. As well as angry attacks on the British delegations, there were demands for resolutions to be voted by the conference, expressing Commonwealth solidarity on key issues.

In November 1959 at the opening of the conference in Canberra, the Australian Prime Minister, Robert Menzies, said:

> One of the great features of these gatherings is that we do not meet to attack each other; we do not meet to exacerbate any difference that may exist; we meet primarily to achieve an understanding of each other and of each other's problems, to get a concentration of mind on the great elements of unity that we have in common, to develop our personal contacts, our personal friendships, and a greater mutual understanding of the parliamentary system in every country represented. That, though it can lead to vigorous discussion, is the kind of meeting that we all like, because its object is not to record differences, not to pass resolutions, not to engage in propaganda, but to achieve understanding and a willingness to assist each other mutually and in a friendly way.[10]

This described well what had always been accepted as the nature and purpose of the Association's plenary conferences. In Jamaica in 1964 this proved to be no longer true and a new acerbic note was sounded.

The 10th Commonwealth Parliamentary Conference, held in Kingston, Jamaica, in November 1964, brought together 124 delegates and 24 Secretaries from 67 branches. The first Chairman of the General Council, Senator A.W. Roebuck, still robust at the age of 86, was present. It had been hoped that all previous Chairmen could come and special invitations were sent, but only four were able to accept. Four Senators from the US Congress were led by Senator John J. Sparkman. The House of Representatives was unable to send a delegation. The associated branch in the Irish Republic declined the invitation.

The Chairman of the General Council was Donald Sangster, the Deputy Prime Minister and Minister of Finance of Jamaica. He had been deeply involved in the Association's activities for some years, and was one of its keenest supporters. As Chairman, presiding not only over the conference sessions but also over the meetings of the Council and the General Meeting, he was outstanding for his tact, fairness and sincerity, and for his ability to defuse situations which seemed about to erupt. All liked and respected him. The fact that the 1964 conference was so successful was due in large part to his contribution as Chairman and host.

The Council first met on 9 November 1964 in Montego Bay. Five further meetings proved necessary and were held later in Kingston. The councillors included a number of distinguished members who had contributed much to the Association or who were to do so in the future. Among them were Dr Lim Swee Aun (Malaysia), Sir Alister McMullin (Australia), Bernard Braine (United Kingdom), Miss Joan Vickers (United Kingdom), Peter Howson (Australia), Florizel Glasspole (Jamaica), Saied Mohammed (Trinidad and Tobago), Senator Ashford Sinanan (Trinidad and Tobago), G. L. Binaisa (Uganda), Hugh Stanley (Zambia) and Shri Krishnamoorthy Rao (India).

The Chairman welcomed the councillors. Then, before any business could be taken, Senator T. M. Chokwe, President of the Senate of Kenya, rose on a point of order. His delegation was embarrassed, he said, by the presence of delegates from Southern Rhodesia, which refused to honour the high ideals of the CPA. He called on those delegates to withdraw. Unless there was a special reason why Southern Rhodesia should remain, the Kenya delegation would be forced to reconsider its position.

The Attorney-General of Uganda, G. L. Binaisa, at once rose in support. The Southern Rhodesian government was defying the British government and all members of the Commonwealth. Other countries, particularly Jamaica and those of Eastern and Central Africa, had, he said, shown the world that many races could live together in one country, enjoying the same rights and owing the same duties.

Councillors from Tanzania, Zambia, Ghana, Nigeria, Ceylon, Sierra Leone, Pakistan, Malaysia and India all spoke in support of the withdrawal of the Southern Rhodesian delegation from the conference. The New Zealand councillor, J. H. George, protested that the Southern Rhodesian Parliament had been elected in accordance with the constitution, conferred by the United Kingdom. The delegation was entitled to be present under the constitution of the Association and should remain.

The discussion lasted nearly two hours. The Afro-Asian councillors presented their case strongly but with dignity and restraint. The Chairman had to rule on the point of order and he did so firmly and persuasively. The CPA conference, he said, had no jurisdiction over the internal affairs of any other country. The Commonwealth Prime Ministers' meeting, in which he personally had taken part, had accepted this position. Further, he emphasised that all present must be presumed to believe in the rule of law and adherence to the constitution. He then read the relevant clauses of the Association's constitution under which it was clear that the Southern Rhodesia branch was entitled to send a delegation. He could not, therefore, accept the point of order. The discussion that the Council had had would, he hoped, achieve the result intended, namely, to let the Southern Rhodesian representative know that nobody on the Council accepted the principle of minority government. He then adjourned the meeting for a coffee-break.

The issue was not raised again when the meeting resumed. All knew that it was bound to arise at a subsequent meeting when the application of the Southern

Rhodesia branch for a change of status was considered. Meanwhile the Australian delegation was disturbed by a rumour that the African group were planning to attack the White Australia policy.

Senator Chokwe as leader of the African bloc continued to assert the African presence. The reappointment of the Salaries and Management Subcommittee was questioned by him, and others joined in support. It was clear that they felt that the Subcommittee was dominated by United Kingdom councillors and they wanted this changed. In the meantime the subcommittee was reappointed.

The Council next met on 12 November 1964 in the Chamber of Gordon House, Kingston. One councillor present wrote: 'This, I suppose, is the most exciting meeting ever held in the CPA.'[11] At the start, Senator Chokwe reported that he had had a cable from Kenya telling his delegation to walk out if not satisfied with events.

The Chairman called on the leader of the United Kingdom delegation, Lord Taylor of Harlow, who had arrived in Jamaica on the previous evening, to open on the agenda item concerning the status of the Southern Rhodesia branch. It was unfortunate that the United Kingdom delegation, which almost invariably has strong leadership, should on this occasion have had an inadequate leader. Lord Taylor, Parliamentary Under-Secretary for Commonwealth Relations and the Colonies, began by saying that he was just an ordinary doctor, who suddenly found himself Secretary of State for Commonwealth Relations at a day's notice and that this was the first speech he had made on the subject. 'It certainly sounded like it,' one councillor observed.[12] The essence of the speech was a plea that members of the Council should do nothing to make the task of the Prime Minister, Harold Wilson, and the British government more difficult.

At once Senator Chokwe replied that, while he did not want to make difficulties for the British government, he could not accept Lord Taylor's request, especially since Ian Smith had just refused to meet a representative of the British government. The Kenya delegation refused to sit in the conference with delegates from Southern Rhodesia. G. L. Binaisa, leader of the Uganda delegation, then pointed out that the Southern Rhodesia branch was really asking for the auxiliary branch status which it had had before the formation of the Federation in 1953. The Council should, he said, reject the application, or it could suspend consideration of the matter for 12 months by which time the situation might have become clearer. Several other councillors from the Afro-Asian group supported this proposal. Others demanded an immediate decision. Any delay, they argued, would lead to the walk-out of many delegates.

The New Zealand councillor, Mick Moohan, stated that the Southern Rhodesia branch had a constitutional right to be represented at the conference. Unimpressed by the high-principled stand taken by many delegates, he went on to say: 'What are we here for in the CPA? We are here to gain information. It was a matter of seeing and understanding the full facts, which were not always reported in the press. In Pakistan he had heard about "Guided Democracy". He would like to learn from the Pakistan delegates what this meant. He thought there were two things – democracy and tyranny, and how could you guide democrats?'

Turning to the Tanzania delegation he said: 'We read in the paper that soon after the revolt in Zanzibar 12,000 Arabs were slaughtered.... We would like to hear from the Tanzanians exactly what happened.' He continued, addressing now the Ceylon delegation. 'Do you know that in Ceylon when we came through we found tens of thousands of Indians who haven't got a vote. Now that is not a nice thing to happen to Indians in the friendly country of Ceylon. But possibly Ceylon will be able to tell us whether this is true or not. All I am doing is seeking information.'[13] His speech was followed by a stream of points of order, lasting until the meeting adjourned for lunch.

The leader of the Southern Rhodesia branch, W. J. J. Cary, opened the afternoon session. He explained that his branch was composed of members from all parties, including Africans, coloured and others who agreed or disagreed with the government of the day. The branch, not the government, had elected the delegation, as under the CPA constitution it was entitled to do.

Florizel Glasspole (Jamaica), then made a statesmanlike speech, urging compromise. He said that, according to the CPA's constitution, the Southern Rhodesia branch had an unanswerable case, but the Council could not consider the matter solely in terms of the constitution. He urged the Council to defer its decision for 12 months, as suggested earlier by G. L. Binaisa (Uganda), and to accept that the branch would continue for the present with the status of an affiliated branch. This would mean that the branch would have only one delegate at the conference.

Feeling that the meeting was nearing a consensus, the Chairman argued persuasively for acceptance of Glasspole's compromise solution. Peter Howson supported him, as did a Kenyan and a Nigerian delegate. At this stage Senator Chokwe protested that he and others who shared his views were not interested in the constitution or the status of the Southern Rhodesia branch. They simply did not wish to participate in the conference if the Southern Rhodesia delegation was present. After the tea-break, while still protesting that the principles for which the CPA had been created should override the constitution, he reluctantly accepted the compromise proposal. It was then approved by the Council.

From the time the delegates arrived in Jamaica there had been intensive lobbying by the African delegates. They took the line that the continued rule by a white minority government in Southern Rhodesia was an affront to all other races. They appealed to the Asian delegates for support, arguing that the Afro-Asian members must unite to eradicate the last remnants of white paramountcy. It was an argument that Asian politicians could not openly reject. But many of them were embarrassed by this approach. Privately they assured fellow delegates from the 'old' Commonwealth that, while publicly they must support the African line, they would do all they could to moderate it and to find a compromise. The Southern Rhodesian delegate was partially ostracised. W. J. J. Cary was the leader, for, expecting to have auxiliary branch status, which would allow two delegates, a black Rhodesian opposition member, M. Mkudu, had been elected as the second delegate. He was severely harassed by the East Africans. They urged him to set up a Mau Mau movement among his people on his return. When Mkudu demurred, he was denounced as a 'black Judas'.[14]

The next meeting of the Council took place on 13 November in Gordon House, Kingston. The Chairman spoke about the Prime Ministers conference, held in London in July 1964. Sir Alexander Bustamente, the Prime Minister of Jamaica, had been indisposed, and he, Donald Sangster, as Deputy Prime Minister, had attended. For some time he had noted that individual Prime Ministers had expressed their support for the CPA, but it was, he felt, opportune for all collectively to pay tribute to the work of the Association. As a result of his initiative, the following reference was contained in the final communiqué of their conference:

COMMONWEALTH PARLIAMENTARY ASSOCIATION

The links between the countries of the Commonwealth are strengthened not only by cooperation between their governments in initiatives of this kind but even more by frequent personal contacts between individuals who share common professional interests.

The Prime Ministers recorded their support for the valuable work which the Commonwealth Parliamentary Association performs in bringing together members of the Parliaments of all Commonwealth countries. The British Government stated that they would be prepared, if other Commonwealth governments would do the same, to increase their contribution to the Association.[15]

The Chairman reported that the British Prime Minister had offered to increase the subvention to the United Kingdom branch by £30,000 a year. While still in London, the Chairman added, he had written to the Finance Ministers of the independent countries of the Commonwealth and to the Premiers and Chief Ministers of all other countries, states and provinces in which there were branches of the CPA, inviting them to respond to the initiative. From replies received to date it was clear that the great majority would take suitable action.

The leader of the Australian delegation, Peter Howson, then spoke of the memorandum, produced by the Australian branch and already circulated to all branches. He explained that, following the release of the communiqué of the Prime Ministers conference, his branch had considered steps to be taken to strengthen the CPA. The communiqué had emphasised the value of the CPA's work in bringing Commonwealth parliamentarians together. His branch wished to propose further action.

The Secretary-General had calculated that, apart from meetings of Commonwealth Ministers and the conferences of the CPA, no more than 2 per cent of the total membership of some 7500, visited another Commonwealth country each year, and of these some two-thirds were coming to or going from the United Kingdom. Peter Howson said that his branch proposed a scheme to increase the scale of visits. It was especially important that there should be more visits of members between the new nations of Africa, Asia, and the Caribbean, and the older nations of Australia, Canada and New Zealand. The scheme would give a Member of Parliament the opportunity to visit another Commonwealth country once every six years. The Australian government was prepared to increase its annual subvention from £7000 to £17,000 for this purpose. The General Council office would coordinate these inter-branch visits. He hoped that other governments would be prepared to give similar support.

The Secretary-General reported that some 20 governments had agreed to increase the subventions to their branches to further the Australian scheme. On his suggestion it was agreed that the scheme should be discussed further in the conference session on 'The Future, Functions, and Role of the Commonwealth Parliamentary Association'.

Regional and area conferences had become an established part of the Association's annual programme. The Council noted that the 8th Australian Area Conference would take place in Tasmania in March 1965 and the 7th Canadian Area Conference in Alberta in August or September 1965. The Chairman reported that the Barbados branch would host the Caribbean regional conference in April 1965. It would be the third conference of the region, the two earlier conferences having been held in 1952 and 1960. Senator Chokwe said that in East Africa they were considering the holding of a regional conference, possibly including Central Africa, in 1965.

The Council had to deal with a heavy agenda which included consideration of publications, information services, publicity and finance. At its final meeting on 21 November it approved the recommendations of the Finance and General Purposes Committee concerning the staff and salaries of the Council office. This review had been undertaken on the initiative of Sir Alister McMullin and Peter Howson. As a result Ian Grey, Deputy Editor and Assistant Secretary-General, was appointed Editor and Deputy Secretary-General on the retirement of S. A. Pakeman on 31 December 1965. In the period 1 July to 31 December 1965 he would carry out the duties of Editor, while Pakeman would continue to serve as Deputy Secretary-General. Further it was agreed that the office of Deputy Editor would be created in place of the existing office of Deputy Editor and Assistant Secretary-General. The post was to be advertised in national newspapers throughout the Commonwealth. At the same meeting the salaries of the council staff were increased. (D'Egville had always kept staff salaries to a minimum.) This review and the consequent improvements were greatly appreciated.

The conference was formally opened on 16 November 1964, in the assembly hall of the University of the West Indies, Mona, Kingston, by the Governor-General, H. E. Sir Clifford Campbell. He had long been an active member of the Association as a Minister, as Speaker of the House of Representatives, and then as President of the Senate. Indeed, he had been in Nigeria in 1962 as a member of the Jamaican delegation, when his appointment by H.M. the Queen as Governor-General was announced.

With full ceremonial the Governor-General was received by the Chairman, Donald Sangster, who presented the Vice-Chairman, W. B. Tennent (New

Zealand). Subsequently he presented the four past Chairmen, who were present, as well as councillors and others. As was now customary, the Chairman spoke and invited the Governor-General to declare the conference open. The Prime Minister and the Vice-Chairman also delivered speeches.

The conference agenda devoted no less than four of the eight sessions to the Commonwealth and the CPA. Two sessions were given to discussion of trade and aid, one to international affairs, and one to the role of Mr Speaker.[16] The discussions were on the whole amicable with far less of the tense racial undercurrents which had marked the Council meetings.

In the session on international affairs Dr K. D. Konoso (Zambia), made a polite appeal to the Australian delegation to persuade their government to 'do away with its white policy and allow races, other than white, to migrate to Australia'.[17] Senator Chokwe (Kenya) stated bluntly that 'the African is very suspicious of the white man' and also of the British, American and Russian imperialists.[18] G. L. Binaisa (Uganda) made a strong speech, asserting the major role which Africa and the recently formed Organisation of African Unity intended to play in world affairs in the future.

At one stage in the session, delegates became restive over the assertiveness of the Africans. Speaking on Commonwealth support for Malaysia in meeting Indonesia's policy of confrontation, R. Cleaver (Australia) said: 'My very good friends from the African states need perhaps to remember that a few less words about Africa and a few more positive words about support for other members of the Commonwealth might not be inappropriate.' This mild admonition drew applause from the conference.[19]

The leader of the Pakistan delegation, Chaudhri Cheema, made a lengthy statement on Pakistan's claim to Kashmir. The leader of the Indian delegation, Shri Krishnamoorthy Rao, made an equally lengthy reply, rebutting Pakistan's claim and asserting India's sovereignty over Kashmir. The Southern Rhodesia delegate, W. J. J. Cary, attempted to explain the situation in his country, but was so frequently interrupted by African delegates that the Chairman intervened in defence of his right to speak. The delegate from British Guiana, criticised British intervention in his country. The discussions as a whole in this session were lively and contentious, but good-tempered.

The session on 'Commonwealth Organisations' was concerned exclusively with the Commonwealth Secretariat and the Commonwealth Foundation. Both organisations had been proposed and approved in principle by the Prime Ministers meeting in July 1964. The background to this development was that some months earlier the British Prime Minister, Sir Alec Douglas-Home, had spoken publicly about 'giving the Commonwealth new meaning and new life'.[20] He made seven concrete proposals, some of which were later realised. The publicity given to this fresh approach to the Commonwealth stimulated other Commonwealth leaders to give thought to the subject. Dr Eric Williams, Prime Minister of Trinidad and Tobago, proposed the formation of five new Commonwealth organs, including a Secretariat. Kwame Nkrumah, President of

Ghana, suggested 'a central clearing-house to prepare plans for trade, aid, and development and serve all Commonwealth members equally'. Mrs Bandaranaike, Prime Minister of Ceylon, suggested 'some sort of conciliation machinery for disputes between members, provided they agreed'.[21] At their meeting the Prime Ministers reached agreement in principle that there was a need for a Secretariat and a Foundation in the Commonwealth.

Surprisingly the older member countries, all of which had in the past opposed the creation of such a central organ, now welcomed the idea of a permanent Commonwealth Secretariat. To Mackenzie King, as Prime Minister of Canada, any form of centralisation within the Commonwealth had been anathema. On 17 July 1964, however, the Prime Minister, Lester Pearson, reporting to the Canadian House of Commons, explained the decision as follows:

> There was one other proposal which appears at the end of the Prime Ministers' communiqué which in some respects is the most interesting of all the concrete proposals made. It became clear from the beginning of the conference that there was a strong desire on the part of the newer countries of the Commonwealth, the newer African countries, to have some kind of Commonwealth machinery, some kind of Commonwealth institution, a Commonwealth Secretariat established for the service of the Commonwealth as a whole. When I say this proposal was in a sense surprising, we remember it is not long since proposals for a Secretariat were regarded with fairly general suspicion as it reflected a tendency towards centralisation which in those early days was interpreted as meaning rule from Downing Street. It is significant to realise that pressures towards this kind of consultative centralisation ... come from the newer countries which in many ways are, or should be, most suspicious of the older members in that regard; but they have no fears of any such implication.... And so we support this proposal.... It is something we should try to work out on a genuine Commonwealth basis, yet at the same time it should be done without interfering with existing channels of communication, without confusing what is already in many respects a very satisfactory method of coordination and exchange of information. We must make sure that the basis of that new Secretariat is sound and that we are adding an institution of value and not simply an additional agency available for the free play of Parkinson's Law ...'[22]

There was some disagreement as to the extent of the functions of the Secretariat. In January 1965 senior officials from member countries met in London and produced a memorandum. In effect it gave the Secretary-General a free hand to extend the activities of the Secretariat in any way subject to his gaining sufficient support from Commonwealth governments. In an editorial *The Times* welcomed the new Secretariat, noting that there was some dissatisfaction with the administration of the British Commonwealth Relations Office and that the Commonwealth in future 'must be more than a British-based, British-inspired institution'.[23] The special appeal of a Commonwealth Secretariat was that it would be an independent entity. No longer would meetings of Prime Ministers and other Ministers be set up by Whitehall. It was part of the emancipation of the new from the old members of the Commonwealth and especially from Britain.

In Jamaica the delegates gave strong but not unanimous support to the creation of the new Secretariat. There were some who advised caution and warned of dangers. The Indian delegate from Rajasthan, Shri R. N. Mirdha, said that the functions to be undertaken by the Secretariat were already taken care of by many existing organisations. He stressed the value of the informality of approach within the Commonwealth which 'has grown and prospered because we have temporised and improvised as occasion demanded. That has lent strength to our relationships and an effort to introduce any rigidity by way of a Secretariat or other way may, I think, militate against this very informal spirit which has bound us up to now.'[24]

In welcoming the new Secretariat, John A. Farr (United Kingdom) said that it should function only in providing an information service. He went on to propose a Commonwealth Parliament. Senator Chokwe (Kenya) expressed full support for the Secretariat and also for the creation of a Commonwealth Parliament. He went further in proposing that the CPA conference might be transformed to provide a Commonwealth Parliament.

The Australian delegate, R. Cleaver, expressed the fear that the Commonwealth was in danger of becoming 'vastly over-organised'. The new Secretariat would be welcome only if it rendered real service to governments. The Commonwealth Foundation, with its task of promoting contacts between members of professional bodies was, however, of great importance. The new member countries were, he said, in desperate need of guidance in many professional fields.

In winding up the discussion Donald Chapman (United Kingdom) delivered a thoughtful and cautionary speech. 'We must not in my view', he said, 'set up bodies which conflict with our existing Parliaments, with parliamentary sovereignty in the individual nations of our great Commonwealth.' The Secretariat should not become a lobbying organisation on governments and Cabinets. He stressed three principles: first, the Secretariat should be small; second, its expenses should be shared by all Commonwealth governments; third, it must work on a thoroughly impartial basis. Further, since the Secretariat must not conflict with any of the Commonwealth governments, its role should be mainly to provide background information and to service ministerial meetings.

All who attended the Jamaica conference were agreed that it was an unforgettable experience. Each of the 19 conferences which the present writer has attended has had its own character. All have been successful, but certain conferences have been outstanding. The Jamaica conference belongs to the category of the outstanding. In Jamaica the friendliness of the people and the beauty of the island, the ability and warmth of the Chairman, Donald Sangster, and of the parliamentary officers, Dossie Carberry, Easton Soutar and Edley Deans, the rich hospitality and concern for the well-being of delegates, and the stimulus of the element of conflict, amicably resolved, were all factors in making it so memorable. There was another, indefinable, element admirably stated by Shri Mirdha from Rajasthan: 'The Commonwealth idea influences in a very subtle way,' he said. 'It is a sort of alchemy, which works in a very subtle but strong way,

Howard d'Egville, first Secretary-General (holding flowers) with staff members (from d'Egville's left), Sidney Pakeman, Betty May and Jack Fowler, arriving in New Delhi for the 1957 Commonwealth Parliamentary Conference.

Gerald Regan (Nova Scotia) signs the Overseas Members Register at the CPA Headquarters.

Donald Sangster (Jamaica).

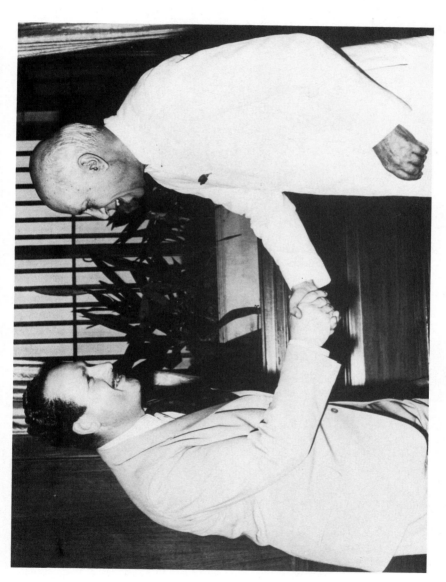

Bernard Braine (UK) and the Indian Prime Minister, Jawaharlal Nehru.

Richard Harrison (New Zealand) pays a CPA courtesy call on Tanzania's
President Julius Nyerere in 1979.

Allister Grosart (Canada).

Bal Ram Jakhar (India).

Tun Tan Siew Sin (Malaysia) presents a leather-bound copy of the 1970 conference Verbatim Report to Alister McMullin (Australia).

Hamilton Maurice of Trinidad & Tobago and the Australian Prime Minister, Harold Holt, at the Association's Headquarters in London.

Peter Howson (Australia).

The 1966 Commonwealth Parliamentary Conference in Ottawa. From left to right: W. W. Kalema (Uganda), Secretary-General Robin Vanderfelt and John Connolly (Canada).

A CPA delegation attends the state opening of Parliament in Kuala Lumpur, 1979. From left to right: Azizul Rahman bin Abdul Aziz (Clerk of Malaysia's House of Representatives), Richard Harrison (New Zealand), Secretary-General Robin Vanderfelt, Isaac Abecasis (Gibraltar), Omar Yoke-Lin Ong (Malaysia), Neil Marten (UK), Musa Hitam (Malaysia) and Charles Kerruish (Isle of Man).

Gerald Ottenheimer (Newfoundland) receives a souvenir of his 1984 Chairman's tour of India from Radha Nandan Jha of Bihar.

and it is here in Jamaica that we feel the influence of this alchemy more than in most places.'[25]

Lack of publicity for the work of the Association, especially the annual conferences, was a matter of concern to the Council and to the Secretariat. The days had passed when Prime Ministers and others looked upon the CPA as providing an ideal forum for making policy statements or expressing new ideas on the Commonwealth, as had happened in the 1920s and early 1930s. The press, radio and television were now preferred. Even Parliament which was the national forum for debate on major issues, was in many countries by-passed. National leaders often chose to speak by radio directly to their peoples rather than by way of their elected representatives. Another reason why the media took little interest in the CPA was that its activities were usually amicable in spirit and so considered to be not newsworthy. Indeed, the Commonwealth itself received scant coverage in the press of member countries, unless there was some serious crisis.

During the conference the *Daily Gleaner*, Jamaica's leading newspaper, gave full coverage to the discussions and interviewed leading delegates. Jamaican radio also broadcast a number of interviews. In the rest of the Commonwealth reporting of the conference was slight or non-existent. Before going to Jamaica the Deputy Editor had discussions in London with the Chief Editors of Reuters, the United Press Agency, the Canadian Press Agency and the London Press Service. All agreed that the conference was an important occasion. Reuters instructed its Caribbean correspondent to cover the whole conference. He sent full daily reports to London. There they were filed and forgotten, while other news, rated more exciting or more important, was circulated.

In Jamaica the Council appointed a subcommittee to consider ways of attracting publicity. It was noted that until 1960 the press had been excluded from CPA conferences and publicity had been discouraged. The London conference in 1961 had admitted the press for the first time. This conference was well reported in the newspapers of most Commonwealth countries. Press coverage of subsequent conferences was on a much smaller scale and soon faded out almost completely.

In considering new approaches the subcommittee welcomed the leaflet on the *Aims, Constitution and Activities of the CPA*. This had been produced in the Secretariat and was intended as a brief introduction for newly elected MPs, the press and others. The subcommittee was not in favour of daily press releases during conferences. They would impose a heavy burden on the small Secretariat of ten members. Moreover such releases would of necessity be selective and delegates who were not mentioned would feel resentful. But it approved a plan to produce within a few days of the close of a conference a short summary of the views expressed. This would be sent to Prime Ministers and other Ministers with a special interest in the subjects considered.

The discussions in Jamaica on Southern Rhodesia proved to be no more than a mild rehearsal for the fury let loose in the conference in New Zealand. The General Council held its first meeting in the Parliament Buildings, Wellington, on

15 November 1965. It dealt with routine business. The Chairman, Blair Tennent, then announced that following the unilateral declaration of independence he had sent a cable to the President of the Southern Rhodesia branch. It read: 'Very sorry indeed to learn of the decision of the Southern Rhodesia government. Under the circumstances sincerely regret must request you not to send delegate to our conference.'[26] Alhaja Shehu Shagari at once expressed appreciation of this action.

The Council then appointed a conference Steering Committee of five. Senator Chokwe (Kenya) moved that two additional members be elected. Six members were nominated. Ronald Ngala (Kenya) and J. P. Gyles (Jamaica) were elected. Dr P. V. J. Solomon, Deputy Prime Minister and Minister for External Affairs, Trinidad and Tobago, who was to play a prominent role during the conference, proposed that 'International Affairs' should be the first, rather than the last item on the agenda. He made this suggestion, he said, because the Rhodesian crisis could well determine the future existence of the Commonwealth. The Chairman explained that, since a strong delegation from the associated group in the US Congress was expected, such a change in the agenda at this late stage might prove inopportune. Arthur Henderson (United Kingdom) argued that the agenda was a matter for the Steering Committee. His motion to this effect was voted down by the African councillors and others. Senator Chokwe proposed that the first day of the conference should be devoted to Rhodesia and that the rest of the agenda should be referred to the Steering Committee.[27] This proposal was approved.

The African delegates thus had their way. Certain councillors, however, and especially those from Asia, were restive over Africa taking the centre of the stage. Dato' Wong Kim Min (Sarawak) protested that the problems of Asia were equally important, and that he could not accept that Asia should play second fiddle to Africa. Southern Rhodesia was, however, the burning Commonwealth issue of the day, and the Africans were a strong and united bloc. The Chairman stated firmly that, since the first day of the conference would be devoted to Rhodesia, the subject could not be brought up again in the two final sessions when 'International Affairs' were discussed.

The Council next met on 29 November 1965. Alhaji Shehu Shagari then moved the following resolution:

> That in view of the fact that the Rhodesia Parliament has condoned the act of rebellion by the illegal Smith regime and actively supported the actions of the said illegal regime it is hereby resolved that the Rhodesia branch be expelled from the Commonwealth Parliamentary Association forthwith and it is further resolved that when a legal and constitutional government is restored to Rhodesia an application for readmission of the said branch to the Association will be duly considered by this Council.

The resolution was carried unanimously.

Venues for future conferences were next considered by the Council. The invitation of the Canadian Prime Minister, Mr Lester Pearson, to hold the 1966 conference in Canada was accepted with acclaim. Senator John J. Connolly,

Leader of the Government in the Canadian Senate and Minister without Portfolio was elected Vice-Chairman. Like Donald Sangster, he was to prove an ardent supporter of the Association and a friend of many parliamentarians throughout the Commonwealth.

In fact, in Jamaica in the previous year, the Northern Ireland branch had issued an invitation to host the conference in 1966. The branch had, however, expressed readiness to withdraw it and to renew it at a later date to be arranged in consultation with the Council.

In Wellington, William Kalema (Uganda) extended an invitation to host the conference in Kampala in 1967. The invitation was unanimously accepted. The Council also expressed appreciation of the letter, brought by Dr Solomon, from the Prime Minister of Trinidad and Tobago, Dr Eric Williams, which stated that he hoped to invite the conference to meet in Port-of-Spain in the near future.

The proposals of the Australia branch for an increase in the number of inter-branch visits were discussed in Jamaica. The leader of the Australian delegation in New Zealand, C. F. Adermann, reported in detail on the proposed scheme and moved a resolution for its approval. It was adopted unanimously.

At its first meeting in Wellington the Council had set up a subcommittee on publications and another on the role of the General Council. At its final meeting on 2 December it dealt with their recommendations. (The report of the subcommittee on the role of the General Council is considered below.)

The subcommittee on publications, meeting under the chairmanship of Dr P. V. J. Solomon, carried out a thorough review. The Editor, who had taken up his duties on 1 July 1965, had submitted proposals for changes in both the *Journal of the Parliaments of the Commonwealth* and the *Report on Foreign Affairs*. The *Journal* had been unchanged during the years of publication. Its presentation was somewhat drab. The contents had been restricted always to summaries of the main proceedings of sovereign Parliaments, until 1961 when it became the practice to include one or two articles in each issue. It was now proposed that the *Journal* should have the short title of *The Parliamentarian* and that a new cover design bearing the symbol of the Mace should be adopted. The new title and format would reflect the editorial policy of devoting the *Journal* wholly to parliamentary rather than to CPA affairs. Among councillors and in the Secretariat some felt that it should be the *Journal* of the Association, reporting major events and discussions, as well as parliamentary matters. It was recognised, however, that there would be difficulties in producing a publication serving both purposes. Bearing in mind the fundamental purpose of the Association of promoting parliamentary government, the subcommittee agreed to recommend that the changes proposed should be adopted, subject to future review. The Council approved this recommendation.

The *Report on Foreign Affairs* had been unchanged in format and editorial policy during its 45 years of publication. It had always been restricted to reports on the affairs of countries outside the Commonwealth. The anomaly was that in disputes involving a Commonwealth and a foreign country, only the latter's policy would be reported. It was assumed that the Commonwealth country's policy would be reported in the *Journal*. This did not always happen. The Editor's proposal was that, following the same editorial policy of impartial and factual reporting, the content of the *Report* should be expanded to include Commonwealth countries. The subcommittee recommended and the Council approved this proposal.

The subcommittee welcomed the leaflet, entitled *Aims, Constitution and Activities of the CPA*. It considered that revised editions should be produced as necessary to meet demands from branches and outside organisations. It also welcomed the publication of the fourth revised edition of the information memorandum on *Payments and Privileges of Commonwealth Parliamentarians*. It agreed that copies should be sent free to all members of the Council and to branch Secretaries, but members and others should be asked to purchase their copies. At the time of mounting world inflation this memorandum was in demand. It provided governments and members with criteria and comparisons in the difficult task of reviewing the salaries and allowances in their own legislatures. The Secretary-General's newsletter, keeping branches informed about CPA activities, was warmly commended. The hope was expressed that branch Secretaries would ensure that it reached all their members.

At previous conferences, and especially in 1964, delegates from the smaller countries had spoken of their need for factual and authoritative data papers, relevant to items in the conference agenda. Delegates from the older Commonwealth countries were briefed and provided with documentation by their ministries. This was not possible in most of the smaller countries. For the conference in Wellington in 1965 the first *Dossier of Conference Data Papers* was produced in the Secretariat. A copy was distributed to every delegate. The dossier was greatly appreciated, and the Council directed that a similar dossier should be produced for future conferences.

The recommendation of the subcommittee concerning the verbatim report of conference proceedings gave rise to considerable debate. Since the first conference of the Association in 1911 a verbatim report had been regularly published as the official record or *Hansard* of the conference. The report had become an expensive production, especially as a copy was sent to every member. It was suggested that the distribution should be limited in future to councillors, branch Secretaries, and delegates as this would effect some economy. Then it was proposed that the report should be discontinued; in its place there should be published a full summary of the conference proceedings. This would mean a considerable economy. The subcommittee finally recommended this proposal.

The Council was divided over the recommendation. Dr Solomon as Chairman pressed the case for abandoning the expensive full report. Delegates would have copies of their own speeches, and a summary would be more likely to be read than the verbatim report. Many councillors disagreed with this argument. They considered that it was incompatible with the dignity of an international organisation like the CPA that it should not publish an official report of its annual conference. It was, moreover, essential that the archives not only of the Association but also of parliamentary and other libraries should contain a full official record of conference proceedings. This was important material for members interested in the CPA and for present and future scholars studying the history of the Commonwealth. A summary, no matter how full and skilfully written, would not meet these needs, and would fail to convey the real content and spirit of the conferences. The economy envisaged was of negligible value compared with the importance of these records for posterity. Dato' Wong Kim Min added that most delegates had had no previous experience of an international conference, and were attending their first CPA conference. By studying the verbatim report they could gain knowledge and confidence. Certain African delegates also spoke of the value of the verbatim reports in providing for new members examples of styles of speeches in Parliament and in conference.

Councillors from the United Kingdom, Canada and Australia spoke in favour of discontinuation; councillors from Africa and other countries argued strongly that publication of the verbatim reports should be continued as an essential part of the documentation of the Association's activities. On a vote in the Council the motion that the reports be continued was lost.

At the General Meeting of the Association on 7 December 1965, however, the Council's decision was overturned. Dato' Wong Kim Min moved a resolution.[28] It was strongly supported by Miss Joan Vickers (United Kingdom), Alhaji Shehu Shagari (Nigeria), Emanuel Shinwell (United Kingdom) and Rev. C.K. Dovlo (Ghana). Dr Solomon stated that his subcommittee and the Council itself had been divided on this proposal. In view of the very strong feeling of the General Meeting he would not attempt to press the matter. Dato' Wong's resolution that the verbatim conference report should continue to be produced was then carried unanimously.

The 11th Commonwealth Parliamentary Conference was opened with the customary ceremonial in the Chamber of the House of Representatives in Wellington on 30 November 1965. It was attended by 123 delegates and 24 Secretaries from 68 branches. Senator J. William Fulbright led a delegation of five from the associated group in the US Congress. The Chairman of the Association, Blair Tennent, invited the Governor-General, Brigadier Sir Bernard Fergusson, to declare the conference open. Following his speech, the Prime Minister of New Zealand, Keith Holyoake, addressed the delegates, recalling that his first experience of the CPA was in attending the 1946 conference in Bermuda. Senator John J. Connolly, the Vice-Chairman, spoke briefly, thanking the Prime Minister and the New Zealand branch for the admirable arrangements for the tours and for the conference.

The first of the 12 sessions of the conference took place on 1 December.[29] The subject was 'Rhodesia'. The opening speaker was Alhaji Shehu Shagari (Nigeria). He spoke with a quiet dignity which made the impact of his speech all the more powerful. He described Africa as a sleeping giant which was now awakening and staring everyone in the face with a challenge. He condemned the 'old-fashioned colonialism' that remained in Rhodesia and South Africa. 'Africans in colonial Africa', he said, 'demand equal rights, justice, and fair play, but are still groaning under the yoke of white supremacy and barefaced oppression while the rest of the world looks on.'[30] He paid tribute to Britain, saying, 'We all admire her noble and wise rule in the encouragement of colonial peoples to regain their freedom in an atmosphere of lasting friendship and equality which we all now enjoy.'[31] But, he continued, one of the greatest mistakes in her colonial policies had been her handling of the Rhodesian situation. British colonial history was replete with examples of the use of force against rebellion within the Empire. Why then had Britain departed from her traditional method of asserting her authority and prestige in the single case of Rhodesia? He suggested that Smith and his government would not have dared to defy the British Crown had they not got the assurance of the British government that force would not be used against them. He would leave the matter of economic sanctions, in which he had no faith, to the United Nations. At this conference, he said, they were more concerned

> with the future of this Commonwealth, which has always regarded Britain with the greatest respect and affection as the mother country; the Commonwealth to which we all freely chose to belong, because we share the same belief in the principles of democracy and the rule of law; the Commonwealth in which freedom, justice, and fair play have been the sacred ideals for which we have fought on the side of Britain in two world wars.... Will Britain now hesitate to fight any more for those principles and this same cause just because a few of her kith and kin are involved.[32]

Britain had been asked time and again to send troops to Rhodesia. 'It is incredible to perceive a great world power in a helpless dilemma for over two weeks in facing her responsibility to bring a handful of rebels to their knees.'[33]

This expression of the African attitude to the Rhodesian situation was reiterated not only by other delegates from Africa but also by delegates from Asia and the West Indies. It was notable that Shri Morarji Desai, the elder statesman who led the Indian delegation, while expressing his belief in non-violence, saw it as the duty of the British government to use force against the rebels in Rhodesia. He suspected, like many of the delegates, that the reason why military force had not been used was racial; whites would not be deployed against whites. Senator Chokwe expressed this view more strongly. The leader of the Malawi delegation, R. D. Chidzanja, spoke moderately. He said that his country benefited economically from its relations with Rhodesia. His government nevertheless gave its moral support to Britain in its task of establishing majority rule in Rhodesia.

An individual voice in the African bloc was that of J. J. Burnside, a white Zambian citizen. He referred to the 40,000 citizens of Zambia, living in Rhodesia, who would be directly involved if force was used. The African delegates who had spoken had used words like 'bloodshed', 'spilling of blood', 'military intervention', and they had no conception of what they meant in terms of human suffering.

The United Kingdom delegation seemed unprepared for this attack and unaware of the strength of African feeling. Its leader, Emanuel Shinwell, was angered, especially by the opening speech. He brusquely dismissed it for 'All the fine sentiments ... accompanied by the usual clichés and, of necessity, platitudes...'.[34] When interrupted, he responded as though dealing with a heckler at the hustings. Dame Joan Vickers made a strong and courageous speech, rebutting many of the allegations made by other delegates. She deplored the constant demand for the use of force and the spilling of blood. This would bring devastation and suffering to all peoples in Rhodesia. In particular she took Shri Morarji Desai to task for advocating force and so forsaking the great Indian principle of passive resistance and non-violence. She asked delegates to support sanctions and negotiations. Indeed, she quoted from the charter of the Organisation of African Unity, which required its members to pursue 'Peaceful settlement of disputes by negotiation, mediation, conciliation, and arbitration'.[35]

Delegates from the 'old' Commonwealth all condemned the rebellion of the Smith regime, but were unanimous in their opposition to the use of force. They supported the position stated by Joan Vickers. E. D. Mackinnon (Australia) said: 'I do suggest to those hotheads who would go in with tanks and guns that we peace-loving delegates here today have a responsibility not to allow such a situation to arise. It is quite obvious that there is a need to appreciate the reality of modern warfare.'[36] Pleas for restraint were made also by H. A. Blaize, Chief Minister of Grenada, and by Dato' Wong Kim Min, Sarawak.

During the day's debate on the Rhodesian situation, it became obvious that there was a clear racial division. Dr Solomon said: 'The dividing-line is sharp between those who support the United Kingdom and those who do not. What form does the line-up take? With disgust and horror I say that it is purely and entirely a matter of colour.'[37]

In these terms Rhodesia presented a severe crisis for the Commonwealth and the CPA. The vehemence of many speakers in the debate suggested that some delegations were ready to pack and depart and that the Commonwealth would suffer a fatal schism. It did not happen. The conference continued with all delegates taking an active part. Within and outside the conference sessions delegates continued to meet and talk together.

On the second day of the conference, discussion began on 'Economic Growth in the Commonwealth', which extended over four sessions. The opener in each session gave an outstanding review of the aspect of the subject to be considered. The speech of Shrimati Dr Anjanabai Magar (Maharashtra) on 'The Growth of Population in Relation to Resources' was especially notable. Indeed, the standard of the speeches of all who took part in these sessions was very high. A clear consensus emerged on the need for and application of technical and financial resources, on greater efforts to secure stabilisation of commodity prices, on agricultural cooperation, and the importance of restraints on population growth.

The tense and angry note which had marked the discussions on Rhodesia in the first two sessions was notably absent. This applied equally to the following sessions concerned with 'Parliamentary Government in the Commonwealth'. All confirmed their faith in democracy. The Africans in particular expressed their determination to build strong and stable democracies in their countries. There was a division of opinion on the one-party state. Some delegates extolled the advantages of such a system in Africa and defended it as democratic. Others saw it as leading to dictatorship and tyranny. Although strong disagreement was expressed, the mood of the conference remained amicable.

A full session was devoted to the Commonwealth Parliamentary Association. The opening speaker was Bernard Braine (United Kingdom) who gave a magisterial review of the developments which would strengthen the CPA in the future. His speech drew tributes from all delegates who took part in the session.

Two aspects of the Association, he said, called for urgent reform – the conference itself, and the lack of continuity in the governing body. Immediately after the Jamaica conference in the previous year a summary of the main views expressed was prepared by the Secretariat and sent to all Prime Ministers and other Ministers closely concerned. In Wellington delegates had had the valuable dossier of data papers, prepared in advance by the Secretariat, and they had certainly helped raise the standard of their discussions. Further, much more time had been allotted to the conference; there were 12 sessions, each of which was longer, so that the overall time allocation was as much as 50 per cent greater than in previous conferences. These were all important developments. A further gain, he suggested, would come from making use of committee sessions for some topics, and the Council had this under consideration.

Bernard Braine then said that he wondered whether there might not be a case for developing the conference into a deliberative assembly along the lines of the Council of Europe, which had an Assembly and a Committee of Ministers. This would, of course, link the conference proceedings more closely with governments. Developments of this kind had been put forward in the CPA over many years. He spoke of the discussions of this idea in the United Kingdom earlier in the year. The Prime Minister, Harold Wilson, had been hopeful that a specific proposal for a Commonwealth Consultative Assembly, undertaken in collaboration with the CPA, would be considered by the Prime Ministers meeting in June 1965. In the event they had not had time to go into the matter fully. He asked delegates if they thought that their Association should pursue the idea further.

He warned, however, that it involved radical changes for several reasons. First, CPA conferences did not debate resolutions, take votes or make recommendations. Secondly, the Association had no formal links with Ministers, although the practice of choosing Ministers to lead national delegations was growing. Thirdly, representation in CPA conferences included delegates not only from sovereign states but also from dependencies which had no international forum in which to voice their views. A further consideration was that the trend in Europe was away from nationalism and towards political and economic unity, while in the Commonwealth the trend was towards sovereign independence and equality of status. Thus the obstacles to the development of the CPA on the lines of the

Council of Europe were perhaps insuperable. But there were features of the Council which could be adapted to the purposes of the CPA, giving its deliberations greater authority.

Bernard Braine strongly supported the proposal of the Australia branch that a small Executive Committee should be created. Meeting at some time between conferences it could draft the agenda and deal with other important business. He suggested, too, that there should be a closer relationship between the agenda and what the Commonwealth Prime Ministers discussed at their meetings. This could be achieved by liaison between the CPA and the Commonwealth Secretariat.

Turning to the role of the General Council, Bernard Braine laid emphasis on the need for greater continuity in its membership. Constructive proposals on this and other matters, put forward by the Australia branch, would be considered closely at the next meeting in Ottawa in 1966.

The remarkable feature of the discussions which followed was the degree of enthusiastic support for the Association. A minority argued that the conference should debate and vote on resolutions. Generally, however, delegates accepted that the CPA was a deliberative, not an executive, organisation, and further that resolutions would be divisive and destructive. Dato' Wong Kim Min (Sarawak), who had taken a very active and constructive part throughout the conference period, made a plea for improved financing of the Association. 'A re-examination needs to be made of our financial resources, if we value this Association of ours,' he said. 'We should look at this as a business organisation or a club. We are all members and if we want this Association to progress then let us not undercapitalize it.... No business or government can operate on a shoestring.'[38]

The first session on 'International Affairs' was opened by the New Zealand Prime Minister, Keith Holyoake. He ranged over the world situation as seen from New Zealand. He dwelt especially on the conflicts in South-East Asia and the menace of Communist China. Dato' Wong Kim Min explained the predicament of Malaysia in facing the hostility of Indonesia. He emphasised interdependence within the Commonwealth and pointed out that, as Malaysia had been prompt to condemn rebellion in Rhodesia and to support sanctions, so he would expect support for Malaysia from fellow nations in the Commonwealth. Other delegates recognised the threats posed by the USSR and Communist China. The leaders of the India and Pakistan delegations had a lengthy exchange over Kashmir, an exchange which most delegates disapproved of in this forum.

The second session on 'International Affairs' was opened by Senator J. William Fulbright, Chairman of the Senate delegation from the United States. He gave a broad review of American policy towards the USSR and Communist China, and explained the situation in Vietnam. In both sessions delegates showed a breadth of view and understanding which was impressive.

In New Zealand, as in Jamaica, there were times of tension when it seemed that delegations would walk out. It had needed only one delegation to take such action, and others would probably have followed. The CPA and the Commonwealth would have been divided and their future endangered. But delegates were reluctant to take such drastic action and to cut themselves off from the Association. One factor in this reluctance was no doubt the alchemy of the Commonwealth. There was also another explanation. It was that CPA gave delegates, especially those from Africa and other newly independent countries, a forum where they could speak freely and as equals. They could belabour their former master, if they felt the need. And many delegates attacked and criticised Britain. They did so with a certain reluctance, in sorrow rather than in anger. The opening speaker in the sessions on Rhodesia had expressed his respect and affection for Britain. Other delegates spoke warmly of Britain and acknowledged their indebtedness. It was, however, the freedom to speak as they felt and as equals that mattered most to the new members in these early years of independence. They had and cherished the freedom, equality, and fellowship which the CPA forum gave them.

Notes

1. In 1956 the eight member countries were the United Kingdom, Canada, Australia, New Zealand, South Africa, India, Pakistan and Ceylon.
2. The new member countries and the year of accession were Ghana and Malaya (1957), Nigeria and Cyprus (1960), Sierra Leone and Tanganyika on the withdrawal of South Africa (1961), Jamaica, Trinidad and Uganda (1962), Kenya and Zanzibar (1963), Malawi, Malta and Zambia (1964), the Gambia and Singapore (1965), Mauritius and Swaziland (1968), Tonga, Fiji and Western Samoa (1970).
3. J. D. B. Miller, *Survey of Commonwealth Affairs, Problems of Expansion and Attrition, 1953-69* (London, 1974), p.18.
4. Ibid., p.159.
5. Quoted by Miller, ibid., p.144.
6. *Loc. cit.*
7. Ibid., p.145.
8. House of Commons Debates, United Kingdom, 8 April 1960, cols. 834-6.
9. Conference Report (Kingston, 1964), p.232.
10. Conference Report (Canberra, 1959), p.5.
11. Peter Howson, *The Life of Politics* (Victoria, Australia, 1984), p.122.
12. *Loc. cit.*
13. Ibid., p.123.
14. Conference Report (Kingston, 1964), p.273.
15. Report of the CPA General Council 1963-64, p.15.
16. **Agenda and Opening Speakers, Jamaica, 1964**
    Trade and Aid, with particular reference to the UN Conference on Trade and Development - R. C. Lightbourne, Minister of Trade and Industry (Jamaica)
    Commonwealth Organisations - Saied Mohammed, Minister of Works (Trinidad and Tobago)
    Educational Cooperation within the Commonwealth - Senator T. M. C. Chokwe, Speaker of the Senate (Kenya)
    The Future Functions and Role of the Commonwealth Parliamentary Association - Peter Howson, Minister for Air (Australia)

The Way Ahead for the Commonwealth – J. H. George, Senior Government Whip (New Zealand)

The Role of the Speaker in Parliament – Lord Morison of Lambeth (United Kingdom)

International Affairs – Enche Mohamed Ghazali bin Haji Jawa, Minister of Lands and Mines (Malaysia).

17. Conference Report (Kingston, 1964), p.238.
18. Ibid., p.250.
19. Ibid., p.254.
20. Miller, *op. cit.*, p.398.
21. *Loc. cit.*
22. Canadian House of Commons, Official Report, 17 July 1964.
23. *The Times*, 4 January 1965.
24. Conference Report (Jamaica, 1964), p.59.
25. *Loc. cit.*
26. Minutes of CPA General Council, 15 November 1965.
27. *Loc. cit.*
28. Report of the CPA General Meeting, 7 December 1965, p.60.
29. **Agenda and Opening Speakers, New Zealand, 1965**

    Rhodesia – Alhaji Shehu Shagari, Minister of Works (Nigeria)

    Economic Growth in the Commonwealth

    (i) The effective use of technical and financial resources for economic development – Professor N. G. Ranga (India)

    (ii) Problems of commodity stabilisation – R. A. Njoku, Minister of Communications (Nigeria)

    (iii) Agricultural cooperation – J. P. Gyles, Minister of Agriculture and Lands (Jamaica)

    (iv) The growth of population in relation to resources – Shrimati Dr Anjanabai Magar, Maharashtra

    Parliamentary Government in the Commonwealth

    (i) Differing party systems – Senator T. M. C. Chokwe, President of the Senate (Kenya)

    (ii) The redress of grievances: the office of ombudsman – J. R. Marshall, Deputy Prime Minister, Minister of Industries and Commerce, Minister of Overseas Trade (New Zealand)

    The Commonwealth Parliamentary Association – Bernard Braine (United Kingdom)

    International Affairs – K. J. Holyoake, Prime Minister of New Zealand; Senator J. William Fulbright, Chairman, Senate Committee on Foreign Relations (USA); A. H. Nordmeyer, Leader of the Opposition (New Zealand).
30. Conference Report (Wellington, 1965), p.1.
31. *Loc. cit.*
32. Ibid., pp.2–3.
33. *Loc. cit.*
34. Ibid., p.13.
35. Ibid., p.40.
36. Ibid., p.45.
37. Ibid., p.27.
38. Ibid., p.254.

15   The Working Party, 1966–68

At the end of the 1960s it seemed that the Commonwealth could not survive for many more years. A series of momentous events appeared to undermine faith in its future.

In January 1966 a group of soldiers brutally murdered the Nigerian Prime Minister, Sir Abubakar Tafawa Balewa, and set up a military regime. Six months later General Ironsi, head of the Federal military government, was assassinated, and was succeeded by General Yakubu Gowon. In Ghana, Kwame Nkrumah was ousted in February 1966 and military rule established. Also in February 1966 President Obote suspended the Ugandan constitution. In March 1967 the army seized power in Sierra Leone. Civil war broke out in Nigeria in July 1967, when Colonel Ojukwu declared the secession of the Republic of Biafra. The war lasted until January 1970. Each of these events imposed a strain on the Commonwealth, which was further aggravated by the continuing failure to resolve the Rhodesian problem.

The Commonwealth was divided over the civil war in Nigeria. The situation was further complicated by the involvement of countries outside the Commonwealth. Britain supported the Federal government, as did the Soviet Union. France, hoping to increase its influence in Africa and especially anglophone Africa, actively aided Biafra. South Africa and Portugal sided with Biafra, and China and Israel gave moral support. Tanzania and Zambia, as well as the francophone Ivory Coast and Gabon, went so far as to recognise the Republic of Biafra. All other African states and the Organisation of African Unity continued to recognise the sovereignty of the Federal government, headed by Gowon.

The Commonwealth Prime Ministers did not seek to intervene or mediate. The Nigerian Federal government insisted that the civil war was a domestic matter. The principle of non-interference in the internal affairs of a member country was observed. It was, however, ignored whenever Rhodesia's minority government was mentioned.

The troubles were not confined to Africa. In August 1965 Singapore separated from the Malaysian Federation and became an independent state. Early in 1969 savage riots broke out between Malays and Chinese in Malaysia, and in May 1969 the Parliament was suspended. The enduring disputes between India and Pakistan led to war in 1965 and again in 1971.

Inevitably all of these events made an impact on the Commonwealth and the attitudes of its members. The African states were seriously divided among themselves and frequently in dispute over local matters. On one objective, however, they were united. This was to establish government by Africans over the whole of the continent south of the Sahara. At one time or another certain African leaders, feeling thwarted, threatened to leave the Commonwealth. They did not do so, because it gave opportunities to publicise their demands and to bring pressure to bear on Britain. Speeches by such leaders as Kaunda, Nyerere, Hastings Banda and Obote were reported by the British media, and there was a body of sympathetic opinion in Britain. France did not allow such freedom to its former colonies. Indeed, by agreement with the francophone states, the African leaders in the Commonwealth refrained from criticising France publicly for trading with Rhodesia and supplying arms to South Africa. They bitterly criticised Britain on both of these scores. Moreover, they made full use of the Commonwealth Secretariat which at times to some observers appeared to act as an African agency. But the African leaders were often intemperate in their language, and they harmed their cause.

In the 1950s British people were gratified and even elated by the way in which colonies in Asia and West Africa had moved to independence within the Commonwealth. Moreover, Britain's relations with them seemed to have been enhanced. During the 1960s this sense of pride and achievement was shattered. The political and economic stability which, it was believed, had been imparted to the African states before independence, was proving to be fragile. Disappointment was turned into resentment and anger by African attacks and criticism over Rhodesia and South Africa, and by the demands for more and more aid at a time when Britain was dogged by economic crises.

Britain was turning increasingly towards Europe. The attempts to join the EEC in 1962 and again in 1967 had failed. Support for joining the Community was, nevertheless, growing in Britain. The old economic links within the Commonwealth were diminishing in importance and the sterling area was soon to come to an end. Many people overseas saw the Commonwealth Immigrants Act 1962, strengthened in 1965, which sharply reduced the influx into Britain of immigrants from Commonwealth countries, as further evidence of Britain's disenchantment with the aftermath of Empire.

Against this background many people in Britain and elsewhere questioned whether the Commonwealth could survive. Within the CPA, however, the question hardly arose. There was no weakening of support for the Association from any region of the Commonwealth. The African branches in particular were enthusiastic supporters. The CPA gave them a valuable forum, but also it was a parliamentary organisation and there could be no doubting the sincerity of the aspiration of African leaders to establish stable and democratic regimes in their countries.

Members of branches, suspended after the overthrow of their Parliaments, always felt isolated and ostracised. On the return of parliamentary rule, one of their first concerns was to revive their branches and return to the parliamentary community. In 1966 the suspended branches in the Federation and the four states of Nigeria, and also of Ghana, suggested to the Council that each should send a senior parliamentary official to the conference as an observer. This would, they claimed, enable these former branches to maintain contact with the Association in anticipation of a return to parliamentary government. The proposition was discussed at length by subcommittees and the full Council. Councillors from Canada and Britain were sympathetic. But others, and especially the African councillors, were insistent that the parliamentary principle should be upheld. They emphasised that the CPA was a parliamentary association, which could not make concessions. The motion, which was finally carried unanimously, read: 'That no action be taken to invite observers to attend the conference this year from Commonwealth countries in which Parliament has been suspended and in which no branch of the Association exists.'[1]

In the late 1960s the intense activity and thought given to the planning of the future of the Association demonstrated the confidence of members in its importance and continued existence. This movement to develop and revitalise the Association began in the meetings in New Zealand in 1965: it gathered real momentum in Canada in 1966.

The General Council met in Montreal on 10 September and then in Ottawa on 26 and 30 September. It appointed the new Finance and General Purposes Committee, and new subcommittees on the General Council and publications as well as the conference Steering Committee. It received reports on the regional conferences which had become annual events and on the 16th Westminster seminar on parliamentary practice and procedure, held in April 1966. It welcomed new branches and changes in branch status. It accepted with acclaim the invitation of the Uganda branch to host the conference in 1967. Such were some of the routine matters that the Council always had to approve, but invariably there was new business.

Recognition of the valuable service given to the Association by S. A. Pakeman was recorded. Dr N. M. Perera (Ceylon) said that he had had the privilege of being Pakeman's pupil in the University of Ceylon and then his colleague in the Ceylon Parliament. After his retirement from Parliament and return to England, he had devoted himself to the service of the CPA. Peter Howson seconded the motion. He paid tribute to Pakeman's contribution as Editor and as Secretary-General at a critical time in the history of the Association. The motion, passed unanimously, read: 'That the General Council of the CPA records its high appreciation of the long and distinguished service rendered by Mr S. A. Pakeman to this organisation.'[2]

The need for some link between the conferences of the Association and the

Prime Ministers' meetings would, it was agreed, be discussed in the plenary session on 'The CPA and the Commonwealth Secretariat'. Several councillors were, however, uneasy about the status and role of the new Secretariat. Arnold Smith, the first Commonwealth Secretary-General, had been invited by the host branch to address the delegates. Peter Howson raised objections. First, he said, Arnold Smith was not a parliamentarian but an official; he could not therefore take part in the conference and his address should be on a separate occasion. This was strongly supported by other councillors, who jealously guarded the parliamentary character of the Association. Secondly, he expressed concern that allowing him to address delegates might create a precedent; it would be more appropriate for him to address the General Council. The consensus of the meeting was, however, that it would be of interest to delegates to hear and question him about the role of the new Secretariat, but that the conference should be adjourned and the address given at a separate, informal meeting.[3]

One of the most important decisions of the Council arose from an initiative of the Commonwealth of Australia branch. This was to carry out a basic review of the purposes and activities of the Association and to set up a Management Committee which would meet not only at the time of the conference but also between conferences. Peter Howson, Sir Alister McMullin and Alan Turner, Secretary of the branch, had originated the proposals after close consultation with Robin Vanderfelt and others in the Secretariat.

A basic review, Peter Howson explained to the Council, was essential. The constitution had been adopted in Uganda in 1960. Since then dramatic changes had taken place in the Commonwealth and were reflected in the CPA. This was illustrated by the growth in the size of the Council. In 1960 25 councillors had attended; in Ottawa just six years later there were 49 councillors, the majority without any previous experience of the Association. Meeting only once a year, the Council could not be expected to provide adequate management. This and other aspects of the functioning of the Association needed re-examination. The Australian submission was that a working party should be appointed to meet once in the following year and to report to the Council in Uganda in 1967.

The General Council unanimously approved without amendment the detailed Australian proposals. It agreed that in composition the working party should be similar to the Management Committee envisaged. It should have its own Chairman and the Chairman of the General Council should be its Vice-Chairman. The other officers of the Council and the three Clause 24 councillors would be members. The four additional members would be elected bearing in mind that all regions should be represented and that the members elected should have a sound knowledge of the Association.

The Council then elected Peter Howson to be Chairman of the working party. The other members elected were Donald Sangster (Jamaica), Dr N. M. Perera (Ceylon) and Senator Hamilton Maurice (Trinidad and Tobago). The councillor from India, K. Hanumanthayia, stated that, while not opposed to the working party and its purpose, he considered it unlikely that his branch would wish to be represented on it. He gave no reason. The Chairman said that the absence of an Indian member would be greatly regretted. He proposed that Shri Hanumanthayia consult his branch on his return to New Delhi and, if it nominated a member, the Council would be pleased to accept him as a member.

Dr Guido de Marco said that Malta with its developing economy could not hope to host a conference of the Association. His branch would, however, welcome the working party to Malta. The Council expressed appreciation for this invitation.

Discussion of the conference agenda took up much of the Council's time. A draft agenda had been drawn up by the Salaries and Management Subcommittee in London in June 1966, and the conference Steering Committee submitted a final draft to the Council for approval. The Chairman explained that, contrary to previous practice, the Steering Committee proposed that international affairs should be discussed at the beginning and not at the end of the conference. Since it was the practice of the host branch to open the debate on this subject, the Canadian Secretary of State for External Affairs, Paul Martin, had agreed to return to Ottawa from the United Nations to open the session. Also a delegation from the US Senate, led by Senator J. William Fulbright, would arrive in time to speak in the following session.

J. S. M. Ochola (Uganda) and J. K. Ole Tipis (Kenya) at once protested that Rhodesia should be discussed first as a separate item. This had been the arrangement at the conference in New Zealand and the precedent should be followed. Several councillors spoke in support. There was, however, no unanimity on this point among the African delegates. L. J. Ngobeh (Sierra Leone) thought that it made little difference when Rhodesia was discussed and he was unwilling to inconvenience the host branch and the Secretariat. William Kalema (Uganda), the Vice-Chairman, supported this view. He added that the Prime Ministers, meeting in Lagos, had achieved nothing and the United Nations had failed. It was unlikely that the CPA conference would have greater success. Other councillors were concerned that the war in Vietnam should be fully discussed. On a vote the agenda, as proposed by the Steering Committee, was approved.[4]

The 12th Commonwealth Parliamentary Conference was opened with customary ceremony by the Governor-General of Canada, H. E. Georges P. Vanier, on 28 September 1966. The speakers were the Chairman, Senator John J. Connolly, the Governor-General, the Prime Minister of Canada, Lester B. Pearson, and the Vice-Chairman, William W. Kalema. The conference was attended by 138 delegates and 26 Secretaries to delegations from 65 branches of the Association. Two Senators, J. William Fulbright and Edmund S. Muskie, came from the US Congress. Special invitations were sent to past Chairmen of the Association, all of whom, except Harold Holt, were present in Ottawa.

At this conference certain topics were taken in committee sessions. Delegates were asked to select one of two topics on which they wished to speak and to serve on that committee. The committee Chairmen reported to a later session of the conference. This was an attempt to break away from the formality of proceedings in plenary sessions and to encourage more active debate.

The first three sessions were devoted to 'The Commonwealth and the World'. Opening the discussion Paul Martin spoke on the problems of direct concern to his country, and especially the war in Vietnam, the Rhodesian crisis, and the role of the United Nations. Three British delegates took the initiative in speaking on Rhodesia in the next session. William W. Hamilton recognised Rhodesia as an important moral issue. He listed the mistakes which in his view the British government had made in its handling of the problem, but asked African delegates to have patience and faith in the determination of the British government to ensure majority rule in Rhodesia. The next British delegate to speak was Nigel Fisher. He explained forcefully the grave implications of using force, as so many Africans urged. He added:

I hope that the pressures upon Britain will not be increased too much by our Commonwealth partners. We, too, are an independent and still a great nation. We do not care to be threatened with walk-outs and withdrawals and with the dissolution of the Commonwealth. There is, indeed, a growing disenchantment with the Commonwealth among certain sections of the British people. I do not agree with it. Indeed, I deplore it, but it exists. Britain's enthusiasm for the Commonwealth should no longer be taken absolutely for granted.[5]

The Kenya delegate, J. K. Ole Tipis, said that Britain was shirking its responsibilities in not using military force to bring down the Smith regime. If Britain could not solve the Rhodesian problem, then it should be passed to the United Nations. One of the most vehement demands for the use of military might was made by an Indian delegate, A. B. Vajpayee, who said that the future of the Commonwealth was at stake. J. S. M. Ochola (Uganda) accused Britain of being half-hearted over the Rhodesian issue and argued that there was no alternative to the use of force. Other delegates from Africa and the Caribbean took the same view. A remarkable exception was the speech of M. H. Blackwood (Malawi) who gave a detailed appraisal of the devastation that the use of force would cause not only in Rhodesia but also in Malawi and Zambia. The leader of the United Kingdom delegation, Arthur Bottomley, who had been directly involved as Secretary of State for Commonwealth Affairs, reviewed the situation and called for Commonwealth support in resolving the Rhodesian issue peacefully.

In the context of this history the discussions in plenary session of 'The Commonwealth: The CPA and the Commonwealth Secretariat' were of special interest. All delegates had before them a note, expanding the agenda item, which read: 'The creation of a link between the CPA and Commonwealth Prime Ministers in their corporate capacity which would, with advantage to both Parliaments and governments, enable matters of interest to the Commonwealth as a whole, but outside the field of domestic policy, to be referred to one body by the other for discussion at their respective conferences.'[6]

On the previous day the Commonwealth Secretary-General, Arnold Smith, had addressed delegates at a special meeting. An experienced Canadian diplomat and an able administrator, Smith was not unmarked by the anglophobia which was a characteristic of Dr O. D. Skelton, the chief adviser on foreign affairs to Mackenzie King and the principal architect of the Canadian diplomatic service. Many delegates considered Smith's address too long and ponderous. His references to 'little Englandism' or neo-isolationism brought prompt comment from Bernard Braine during the question period. There was also unease in the minds of several delegates that he might see himself as not only the servant of the collective governments of the Commonwealth but also as an initiator of ideas and in a position to determine matters which were properly the responsibility of governments. Smith's reply that he saw himself entirely as the servant of governments did not assuage the unease.

The leader of the Australian delegation, Peter Howson, opened the session on 'The CPA and the Commonwealth Secretariat' on an optimistic note. He found, he said, a change in the mood of the conferences; the tensions which had existed in Jamaica in 1964 had tended to disappear. In Ottawa there seemed to be a greater realisation that they were all now a partnership without the British dominance which some emerging nations had felt.

The note, added to the agenda item on the suggestion of the Australian delegation, was, he explained, intended to establish whether there was a consensus in favour of a closer link between the CPA and the Commonwealth Prime Ministers. This idea had been raised on several occasions, most notably by Harold Holt in 1959 and by Harold Wilson in 1965. Delegates at the conference, he said, represented their constituencies. It was important, therefore, that their views, as expressed in the sessions, should be distilled by the CPA Secretariat and conveyed to the Commonwealth Secretary-General for incorporation in the notes and data papers, prepared for the meeting of Prime Ministers. Such information would also help to remind the Commonwealth Secretariat of the limitations of its role. He added that there could be no suggestion of the CPA being taken over by the new Secretariat. It was an organisation serving governments, while the CPA embraced parliamentarians of all parties.

Many delegates warmly supported the Australian proposal. Senator Allister Grosart (Canada) made a number of comments which were especially perceptive. He was not, he said, apprehensive that the new Secretariat might seek to take over the CPA. It had already absorbed two major Commonwealth organisations, increasing its staff from 40 to 140 in the process. The danger he saw was that the CPA might allow itself to be downgraded by default as a Commonwealth organisation. The CPA should make it clear that it was different from the other 200 or more Commonwealth organisations. He proposed 'that we resolve at this conference to commence an upgrading of our organisation in the Councils of the Prime Ministers and of our Secretariat to the level of the Commonwealth Secretariat'.[7] He went on to recommend that the Prime Ministers should be asked to increase their contributions to the Association. The CPA Secretariat had a staff of only ten and should be expanded. He expressed amazement at the extent of the responsibility that this small staff shouldered.

The United Kingdom delegates considered the Australian proposal unrealistic. Their opposition was expressed by Charles Pannell and William Hamilton with a bluntness which other delegates found abrasive and discourteous. Charles Pannell urged that the conference should not 'rise above itself and give itself an arrogance that is not merited by its power'.[8] He stated that the British delegation was, in fact, 'a United Kingdom fourth XI, batting away from home ... and to suggest somehow or other that the Prime Ministers have to come back to consult us is derisory'.[9] He feared that in the Commonwealth Secretariat a new empire had been created. The Australian proposal would, he suspected, 'result in new machinery and more officials ....This is Parkinson's law with a vengeance.'[10] He went on to criticise the conference discussions as a 'futile exercise'.[11] Lord Shepherd spoke later to mollify the remarks of his two colleagues. Bernard Braine, winding up the discussion, said that he could find no real consensus beyond a general agreement that a close but wholly informal link should be established between the two Secretaries-General. This was a matter which the working party would surely consider.

The General Meeting of the Association took place in Ottawa on 3 October. In the discussion on the accounts, James Walker (Canada) spoke about the escalating cost of hosting the annual conference. If this continued, few countries would be able to afford to be host. This was a problem to be examined by the working party. One suggestion he would make was that delegates should be provided with economy class tickets, for this would effect a large saving. The subsidising of the host branch from Council funds was another suggestion to be examined. An overall review of branch contributions was also needed. He considered that the United Kingdom was contributing to a far greater extent than was reasonable.[12]

William Hamilton (United Kingdom) expressed strong agreement. He added: 'It seems to me that the contribution made by the UK is an unduly large proportion of the total cost. It angers us who represent the United Kingdom to come here and find we are being kicked in the teeth all along the line and then having to foot the bill for the privilege ...'.[13]

The New Zealand delegate, John Gordon, said that as New Zealand was the last country to pay the full bill for a conference he would like to assure delegates that the people of the country had been delighted to host it and that it had imposed no undue burden on New Zealand's taxpayers.

Discussion followed on the financing and planning of conferences. Lord Shepherd (United Kingdom) intervened to point out that British delegates came to conferences as individuals. The speech of William Hamilton in the previous day's proceedings, which had attracted wide coverage in the Canadian press, had expressed his own views and not those of the United Kingdom delegation. Lord Shepherd said that he considered that the conference had been a valuable experience for all. He felt, however, that the financing of all CPA activities should be reviewed. The Gibraltar delegate, S. A. Seruya, spoke of the importance of the CPA, and especially of the United Kingdom branch to his country. He praised the work of the Secretariat in London. He suggested that branches, grouped in regions, might share the cost of conferences held in their region.

One detail in the report of the Chairman of the Council to the General Meeting took up considerable time. This concerned the composition of the working party. The Labour Party members of the United Kingdom delegation suddenly realised that, while their branch had two members on the working party, which was double the number from any other branch, both were from the Conservative Party. This had happened fortuitously. Charles Pannell was indignant. Other delegates suggested that it was for the United Kingdom branch to put its own house in order.

The Chairman of the working party, Peter Howson, welcomed the fact that the Council and the General Meeting had agreed on the need for this basic review. He regretted, however, that the composition of the working party, already approved by the Council, had now been reopened. He pointed out that the Australian proposals had been sent to the United Kingdom branch on 11 July and that it had had three to four months in which to examine them. In its original proposals the Treasurer had not been included, because the Clause 24 councillor from the United Kingdom would serve on the working party. There was no valid reason why the branch should have an extra member. The inclusion of the Treasurer had been proposed by the Chairman and agreed by the Council. Nigel Fisher, the newly elected Treasurer, said that to resolve the problem he would withdraw from the treasurership and thus from the working party. The meeting agreed that it should be left to the branch to nominate another member to serve as Treasurer.

The final membership of the working party, which met in Malta from 22–26 May 1967 under the chairmanship of Peter Howson is set out in the notes to this chapter.[14]

The opening ceremony for the working party took place in the Tapestry Chamber of the Palace, Valletta, on 22 May. The Speaker of the House of Representatives, Dr A. Bonnici, welcomed the members on behalf of the Prime Minister and the Malta branch. The Chairman of the working party, Peter Howson, expressed thanks on behalf of the General Council and of the members present. He outlined the problems facing the Commonwealth and the CPA, and also the terms of reference of the working party.

This was the culmination of six months of intensive preparation in the Secretariat. Robin Vanderfelt, Ian Grey, Jack Fowler and Betty May had between them produced memoranda on every aspect of the Association's organisation and activities. These papers gave not only the historical background, but also the problems and suggested solutions, and a full statement of the financial policies in the past and estimates of future needs. There were also papers on the conferences of Commonwealth Speakers, relations with the Prime Ministers' meetings and with the Commonwealth Secretariat.[15] The memoranda were a notable contribution, achieved in addition to their usual work and responsibilities. All agreed that this work had been amply justified.

The meetings of the working party were stimulating and memorable.

They brought together members from ten countries, representative of the Commonwealth as a whole. Meetings of this kind under the guidance of a firm but sympathetic chairman can develop a sense of partnership. Members of the working party together with the Secretariat under its Chairman had this relationship. Each member contributed, discussed and finally agreed the recommendations to go forward to the Council. The contributions of Peter Howson, Senator John J. Connolly, Bernard Braine, Senator Hamilton Maurice and Ronald Ngala (Kenya) were especially valuable.

The working party's report charted the course of the Association over the following 15 years. In presenting this report to the Council and the General Meeting in Kampala, Peter Howson said that the general approach was, as set out in the introductory note to the report, as follows:

The CPA serves the basic purpose of fostering respect for, and knowledge of, the fundamentals of democratic government, but it also has special significance in bridging racial, cultural, and economic divisions in the world. One of the gravest threats today is the trend toward alignment of nations by race and levels of economic development. The Commonwealth, and at its core, the CPA, both multiracial and multinational in character, play an influential part in bringing together peoples of every race, nationality, religion, and culture on a basis of mutual understanding and respect. This is a purpose which the Association, with its long and successful experience of multiracial relationships, is uniquely equipped to promote.... But to maintain its dynamism the Association must keep its activities under constant review, and seek new means of furthering its objectives.[16]

The Council then considered the four main sections of the report. It approved the recommendation that an Executive Committee should be set up, taking over the functions of the Finance and General Purposes Committee, and meeting at least twice a year. It approved also the composition and terms of reference of the Committee.

Dealing with finance, Peter Howson stated that in recent years the Association had been overspending. In 1964 the deficit had been £3000, but in 1966 it was £12,980. The Finance Officer, Jack Fowler, had prepared estimates for the next five years. From these figures it was clear that an additional income of £55,000 would be needed each year for the period 1969–73. This took into consideration the cost of travel for the new Executive Committee, and the further proposal that a subvention should be available to assist smaller branches to host conferences. Thus an increase in branch contributions was unavoidable. The working party then examined in detail all possible economies. It recommended that in future fares for delegates should be provided on an economy class instead of first class basis. Branches wishing their delegates to travel first class would have to pay the difference in cost. This would reduce the additional income needed to about £25,000. In revising the branch contributions it had been found that some were out of balance, and the contributions of the Australian and Canadian branches had been increased. The proposal that delegates travel economy class met with some opposition, but finally this and the other recommendations were approved.

The working party considered, after reviewing the publications of the Association, that all, except the *Report on Foreign Affairs*, should be classed as obligatory and be continued. It recommended, too, that a proposed *Handbook of Commonwealth Parliaments* should be produced, subject to finance being approved in the 1969–73 estimates. It was felt, however, that the need for the *Report on Foreign Affairs* was declining and that an up-to-date leaflet sent monthly by airmail to members, would be more effective. The Editor had been asked to produce a sample issue of a leaflet, to be called *News of the Commonwealth*, which had been circulated to members of the Council for their comments. Meanwhile the Editor was authorised to mount a sales campaign to increase subscriptions to the *Report*. The result would be reviewed by the Executive Committee in 1968 when it would reach a decision on its continued publication.

The working party considered relations between the CPA and the Secretariat and the Commonwealth Prime Ministers. It also noted the various proposals that had been made from time to time for developing these relations. It recommended that the Association must remain free and independent of governments. Liaison between the two Secretariats should be maintained on a friendly but wholly informal basis. Finally it considered that the existing channels of communication between the CPA and governments either through direct contact with Prime Ministers or through Ministers taking part in its activities should be maintained. No recommendation was made concerning the creation of a special link between the Association and the Prime Ministers' Meetings or for the development of a Commonwealth Consultative Assembly.

An exhaustive examination of the work of the General Council and its Secretariat as well as the planning of conferences and tours was carried out. All the recommendations under these and other headings, together with consequential amendments to the constitution, were adopted without amendment by the General Council and then by the General Meeting.

The Council then elected the Chairman and the seven regional representatives of the new Executive Committee. By unanimous vote Peter Howson was called on to serve as the first Chairman for a three-year term.[17] At the General Meeting the leader of the Mauritius delegation, Hurrypersad Ramnarain, extended an invitation for the Executive Committee to hold its first meeting in his country. Members from Gibraltar and Jersey also offered to host future meetings of the Committee.

The working party's review of every aspect of the CPA's role and activities as well as its clear recommendations undoubtedly gave a new vigour and direction to the Association. The Executive Committee was to prove a major development. Its mid-year meetings enabled this small group of members to concentrate without distractions on its agenda, and to serve as a real management committee.

The 13th Commonwealth Parliamentary Conference was held from 26 October–1 November 1967 in the Committee Room Suite of Parliament House, Kampala. It was attended by 129 delegates and 21 Secretaries to delegations from

64 branches of the Association. After the customary ceremonial, the formal opening of the conference was carried out by H.E. Dr Milton A. Obote, President of the Republic of Uganda.

In a long and eloquent speech Dr Obote dwelt first on his country's absolute commitment to parliamentary democracy. 'Uganda has chosen this particular form of government', he said, 'because we strongly believe that it is the only form that will enable us to develop and build our country and nation in such a way that the hopes and aspirations of man and conditions which allow him full development are based on or fulfilled through his own decisions, as expressed by his freely elected representatives.' He said that Ugandans regarded the invitation to host the conference, extended in New Zealand in 1965, as forming, in his words, 'a moral contract between Uganda and the Parliaments of the Commonwealth. The principal clauses of that contract were the registration of our choice of the form of government we want to establish in our country and a promise to the Parliaments and peoples of the Commonwealth that it is our determination to develop here effective parliamentary institutions.'[18]

Dr Obote expressed his faith in the value of the Commonwealth.

The fact that the Commonwealth has given a forum to so many countries to discuss their problems, and no other organization or club has done so or is even able to do so without raising of voices and perhaps creating an atmosphere of bitterness, is itself a credit to the Commonwealth and an indication of its usefulness in promoting understanding and cooperation among nations.[19]

The great danger was, he said, that the Commonwealth would become tarnished and cease to exist. 'The nerve centre of this danger is in Africa in general and in Rhodesia in particular.'[20] He went on to indict Britain fiercely for failing to enforce the principle of one man one vote. Time was running out, he said, and Africans would soon pursue their rights on the principle of 'one man one gun'. He feared that they were witnessing the end of the Commonwealth. It was this last part of his oration which set the bitter tone of the first two sessions of the conference in which 'Africa in World Affairs: World Peace' was discussed.[21]

Uganda's Minister of Foreign Affairs, Samuel Odaka, in an impressive speech, opening the first session, reviewed the liberation movement in Africa. He saw a danger that racial conflicts would escalate throughout the continent as a result of the struggle of Africans for their freedom in Rhodesia and South Africa. In the face of such a danger he questioned whether Britain could continue its refusal to use military force in Rhodesia. The African and Asian delegates with mounting fervour called on Britain to send troops to destroy the Smith regime. Dr Sanjiva Reddy, Speaker of the Lok Sabha, India, said: 'When the President said yesterday that "one man one gun" is the only solution now because we have failed to give one man one vote, he was expressing the sentiments of every country, not only in Africa but also outside Africa.'[22]

The British delegates, including George Thomson, Secretary of State for

Commonwealth Affairs, who was leader of the delegation, were restrained in their speeches. They stressed the difficulties and dangers of a military invasion of Rhodesia, which might lead to war with South Africa. They stated frankly that no British government would have the support of the British people for such action. Moreover, the use of force would divide the Commonwealth itself. They affirmed the British determination to ensure majority rule in Rhodesia.

British explanations and assurances had no effect. Indeed, Dr N. M. Perera (Ceylon) delivered what can only be called a tirade against Britain.[23] Senator J. E. Marriott, leader of the Australian delegation, was moved to protest against the intemperate speeches throughout the debate which, he said, 'has been literally punctuated with accusations and vilifications of Great Britain.... The more I hear of this debate the more I fear for the possibility of value proceeding from the discussions of the CPA in future.'[24] S.R. Ramsden (Queensland) expressed his disappointment in the mood of the conference. He recalled that in his speech at the opening the President had spoken of their freedom to talk about their problems without raising their voices and without bitterness. 'We have', Ramsden said, 'heard all sorts of bitterness and acrimony.'[25]

Tensions diminished in the following sessions. The emotive Rhodesian issue gave way to discussions in committee on 'Aid to Developing Countries' and 'Parliamentary Institutions'. The intractable problem of the widening gap between the developed and the developing countries was considered in all aspects and many delegates made appeals for more aid. In the committee session on 'Parliamentary Institutions' the earnest and well-informed speeches by delegates from the newly independent countries, especially in Africa, were impressive. All expressed their fervent and sincere concern to uphold the rule of law, the rights of their citizens, and the dignity of Parliament.

The final sessions were devoted to the 'Commonwealth and the European Economic Community'. George Thomson (United Kingdom), in opening, explained British policy and the impact that British membership of the EEC was expected to have on the Commonwealth. He gave a firm undertaking that in the negotiations with the Community Britain would do all in its power to protect the interests of Commonwealth members and especially of New Zealand. While all delegates recognised that it was Britain's right to decide, many were concerned about the effect on their markets in Britain.

The Ugandan Foreign Minister, Samuel Odaka, in what a British delegate described as 'a most statesmanlike and understanding speech', strongly upheld Britain's right to do whatever was best in its interests. He paid tribute to Britain for the concern it showed for the interests of other member countries and for openly discussing the matter in the conference. He personally did not believe that Britain's accession to the EEC would mean the end of the Commonwealth. He added that primary-producing countries, like Uganda, must be realistic in pursuing new markets. Roy McNeill (Jamaica) spoke of the anxieties of the Caribbean countries. They were satisfied, however, that Britain would use its best endeavours to protect their interests.

In summing up the discussion Peter Howson spoke of the issues of trade and aid that would arise when Britain was part of the EEC. He then referred to the underlying question, which he defined as follows:

> The question that I believe emerges from this debate is that if Britain goes into Europe and adopts the same introverted, inward-looking policies that are being shown by other members of the Six, then I believe there will be a real danger for the future of the Commonwealth and particularly the future of the Commonwealth Parliamentary Association. But if on the other hand it goes into Europe determined to convert that European regionalism into an outward-looking world force prepared to play a very real part in world problems and really developing into a Third World Force, as was stated by Mr George Thomson, then I believe all the members of the Commonwealth here will be grateful for the step Britain has taken.[26]

The Uganda conference was a stimulating and valuable experience for all who took part. Far from bringing the CPA and the Commonwealth to the point of dissolution, it seemed to strengthen the sense of community within the Association. The speech of the Ugandan President and many of the speeches on the Rhodesian issue were emotional and intemperate. But they demonstrated the strength of African feeling. Moreover, the African delegates were able to express themselves freely and to criticise Britain. The British delegates spoke and behaved with dignity and restraint which commanded respect. In the following sessions the discussions were earnest and frank, but courteous. Away from the conference cordial relations prevailed. The Chairman, William Kalema, and the leader of the Uganda delegation, Samuel Odaka, contributed much to the goodwill which flowed from this conference.

At the close of the General Meeting in Kampala on 1 November 1967, a warm tribute was paid to the late Sir Donald Sangster, who had become Prime Minister of Jamaica only a few weeks before his death on 11 April 1967. He was saluted as a great parliamentarian who had been throughout his long political life a fervent supporter of the Association and all that it stood for. His address to delegates in Ottawa on 28 September 1966 was recalled and the following passage was read out:

> Many people have said in the past that we have a unique association, covering some eight hundred million people from many parts of the world, from many races, many religions, and many cultures. I believe the Commonwealth has a mission in the world. The United Nations is multilingual, but we, fortunately, can speak one language; we can understand each other.... We ought to be able to exercise a greater influence on world affairs than we are doing. We have the ability, we have the resources. Despite the recent establishment of a Commonwealth Secretariat, I do not think there is a greater organization in the Commonwealth than the Commonwealth Parliamentary Association because, in the last analysis it is we, the Members of Parliament, who have to decide the fate of our own countries.[27]

On behalf of the Jamaica branch Roy McNeill responded. Delegates then stood in silence as a mark of respect to the memory of a good friend.

At the end of the conference in Kampala, L. O. Pindling, Premier of the Bahamas, was elected Chairman of the Association. The Council was unable to elect the Vice-Chairman, since the venue of the 1969 conference was not certain. The Pakistan branch had been expected to host the conference in 1969, but, since national and provincial elections were to be held later in that year, it had been unable to extend an invitation. Trinidad and Tobago was to be host in 1970. At the request of the Chairman, Dr Eric Williams, the Prime Minister, agreed to advance its invitation to 1969. Subsequently Gerard Montano, Minister of Home Affairs and Personnel and Leader of the House of Representatives, was elected Vice-Chairman.

The Executive Committee held its first meeting in Mauritius from 4–7 June 1968.[28] The opening ceremony was performed by the Speaker of the Legislative Assembly, H. R. Vaghee. It was attended by the Governor-General, Sir John Shaw Rennie, by the Prime Minister, Sir Seewoosagur Ramgoolam, and other Ministers and members of the legislature.

The Committee of 15 had 6 new members, and from the start all worked well together. The agenda for the conference to be held in Nassau was drafted in greater detail. At the same time it was made more forceful by including contentious subjects, like race relations, which had been avoided in the past.

The ruling of the Council at its meeting in Montreal in September 1966 that observers should not be invited to attend the conference from branches in abeyance was reviewed by the Executive Committee. It took a firm line in endorsing the principle that the maintenance of parliamentary government was fundamental to the existence of the Association and of its branches. The invitation of observers from such defunct branches would offend against this principle. The Committee went further in recommending that this decision should be widely publicised so that the Association's commitment to the principles and practices of parliamentary democracy was generally understood. It was, indeed, this commitment that gave the CPA its strength and following.

The idea of establishing a special link between the CPA and the meetings of Prime Ministers was modified, rather than abandoned. The Committee adopted a resolution which read:

> That the Prime Ministers should express their strong support for the CPA and the further development of its activities, as set out in the Report of the Executive Committee of its General Council after the meeting in Mauritius, and especially endorse its valuable work as an association of Parliamentarians, united irrespective of race, religion, and culture in the Commonwealth.[29]

The Prime Minister of Mauritius, Sir Seewoosagur Ramgoolam, a staunch friend of the Association, had agreed to propose the inclusion of this resolution in the agenda of the forthcoming meeting of Prime Ministers. Members of the Committee were asked to seek the support of their own Prime Ministers for the resolution. The purpose was to gain greater attention and more finance as well as wider publicity and influence for the Association.

Members of the Committee and particularly its Chairman, Peter Howson, had been active in seeking invitations well in advance to host the annual conference. At the Mauritius meeting the Committee was able to note the following venues: 1969, Trinidad and Tobago; 1970, Pakistan; 1971, Australia; 1972, Zambia; 1973, United Kingdom; 1974, Ceylon. Venues for the mid-year meetings of the Committee were also noted. Gibraltar and Jersey had already issued invitations. A meeting in Sierra Leone was considered desirable, since parliamentary government had been restored there recently. It was further agreed that enquiries should be made of the branches in Singapore, Fiji, Lesotho, Botswana, Swaziland, British Honduras and Bermuda, as to their readiness to host meetings of the Committee.

The desirability of conferences of Presiding Officers was under active consideration in several Commonwealth legislatures in the late 1960s. Since the 1920s conferences of Presiding Officers in the legislatures of India had been taking place on a regular basis. They had proved valuable in enabling Speakers and Presidents, especially those newly elected, to discuss standing orders, privilege, and indeed every aspect of the machinery of Parliament. The discussions contributed to greater efficiency in the use of parliamentary time and the running of legislatures generally.

In 1964, following the meeting of Prime Ministers, Donald Sangster had written to his fellow Finance Ministers, proposing that they increase grants to their branches. In his letter he had emphasised the need for more contacts between Commonwealth MPs. He had added: 'I believe, too, that the institution of Parliament would be strengthened by periodic conferences of Speakers and conferences of Clerks, which the CPA could promote or assist in promoting.'[30]

Kenya was first to respond to this suggestion. Humphrey Slade, Speaker of the Kenyan House of Representatives, jointly with the Speaker of the Senate, T. M. Chokwe, invited Speakers and Clerks of Parliaments in Eastern and Central Africa to attend a conference in Nairobi on 12–14 August 1964. Invitations were extended also to Robin Vanderfelt, Secretary-General of the CPA, and to Charles Gordon, who was then Fourth Clerk-at-the-Table at Westminster. Nine Speakers and seven Clerks attended this conference. The opening ceremony was performed by Jomo Kenyatta, Prime Minister of Kenya, who said in the course of his speech that 'The importance of Speakers of the Parliaments whose countries have just gained independence or are about to gain independent status to meet and exchange ideas and share their experiences cannot be exaggerated'.[31] Humphrey Slade was a learned and dedicated parliamentarian. He played a leading role in this conference and, as a senior Kenyan Clerk, was to write later, he 'laid the foundation stone of parliamentary democracy during the first six years of Kenya's independent Parliament'.[32]

Support for such conferences gained impetus in 1965, when 40 Presiding Officers assembled in London for the celebration of the 700th anniversary of

Simon de Montfort's Parliament. Meeting during the celebrations they agreed 'that regional conferences possibly with a few guest Speakers from elsewhere might profitably be arranged at intervals of two or three years, with conferences comprising the whole Commonwealth somewhat less frequently'.[33]

Conferences or informal meetings of Speakers took place in Ottawa in September 1966 at the time of the conference, when as many as 18 Speakers were present as delegates, and also in Lusaka in May 1967, and in Kampala in October 1967. Two further developments of importance were the first conference of Australian Presiding Officers and Clerks, which took place in Canberra in January 1968, and the meeting of Presiding Officers of the Caribbean in Barbados in June 1968.

Meanwhile the Speaker of the Canadian House of Commons, Lucien Lamoureux, enthused by the success of the informal meeting in Ottawa in 1966, proposed to Westminster that conferences of Speakers of the Commonwealth should be held at two-yearly intervals. He took the initiative in planning to host the first conference in Ottawa in September 1969. The Speaker at Westminster welcomed the Canadian proposal, but suggested that the conferences should take place at 3–5-yearly intervals and that the first conference should be in 1970.

The Executive Committee reviewed the proposals in the context of the overall activities of the CPA. It recommended that regular conferences of Commonwealth Speakers should be encouraged at 4–5-yearly intervals. It noted that the CPA did not have sufficient funds to support them financially, but would welcome their being held under CPA auspices. It added that, if Speakers' conferences were arranged independently, they should not take place as in Ottawa and in Kampala, at the time of the CPA conferences, since they distracted delegates and posed difficulties of organisation. The recommendations revealed a cautious attitude, reflecting the view of the United Kingdom rather than of the Commonwealth as a whole. Certain Speakers resented this. As a result it was decided that their conferences would be held at 2–3-yearly intervals and independently of the CPA.

The 17th course on parliamentary practice and procedure was held at Westminster on 1–16 May 1968. The Committee agreed that these practical courses, hosted jointly by the General Council and the United Kingdom branch, were among the most valuable activities of the Association. They promoted the understanding and the efficiency of Parliaments. They also brought together some 25 members in a multinational delegation and so furthered the policy of increasing contacts between Commonwealth members. A tribute to the excellence of these courses came in the form of repeated proposals that two courses should be held each year. On each occasion the United Kingdom rejected the proposal on the ground that it would be difficult to fit a second course into the crowded programme at Westminster. The Committee welcomed reports that the Australian and Canadian branches were planning to hold similar courses in their regions.

The Committee carried out the annual review of the journals, reports and other papers, produced in the Secretariat. It warmly commended *The Parliamentarian* and directed that it should be expanded further. It approved all other publications, except the *Report on World Affairs*, The working party had questioned whether it should be continued. In Mauritius the Executive Committee discussed it at length. Certain members expressed the view that it was comprehensive and informative. It was of special use in the developing countries where such information was not readily available. The majority of members, however, considered that, since the *Report* was published quarterly and sent by surface mail, it was always out-of-date by the time it reached most members. It was then of value only for reference. The division of views was broadly between those members who had ample information resources in their own Parliaments and those from developing countries which lacked them. Finally the Committee agreed by a majority of 7 to 4 with two abstentions to recommend to the General Council that on grounds of economy the *Report* should cease publication on completion of the current volume. If the Council approved this recommendation, the Committee would consider then the publication of a monthly airmail newsletter, *News of the Commonwealth*, containing items of Commonwealth and parliamentary news.

The Committee finally examined the finances of the Association. The calculations of the working party had been upset by the devaluation of sterling. By changing to the provision of economy class fares for delegates, however, the deficit in 1968 was estimated to be approximately £7700. The Committee also noted the estimates for 1969–73, prepared by the Finance Officer, Jack Fowler, which showed an overall excess of income over expenditure of £8665. These estimates together with proposals for small increases in the salaries of senior staff of the Secretariat, were submitted to the council in Nassau.

The first meeting of the Executive Committee had demonstrated its value. It gave early consideration to important matters which in the past had been delayed until the annual Council meetings. It was noteworthy how at the mid-year meeting 15 members, representative of the Commonwealth, were able to concentrate on and discuss impartially the business and problems of the CPA. It provided, in fact, an impressive example of Commonwealth cooperation and unity.

The management of the Association was, however, still cumbersome. The Executive Committee had to report to the General Council which in turn had to report to the General Meeting. The small Secretariat was hard pressed to produce the minutes and reports of the respective organs. Too much time was taken to reach decisions and then to implement them. The urgent need for reforms soon became apparent.

From Mauritius the Chairman of the Association, L. O. Pindling, the Chairman of the Executive Committee, Peter Howson, with Mrs Kitty Howson, accompanied by Ian Grey, visited Kenya. They had meetings with the Speaker, Humphrey Slade, with the Vice-President Daniel arap Moi, and with the Attorney-General, Charles Njonjo. They were presented to the President of

Kenya, Mzee Jomo Kenyatta, and to Ngwazi Dr H. K. Banda, President of Malawi, who was then on an official visit to Kenya.

From Nairobi they flew to Pakistan on a four-day visit to meet members of the National Assembly and to discuss arrangements for the 1970 conference. The Pakistan branch had been in abeyance but had been revived and readmitted to membership of the Association in 1963. The President, Mohammed Ayub Khan, received the guests and confirmed that Pakistan would host the conference as agreed. He nominated the Minister for Law and Parliamentary Affairs, S. M. Zafar, to serve as Vice-Chairman in 1968–69 and as Chairman in the following year.

This involved an amendment to the Association's constitution. Pakistan had adopted a presidential system of government under which Ministers were excluded from membership of the National Assembly. They had all rights and privileges of members, but not the right to vote. Further a member who became a Minister was required to resign his seat in the National Assembly. The constitution of the Association provided in Clause 8 that only members of a legislature were eligible for membership of a branch and so of the Association. Ministers in Pakistan not being members were thus excluded. The Executive Committee in Nassau agreed to recommend to the Council adoption of the following amendment to Clause 8:

> Notwithstanding the above the General Council of the Association shall have authority to admit to full membership of a branch on the recommendation of the Executive Committee of that branch any Minister who, while not a member of his legislature is carrying out parliamentary and ministerial duties.[34]

Meetings of the General Council were usually earnest but cordial. Opposing views were sometimes argued, but without heat. This did not apply during the Council's meetings in Nassau on 27 October and on 1 and 5 November 1968.

One of the first items to be considered by the Council was the amendment to the constitution which would admit Ministers in Pakistan to membership of their branch. Mohammed Bash Taqi, the councillor from Sierra Leone, at first strongly opposed it. He argued that it violated a basic principle of the CPA that every member must be an elected representative of the people and not merely an appointee. The Chairman pointed out that a major difference between the Pakistani and the US constitutions was that Ministers could not sit in either House of Congress and could appear before a committee only on the invitation of either House. Further, members of non-elective second Chambers, like the House of Lords and the Canadian Senate, had always been entitled to membership of their branches. Bash Taqi nevertheless maintained that acceptance of people from outside the legislature, who would represent the CPA, was a violation of a fundamental principle and a dangerous precedent. After further discussion, however, the amendment was adopted by a large majority.

The Council approved the agenda and all the arrangements for the conference.

An innovation was that the proceedings would be broadcast live by Bahamas Radio. At the meeting on 1 November, it received various reports on CPA activities. In the discussions on the Westminster course on parliamentary practice and procedure and plans to hold similar courses in Australia and Canada, Eric Gairy, the Prime Minister of Grenada, proposed a further development. It would, he said, be more realistic and valuable if a team of experienced members could visit a country, holding a course in which all local members could take part. A team from Westminster, for example, could visit five or six Parliaments in the West Indies and a great many members would benefit.

The recommendation of the Executive Committee that publication of the *Report on World Affairs* should be discontinued was discussed at length. A number of delegates found the *Report* valuable and were reluctant to see it abandoned. Others expressed the criticisms which had already been noted by the Committee. Then came allegations that the *Report* was misleading and gave 'a false representation of affairs in each state'.[35] Dr N. M. Perera called it 'an insult to the Association ... with out-of-date information, often inaccurate'.[36] This was the first time that Dr Perera, although present both at the working party and the Executive Committee meetings, had voiced such criticisms. Roy McNeill (Jamaica) complained of 'an ill-founded and inaccurate report' of an incident in his country.[37]

The Editor explained that the condensed reports were contributed by correspondents in each region who were respected and well-informed. He had during his editorship received two complaints of inaccuracy in the *Report*, only one of which had proved justified. Others then spoke in defence of the *Report*. The allegations reflected the sensitivity of members, especially from the newly independent countries, and the difficulty of producing a quarterly report, acceptable to all members. There was a clear majority in favour of discontinuation and the recommendation of the Executive Committee was approved.

After noting the estimates for 1968 and 1969, both of which anticipated a credit balance, several councillors questioned whether the increases in branch contributions, approved in Kampala in 1967, were now necessary. The Treasurer explained that they would not become operative until 1969. There would be a saving of some £6000 from closure of the *Report on World Affairs*. The Association was at last in credit and this should be maintained.

Dr Megat Khas stated that the Malaysian branch objected to the increase and had informed the Council by letter in Kampala. The Chairman said that the letter had been noted, but the Council had nevertheless agreed to ask branches to increase their contributions. More than 90 per cent had agreed; no branch had yet refused. Dr Megat Khas replied that his branch would not pay the increase. He went on to complain about the expenditure incurred by the office and staff of the General Council. 'An organisation such as the CPA could not and should not attempt to maintain an expensive staff, nor could the CPA afford to continue undertaking expenditure on the unnecessary travel of staff and officials.'[38] He asked for an investigation to establish whether the Secretariat had too many staff.

The Chairman replied that at its last meeting the Executive Committee had agreed unanimously to examine the need to increase the staff of the Secretariat.[39]

The Chairman then reported that the Committee had also agreed to recommend a new range of salaries for the senior staff. The Treasurer explained that the cost of salaries for the five senior members of staff as on 1 January 1968 was £12,230. The total cost of the increases proposed would take this figure to £14,080, a rise of £1850 as from 1 January 1969.

Dr Ng Kam Poh (Malaysia) said that he wished it to be recorded that in the Executive Committee he had objected to the increases in salaries. B. K. Bataringaya (Uganda) expressed his great respect for the staff and considered that they deserved the thanks and congratulations of the Association. He thought, however, that the terms of service of the staff should be examined by the Committee and printed in book form.

Speaking on the salary increases, Sir John Cramer (Australia) drew attention to the responsibility resting upon the Secretariat: 'Upon it', he said,

> depended the success or otherwise of the Association. . . . From year to year the burden was carried by the Council's Secretariat in conjunction with a number of non-paid people – Clerks of Parliament – who acted as branch Secretaries. Members of Parliament changed from time to time, but the Secretariat continued. The whole issue was really one of the value of the Secretariat to the Association, and in present day circumstances to have a salary bill of £14,080 to carry out the responsibility and the work involved was to him astounding. The Council should accept the recommendation of the Committee and be thankful that they had people of the calibre they had in the Secretariat.[40]

Eric Gairy (Grenada), supporting this view, said that the proposed increase in salaries was 'just a joke. The Association was not paying salaries commensurate with the responsibilities of the Secretariat'.[41]

The Council then approved, Malaysia dissenting, the motion to accept the recommendation of the Executive Committee. It approved also a motion that the terms and conditions of service of the Secretariat be examined by the Committee at its next meeting in Gibraltar.

One of the last acts of the Council in Nassau was to elect a councillor in terms of Clause 24 to succeed Bernard Braine who had completed his three-year term. Four members were nominated and Mohammed Bash Taqi (Sierra Leone) was finally elected.

The retirement of Bernard Braine was a loss to the CPA. Over a period of 14 years he had been an active member, taking a major part in every important occasion. As a United Kingdom councillor, as a Clause 24 councillor, and a member of the working party, he gave to the CPA devoted service at a time when it was evolving rapidly. Of all the parliamentarians who have contributed importantly to the Association, certain deserve special mention in this history: Bernard Braine belongs to that group.

The General Meeting of the Association, held on 28 October and 8 November 1968, was uneventful. One item of business, however, merited special notice. This was the tribute to Harold Holt, the former Chairman of the Association and late Prime Minister of Australia, whose tragic death took place on 17 December 1967. Bernard Braine spoke on behalf of the Association. He recalled that he had first served on the Council under his Chairmanship in Nairobi in 1954. He had also had the stimulating experience of travelling the length and breadth of the African continent with him. Harold Holt was, he said, a natural leader but with the rare quality of evoking affection as well as respect. He cared for people and never forgot old friends. A politician and also a parliamentarian, like the late Donald Sangster, he gave richly to the Association in which he believed. Sir John Cramer responded on behalf of the Australian branches. The members then stood in silence as a mark of respect to his memory.

The 14th Commonwealth Parliamentary Conference, held in Nassau from 1–8 November 1968, was stormy. It was opened with customary ceremony by the Governor of the Bahamas, Sir Francis Cumming-Bruce, on the invitation of the Chairman, L.O. Pindling, Prime Minister of the Bahamas. Delegates, numbering 120 with 25 Secretaries to delegations, represented 64 branches of the Association. Notable among members of the United Kingdom delegation was Mrs Margaret Thatcher, then a member of the Opposition.

The first three sessions were concerned with 'World Security'.[42] Again, Rhodesia was the subject of fiery speeches. B. K. Bataringaya (Uganda) condemned Britain's refusal to use military force, while sending arms to Gowon's Federal government in Nigeria and helping in the suppression of the Biafra rebellion. It meant, he said, that Britain would provide arms to suppress a black rebel, but not for use against the white rebels in Rhodesia. Delegates from Lesotho and Malawi spoke boldly against the use of force in Rhodesia, explaining that their nationals would suffer most in any war. Most others from Africa, Asia and the Caribbean deplored Britain's failure to send troops or to resolve the crisis.

The speeches became more and more vituperative. Opening the second session Humphrey Mulemba, leader of the Zambia delegation, spoke with strong emotion and threatened that Africa might turn to Russia or China for support against the Ian Smith regime. Like others he was voicing the deep frustration of Africans at their own impotence and their anger over Britain's failure to resolve the problem. Another underlying factor was that delegates from the newly independent countries still looked on Britain as a great power and one that upheld higher moral principles than other powers: they now felt let down.

Dr Sanjiva Reddy (India) observed that all were agreed that the principle of one man one vote must be established in Rhodesia. This had been fully discussed in the last three conferences. The CPA could not take decisions that would solve the problem: it was a matter for heads of government. The conference should be devoting the time to parliamentary matters. Goronwy Roberts, leader of the United Kingdom delegation, wound up the session with a long placatory speech, which seemed to incense the African delegates.

At the opening of the third session the Chairman read out a letter of protest from the Zambian delegation. Conference practice was that the speaker chosen to open a session was allowed 20 minutes; all subsequent speakers had 10 minutes. Humphrey Mulemba, opening the session, was exceeding his 20 minutes by 4 minutes when the Chairman, Lynden Pindling, interrupted him. A tolerant Chairman he had, in fact, allowed two other delegates to exceed the limit. The Zambian complaint was that Goronwy Roberts had spoken for 14 minutes and then an extra 10 minutes without interruption. It was the fact that the United Kingdom delegate had taken extra time for a speech which was appeasing in content, that angered the Zambian and other delegates. The protest was discussed for nearly an hour. All delegates were anxious, however, to avoid a motion of censure on the Chairman, and all went out of their way to express their full confidence in him. Finally Humphrey Mulemba, after bitter criticism of another United Kingdom delegate who had intervened, asserted that he had merely wished to draw the attention of the chair to the incident. The session then continued.

Delegates divided into Committees, which sat concurrently during the next two sessions. One Committee, chaired by Bernard Braine and then by Sir Frederic Bennett (United Kingdom) discussed 'Aid – How Effective?'. The other Committee, chaired by the Vice-Chairman, Gerard Montano, considered 'Parliamentary Government – Where is it Heading?' In the Committees and the subsequent plenary sessions there were many thoughtful and well-informed speeches and the discussions were of a high standard. Certain delegates, however, spoke with a truculence that soured the mood of the meeting. Dr N. M. Perera (Ceylon), a kindly man in his personal relations, who described himself as 'an innocuous Trotskyist', was prone in conference to speak critically, even violently, against Britain and the developed countries. Victor Grant, leader of the Jamaica delegation, spoke more frequently than any other delegate. He was articulate, even eloquent at times, but often vituperative. In the session on 'Racial Harmony' he lashed out not only at Britain, but also at Australia, Canada and the United States, accusing all of practising racial discrimination. An Australian delegate, Fred Daly, who spoke after him, said: 'His speech made no contribution towards solving this great human problem but rather aggravated our difficulties.'[43]

Margaret Thatcher had been angered by the constant attacks on Britain, but in conference she spoke with great moderation. During the session on 'Racial Harmony', she expressed her view of the conference when she said:

> Mr Chairman, we have had a very good debate through the whole conference. The purpose of controversy is to grow together by discussion of differences and not by accentuating differences to grow further apart. I think that one fault of this conference has been that we have tended to look at everything in terms of black and white, when we all know there are far more sophisticated political reasons behind most problems. I hope that in the short time left to us we will use our freedom of speech constructively to grow together and not further apart.[44]

It was a stimulating and at times difficult conference. African problems provided the dominant themes, whether on the Rhodesian crisis or on aid. As in previous conferences the division appeared to be racial. This did not, however, prevail away from the conference sessions. Delegates were accommodated in adjacent hotels and were constantly brought together. The tendency to keep in groups was gradually broken down. The Chairman, Lynden Pindling, was a warm and generous host, mingling among them. Members of the Secretariat, too, made an important contribution to the general sense of fellowship. They were in constant contact with the delegates and Secretaries to delegations, many of whom they could count as personal friends.

At a time of great stress within the Commonwealth, the Association had again provided a forum in which conflicting views and the tensions to which they gave rise could be freely discussed. This was achieved, moreover, without walk-outs, breakdowns or disruptions in relations between delegates and member countries.

Notes

1. General Council Minutes, 10 September 1966.
2. General Council Minutes, 30 September 1966.
3. Arnold Smith and his successor, Sridath Ramphal, have attended CPA conferences as observers whenever their commitments permitted. They have been invited to address delegates, but not in conference. A separate meeting has been arranged. Their speeches and the record of the question period have been printed as appendices to the official reports of conference proceedings.
4. **Agenda and Opening Speakers, Ottawa, 1966**
   The Commonwealth and the World - Paul Martin, Secretary of State for External Affairs (Canada)
   Parliamentary Government in the Commonwealth - in committee
   Commonwealth Self-help - Trade and Aid - in committee
   The CPA and the Commonwealth Secretariat - Peter Howson, Minister for Air and Minister assisting the Treasurer (Australia)
   Commonwealth Self-help - Trade and Aid, in plenary session - Lord Shepherd, Government Chief Whip, House of Lords (United Kingdom)
   Education and Technical Assistance - consideration of the report of the first committee on Trade and Aid
   Parliamentary Government in the Commonwealth - consideration of the report of the committee session
   Commonwealth Self-help - Price Stabilisation, in plenary session - Shri M.P. Bhargava, Vice-Chairman of Rajya Sabha (India); Miangul Aurangzeb (Pakistan).
5. Conference Report (Ottawa, 1966) p.21.
6. Ibid., p.245.
7. Ibid., p.253.
8. Ibid., p.260.
9. *Loc. cit.*
10. Ibid., p.263.
11. *Loc. cit.*
12. Report of the General Meeting (Ottawa, 3 October 1966), pp.53–4.
13. Ibid., p.257.

14. **Members of the Working Party**
   Chairman – Peter Howson (Australia); W. W. Kalema (Uganda), Chairman of the Association, John J. Connolly (Canada), Bernard Braine (United Kingdom), Malcolm MacPherson (United Kingdom), Roy McNeill (Jamaica), J. Hamilton Maurice (Trinidad & Tobago), Ng Kam Poh (Malaysia), R. G. Ngala (Kenya), N. M. Perera (Ceylon), Guido de Marco (Malta) and Vincent Moran (Malta).
15. The papers are published as the supporting memoranda to the report of the working party, bound with the report of the General Council, 1966–67.
16. Report of the Working Party (Valletta, 1967), p.5.
17. **Members of the Executive Committee**
   Chairman of the Committee – Peter Howson (Australia); L. O. Pindling (Bahamas), A. G. Montano (Trinidad & Tobago), represented at meetings by Hamilton Maurice, W. W. Kalema (Uganda), Malcolm MacPherson (United Kingdom), Bernard Braine (United Kingdom), R. G. Ngala (Kenya), N. M. Perera (Ceylon), M. Sipalo (Zambia), N. Sanjiva Reddy (India), A. E. Allen (New Zealand), John J. Connolly (Canada), Ng Kam Poh (Malaysia), George Thomson (United Kingdom) and Roy McNeill (Jamaica).
18. Conference Report (Kampala, 1967), p.xvi.
19. Ibid., p.xvii.
20. Loc. cit.
21. **Agenda and Opening Speakers, Kampala, 1967**
   Africa in World Affairs: World Peace – S. N. Odaka, Minister of Foreign Affairs (Uganda); James E. Walker (Canada)
   Aid to Developing Countries: Food Resources and the Population Increase – A. P. Appanna, Deputy Minister for Industries (Mysore)
   Parliamentary Institutions: Erosion of Parliamentary Authority by the Executive and Through Subordinate Legislation – Senator J. E. Marriott (Australia)
   Aid to Developing Countries: Investment in Developing Countries of the Commonwealth – R. E. Wallace (Trinidad & Tobago)
   Parliamentary Institutions: The Breakdown of Parliamentary Institutions in Parts of the Commonwealth – R. G. Ngala (Kenya)
   Aid to Developing Countries: Scientific Research and Development Services – J. A. Pettitt (Australia)
   Parliamentary Institutions: the Press in a Parliamentary Democracy – N. J. Bissember, Minister for Parliamentary Affairs and Leader of the House (Guyana)
   The Commonwealth and the European Economic Community – George Thomson, Secretary of State for Commonwealth Affairs (United Kingdom); Roy McNeill, Minister of Home Affairs (Jamaica).
22. Conference Report (Kampala, 1967), p.10.
23. Ibid., pp.36–7.
24. Ibid., p.44.
25. Ibid., p.53.
26. Ibid., p.269.
27. Conference Report (Ottawa, 1966), pp.38–9; Report of the General Meeting (Kampala, 1967).
28. Report of the Executive Committee (Mauritius, 1968), p.12.
29. Report of the General Council (1967–68), p.60.
30. Loc. cit.
31. Report of the Conference Proceedings of Speakers and Clerks of Parliaments of Eastern and Central African Territories (August 1964), p.8.

32. From a private source.
33. General Council Minutes, 27 October 1968.
34. General Council Minutes, 1 November 1968.
35. *Loc. cit.*
36. *Loc. cit.* The report was, in fact, accurate. The event was one in which the government appeared to be at fault. Roy McNeill objected to this being reported.
37. *Loc. cit.*
38. General Council Minutes, 5 November 1968.
39. *Loc. cit.*
40. *Loc. cit.*
41. *Loc. cit.*
42. **Agenda and Opening Speakers, Nassau, 1968**
    World Security – John J. Connolly (Canada); Humphrey Mulemba, Minister of State for the Cabinet and Public Service (Zambia); S. M. Zafar, Minister for Law and Parliamentary Affairs (Pakistan)
    Aid – How Effective? – in committee – James J. Webster (Australia); Sir Frederic Bennett (United Kingdom)
    Parliamentary Government – Where is it Heading? – in committee – Robin Turton (United Kingdom); Philip Saliba (Malta)
    Problems of Economic Growth – J. F. Luxton (New Zealand); Robin Turton (United Kingdom)
    Racial Harmony or Conflict: Which Way for Mankind? – Kendal G. L. Isaacs (Bahamas); B. L. B. Pitt, Minister of State in Ministry of Prime Minister (Trinidad & Tobago).
43. Conference Report (Nassau, 1968), p.277.
44. Ibid., p.264.

16 Into the 1970s, 1969-70

The 1960s had been a troubled decade in Africa and other regions of the Commonwealth. The 1970s were to prove no easier. The Commonwealth nevertheless continued to demonstrate an extraordinary cohesion and capacity for survival.

The reasons for this survival were numerous and are still relevant today. They included the remarkable personal influence of the Monarch as Head of the Commonwealth and the use of English as the means of communication. They included also the fact that the developing nations, while attacking Britain over Rhodesia and South Africa, could continue to look to Britain as the main source of aid. There remained, too, a strong respect for the law and order and stable parliamentary government maintained in the United Kingdom, and even an abiding affection for the former imperial power.

Yet another factor was that the Commonwealth was a community in which shared background and principles allowed members to meet, discuss and dispute more readily than in the United Nations and other international organisations. It was, for example, noteworthy that anglophone Africans were seldom at ease with their francophone neighbours, as they were with their fellow members of the Commonwealth. The cohesion and survival of the Commonwealth also owed a great deal to another factor which was not widely publicised nor indeed widely recognised. This was the frequent contacts between people with common interests, provided by the non-governmental organisations and especially the CPA.

At the beginning of the 1970s the CPA was developing strongly and extremely active. The Executive Committee was the main source of the new vitality, which owed much to the drive of Peter Howson, its Chairman. The Committee met in Gibraltar from 26-30 May 1969. Gerard Montano, Chairman of the Association, reported the arrangements for the conference to be held in Trinidad and Tobago in October 1969.

The Committee noted with pleasure the reference to the CPA in the communiqué, issued after the meeting of the Commonwealth Prime Ministers in January 1969, which read:

The meeting also expressed appreciation of the valuable contribution to the strengthening of Commonwealth cooperation and understanding being made by the Commonwealth Parliamentary Association. As an independent association of Parliamentarians it provides unique opportunities for the sharing of experience, the discussion of common problems, and the development of personal links to the benefit of both of its members and the people they represent.[1]

This tribute had been made on the initiative of the Prime Minister of Mauritius, Sir Seewoosagur Ramgoolam. It was not, however, followed up by requests to the individual Prime Ministers for greater financial support as in 1964, and during the 1970s the finances of the Association were a source of real problems.

Venues for future conferences were discussed at length. Pakistan had offered to host the conference in 1970, as the President, Ayub Khan, had confirmed personally to Peter Howson in 1968. Parliamentary government had been suspended there in March 1969. It was expected to be restored early in 1970. The Committee's view was, however, that this would allow too little time to make adequate arrangements. Alternative venues were considered. It was hoped that Australia would bring forward its invitation from 1971 to 1970. The probable venues were then as follows: 1969, Trinidad and Tobago; 1970, Australia; 1971, Pakistan; 1972, Zambia; 1973, United Kingdom; 1974, Sri Lanka (Ceylon).

The expansion of regional and area conferences and of seminars received special attention. The first African regional conference had been held in Lusaka in April 1969. Further conferences were to take place in 1970 in Sierra Leone, in 1971 in Malawi, and in 1972 in Mauritius. The Committee received reports on the 6th Caribbean regional conference, held in Antigua earlier in May 1969, and on the 10th Australian area conference, held in Sydney in April 1969. The 10th Canadian area conference was to be hosted by Newfoundland in July 1969, and the Isle of Man was to host the first conference of the United Kingdom and Mediterranean region in September 1969.

The Committee also took notice of two conferences which, while not held under CPA auspices, were of special interest. They were the second conference of Australian Presiding Officers and Clerks-at-the-Table, held in April 1969, and the conference of Commonwealth Speakers, which the Speaker of the Canadian House of Commons was to host in Ottawa in September 1969.

The 18th course on parliamentary practice and procedure, which included visits to Northern Ireland and the Isle of Man, had taken place at Westminster from 23 April–9 May 1969. This course continued to be one of the most valuable events in the Association's calendar. The Committee was now also keenly interested in seminars in other countries. At the General Meeting in the Bahamas in 1968, the Premier of Grenada, Eric Gairy, had suggested that seminars would be of more value if a team of experienced parliamentarians could visit smaller countries, leading discussions on practice and procedure, which would benefit all members of the legislature. The pilot seminar was planned to take place in Grenada in July 1969, when a team of two members and a senior Clerk from Westminster and a similar team from Ottawa would take part. From Grenada they were to fly to the Bahamas to conduct another seminar. In Australia and Fiji seminars were under active consideration. Thus the Association's programme in 1969 gave impressive evidence of the increasing scale of its activities.

The 15th Commonwealth Parliamentary Conference took place at Chaguaramas, Trinidad and Tobago, in October 1969. It was preceded as usual by meetings of the Executive Committee and the General Council. One of the Council's first items of business concerned the venue of the 1970 conference and the election of the Vice-Chairman. In Pakistan the National Assembly had been dissolved and the branch suspended. S. M. Zafar, elected Vice-Chairman in Nassau, automatically vacated the office. Australia had agreed to host this conference. Sir Alister McMullin, President of the Australian Senate, was unanimously elected in his place. All who could recall his service to the Association as its Chairman both in 1959–60 and 1969–70 as a Clause 24 councillor, welcomed his return to office. Members of the Secretariat to whom he had always been a warm and helpful friend were especially pleased. The Secretary-General at once sent a cable inviting him to come to Trinidad at his earliest convenience. He arrived five days later.

The Council accepted with appreciation Zambia's invitation to host the 1972 conference. It came in a letter from Kenneth Kaunda, President of the Republic.[2] The Chairman of the Executive Committee, Peter Howson, reported that, when in London in June 1969, he had called on the Prime Minister, Harold Wilson. He had confirmed the invitation, extended by George Thomson in Nassau, to hold the conference in London in 1973.

At its meeting on 11 October 1969 the Council welcomed the delegation from Ghana, which had just arrived in Port-of-Spain. One of the first acts of the newly elected Parliament of Ghana had been to pass a resolution to revive its branch. Next, it had chosen its delegates and within a few days they had set out to attend the conference.

The seminar in Grenada, in which the Executive Committee had taken a keen interest, had taken place on 14–18 July 1969. Neville Bissember (Guyana), the Caribbean Regional Representative, had attended it. He reported now to the Council that it had been a great success. The discussions and exchanges of views had been lively in all sessions. The presence of the Chairman of the Association, Gerard Montano and his participation in the first three sessions, had been welcomed. The Premier of Grenada had taken an active part in the discussions, as had other local Ministers and members.

Neville Bissember recommended that seminars of this kind should be arranged more frequently. It was, he said, important that members of smaller legislatures should be able to discuss parliamentary matters with experienced visitors. Such discussions helped them to put their own problems into perspective, while encouraging them to review their procedures and to make their legislatures more efficient.

In summing up the discussion that followed, the Chairman of the Council said that seminars were clearly valuable and central to the main purpose of the

Association. Unless more money could be found, however, they would have to be curtailed. Having held a seminar in Grenada in 1969, the CPA should try to hold the only seminar it could afford in 1970 somewhere in Africa. Thus the project of local seminars was virtually set aside for lack of finance.

The General Council had elected Sir Frederic Bennett to be Treasurer in succession to Malcolm Macpherson. Bennett had the advantage of being a financier. He reported to the Executive Committee in Gibraltar that he had negotiated with a merchant bank a favourable rate of interest on the Association's funds. Further he suggested two approaches which would avoid payment of British taxes. The first was to register the Association as a charity. He had consulted the Charity Commissioners in London and had been advised that the constitution of the Association could be revised to meet their requirements without detracting from its aims and functions. The second course involved the initial payment of all CPA income, less the amount paid by the United Kingdom branch, through the Jersey branch, thus avoiding UK taxes. This was a procedure about which he would have to consult the British Commissioners of Inland Revenue.

As recorded in the Executive Committee's report of its meeting in Gibraltar in 1969,

> The Chairman on behalf of the Committee expressed warm appreciation for the masterly manner in which the Hon. Treasurer had handled the reinvestment of the funds and had reviewed the finances of the Association. It was agreed that since the financial arrangements discussed would spread beyond the Hon. Treasurer's term of office, he should be appointed as Honorary Financial Adviser to the Committee until these arrangements were concluded.
>
> In further discussion, the view was strongly expressed that the existing system whereby a new Hon. Treasurer was appointed annually irrespective of his qualifications as a financier should be reviewed. It was essential that the Association's funds should be expertly handled and, since this was the function of the Hon. Treasurer, the appointment of suitably qualified Members to this office was of overriding importance.[3]

At its meeting in Port-of-Spain on 11 October, the Council elected Sir Alfred Broughton, nominated by the United Kingdom branch, to be Treasurer for the year 1969–70. It also co-opted Sir Frederic Bennett to serve for 12 months as Hon. Financial Adviser. This second appointment was certainly necessary, for Broughton openly confessed that he knew nothing at all about finance.

One topic which took up much of the Council's time and nearly all of the time of the General Meeting, held on 15 October 1969, concerned the presence of wives of delegates at conferences of the Association. The long-standing convention was that wives or spouses did not accompany delegates, but it was increasingly broken. The Executive Committee took the view that the matter should be reconsidered.

This was in no sense a frivolous matter, but one of real concern. Howard d'Egville had done all in his power to discourage delegates from bringing their spouses to CPA meetings. He had been generally successful. He maintained strongly that the conferences were working events. Each delegate was expected to participate in the sessions and to have serious exchanges with other delegates away from the conference floor. Members did not take their wives to Parliament and should not take them to CPA conferences. The presence of wives would, moreover, be a distraction from work, leading to shopping expeditions, sight-seeing, golf and other demands on delegates' time. Furthermore, if wives accompanied the delegates, it would encourage the flippant idea that attendance at a CPA conference was a jaunt or joyride, a plum to be offered to the faithful party member. Another factor was that the presence of wives would add to numbers, putting pressure on accommodation, arrangements for tours, and transport. The councillor from New South Wales, R. F. Jackson, asserted that the following year in Australia it would be impossible to accommodate all delegates in the one hotel, which was always the objective, if wives came, and there would be difficulties with transport. He urged that the convention should be maintained.

On a vote 32 of the 55 members of the Council approved the following resolution: 'That this General Council of the CPA resolves that the presence of wives or husbands of delegates, as the case may be, at annual conferences of the CPA is not in the best interests of the aims and objects of the CPA.'[4]

Discussion of this resolution in the General Meeting was lively and at times heated. Again R. F. Jackson urged support of the Council's resolution. Now he was opposed by two other Australian delegates. E. J. Harrison, a member of the Australian Federal branch, and the Queensland delegate, C. M. Hughes, who said that he had been married just four weeks, dismissed the resolution as archaic. The leader of the Bermuda delegation, Mrs. L. M. Browne-Evans, spoke forcefully against the resolution. Women usually made real contributions to their husbands' political careers, she said, and were not distractions. Each branch should make its own ruling. Hamilton Maurice (Trinidad and Tobago) favoured the attendance of wives, adding, 'I do not see how the presence of wives affects the aims and objects of our Association.'[5]

An amendment to the Council's resolution was moved, 'That the question of wives or husbands accompanying delegates be left entirely to the discretion of the delegates, on the clear understanding that any expense incurred in connexion with the wife or husband accompanying the delegate shall not be an expense against the CPA but shall be entirely the financial responsibility of the delegate.'[6] On a show of hands, 46 delegates voted for and 25 votes against the amendment, which was thus carried.

The conference was opened at Queen's Hall, Port-of-Spain, on 13 October with customary ceremonial by the Governor-General of Trinidad and Tobago, Sir Solomon Hochoy. The Chairman of the Association, Gerard Montano, the Prime Minister of Trinidad and Tobago, Dr Eric Williams, and the Vice-Chairman, Sir Alister McMullin, all made speeches. Gerard Montano, who always expressed himself with great clarity, spoke of the Association as follows:

The CPA is, in fact, a unique organisation. Through it, Members of Parliament from all parts of the Commonwealth are able to meet to discuss common problems, to grow in understanding and, I venture to say, in stature. The plenary conferences, which are held annually in different parts of the Commonwealth, enable them to see at first hand the problems of those countries. This direct contact and often the realisation that problems are common to many other countries, in itself provides a bond of understanding and often results in mutual help.

The CPA is sometimes referred to as a club. I believe that our Association is of much greater importance. The obligation of a member of a club is to pay his dues so that he may enjoy its facilities, but in the CPA we are bound by much stronger bonds, and have a deeper purpose. As parliamentarians we are committed to the democratic process and we have the special responsibility of serving the people who have elected us, and of serving our countries. Through our membership of the Association we are strengthened and helped in this process.[7]

The conference brought together 135 delegates and 25 Secretaries to delegations from 68 branches of the Association. From the associated group in the US Congress two Senators and two Representatives attended. The Association was especially pleased to welcome again Senator J. William Fulbright. The conference sessions were held at Chaguaramas in the admirable new conference centre, which had been completed only on the day before the first session opened.[8]

The first agenda item, 'Economic Development', was discussed with great breadth and authority. Delegates struck a note of realism. This was notable, too, in the fifth and sixth sessions when 'The Commonwealth and World Security' was the subject. The opening speaker, Shafiq Arain, leader of the Uganda delegation, reviewed the troubled state of the world. He then spoke of Africa's problems and especially of Rhodesia. On this critical issue he spoke frankly, but with restraint. Several African delegates repeated earlier attacks on Britain. Certain of those present felt that these speeches were for the record, and that these delegates now recognised that the use of force by Britain was not practicable. The delegates from Lesotho, Malawi and Swaziland condemned their demands for military action by Britain. The discussion on Rhodesia was markedly more moderate than the discussions in Kampala in 1967 and Nassau in 1968.

The two sessions on 'New Concepts in Race Relations' were muted in tone. Several delegates delivered set speeches on how well they were coping with racial problems in their own countries. Indeed, Bernard Soysa (Ceylon) commented: 'I must confess to my fellow delegates here that in regard to this problem of racial discrimination I feel that all nations speak with a voice of guilt. There is a certain hesitancy in utterance when we come to discuss this problem.'[9]

Three subjects were taken in Committees, meeting concurrently. The Chaguaramas centre provided ideal accommodation for such smaller meetings, and these sessions were the highlights of the conference. Each Committee had a rapporteur and their reports were presented in the final plenary session.[10] This was, indeed, a successful conference. All who attended cherished memories of the friendship and hospitality, and especially of the part played by the Speaker, Arnold Thomasos, the President of the Senate, Hamilton Maurice, and the Clerks, Rex Latour and Emman Carter.

The Executive Committee met next on 1–5 June 1970, as the guest of the Jersey branch. In reviewing the work of the Association since the meetings in Port-of-Spain, the Committee gave close attention to two underlying needs. The first was to involve as many of the 7000 members as possible directly in CPA activities. Much had been achieved by the expansion of regional and area conferences and exchanges of delegations. Australia, Canada and the United Kingdom had been very active in sending and receiving delegations of members from other branches. It was noted, however, that a number of the smaller branches were unable to take part in such activities for lack of funds. The Committee agreed a proposal, made by Sir Alister McMullin, Chairman of the Association, to recommend the setting-up of a special fund to assist them.

The other need was to make far greater use of the seven regional representatives. In the course of his three-year term each representative should aim to visit every branch in his region encouraging the members to take a more active part in its work, and generally to stimulate CPA activity. This concept of the role of the regional representatives was sound, but results varied from region to region. Success depended on the calibre and commitment of the representative and on the amount of time which as an active politician and member of his legislature he could devote to the CPA.

The Committee gave close attention to arrangements for the conference to be held in Canberra in October 1970. A subcommittee under the chairmanship of Wesley Nyirenda (Zambia), who was held in warm and high regard by all members, drafted a full agenda. The Committee noted that Arnold Smith, the Commonwealth Secretary-General, had accepted the invitation to attend as an observer. It was agreed to suggest to him that, rather than deliver an address, he should circulate a short written statement on the work of the Secretariat on the basis of which delegates could ask questions on matters of interest to them. In the event Arnold Smith was unable to attend and sent his deputy, T. Gooneratne.

In meetings of the Executive Committee and of the General Council proposals for the expansion of CPA activities usually took the form of more conferences and more contacts between members from all parts of the Commonwealth. Visits to branches by the officers of the Association and regional representatives in particular were being encouraged. The fundamental purpose of the Association of promoting the understanding and strengthening of parliamentary institutions tended to be overlooked.

The development of seminars on parliamentary practice and procedure was of great importance. It was, however, coming forward slowly. The Westminster course, called a seminar as from April 1970, took place with great success each year. A seminar for the African region was planned for August 1970 in Kenya. The Australian branches hoped to launch their first seminar in 1971. Canada was to introduce seminars in November 1973. India, so often ahead in providing facilities for members of its legislatures, held regular orientation seminars. They were organised by the Institute of Constitutional and Parliamentary Studies with the full support of the Speaker of the Lok Sabha.

Overall, however, the work of the Association in the parliamentary field was too limited. Many Commonwealth countries continued to need information and assistance, as their legislatures evolved. This applied especially to the newly independent countries in Africa. Tribal rivalries and popular expectations of miracles on attainment of independence, as well as economic problems, gnawed at the roots of their parliamentary systems. The bold experiment of the one-party state was introduced. It was argued that this was a truly democratic system and suited to African conditions, but it remains an experiment. In West Africa, the army, lowering in the background, has used its military strength to overthrow democratic regimes in the arrogant and mistaken belief that soldiers can manage better than the representatives elected by the populace.

Throughout these tribulations a great many Africans continued to long for the opportunity to work towards stable parliamentary government. The Clerks of the Overseas Office at Westminster gave advice and help, and Clerks like Barnett Cocks, David Lidderdale, Charles Gordon, Kenneth Bradshaw, Michael Lawrence, Clifford Boulton, Michael Ryle and John Sweetman, have in their friendship and support aided Clerks and members throughout the Commonwealth. The practice of Clerks attending for short periods on attachment at Westminster had been established. This practice was taken up by the Clerks' department in Canberra, Delhi, Ottawa and Wellington. There were, however, some 85 legislatures, and they also looked to the CPA for information and assistance.

At its meeting in Jersey the Executive Committee considered a paper, submitted by the Editor, proposing the creation of a Parliamentary Information and Reference Centre. It would be formed by the reorganisation and expansion of the materials held in the Secretariat. The proposal was, in fact, a further development of Howard d'Egville's idea that the CPA must always maintain an information service for all branches. This service had, however, operated on a small scale.

The new proposal envisaged the creation of a central assembly-point for documentation on Commonwealth Parliaments and kindred legislatures. In planning the project the Editor had visited the headquarters of the Inter-Parliamentary Union in Geneva. There he was given all assistance in examining the International Centre for Parliamentary Documentation, which the IPU has maintained for many years. He also discussed it with the Librarians of the House of Commons, the Australian and Canadian Parliamentary Librarians, and others professionally engaged in this field. All had welcomed the project, for no such bank of materials on Commonwealth legislatures existed. It was recognised, too, that the Secretariat in London was ideally placed to develop it.

The purpose of the Centre was to provide a prompt information service for Speakers, members, and parliamentary officials, and indeed for all *bona fide* students of Parliament. It would also produce memoranda, bibliographies and other documentation, giving comparative information on aspects of Parliaments and their practices.

The Committee welcomed the proposal and approved the appointment of a part-time librarian/archivist to assist in establishing the Centre. It added, on the instigation of the Treasurer, the caveat that the Centre should not become an excessive burden on the finances of the Association. In fact, the cost of the Centre, which came into operation on 11 January 1971, was minimal. The generous cooperation of members, Clerks and parliamentary librarians throughout the Commonwealth in response to the acquisition letters sent out by the Editor ensured a steady flow of parliamentary papers free of charge.

The creation of this Centre owed a great deal to the support of Sir Alister McMullin. He had been closely involved in the formation of the Australian National Library in Canberra and in kindred projects. He believed that the new CPA Centre would be invaluable. Indeed at the meeting of the Council which approved the Executive Committee's decision, he announced that the Australian government would make a donation of books to it. In subsequent years the Australian branch has made special donations to the Centre for further acquisitions. The progress of the Centre is discussed in a later chapter.

The senior staff of the Secretariat remained almost unchanged after the departure of Howard d'Egville. S. A. Pakeman retired at the end of 1965, but Robin Vanderfelt, Ian Grey, Jack Fowler and Betty May provided a continuity which was important to the work of the Association. On 31 July 1970, however, the Deputy Editor of Publications, Louis Marriott, resigned to return to Jamaica, his homeland. He had been appointed from among a large number of candidates and had taken up his duties on 26 July 1965.

Louis Marriott possessed remarkable abilities as a writer and administrator. Unfortunately, he could not settle down to life in England. Before leaving the Secretariat he presented to the Secretary-General a paper on 'Proposals for Modernisation' of the Association which was circulated to members of the Executive Committee. The paper was forthright in its comments. He wrote that the CPA was 'more Anglocentric than Commonwealth-oriented, and that its activities are not worth the annual expenditure of more than £100,000 of Commonwealth taxpayers' money'.[11] Changes which were in his view necessary included far greater emphasis on parliamentary matters in the Association's activities and especially in the annual conference. He argued that no real purpose was served by discussion of world issues. Such discussion divided delegates into opposing camps. Furthermore, the Association lacked authority and influence with governments to implement ideas which might emerge.

The paper was the outcome of much thought and contained proposals of value, many of which have since been adopted. It was vitiated, however, by its somewhat abrasive style. Louis Marriott's departure was nevertheless regretted by those who worked most closely with him, namely the Editor and Sue Burchett, then the Publications Secretary, who later was to be appointed Assistant Editor.

The 16th Commonwealth Parliamentary Conference was held in Canberra from 2–9 October 1970. Altogether, 154 delegates with 22 Secretaries to delegations represented 70 branches of the Association. The opening ceremony took place in the Senate Chamber on 2 October. Sir Alister McMullin as Chairman of the Association invited the Governor-General of Australia, Sir Paul Hasluck, to deliver the opening address. This was followed by speeches by the Prime Minister, John Gorton, by the Premier of Queensland, J. Bjelke-Petersen, and by Wesley Nyirenda. There were eight plenary sessions and two sessions during which three committees sat.

A small incident threatened to cast a cloud over the Canberra conference. On 2 October 1970, as part of the opening ceremony, the national flags of all the nations represented were unfurled on flagpoles in front of the Parliament House. During the night the Zambian flag was blown down in a high wind. K. H. Nkwabilo, leader of the Zambian delegation, called on the Chairman of the Association on the following morning, 3 October, to protest. He charged Australia with directly insulting Zambia and announced that his delegation was returning forthwith to Lusaka. Sir Alister McMullin and Peter Howson tried to dissuade him, but Nkwabilo was obdurate and refused to consult with his President by telephone or cable. Five senior members of the Executive Committee – Gerard Montano, Dr G. S. Dhillon, Ong Yoke Lin, James Walker and George Thomson – called on the Zambian delegates, but were unable to persuade them to remain.

In the afternoon Peter Howson personally delivered a letter of apology together with the police report on the incident, which stated that the halyard had frayed and broken in the high wind. It also revealed that other national flags had fallen and had been replaced. In the course of the second session Sir Alister McMullin reported to all delegates on the incident, and made a full public apology to the Zambian delegation on behalf of the Australian branches and as Chairman of the Association. Nothing would move Nkwabilo to stay.

On 4 October 1970 Sir Alister McMullin and Peter Howson drove to the airport to bid farewell to the Zambians. Wesley Nyirenda was obviously unhappy about the withdrawal, but evidently unable to overrule the other members of the delegation. He expressed the hope to Peter Howson that he would see him at the conference in Lusaka in the following year.

On 8 October, however, a cable was received from Zambia's President. It expressed appreciation of the election of R. M. Nabulyato, Speaker of the National Assembly of Zambia, to the office of Chairman of the Association. It went on to state that 'Zambia will not be in a position to host next year's general conference. This decision of the Zambian government has been very reluctantly taken and is deeply regretted, but recent developments in the Commonwealth Association and on the world scene as a whole have left Zambia with no other alternative in relation to this matter.'[12]

A special meeting of the General Council was convened on 8 October and a Special General Meeting on 9 October. The business of these meetings was to rescind the election of Speaker Nabulyato, since by long-standing convention the

Chairman of the Association had to be a national of the country hosting the conference. A cable was drafted and approved by the General Meeting, advising President Kaunda of this fact. It was agreed, too, that Sir Alister McMullin should be acting Chairman until the venue of the 1971 conference was known and it was possible to elect a new Chairman by postal ballot. Tan Sri Ong Yoke Lin (Malaysia), the Regional Representative for South-East Asia, was asked to approach his government about the possibility of Malaysia hosting the 1971 conference. Finally the General Meeting passed unanimously a resolution, regretting the withdrawal of the Zambian delegation, but absolving the Australian government and branches from any responsibility for the incident, and recording deep appreciation of the hospitality and the excellent arrangements provided for the conference. Subsequently Malaysia generously agreed to host the 1971 conference and Tun Tan Siew Sin, the Minister of Finance, was elected Chairman of the Association.

The withdrawal of the Zambian delegation did not interfere with the business conducted by the General Council or with the conference. It was regretted by all delegates and seen as unreasonable. It even caused embarrassment to some African delegates and may even have influenced them to speak with more restraint in the session on Africa. The incident might, nevertheless, have provoked serious discord among delegates but for the prompt and frank diplomacy of Sir Alister McMullin and Peter Howson.

The three-year term of office of the Chairman of the Executive Committee, Peter Howson, came to an end in Canberra. A number of members, including Speaker Dhillon, Ong Yoke Lin and Arthur Bottomley, pressed him to stand for a second term. His own Prime Minister, John Gorton, urged him on more than one occasion to stand again. Had he done so, he would undoubtedly have been re-elected.

Peter Howson declined. He explained that he had taken on the task of revitalising the CPA at the request of Harold Holt. He had served his full term and now felt strongly that another member should be elected to succeed him. He argued, too, that if he were to stand again it would create a bad precedent, which would prove damaging to the Association in the future. There were, moreover, three outstanding members who were interested in the chairmanship and who would serve the CPA well. They were the Canadian Minister of Justice and Attorney-General, John Turner, the Zambian Minister of Education, Wesley Nyirenda, and the immediate past Chairman of the Association, Gerard Montano.

In the event an election proved unnecessary when the Council met on 5 October. Nyirenda had withdrawn as a candidate on 4 October when he departed with the Zambian delegation. John Turner decided that he would not stand. Gerard Montano was then elected unanimously.

Warm tributes were paid by the Executive Committee, the General Council and the General Meeting of the Association to Peter Howson. His energetic and dedicated chairmanship of the working party and then of the Executive Committee had brought impressive results. In the General Meeting the motion was moved 'that this plenary session puts on record its deep appreciation to Mr Peter Howson for the work which he has done as Chairman of the Executive Committee over the past three years'.[13] The motion was adopted with acclamation. All members of the CPA owed him a great debt of gratitude.

At its meeting on 5 October the Council elected four regional representatives. It also elected Bryant Godman-Irvine as Treasurer. Sir Frederic Bennett, the Hon. Financial Adviser, was co-opted for a further 12 months. Dr N. M. Perera had completed his three-year term as a councillor under Clause 24 of the constitution. Sir William Aston, Speaker of the Australian House of Representatives, was nominated to fill the vacancy. It was agreed, however, that he should be co-opted after the retirement of Sir Alister McMullin. Dr G. S. Dhillon (India) was then nominated in his place and elected.

A number of constitutional issues had been raised in the Executive Committee in Jersey and were discussed further by the Council in Canberra. It was necessary to amend the constitution to permit registration of the CPA as a charity under British law. The categories of branches, as set out in the constitution, stood in need of review, especially to meet requests from Jersey and the Isle of Man. The Trinidad and Tobago branch questioned the need for Clause 24 councillors – the 'three wise men'. It proposed that they should be abolished and that additional regional representatives be appointed in their place.

The Council noted that the last major review of the constitution had taken place in 1961. In Canberra it appointed a subcommittee under the chairmanship of Gerard Montano, Chairman of the Executive Committee, to carry out a comprehensive review of the constitution and to make recommendations.

The first plenary session on 2 October, concerned with East Asia, and the Pacific and Indian Oceans, was opened by Phillip Lynch, Minister of Immigration and leader of the Australian delegation. He explained Australia's interests and policies in this vast area. K. H. Nkwabilo (Zambia) was critical of US intervention in South-East Asia, as were Thomas Uren, an opposition member in the Australian Parliament, and Stanley Tillekeratne (Ceylon).

The subject of the second session was Southern Africa. The opening speaker was B. K. Adama, leader of the Ghana delegation. He condemned the white regimes in Rhodesia and South Africa, and argued that Britain must use force in Rhodesia. Several African, Indian, Canadian and Caribbean delegates were critical of Britain's proposal to sell naval equipment to South Africa.

A. M. Nyasulu, leader of the Malawi delegation, forcefully asserted the Malawi view that the only way to resolve the South African and Rhodesian problems was by promoting contacts between the African states and the white minority governments. Malawi had diplomatic relations with South Africa. In May 1970 its Prime Minister, J. Vorster, had come to Malawi for talks. This was, he said, the way ahead. M. H. Blackwood spoke strongly in support of this policy. The third Malawi delegate, Richard Sembereka, was outspoken about countries which dismissed sanctions as useless against Rhodesia and South Africa and demanded that Britain use force, while they were covertly trading with both countries. It was an interesting discussion and without the bitterness and heat which had marked sessions in 1965 and 1966 on this subject.

The committee sessions were again among the highlights of the conference. They came closer to informal debate and discussion. Many of the contributions were outstanding. All delegates in the sessions on conservation congratulated Mrs Jill Knight on her opening speech. Shrimati Sushila Rohatagi (India) delivered a well-informed address in opening the session on population growth. Arthur Bottomley spoke with authority when he began the discussion on parliamentary democracy.[14]

During the conference several delegates were critical of Australia's treatment of the aboriginals. The immigration policies of Australia and Britain also came under attack. The criticisms, exchanges and explanations were, however, good-tempered. Indeed the conference was both eventful and successful. It was made more memorable by a new feature. The closing ceremony was held at sunset outside Parliament House on the evening of 9 October. The flags of the nations represented were slowly lowered as the Royal Australian Navy Bank sounded the Beat Retreat. Many delegates were moved by this ceremony.

Notes

1. Report of the Executive Committee (Gibralter, 1969), p.11.
2. Minutes of the General Council Meeting, 11 October 1969.
3. Report of the Executive Committee (Gibraltar, 1969), p.24.
4. Minutes of the General Council Meeting, 11 October 1969.
5. Report of the General Meeting (15 October 1969), p.96.
6. Ibid., p.97.
7. Conference Report (Trinidad & Tobago, 1969), pp.xv–xvi.
8. **Agenda and Opening Speakers, Trinidad & Tobago, 1969**
   Economic Development: i. Impact of debt burdens on developing countries; ii. Effect of import restrictions on developing countries; iii. Regional developments (a) CARIFTA; (b) East African Community; (c) EFTA. Openers: Bernard Soyza (Ceylon) and Kamaluddin Mohammed, Minister of West Indian Affairs (Trinidad & Tobago)
   The Commonwealth and World Security: i. Rhodesia and other African problems; ii. Security problems in the Caribbean; iii. The future of dependent territories; iv. Vietnam and other South East-Asian problems. Openers: Shafiq Arain (Uganda) and George Thomson, Chancellor of the Duchy of Lancaster (United Kingdom)
   New Concepts in Race Relations: i. Elimination of discrimination: enforcing UN resolutions on human rights; ii. Commonwealth immigration policies; iii. Security of minorities in multi-racial countries. Openers: Nathan Munoko (Kenya) and Allan Douglas, Minister of Youth and Community Development (Jamaica)
   Future of Parliamentary Democracy: i. Relations of the member with the executive and the electorate; ii. Strengthening of parliamentary democracy in developing countries; iii. Relations of governments with semi-governmental institutions. In committee
   The Pattern of Unrest: Youth in Revolt: i. Influence of communications media; ii.

Influence of political factors; iii. Influence of racial and economic factors. In committee

Future of the Commonwealth: i. PMs' meetings; ii. Organisations of the Commonwealth – CPA, Commonwealth Secretariat, Voluntary and non-governmental Commonwealth organisations; iii. Commonwealth Court of Appeal; iv. Commonwealth participation in international organisations. In committee.

9. Conference Report (Trinidad & Tobago, 1969), p.138.
10. Ibid., pp.156–66.
11. CPA archives.
12. Minutes of the General Council, 8 October 1970.
13. Report of the General Meeting (Canberra, 7 October 1970), p.124.
14. **Agenda and Opening Speakers, Canberra, 1970**

International Affairs and Defence: a. East Asia, the Pacific and Indian Oceans. Opener, P. R. Lynch (Australia); b. Southern Africa, Rhodesia and South Africa. Opener, B. K. Adama (Ghana); c. West Asia, Middle East and the Mediterranean: Détente and disarmament. Opener, Sammy Abela (Malta)

The Paliamentarian: a. The parliamentarian and his responsibility and loyalty to the constituency, the party, the Parliament, and the government; b. Pressure groups as sources of democratic participation in Parliament. Opener, Dr G. S. Dhillon (India)

Partners in Development: Aid – public sector: i. Education; Exchange of technical know-how; ii. Infrastructure. Opener, H. E. Strom (Alberta). *Aid – private sector*: i. Investment; ii. Exchange of technical know-how. Opener, I. E. Omolo Okero (Kenya)

Conservation and Pollution: a. Conservation and environmental control; b. Urbanisation. Opener, Mrs Jill Knight (United Kingdom)

Trade and Economic Development: a. EEC and its possible impact on Commonwealth countries. Opener, J. F. Luxton (New Zealand). b. Regional communities and commodity agreements. Opener, Dato Lee (Malaysia)

Population Growth: Opener, Shrimati Sushila Rohatagi (India)

Race Relations: Economic Disparities and Social Inequalities: Opener, S. M. Shah (Trinidad & Tobago)

Parliamentary Democracy: Its Capacity to Meet the Challenge of: a. Internal and external subversive tactics and techniques; b. Industrial unrest. Opener, A. Bottomley (United Kingdom)

Parliamentary Democracy: c. The protest of youth; d. Poverty; e. General turmoil. Opener: T. M. Forrest (Jamaica).

17 A Time of Constraints, 1971–73

The year 1971 opened on a discordant note. In January the Commonwealth Heads of Government met in Singapore. The mood of the meeting was tense. The Rhodesian crisis was no nearer to solution, and the decision of the British government to renew the sale of naval equipment to South Africa had infuriated most of the African leaders. Britain's concern about the defence of the busy Cape route to the Indian Ocean, where the Soviet navy had already established a strong presence, was not appreciated. The African states demanded that this, and indeed all, trade with South Africa be halted. Certain African leaders threatened to withdraw from the Commonwealth over this issue.

The CPA was unaffected by the acrimony of the Singapore meeting. While Milton Obote, the President of Uganda, was attending the meeting in Singapore, General Idi Amin seized power. Uganda remained a member of the Commonwealth, but the overthrow of Parliament automatically resulted in the suspension of the branch. There was also trouble in other parts of the Commonwealth which raised problems.

The Constitutional Subcommittee, appointed in Canberra in 1970, met in London on 6–8 February 1971. Gerard Montano took the chair, and the members who were able to attend were James Walker (Canada), Guido de Marco (Malta) and Sir Frederic Bennett (United Kingdom).

The venue for the next meeting of the Executive Committee was uncertain. Sierra Leone had extended an invitation, but a state of emergency had since been declared there. Moreover, M. O. Bash-Taqi, a much respected member of the Executive Committee, had resigned from the government and was being held in detention. Alternative venues considered by the subcommittee were Malta, Prince Edward Island, the Cayman Islands, the Isle of Man and London. It was finally arranged that the Committee would meet in Charlottetown, Prince Edward Island.

The future chairmanship of the Executive Committee was also in question. Gerard Montano warned the subcommittee in London that he might become ineligible to serve. Trinidad and Tobago had been troubled for some weeks by violent demonstrations and widespread looting in Port-of-Spain, instigated by supporters of the 'Black Power' movement who claimed that black people in Trinidad and Tobago were discriminated against by those with lighter skins and of other races. On 21 April 1971 the government declared a state of emergency, and the same day part of the 800-strong Trinidad and Tobago Regiment mutinied. The 2000 members of the police force and 160 coastguards remained loyal to the government. Three days later, the mutiny collapsed; and early in May Parliament was dissolved.

In the general election which followed on 24 May, Eric Williams' People's National Party won all 36 seats in the Parliament. Gerard Montano had decided, however, not to stand for re-election. He was thus no longer a member of his branch. The Executive Committee was nevertheless unanimous in co-opting him to attend its meeting in May 1971 to present the constitutional proposals to which he had given much thought.

Prince Edward Island proved to be an ideal venue for the Committee's meetings, which took place on 24–28 May 1971. There was a full agenda, and Tun Tan Siew Sin, Chairman of the Association, was an admirable acting Chairman of the Committee. A full report on the advanced arrangements for the conference in Malaysia in September 1971 was noted with special pleasure because so much had been achieved in a short time.

The attendance of observers at the conference was again considered. A request had been received from the Clerk of the suspended National Assembly of Uganda, E. T. A. Ochwo, who had written that, although the military government had dissolved Parliament, it had left the office of the Clerk intact. He suggested that one or two members of the Clerk's department might be permitted to attend as observers. Similar requests had been received in 1966 from the suspended branches in Ghana and Nigeria and had been refused. In 1968 the Executive Committee had re-examined the principle underlying this decision and the General Council had unanimously approved its recommendation that observers should not be permitted from branches in suspension. This principle had been endorsed by the General Meeting in Canberra in 1970. The request from Uganda was denied.

The Committee carried out its customary review of the Association's activities, receiving reports on regional and area conferences, exchanges of delegations, visits to branches by officers and officials, seminars, publications and information services. It considered also plans for the future. One problem was the venue for the 1972 conference. It had been hoped that Pakistan would be the host country. But there was now no likelihood that parliamentary government would be restored there in the near future. Pakistan was therefore not eligible to host the conference.

Some three weeks after the invitation from Malaysia had been accepted, the Malawi branch had invited the Association to meet there in 1971. The Committee was, however, hesitant about accepting this invitation, if it were reissued for 1972. The reason was that in 1970 the Malawi branch had had to cancel a conference of

Speakers of the African region because the majority of branches had boycotted it. The venue for the 1971 African regional conference had been switched from Malawi to Mauritius, because another boycott was feared. The Committee requested the Secretary-General to approach the following branches in the order listed about hosting the 1972 conference: Malta, Ghana, Bermuda, Barbados, Alberta.

A major item on the Committee's agenda was the amendment of the constitution of the CPA. The Committee discussed the recommendations, presented by Gerard Montano, and finally approved them for submission to the General Council and the General Meeting in Kuala Lumpur.

The size of the Secretariat had remained virtually unchanged since the early 1960s, despite the great increase in the activities of the Association. In Canberra in October 1970 the General Council agreed to the creation of the new post of Assistant Secretary-General. Applications were invited from all regions of the Commonwealth and from a total of nearly 500 received, a short-list of 9 was submitted to the Executive Committee in Prince Edward Island. The candidate chosen was Palitha Weerasinghe. He was well qualified for the post. A barrister, he had been Crown Counsel in the Department of the Attorney-General, Ceylon, from 1955 to 1964. He had then been appointed Clerk-Assistant of the Senate and Clerk in 1970. He took up his duties in the Secretariat on 1 August 1971. The General Council had also approved the appointment of an Assistant Editor of Publications. A Canadian, Joanne Fahey, an honours graduate from Queen's University, Ontario, was appointed.

The Hon. Financial Adviser, Sir Frederic Bennett, had been very active, as he reported to the Committee. He had visited New Delhi after the conference in Canberra and had had successful negotiations with the Indian government over the Association's blocked rupee account. The background was that some twenty years earlier d'Egville had, with the Council's approval, arranged that Indian contributions to the CPA could be paid in rupees and held in a blocked account. This was done to assist India at a time of severe exchange difficulties. The credit in this account now amounted to some £13,000.

In New Delhi, Sir Frederic Bennett said, he had found friendly cooperation. It was agreed that in future India would pay its dues in sterling or other negotiable currency. A series of payments would reduce the capital sum to £10,000. This would be used as a contribution to expenses when India next hosted the conference, and no claim would be made for the subvention of £10,000 from the Association.

The subvention available to a branch hosting a plenary conference had been recommended by the working party and approved by the Council. The intention was that £5000 should be provided in the estimates each year in the expectation that a subvention of £10,000 would be claimed only every second year. It had become the practice, however, for the host branch to claim the full amount each year – indeed, a subvention of £20,000 was made available to Malaysia in 1971, since it had hosted the conference as recently as 1963, and had come to the aid of the Association at short notice.

At the time of the Canberra conference in 1970 Sir Alister McMullin had stated that Australia would not claim the £10,000, but would want it to be paid into a trust fund. The income from the fund was to be used to assist smaller branches to play a greater part in the activities of the Association. Sir Frederic Bennett proposed that the trust should be incorporated under Jersey law in order to avoid paying UK tax on the income. He and the Treasurer made fuller reports on these and other financial arrangements to the General Council.

The General Council met in the Chamber of the House of Representatives, Kuala Lumpur, on 5, 11 and 16 September 1971. Following usual practice, it reviewed the preparations for the conference. It also accepted the invitation from Malawi to host the conference in the following year, fears of a boycott by certain African branches having been allayed.

The Council then dealt with the chairmanship of the Executive Committee. This was unusual. The election of officers of the Association and members of the Committee was one of the last items on the agenda. This allowed councillors to consider and discuss the potential candidates before the elections. In Prince Edward Island the Executive Committee had elected Sir Frederic Bennett as its Acting Chairman. At the meeting on 5 September 1971 Felix Bandaranaike formally proposed that he be elected Chairman for the rest of Gerard Montano's term of office. Roy McNeill (Jamaica) seconded and the Council approved the proposal.

The Council discussed at some length relations between the CPA and the AIPLF (Association Internationale des Parlementaires de Langue Française). The AIPLF had been established in 1967. In the planning stage Robert Moinet, Chef de la Division du Protocole et des Relations avec les Parlements Etrangers, and Xavier Deniau, Secrétaire Général Parlementaire, had called at the Secretariat and had had lengthy discussions with the Secretary-General and the Deputy Secretary-General about the purposes, organisation and activities of the CPA.

In January 1971, M. Moinet and M. Deniau again visited the Secretariat. They pointed out that the AIPLF was now firmly established. It had held two conferences, the first at Versailles, and the second in the Ivory Coast. A third conference would take place later in the year. They had invited observers from the CPA to attend their conferences. Now they proposed a closer, more formal relationship between the two Associations in which they would exchange information and observers. The AIPLF was already active in Commonwealth countries in which there were French-speaking MPs – Canada, Mauritius, Jersey and the Seychelles.

The Executive Committee did not favour such close links. It was felt that the AIPLF had no parliamentary purpose, and that it had been set up primarily to promote the French language and culture. The CPA should adhere strictly to its objective of promoting parliamentary democracy, as understood in the Commonwealth. Close links with the AIPLF would not contribute to this objective. At the same time it was recognised that rejection of the French proposal might prove embarrassing to Canada and other countries involved in the AIPLF. Nevertheless on a vote of 9 to 2 the Committee agreed to recommend to the Council that the proposed closer relations should not be approved.

At the Council's meetings in Kuala Lumpur this recommendation was questioned. Senator Allister Grosart (Canada) suggested that the Association was becoming inward-looking. The existing relationship between the CPA and the IPU provided a precedent. He asserted that the AIPLF was primarily parliamentary, although it had cultural overtones. Moreover, the AIPLF would be the guest of the Parliament of Canada and the National Assembly of Quebec at its forthcoming conference. The Council agreed that for this and other reasons the Executive Committee should be asked to review its recommendation at its mid-year meeting in 1972.

The reports of the Treasurer and the Financial Adviser on the finances of the Association were optimistic. In the year ending 31 December 1970 there had been a surplus of £15,000. The revised estimates for 1971 forecast a surplus of £7550. One of the councillors drew attention to the facts that in 1969 and 1970 expenditure had been £127,000 and £134,000, and it was estimated to reach £157,000 in 1971. Expenditure was rising regularly, while income showed only a small increase.

Sir Frederic Bennett explained that the release of the blocked rupees and the future payment of the contribution of the Indian branches in sterling would improve income. He stated further that with the help of the Jersey branch the funds from branches had escaped the burden of UK taxation, and had earned £7500 in interest. He assured the Council, that, unless something extraordinary happened, there should not be any need to increase branch contributions for a long time to come.

Presenting the Executive Committee's recommendations on finance, Sir Frederic Bennett said that in 1969 the Council had agreed that £2000 should be set aside each year to assist towards the expense of hosting regional conferences and seminars. The Committee now recommended that as from 1972 this should be increased to £5000, but that the expenses of regional representatives, travelling on behalf of the CPA, should also be met from this sum. Finally he reported that, as a result of the improved financial position, the Committee could permit a far wider distribution of the Association's publications.

The General Meeting, held on 15 September 1971, was taken up almost entirely with discussion of finance and of the amendments to the constitution. Again the Treasurer, Bryant Godman Irvine, was optimistic, stating that the financial position of the CPA in the coming years was 'not quite so rosy, but ... I would say there is nothing really to worry about'.[1] Sir Frederic Bennett forecast that the Association could expect to move into deficit in 1972. He would not, however, consider any proposals for increases in branch contributions. He ended his report on a sanguine note: 'In conclusion, Mr Chairman, I would only say that, as the situation is at present, if we take the steps I have outlined, the picture does not look too rosy; nevertheless, as a result of all these steps, although it is always dangerous to forecast, I think I can say that it will be quite a considerable time before we have to think about increasing contributions from any delegation here today.'[2] Several members at the General Meeting warmly congratulated the Treasurer, the Financial Adviser and the Finance Officer on their handling of the Association's finances.

Certain amendments to the constitution were required so that the Association could be registered as a charity under British law and thus be exempt from tax. Other amendments were intended to simplify the categories of branches and to clarify the powers of the General Council and its Executive Committee.

A significant amendment concerned the Treasurer. At the meetings of the Constitutional Subcommittee in London in February 1971, Sir Frederic Bennett submitted that the election of a new Treasurer each year was unsatisfactory. He should continue to be a member nominated by the United Kingdom branch, but should have a longer term of office. He observed that 'it was quite possible that an occasion might arise where neither of the two United Kingdom councillors had any financial experience and therefore it ought to be possible for the Council to elect another member of the branch who was suitably qualified'.[3]

A new clause was drafted, which read:

The General Council shall elect as Honorary Treasurer a member with suitable financial qualifications and ability of the Executive Committee of the branch in the legislature of the country in which the headquarters of the Association are situated. His term of office shall normally be three years, subject to annual re-election. If the Honorary Treasurer so elected is not a representative of his branch on the General Council he shall not be entitled to vote at meetings of the Council or at the General Meeting.[4]

In the General Meeting, however, this draft clause was amended. Arthur Bottomley, the United Kingdom councillor, requested the deletion of the words 'with suitable financial qualifications and ability'. The General Council proposed deletion of 'subject to annual re-election'. Both amendments were approved. The United Kingdom branch wanted the reference to financial qualifications removed so that it would be free to nominate any member of its Executive Committee to this office. It was concerned to continue observing its convention of alternating the office between Conservative and Labour members, irrespective of financial qualifications. It was a political consideration, and some members considered that the finances of the Association suffered as a result.

In the revised constitution, Clause 37 required that there should be a quinquennial review of the contribution of each branch to the Association. Sir Frederic Bennett informed the General Council that the last major review had been carried out by the working party in Malta in 1967. He proposed that the Executive Committee should conduct the next review at its mid-year meeting in 1972.

The provision for a quinquennial review envisaged branch contributions being adjusted only at five-year intervals. If adopted, its effect would have been disastrous. The 1970s were a period of mounting inflation. Air fares in particular were increasing rapidly. Fares for delegates to the conference in 1971 came to £67,340 out of a total budget of £161,297, and in 1972 the fares were £69,298 in the budget of £170,639. The CPA had no control over this major item of expenditure, other than by reducing the frequency of conferences and/or the number of delegates. Debarred from raising branch contributions, the Committee and Council cut back on other CPA activities.

At its final meeting the General Council elected Aleke Banda, Minister of Finance and Minister of Information, Malawi, to be President of the Association for the year 1971–72. It also elected Sir Alec Douglas-Home, Secretary of State for Foreign and Commonwealth Affairs, United Kingdom, as Vice-President. The new titles had been introduced in the revised constitution, thus avoiding confusion with the Chairman of the Executive Committee. Bryant Godman Irvine was elected Treasurer for a three-year term.

The 17th Commonwealth Parliamentary Conference took place in the Parliament Building, Kuala Lumpur, from 13–17 September 1971.[5] It was attended by 152 delegates and 23 Secretaries to delegations, representing 70 branches of the Association. The conference was formally opened on 13 September by H. M. the Yang Di-Pertuan Agong. It was an occasion of customary Malaysian splendour.

In inviting H. M. the King to deliver the opening address, Tun Tan Siew Sin recalled that Malaysia had had the honour of hosting the 9th Commonwealth Conference in 1963. He expressed his faith in the Commonwealth and the CPA. He had attended several meetings of Commonwealth Finance Ministers. The CPA was, however, unique in bringing together members of Parliament, rather than governments. 'There is no substitute for direct personal contacts of this kind,' he said, 'and our meetings are enhanced by their parliamentary basis. In carrying out this function, our Association is not only unique: it also in my view serves as one of the strongest links binding the Commonwealth.'[6] In declaring the conference open, H. M. the Yang Di-Pertuan Agong also expressed Malaysia's strong faith in the Commonwealth and the CPA. The Prime Minister, Tun Haji Abdul Razak, welcoming delegates, reviewed the political and economic advance of Malaysia since independence. On behalf of the Vice-President, Richard Sembereka, leader of the Malawi delegation, expressed the thanks of the delegates to H. M. the King and to the Prime Minister.

The first of the three sessions on 'The Commonwealth and Problems of World Security' was concerned with South-East Asia and the Indian Ocean. Tun Dr Ismail Alhaj, Deputy Prime Minister and Minister of Home Affairs (Malaysia) opened with a review of the problems of security in the area. He was followed by Senator Donald Cameron (Canada) who sharply criticised the British policy of supplying arms to South Africa. Next, Arthur Bottomley (United Kingdom) spoke with feeling about Pakistan and India and the rift between East and West Pakistan. India was coping with the grave problem of refugees from West Bengal, where famine threatened the lives of thousands. Britain had given £8 million to India and £1 million to Pakistan to help alleviate the situation. The problem should, however, be shared by all Commonwealth countries. His appeal was supported by Dr G. S. Dhillon, Speaker of the Lok Sabha (India), who explained in greater detail the conflict between West and East Pakistan and India's involvement.

In the second session the subject was 'The Impact on the Commonwealth of Recent Events in Southern Africa and the Rest of Africa'. I. F. Omolo-Okero, leader of the Kenya delegation, opened the discussion with a fine speech which aroused in many delegates a new sympathy and understanding of the African viewpoint. He spoke of the impact of Portuguese colonialism, of racial oppression in South Africa, and of the Rhodesian predicament. The delegates from Tanzania, S. M. Wassira, and Zambia, J. B. Kanyuka, made bitter attacks on South Africa and were highly critical of British policies. Dame Joan Vickers referred to the lack of realism in Kanyuka's speech, reminding him that his country had recently increased its trade with South Africa. She defended the right of the British government to act in any way it considered necessary to give effect to its global defence policy. Richard Sembereka restated Malawi's policy of promoting dialogue with South Africa, which had been consistently expressed at previous conferences. On this occasion, however, the leader of the Tanzanian delegation, J. J. Mungai, strongly criticised Malawi's President and system of government as being undemocratic.

The third session had been intended for discussion of the Middle East and the Mediterranean. But the problems of Southern Africa kept intruding. Indeed, Anthony Kershaw, leader of the United Kingdom delegation, felt obliged to open the session with a statement of British policy towards Rhodesia, supporting the earlier speeches by Dame Joan Vickers and Arthur Bottomley. He went on to speak about the Arab–Israeli conflict and the growth of Soviet naval power in the Mediterranean. The speeches of other delegates tended to follow this pattern in what proved to be an interesting and wide-ranging discussion.

In six sessions delegates were divided into two committees, which sat concurrently. The discussion of challenges to parliamentary democracy was especially relevant at this time in Africa. Two of the committee sessions on economic development focused attention on Britain and the EEC. The opening speaker, H. C. Templeton (New Zealand), and indeed most of those who followed, showed understanding of Britain's reasons for seeking to join the Community. At the same time several delegates expressed concern about the probable loss of trade preferences and access to the British market. The admirable contributions of the United Kingdom delegates – Anthony Kershaw, Arthur Bottomley, Douglas Houghton, Kenneth Baker and John Mackie – sought to clarify and answer the questions raised, so far as it was possible at this stage of the negotiations.

The practical approach of speakers in the last two sessions was notable. The subject was 'Problems of the Environment: Pollution and Control; Preservation of

Endangered Wildlife; Population Growth; Urbanisation'. The subject had been included in the agenda at the request of the Canadian branch. George J. McIlraith, leader of the Canadian delegation, and Senator Allister Grosart (Canada) in particular dwelt on the magnitude of the problem and the urgent action needed in all parts of the world. It became clear during these sessions that many delegates were unaware of the damage to the environment occurring in their own countries. The discussion undoubtedly aroused their interest and concern.

The year 1972 witnessed an unusual situation in which the Executive Committee appeared to be out of step on several issues with the General Council and the General Meeting of the Association. The Committee met in Singapore on 11–13 and on 14 May. The Speaker of the Singapore Parliament, Dr Yeoh Ghim Seng, presided at the opening ceremony. Sir Frederic Bennett and the President of the Association, Aleke Banda, responded to the speech of welcome.

In its meetings the Committee dealt with its usual business and made a number of recommendations for consideration by the Council in Malawi later in the year. It carried out the quinquennial financial review and in its report to the Council it endorsed the Chairman's statement to the General Meeting in Kuala Lumpur that no increase in branch contributions would be required in the foreseeable future. It recommended, therefore, that the existing basic annual contributions due from main and auxiliary branches be confirmed. The contribution of £3500 for a main branch formed in a national Parliament, was based on £875 for each delegate whom the branch was entitled to send to the plenary conference. An auxiliary branch, formed in a legislature in a country not yet completely self-governing or without a majority of elected members, contributed £1600, based on £800 for each delegate. This recommendation was subject to the proviso that no change be made in the scale of branch representation at conferences. But branches contributing less than £200 per annum, which entitled them to send a delegate every fourth year, were to be assisted from the CPA and Associated Purposes Trust Fund which had now been established.

The Committee reviewed the publications and information services. It expressed high appreciation of the standards maintained in the articles and their presentation in *The Parliamentarian*. It approved the Editor's report on the further development of the Parliamentary Information and Reference Centre. It welcomed the proposal that the first monograph to be produced in the Centre would be a revised edition of the *Payments and Privileges of Commonwealth Parliamentarians*, retitled *Salaries and Allowances of Commonwealth Parliamentarians*. The demand for comparative material of this kind was constant. The Editor reported that he hoped to be able to publish the book by the end of the year. The Committee allocated £750 to meet printing costs.

A new venture, approved by the Committee, was the Library Support Fund. The Editor drew attention to the fact that, while parliamentary libraries and research services were developing rapidly in the larger Parliaments, many of the smaller legislatures lacked even the most basic reference material. A task undertaken in the Centre was the compiling of lists of books which could form the nucleus of a reference library. He proposed a modest scheme to provide such legislatures with the basic books upon which a reference library could be built. The Committee allocated the sum of £250 to the fund. All branches were to be informed. The donation of books to a maximum cost of £50 in each case could then be made to legislatures in order of their application.

The General Council met in Blantyre, Malawi, on 14, 23 and 25 October 1972. On the question of invitations to other organisations to send observers to CPA conferences, it noted the Executive Committee's recommendation that such invitations should be confined to international organisations which were themselves representative of democratically elected members of legislatures and whose aims included all or some of those of the CPA. The Council then approved the Committee's proposal, reversing its previous decision, that there should be an exchange of observers with the AIPLF. It also agreed on the motion of Guido de Marco (Malta) and Dr G. S. Dhillon (India) that relations should be established with the European Parliament and/or the Council of Europe, which should be invited to send observers to CPA conferences.

The Association's finances were the major business of the Council's meetings. The Treasurer reported that the estimates for 1972 showed an excess of expenditure over income of £13,770. The year had started with a credit balance of £22,767, which meant that 1973 would open with a credit balance of just under £9000. If the 1972 level of expenditure was maintained in 1973 and no economies made, the Association would begin 1974 with a debit of £4000, and with an assumed increase in expenditure in 1973 of at least £5000, economies totalling £9000 had to be found. In these estimates, moreover, no allowance had been made for inflation and devaluation.

The Executive Committee had met earlier in Blantyre. It had expressed concern about the rising cost of printing. It had proposed therefore that *The Parliamentarian* should no longer be circulated free to members who requested it, but that they should be asked to pay half the charge to outside subscribers, then £2.50 for four issues.

M. H. Blackwood (Malawi) said that charging members for the journal was the wrong approach. The best solution would be a levy of £1.50 on each member. H. B. Turner (Australia) and Senator Allister Grosart (Canada) agreed that the widest possible circulation of the journal was essential. Dr K. M. de Silva (Sri Lanka) said that it was the annual conference that made the CPA a living force to its members. But the one thing that was constantly before the membership was *The Parliamentarian* and the Council should discuss not whether the Association could afford it, but the fact that it must afford it. Other suggested economies were that the conference should be biennial rather than annual, and that ways should be found to make savings on air fares, the largest single item of expenditure. Before adjourning for lunch, however, the Council decided to reject the Committee's recommendation to charge for *The Parliamentarian*. When the meeting resumed the Treasurer stated that the Executive Committee would meet again and report to a further meeting of the Council.

Reports on regional conferences, exchanges of delegations, and seminars were noted. The Council welcomed a detailed account of the first Australian seminar, held on 10–23 September 1972 in Canberra, Hobart and Melbourne. The Chairman of the Executive Committee, Sir Frederic Bennett, gave an account of his travels on behalf of the CPA in which he had made two world tours, visiting almost a third of the branches throughout the Commonwealth. The Council elected Sir Alec Douglas-Home to be President of the Association for 1972–73, and Felix Bandaranaike (Sri Lanka) to be Vice-President.

A further meeting of the General Council took place on the evening of 25 October 1972 to consider fresh proposals on finance from the Executive Committee. It had before it a long report explaining the various options considered, and giving the Committee's final proposal that a 20 per cent cut in expenditure should be made on contributions to assist branches hosting regional conferences and seminars, on overseas visits by officers and officials, and on publications as a whole. This would, it was estimated, meet the needs of the Association in 1973.

H. B. Turner (Australia) said that the Association would have the greatest difficulty in carrying on its work into 1974 without increased contributions from branches. He suggested that the Committee should reconsider its recommendations on the quinquennial financial review and present in 1973 a plan, dealing with the inflationary situation. Replying to this proposal Sir Frederic Bennett said, 'he could only ask Mr Turner to accept the Executive's word that it would be very very difficult, if not impossible, to accede to any such request in the immediate future, since they would find the greatest difficulty in getting a unanimous response'.[7] With great reluctance the Council adopted the Committee's recommendation.

The General Meeting of the Association was held on 26 October 1972. The main business was consideration of the report of the Council on the recommendations of the Executive Committee. H. B. Turner (Australia) at once raised the subject of the quinquennial review. Inflation and rising costs meant that the CPA could not carry on as in the past. Already they were drawing on reserves. His proposal was 'that the Executive Committee should consider the position very seriously and come up with proposals at the next meeting to increase the revenues so that we may carry on with activities on the existing basis. . . . I do not believe that we can wait any longer, that we can wait even to the next quinquennial review to do this; the matter is urgent.'[8]

Harold Winch (Canada) then spoke. He had been a staunch, even impassioned, supporter of the CPA over many years, his interest having been aroused by Howard d'Egville in the early 1950s. Although now very ill he spoke with the clear resonant voice of an orator. He deplored any talk about curtailing the existing activities. That was a defeatist attitude:

With the seriousness of the problems facing nearly all countries throughout the world and the future problems which are undoubtedly going to arise, now is the time for the

CPA not to be curtailing, but to be increasing its activities, so that our work and our understanding can be greater, so that we can have a greater influence in the world and in the solution of its problems.[9]

As the Treasurer of the Canadian branch for many years, he had had to submit his budget each year to the Speaker and the Treasury Board. Every time he had pointed out that his branch had to meet increasing costs and, because of the importance of the CPA, more money was needed for greater activity. Never had the CPA in Canada been denied the increases by the Speaker and the government.

> I plead with delegates to take the position that now is the time to ask for the required money to meet the expenditure of the CPA; to send the message to all our branches and ask them to take it up with their governments. I ask them also to point out the need for expansion, the need for a greater CPA, and to ask for more money not only to maintain our present level of activities, but to expand.[10]

It was a stirring speech which lifted the mood of the meeting.

The Chairman of the Executive Committee responded with caution. The Committee would, he said, 'consider, with a view to putting them before the General Council next year, which is the proper time and the only time to do so, all the proposals which have been made, including the possibility or feasibility or the desirability of increasing annual contributions'.[11] This response angered many members. M. H. Blackwood (Malawi) said that he would support the proposed 20 per cent cut for one year, but he found it 'extremely unpalatable'.[12] He referred to the statement in the report of the General Meeting in 1971 that 'It should also be possible to finance a wider distribution and expansion of CPA publications'. And he added: 'Here we are going straight back on that and reducing them.'[13] He quoted also the statement of the Financial Adviser in Kuala Lumpur in 1971, that it would be a considerable time before there would be any need to increase branch contributions. He then moved that the section in the report of the Executive Committee, dealing with the quinquennial financial review, be deleted. In rejecting this recommendation, the General Meeting would free the Committee, he said 'to get on with the review and plan our finances properly'[14] without waiting until 1977.

H. B. Turner (Australia) supported Blackwood. He stated bluntly 'that larger contributions should be sought as quickly as possible so that we can carry on our activities and perhaps even expand them'.[15] The motion proposed by Blackwood and seconded by Turner was passed unanimously. The Secretary-General commented that the deletion of this part of the Committee's report was 'essential unless the CPA was to be a financial prisoner for five years'.[16] He spoke with a feeling of deep relief.

The 18th Commonwealth Parliamentary Conference took place in the Kwacha Conference Centre, Blantyre, Malawi, on 20–26 October 1972.[17] It was attended by 141 delegates and 23 Secretaries to delegations, representing 73 branches of the

Association. It was opened with customary ceremonial by H. E. the Life President of the Republic of Malawi, Ngwazi Dr H. Kamuzu Banda. In inviting the President to declare the conference open, Aleke Banda spoke of the role of the CPA in promoting understanding and strengthening the Commonwealth. He continued:

> but the CPA has another function closely allied with it; that is the strengthening of our parliamentary institutions. Parliament can never be at a standstill. It must be a living institution, evolving to meet the needs of its people and its country. A Parliament which is not constantly reviewing, improving, and evaluating its methods and procedures is in danger of becoming static and failing to serve its people.[18]

The Life President delivered a long and discursive oration. He paid tribute to Arthur Bottomley, the deputy leader of the United Kingdom delegation, who as Secretary of State for Commonwealth Relations and in his continued interest while in opposition, had gained the respect and friendship of Ministers and members throughout the Commonwealth and especially in India and Africa. Dr Banda then explained Malawi's parliamentary government as a mixture, containing elements of African village life and elements from Westminster and Downing Street and from Capitol Hill and the White House. He dwelt extensively on British history and the lessons to be learnt from it. Finally, he stated that the Rhodesian crisis and the sale of arms to South Africa were stale issues. Lady Tweedsmuir, the leader of the United Kingdom delegation, speaking on behalf of Sir Alec Douglas-Home who was unable to be present, expressed the thanks of the delegates to the Life President and the people of Malawi.

The first three plenary sessions of the conference were devoted to 'The Commonwealth and World Security: a. Africa; b. Asia; c. Europe'. The intention was that each session would be concerned with one region, but African matters often intruded. The tone of the discussion was, however, more restrained than in previous conferences, and there was a greater breadth of approach to world affairs. Many African delegates appeared to be on the defensive. In part this was because they were in Malawi which had always followed its own independent policies towards Southern Africa, but there were other reasons, as expressed by delegates in the course of the sessions.

The opening speaker in the first session was J. D. Msonthi, leader of the Malawi delegation. He sought to put African problems in the perspective of world security. He urged strongly the need to identify the areas of disagreement and then to engage in frank dialogue about them. 'The liquidation of the white man in Southern Africa has been suggested by some militants as a solution to the existing problems,' he said, and he went on to dismiss such suggestions as old-fashioned, impractical, immoral and misguided.[19] Other African delegates considered that dialogue was out of the question and those from Tanzania and Kenya strongly criticised British handling of the Rhodesian problem. They no longer demanded the use of force, realising now that Britain was firm in rejecting it, and further that in this Britain probably had the support of the majority of Commonwealth countries.

The speech of G. A. Walsh, the leader of the New Zealand delegation, proved a turning-point in the discussion. Delegates were, he said, concerning themselves with problems in the short term. He suggested to the Africans that they should look further ahead. The African continent was well endowed with land and with resources. African states could help themselves by developing their resources to provide a better life for their people. Security was not to be found in guns: ultimate security would be found in proper provision for men on earth.

Albert Henry, leader of the Cook Islands delegation, was forthright. He suggested that racialism had become a two-edged sword. 'Is it possible, I ask, that we, the coloureds, are now beginning to discriminate against our white brothers?' He continued: 'With humility I suggest that a third threat to the security of Africa would be a refusal by Africans to objectively analyse themselves.... It is all too easy these days to find scapegoats. You know if the country is not going well, you blame racialism. This becomes a scapegoat. Everybody must agree with you on the subject – they wouldn't dare disagree...'[20] On the question of South Africa he expressed full agreement with Malawi's policy.

M. H. Blackwood (Malawi) took up the point made by N. W. Munoko, leader of the Kenya delegation, that fear of an African government by whites in those countries still under their control was part of the problem. 'What is required,' he said, 'is an example of good, fair, just, and stable government and racial tolerance in the newly independent countries of Africa.'[21] The delegate from Nova Scotia, G. M. Mitchell, also noted that the policy of apartheid was largely based on fear.

> I think that perhaps one of the best ways to deal with the problem is to have those countries which have recently become independent set an example in the way they govern their new states, treating all minorities with justice and equality. I think that they must make it clear that any danger of military coups is past and that changes in government can take place on this continent as one delegate said by way of a ballot box and not by way of a bullet.[22]

J. G. O'Brien (New Zealand) observed in the following session that, while condemning racialism, African delegates were silent about racialism in Uganda. A Malaysian delegate, Raja Nong Chik, had spoken out against General Amin's treatment of Asians in Uganda. Dr G. S. Dhillon welcomed these comments. India had supported every movement in Africa against racialism, but he found events in Uganda a serious setback to the struggle for racial equality. He called on African leaders to condemn Amin's ruthless regime.

Enche Musa bin Hitam (Malaysia) opened the second session, the subject of which was Asia. In an able speech, dealing primarily with the South-East Asian region, he spoke of the shift from bipolarity to multipolarity in the world power structure. Noting this shift the Foreign Ministers of ASEAN, meeting in Kuala Lumpur in November 1971, had stated their determination to secure recognition of South-East Asia as a zone of peace and neutrality. The Kuala Lumpur Declaration expressed the resolve of their governments to avoid another Vietnam in their region. Arthur Bottomley (United Kingdom) commented that it would be unwise to rely on securing from the Soviet Union, China and the United States a guarantee of the security of this particular region. The best way to secure peace in Asia was, in his opinion, by having a powerful united subcontinent of India. These themes, and the recognition of the Indian Ocean as a zone of peace, were the chief matters raised during the rest of the session.

The third session was concerned with Europe and the Mediterranean. In opening Dr V. Moran (Malta) spoke of Europe as an integral strategic region. The Mediterranean which had in the past been dominated by a single power, now had a US naval presence, which was challenged by growing Soviet naval strength. The speeches in this session tended to be discursive.

In the fourth and fifth sessions delegates were divided into two committees, sitting concurrently. One discussed 'Social Problems' – specifically, population growth, the threat of pollution and the eradication of drug addiction and trafficking. The other discussed 'Economic Problems' under the headings of Britain and the EEC, UNCTAD, the role of the public and private sectors in development, and the role of youth in economic development.

A feature of the agenda was that the last four plenary sessions were devoted to 'Parliament's Role in the Modern World'. At previous conferences certain delegates, and in particular the Indian delegates, had complained that too much time was given to political and economic issues. The conference was straying from parliamentary affairs which were central to the CPA's activities. This view was reflected in the agenda in Malawi.

G. Kennedy (Quebec) opened the first of the four sessions. He spoke on 'Internal and External Challenges to Parliamentary Democracy'. He identified the three main challenges as being, first, the need to adapt parliamentary practices and procedures to the requirements of contemporary conditions; second, the weakness of parliamentary control over civil servants; third, the erosion of Parliament's authority by the Executive. Subsequent speakers mentioned other challenges, but in the main they discussed these three threats. It was a frank discussion which underlined the fact that, even allowing for the different systems in operation, the basic problems were similar.

The following session had as a subheading 'Improving Parliamentary Efficiency' and 'Bringing Parliament Closer to the People'. The leader of the Australian delegation, H. B. Turner, opened this session with an impressive speech. He stressed that the most important need was that the Executive should provide adequate information to members through parliamentary papers, backed up by an effective research service with special facilities for opposition members. He also argued for the development of an effective committee system, and he cited as an example the five new Estimates Committees in the Australian Senate. He advocated, too, that Parliaments should give urgent consideration to televising their proceedings.

This speech introduced a lively discussion. Arthur Bottomley (United Kingdom) spoke of his experience as Chairman of the Select Committee on Race Relations and Immigration. Senator Allister Grosart (Canada) explained the work done by Committees of the Canadian Senate. Many of the practical themes, introduced by H. B. Turner, carried into the following session on 'The Function of the Parliamentarian and his Recognition by Society'. The final session on 'Protection of Minority Interests' was more political in content.

The General Council and the General Meeting, sitting in Malawi, had lacked their usual harmony, but the conference was an undoubted success. Although it was meeting in Central Africa, the problems of Southern Africa had not dominated the discussions on Commonwealth and world security. South-East Asia and India received more of the attention that they merited. Moreover, relations among the delegates were cordial. Much of the credit for this belonged to the President, Aleke Banda, a man of striking ability and personal charm, and to Malawi's Speaker, A. M. Nyasulu, who was active in supporting him.

The next mid-year meeting of the Executive Committee took place in Georgetown, Grand Cayman, on 30 April–3 May 1973. The ceremonial opening of the meeting was conducted in the Chamber of the Legislative Assembly by H. E. the Governor, K. R. Crook. The President of the Association, Sir Alec Douglas-Home, was unable to be present, and Sir Bernard Braine served in his place. J. D. Msonthi (Malawi) represented Aleke Banda.

The Committee's agenda contained not only the routine items of business but also a quinquennial review of CPA activities and the financial matters referred back to the Committee by the General Meeting in Malawi, as well as Australian proposals for amendments to the constitution. The recommendations on these and other matters were considered by the General Council in London.

In pursuit of economies the Committee carried out a searching review of publications and information services. The Editor referred to the decision to impose a 20 per cent cut on publications in 1973. He pointed out that he had no control over the reports of the Committee, the Council, the General Meeting and the conference, and other publications which were obligatory. It meant, in fact, that *The Parliamentarian* must bear most of the cut. He reminded the Committee that until the 1950s the Association had published three journals and a monthly commentary on foreign affairs. Of these publications only one, *The Parliamentarian*, remained. Certain new commitments, limited and specialised in scope, had been undertaken, such as data papers for delegates to conferences, summary reports of conference proceedings, a leaflet on the aims and activities of the Association, and a manual of CPA practices, but they did not reach the general membership.

The Committee agreed that its members should make special efforts to procure advertisements for *The Parliamentarian*. Such revenue would, it was hoped, lessen the impact of the 20 per cent cut. The summary and the verbatim reports of the conference were, it was agreed, both essential. The summary was important, especially because it was sent by airmail to Prime Ministers and Ministers soon after the ending of the conference. It was decided, however, that this short summary should not be printed but mimeographed as an economy. The Committee's own report should also be reproduced in the same way. The new edition of the manual of CPA practices should not be printed, but gummed slips, giving the amendments needed after the Malawi meetings, should be inserted into the old edition. The new up-to-date version of *Salaries and Allowances of Commonwealth Parliamentarians* was warmly welcomed. The Committee decided, however, that as an economy it, too, should be published in mimeographed form, and not printed.

The meeting sharply illustrated what Harold Winch in Malawi had called the negative, defeatist attitude towards the work of the Association. Economies, although damaging, were to be preferred to raising branch contributions. There was a process of chipping away in search of economies. The lack of bold expansionist approach which had plagued the CPA over many years was never more evident.

At the meeting the Editor recalled that, when the Parliamentary Information and Reference Centre was set up, it was envisaged that its functions would include the organisation of specialist study groups to consider in depth major parliamentary topics and publication of their reports. It was, he submitted, of vital importance to develop further the Association's work in promoting the study of parliamentary institutions. A subject which was both topical and crucial was 'Parliament and the Scrutiny of Science Policy'. It was generally accepted that Parliaments were not able to carry out effective scrutiny of the policies and the vast funds committed in this field. Concern was being expressed on this score in the United States, Canada, Australia and the United Kingdom. It was a subject on which the CPA could make a positive contribution. He then gave details concerning the organisation and estimated cost of such a study group. The Committee welcomed the proposal in principle, but doubted whether the necessary finance could be raised.

The General Council met in London on 9 and 15 September 1973. The President of the Association, Sir Alec Douglas-Home, was, as had been expected, so heavily committed to his ministerial duties, that he was unable to preside at these meetings. Indeed, Sir Bernard Braine, as Deputy Chairman of the UK branch Executive Committee had carried the main responsibility in the organisation of the conference programme. Moreover, it was he who in an impressive speech welcomed the delegates in the Royal Gallery on the morning of 10 September 1973. The Vice-President, Felix Bandaranaike, took the chair at the council meetings. Enche Musa bin Hitam (Malaysia) could not attend, and Senator Dr Mahathir bin Mohammed served as South-East Asia representative. C. A. Thomasos, Speaker of the House of Representatives (Trinidad and Tobago), deputised for B. L. B. Pitt.

The Council noted with pleasure the reference to the CPA in the communiqué of the Heads of Government meeting which had taken place in Ottawa in the previous month. It read:

Heads of Government noted with appreciation the contribution by the Commonwealth Parliamentary Association in promoting contacts between members of Parliament of Commonwealth countries at annual conferences and providing a forum for them to exchange views and discuss matters of common interest at regional and international levels thereby furthering Commonwealth ideals and interests.[23]

The Executive Committee in Grand Cayman in May 1972 had discussed relations between the CPA and the Heads of Government meeting. It had taken the view that no attempt should be made to establish a special relationship. At the same time members of the Committee had undertaken to speak to their own Heads of Government to ensure that the work of the Association was noted in their meetings.

The Prime Minister of Sri Lanka, Mrs Bandaranaike, had, the Chairman reported, taken the initiative in obtaining the agreement of all present to the inclusion of this reference to the CPA in the communiqué. The Chairman said that it was especially welcome because the meeting was attended by the Heads of Government in countries with parliamentary regimes and also of some at present deprived of parliamentary institutions. It was important that the latter countries should be constantly made aware of the CPA and the importance which it attached to parliamentary government.

Proposals from the Commonwealth of Australia branch were a major subject of discussion in the Council and the General Meeting. Fred Daly presented the resolutions with admirable clarity. He explained that state and provincial branches were poorly represented on the Council, compared with auxiliary and unitary main branches. Members of state/provincial legislatures in India numbered 3371, in Canada 650, in Malaysia 362, and in Australia 547; each had only one representative on the Council. Thus India had 13 branches, and a branch could expect to appoint a councillor once in 13 years; Canada with 10 provinces, once in 10 years; Malaysia with 10 states, once in 10 years; Australia with 6 states, once in 6 years. The main branch in Jamaica, with 53 members, had two councillors each year, as did Tanzania with 89 members, and New Zealand with 87. Of the auxiliary branches examples were Bermuda, and the Cook Islands, each of which appointed a councillor every year. The Australian branch considered this representation out of balance. It proposed that state/provincial representation be increased as follows: Indian states, 4 councillors; Australian states, 2; Malaysian states, 3; Canadian provinces, 3.

The second resolution was that Clause 19 (formerly Clause 24) councillors should be abolished, that the regions should be reduced from 7 to 5, but that 2 representatives should be elected from each region, and finally that the immediate past Chairman should not in future be a member of the Executive Committee. Thus any increase in the size of the Committee would be avoided.

Fred Daly explained further that the existing system meant that the Australian branch would have to wait another 20 years for representation on the Committee, and this was unsatisfactory. The CPA itself suffered from this arrangement. The

Australia branch was among the most active and efficient in the Association, and a representative from that branch on the Committee would undoubtedly be an asset. Indeed, the Australia branch was seeking a permanent place on the Committee, such as the Canadian branch had.

This was, however, opposed by other branches. The proposals had been rejected by a large majority at the Australasian regional conference. At the Council meeting, R. D. Muldoon (New Zealand) said that any suggestion that the Australian branch, because of its size, should play a more important role or have some form of permanent representation, was entirely unacceptable to New Zealand. This view was supported by councillors from branches in the Caribbean and the Pacific Islands.

The Chairman, Felix Bandaranaike, made attempts to postpone a decision until the meetings of the Council and the General Meeting in 1974. Fred Daly rejected such attempts. His branch had, he said, placed its proposals before all branches and had given notice as required by the constitution. He added that he accepted the Executive Committee's recommendation that there should be no contraction of the regions from 7 to 5. The outstanding proposals should be submitted to the General Meeting which alone could approve amendments to the constitution.

The General Meeting took place on 20 September 1973 with the President of the Association, Sir Alec Douglas-Home, in the chair. Fred Daly and certain other members of the Australian delegation had been unexpectedly recalled for an important constitutional vote in Canberra. The amended proposals were, however, ably presented to the meeting by A. J. Forbes, who remained. The motion which he moved was as follows:

> That this meeting requests the General Council to change the structure of the Executive Committee so that:
> (a) the existing seven regions shall, in future, nominate two representatives each to the Committee, except that the region within which the Treasureship is located shall have only one regional representative, and
> (b) each region shall continue to nominate its representatives by methods of its own agreed determination, for endorsement by the General Council, and
> (c) the Immediate Past President shall cease to be a member of the Committee.[24]

The motion was approved unanimously. It did not, however, give the Australian branch the permanent or even more frequent representation on the Executive Committee that it wanted. It was, indeed, a reflection of the eagerness of the branch to have a more positive role in the work of the Association, as it had had in the 1960s. The matter was to be raised again, this time successfully, in the 1980s.

Future venues for conferences were noted by the Council: Sri Lanka, 1974; India, 1975; Mauritius, 1976; and Canada, 1977. The New Zealand branch indicated that it would host the conference in 1979. The Council noted also that the Executive Committee would meet in Western Samoa in 1974 and in the Isle of Man in 1975.

The Council approved the reports of the Committee on the quinquennial review of the Association's activities and on the current financial position. The Treasurer explained an increase in the income. It resulted from the formation of new branches, from higher contributions from certain branches which had changed in status, and from interest on the investment of branch contributions received early in response to an appeal by the Committee. The improved income, together with the 20 per cent cut, meant that a credit balance of about £21,500 would be carried forward to 1974.

In the quinquennial financial review, however, the Committee had noted that expenditure had shown an average annual increase of 10 per cent over the years 1969–73. If that rate of increase continued, an additional annual income of £50,500 would be needed to maintain CPA activities at their current level. The Committee therefore recommended an increase of 20 per cent in branch contributions with effect from 1 January 1975. The Council unanimously approved this recommendation.

Among the last items of business was the election of officers of the Association and regional representatives. The new President was Stanley Tillekeratne, Speaker of the National State Assembly, Sri Lanka. The Vice-President was Dr G. S. Dhillon, Speaker of the Lok Sabha, India. Bryant Godman Irvine's term of office had ended and the Council elected the United Kingdom branch nominee, Arthur Bottomley, to succeed him as Treasurer.

The election of the Chairman of the Executive Committee was keenly contested. Sir Frederic Bennett had been elected to serve for the remaining two years of Gerard Montano's term of office. Many councillors considered that he was entitled to a final year in office. He had been an active Treasurer, Financial Adviser and Chairman, who had brought financial expertise to bear on the Association's finances. His major contribution had been to have the Association registered as a charity and thus exempt from United Kingdom taxes. In the days leading up to the election there was energetic lobbying among the delegates. The other candidate for the chairmanship was Gerald Regan, the Premier of Nova Scotia, and by 33 votes to 26 he was elected.

The 19th Commonwealth Parliamentary Conference took place in London on 12–21 September 1973.[25] It was attended by 166 delegates and 25 Secretaries to delegations, representing 85 branches of the Association. The Kindred Group in the US Congress was represented by Senator J. William Fulbright. Michael F. Kitt and Gerald L'Estrange, from the group in the Parliament of the Irish Republic, attended as observers. M. Xavier Deniau and M. Robert Moinet were the observers from the AIPLF. The Council of Europe was represented by the Deputy Clerk, G. Adinolfi, and the IPU by the Assistant-Secretary General, Pierre Cornillon. The Earl of Bessborough and Maurice Dewulf represented the European Parliament. The Commonwealth Foundation was represented by its Director, John Chadwick. The Commonwealth Secretary-General, Arnold Smith, attended and also addressed the delegates at a separate meeting.

The opening of the conference took place with great ceremony in Westminster

Hall on 12 September 1973. H. M. the Queen and H. R. H. Prince Philip were present. H.M. the Queen graciously delivered the opening address. The delegates, Secretaries to delegations, observers and some 1600 guests filled the Hall. With the State Trumpeters, the Queen's Bodyguard of the Yeomen of the Guard, and the Bodyguard of the Honourable Corps of Gentlemen-at-Arms in positions below the great stained glass window at the south end and behind their Majesties and the delegates and guests seated in front, Westminster Hall was a splendid sight, and the occasion was vested with a certain majesty of its own.

The President, Sir Alec Douglas-Home, invited the Queen to declare the conference open. In the course of her speech she referred to the importance of the Commonwealth in promoting bridges of communication. She continued: 'Your Association provides such a bridge while, at the same time, strengthening parliamentary government in which all of us present in this Hall believe.'[26]

The Prime Minister, Edward Heath, and the Vice-President, Felix Bandaranaike, also spoke. In expressing thanks to H. M. the Queen, Edward Heath closed on a personal note:

> Twenty years ago, as a fairly new member of Parliament I attended the CPA conference in Nairobi. That made an unforgettable impact on my mind. The opportunity to see the life of other Commonwealth countries, the discussions in the parliamentary Chamber and above all perhaps the innumerable talks we had gave me an understanding of our common interests, as well as the differences which exist between us, for which I have been ever grateful. And the friendships forged in this way have often been renewed in the capitals of the Commonwealth and are regularly refreshed at Christmastide and New Year.[27]

'The Enlarged European Community and the Commonwealth' was the subject of the first two plenary sessions. It was a topical subject and on the minds of all delegates, for at the beginning of 1973 Britain had finally joined the Community. Indeed, in the course of the debate one delegate, J. R. F. Richardson (Trinidad and Tobago) said,

> This is probably one of the most important CPA conferences we have ever had, in that it comes at a crucial time in the history of the Commonwealth, of the United Kingdom, and of some of the developing countries, particularly in the Caribbean area. The United Kingdom must have been conscious when she was thinking of gaining entry into the EEC that it would shake the confidence of individual members of the Commonwealth in the United Kingdom's good intentions. But this is a *fait accompli* and we in the Caribbean area must adjust.[28]

The opening speaker was Julian Amery (United Kingdom). He made an apt reference to the role played by his father, Leo Amery, in the creation of the CPA:

> The main architect of the Commonwealth Parliamentary Association was Sir Howard d'Egville, but it was a proposal by my father, put forward at the time of the Coronation of King George V, which led to the first conference of delegates from the Parliaments of

what were then called the self-governing colonies, and it was from that conference that our Association sprang. My father was in later years several times Chairman of the Association, but he was also a founder member and Vice-President of the United Kingdom branch of the European movement.[29]

Julian Amery then gave the background to the European movement, an idea launched by Winston Churchill's call in 1946 for a united Europe. He explained next his view of the likely impact on the Commonwealth of Britain's accession to the Community, stressing that it would not be inward-looking in its policies. He expressed the hope that the CPA would forge close links with the European Parliament. It was an impressive speech, unfolding his vision of the EEC in the years ahead and the prospects for future relations of Commonwealth countries with Britain and the EEC.

The delegates who followed voiced their anxieties. Indian delegates explained the dire effects of this development. Britain continued to be the largest market for many of India's products. The loss of Commonwealth preferences and other trade advantages in the United Kingdom, following its entry into the EEC, would be serious, unless special safeguards were negotiated. The leader of the Malaysian delegation, Richard Hoh Ung Hun, explained similar anxieties about Malaysia's traditional exports to the United Kingdom. Senator Dr Mahathir bin Mohammed said, 'We in Malaysia have a certain impression of the EEC. We see the EEC as a coming together of some of the richest, most powerful, and most technologically advanced nations of the world. They have come together so that they may protect their interests. Today their interests are centred around their economic well-being.'[30] When forming the EEC, the countries concerned talked about dismantling barriers, but inevitably they erected more barriers against the developing countries. He illustrated this with a reference to Malaysia's export of canned pineapple.

Arthur Bottomley (United Kingdom) argued strongly that Britain's entry into the EEC would enable it to play a more powerful part in the Commonwealth and to benefit all of its members. Delegates from the primary-producing countries were not, however, persuaded. The leader of the New Zealand delegation, J. L. Hunt, said that the economic future of his country was at stake. R. D. Muldoon (New Zealand) made a speech remarkable for its breadth and perception. He had, he said, always supported Britain's joining the EEC. Moreover he saw a continuing New Zealand association with the British economy as far ahead as it was possible to foresee. In the future a strong Britain would inevitably mean a stronger New Zealand. But he warned of major obstacles to be overcome by Britain and the EEC, which must not become inward-looking.

Christopher Brocklebank-Fowler (United Kingdom) spoke very positively about Britain's role in the EEC, and rejected the criticisms and doubts expressed by other delegates. He said, too, that it was no use bemoaning the loss of their protected trade. Commonwealth countries should come together to consider what pressures they could exert on the EEC. Certain other members of the United

Kingdom delegation, however, spoke forcefully against Britain's membership of the Community.

Dr G. S. Dhillon (India) opened the first of the two sessions on 'World Security'. He deplored the great increase of armaments in the world and condemned the arms race between the major powers. The United Nations had declared the 1970s to be a decade of disarmament, but to no avail. He welcomed, however, the general détente following the agreement in Moscow between the US and the USSR. Moreover, in the Indian subcontinent the governments of India, Pakistan and Bangladesh had reached agreement to resolve their differences and to work together for peace and security in the region.

Sir Bernard Braine paid tribute to Dr Dhillon's speech. He went on to emphasise that Britain had joined the EEC not just for economic but also for political reasons. The Community offered real opportunities for securing a more orderly development of international political and economic relations. But he warned that the most pressing and terrifying problem facing mankind in the next two decades was world poverty.

Senator J. William Fulbright (United States) in a statesmanlike speech, asked delegates not to dismiss the United Nations prematurely as an idle dream. The anomaly of their age was the spread of nationalism at a time when the problems of the human race had become truly global. One unprecedented problem which could be dealt with only by cooperative international effort was the population explosion. This explosion negated the effect of economic development in many of the less developed countries. The United States was concerned to give aid, but was increasingly frustrated because it was impossible within its means to keep up with the increase in population in recipient countries.

Senator Dr Mahathir bin Mohammad (Malaysia) spoke about the realisation of governments in South-East Asia that they could rely on none of the powers to maintain security in their region. They had therefore embarked on a new policy of making it a region of neutrality. If this concept were to become universal, the problem of security for the world would be largely diminished.

James Johnson (United Kingdom) alerted the conference to the dangers lying ahead in the oceans and seas of the world. The contents of the oceans and the ocean floor belonged to mankind and he did not want to see a carve-up of them by the powerful nation-states. He urged delegates to press their governments to prepare well for the third Law of the Sea Conference, taking place in Santiago in the following year. This appeal was strongly supported by Lloyd R. Cruse (Canada), who explained the deep interest of Canada in this issue.

In the committee sessions delegates considered more closely the economic consequences arising from Britain's entry into the EEC. They also discussed regional economic arrangements and international monetary reform. Further committee sessions were devoted to a range of social problems. In one plenary session, 'The Future of the Smaller Territories of the Commonwealth', and in another plenary session Commonwealth immigration policies were discussed. The exchanges in these committee sessions, as in these two plenary sessions, were extremely well-informed and valuable. Special mention should be made of the contributions of R. D. Muldoon (New Zealand), Christopher Brocklebank-Fowler (United Kingdom), O. G. Migure (Kenya), and others on economic inter-dependence, which were stimulating and at times brilliant.

In the three final plenary sessions the subject was 'Parliamentary Government: 'Where is it Heading?', considered under five specific headings. The discussions were thoughtful and earnest leaving no doubt about the commitment of all delegates to some form of parliamentary government.

This was an important and influential conference. The calibre of delegations was high. Many of the speeches were outstanding contributions to the under-standing of the problems of world security and those in the economic, social, and parliamentary fields, and, indeed, would merit republication for a wider audience.

Notes

1. Report of General Meeting (Kuala Lumpur, 15 September 1971), p.106.
2. Ibid., p.110.
3. Minutes of Subcommittee Meeting, 6–8 February 1971.
4. Proposed amendments to the constitution of the CPA (June 1971), pp.14B–15B.
5. **Agenda and Opening Speakers, Kuala Lumpur, 1971**
   The Commonwealth and Problems of World Security – Tun Dr Ismail Alhaj bin Dato Haji Abdul Rahman, Deputy Prime Minister and Minister of Home Affairs (Malaysia); I. E. Omolo-Okero, Minister of Health (Kenya); J. A. Kershaw, Parliamentary Under-Secretary, Foreign and Commonwealth Office (United Kingdom).
   Challenges to Parliamentary Democracy – George Rajapakse, Minister of Fisheries (Ceylon); R. C. Wright, Minister of Works (Australia); M. S. Gurupadaswamy (India).
   Economic Development – H. C. Templeton (New Zealand); B. L. B. Pitt, Minister of National Security (Trinidad and Tobago); Roy McNeill, Minister of Home Affairs (Jamaica).
   Problems of the Environment – George J. McIlraith (Canada); Allister Grosart (Canada); Sir Abdul Razak Mohamed, Minister of Housing, Lands, and Country Planning (Mauritius); Dato Ong Kee Hui, Minister of Technology (Malaysia).
6. Conference Report (Kuala Lumpur, 1971), p.xvii.
7. Minutes of General Council, 25 October 1972.
8. Report of the General Meeting (26 October 1972), p.96.
9. *Loc. cit.*
10. Ibid., p.97.
11. Ibid., p.98.
12. Ibid., p.99.
13. *Loc. cit.*
14. *Loc. cit.*
15. *Loc. cit.*
16. *Loc. cit.*
17. **Agenda and Opening Speakers, Blantyre, Malawi, 1972**

The Commonwealth and World Security – J. D. Msonthi, Minister of Education (Malawi); Enche Musa bin Hitam (Malaysia); Dr V. Moran (Malta).
Social Problems of Today – Dr G. S. Dhillon, Speaker of the Lok Sabha (India); Allister Grosart (Canada); W. Szeto (Hong Kong).
Economic Problems – Baroness Tweedsmuir, Minister of State, Foreign and Commonwealth Office (United Kingdom); N. W. Munoko, Assistant Minister of Local Government (Kenya); Dr C. R. De Silva, Minister of Plantation Industry and Minister of Constitutional Affairs (Sri Lanka); P. A. M. Manning, Parliamentary Secretary, Ministry of Petroleum and Mines (Trinidad and Tobago).

18. Conference Report (Malawi, 1972), pp.xvii–xviii.
19. Ibid., p.2.
20. Ibid., pp.21–2.
21. Ibid, p.24.
22. Ibid., p.67.
23. Minutes of General Council, 9 September 1973.
24. Report of General Meeting (London, 1973).
25. **Agenda and Opening Speakers, London, 1973**
    The Enlarged European Community and the Commonwealth – Julian Amery, Minister of State for Foreign and Commonwealth Affairs (United Kingdom); L. E. Ward (Barbados).
    World Security – Dr G. S. Dhillon, Speaker of the Lok Sabha (India); Sillah S. Koroma, Minister of State (Sierra Leone).
    Economic Problems – panel sessions.
    Social Problems – panel sessions.
    Future of the Smaller Territories of the Commonwealth – J. R. Plowman, Minister for Government Organisation (Bermuda).
    Commonwealth Immigration Policies – S. Senarath, Deputy Minister of Irrigation, Power and Highways (Sri Lanka).
    Parliamentary Government: Where is it Heading? – H. de B. Forde (Barbados); Allan J. MacEachen, President of the Privy Council and Leader of the Government in the House of Commons (Canada); Kultar Chand Rana, Speaker of the Legislative Assembly (Himachal Pradesh, India).
26. Conference Report (London, 1973), p.5.
27. Ibid., p.7.
28. Ibid., p.59.
29. Ibid., p.13.
30. Ibid., p.40.

18 A New Mood, 1974–76

For many members of the CPA Britain's accession to the EEC in 1973 appeared as a watershed from which the Commonwealth and the Association itself would emerge in some changed form or even disappear gradually. This did not happen. But the possibility that it might happen was certainly in the minds of many delegates during the London conference. This thought had the effect within the CPA of bringing a new surge of support from its branches and members. Indeed, support for the Association was never stronger than in the 1970s.

The meeting of the Executive Committee in Apia, Western Samoa, on 13–17 May 1974, gave evidence of a new direction. The opening ceremony was performed by the Head of State, H. H. Malietoa Tanumafili II, in the Chamber of the Maota Fono (Parliament House). The proceedings began with ceremonial choral singing and dancing. The Speaker, Toleafoa Talitimu, pronounced an invocation. The Salelesi (Serjeant-at-Arms) then gave his 'taulaga', a special chant to banish evil spirits before the deliberations began.

H. H. the Head of State spoke of the benefits Western Samoa had derived from membership of the Commonwealth. He also expressed gratitude to the CPA for enabling Samoan parliamentarians to attend meetings overseas where they could exchange views with members from other countries. The Prime Minister, Fiame Mataafa, said that Western Samoa's involvement in the activities of the Association had widened its outlook. Through lack of contact with neighbours Western Samoa tended to forget that there was a larger world beyond the seas 'with problems essentially identical with our own and with solutions relevant to problems we are now feeling. . . . We are so small and so far away from other areas of the world that we often seem to exist only as figments of the imagination of Hollywood.'[1] The Chairman of the Committee, Gerry Regan, in his speech of thanks said, 'Nowhere in the world have I seen a Parliament Building more strikingly national in more attractive surroundings and providing every facility in which your elected representatives are able to deliberate the important matters of the day.'[2]

The occasion, like other events in the programme, admirably prepared by the

Cierk of the House, George Fepulea'i, expressed the warmth and friendliness and the traditional courtesies of the Samoan people. Members of the Committee and the Secretariat staff were able to see the beauty of the islands, still quite unspoilt, and to feel something of the spirit of Western Samoa, where age-old Polynesian customs are cherished and maintained. The experience was moving and unforgettable.

The membership of the Committee brought a fresh approach. The new Chairman, Gerry Regan (Canada), introduced an informal, relaxed mood and a certain gusto into the meetings. He allowed discussions to range widely, but had an intuitive understanding of the feelings and views of every member and of the Secretariat, and he was adept at closing each discussion with a lucid expression of the consensus, acceptable to all present. Senator Allister Grosart (Canada) was now a member of the Committee. He was a man of vision and applied a trenchant mind to the urgent problems of the Association. Another new member was Senator Wilfred Krichefski (Jersey), an active supporter of the CPA. The Committee also benefited from the contributions of Dr G. S. Dhillon (India), Arthur Bottomley (United Kingdom), Roy McNeill (Jamaica) and Dr Mahathir bin Mohammed (Malaysia), all with long experience of the Association.

Finance was the principal item in the Committee's agenda. The year 1973 had closed with a credit balance of £38,749. The estimates forecast a deficit of £32,975 at the end of 1974, thus reducing the credit balance to only £5774. World inflation, and in particular the sharp increase in air fares of 26 per cent, expected to rise soon to 30 per cent, were mainly responsible. Several areas in which economies might be made were discussed, but Dr Dhillon pointed out that the ultimate solution must be found in further increases in branch contributions. Finally, on the proposal of Allister Grosart, the Committee appointed a Finance Subcommittee of three members: Allister Grosart, Arthur Bottomley and Wilfred Krichefski. The subcommittee was to hold preliminary meetings in Apia and subsequent meetings in London. It was to examine the 1974 estimates and the financial position of the Association generally, and to report to the Committee in Sri Lanka.

The subcommittee carried out a thorough and realistic review. Its report, as well as proposals for further amendments to the constitution and other business, were considered by the Committee and its recommendations went forward to the General Council.

The meetings of the General Council took place in Colombo, Sri Lanka, on 2 and 9 September 1974. The review of the Association's activities during the preceding 12 months was, as always, an important part of the agenda. The 21st parliamentary seminar at Westminster, and regional seminars in Canada and Australia as well as the Canadian, Caribbean, African and the UK and Mediterranean regional conferences, were noted. The biennial conference of Commonwealth Caribbean Presiding Officers and Clerks had been held in Bermuda. The officers of the Association, the regional representatives, and members of the Secretariat reported on their visits to branches. There were also extensive exchanges of delegations between branches. Delegations from Australia had visited India, Bangladesh, Sri Lanka and the United Kingdom. India had sent a ten-member delegation to Australia. The United Kingdom branch had sent 40 of its members on overseas visits to 20 branches. It had also in addition to the seminar at Westminster received a delegation of 23 members from 14 overseas branches. The Canadian branches had received a delegation of 13 members from the UK and Mediterranean region and had in turn sent a delegation, led by their Presiding Officers, to the region. The Malawi branch had received a visit of members of the Solomon Islands branch, which, prior to independence, wanted to study Malawi's constitutional and economic development.

Such conferences, seminars and exchanges were part of the vast pattern of visits and personal contacts between members of legislatures throughout the Commonwealth each year. The CPA promoted and made such contacts possible. They usually attracted little attention from the media and often passed unnoticed. But this was the CPA in action and from these contacts it drew much of its strength and support.

The most urgent matter on the agenda of the General Council was finance. In presenting the subcommittee's report, the Treasurer stated that a projection of expenditure and income for the five-year period 1974–78 forecast a total deficit of £113,000. This estimated deficit included £20,000 transferred to the operating credit balance forward, which the Committee considered to be the minimum credit balance to be kept in hand. Prompt action was needed if the Association was to avoid bankruptcy.

The Committee recommended certain economies to balance the budget in 1975 and 1976. The cutbacks were not proposed in any of the service activities of the Association but in the general area of annual conferences. The reason was that, since delegates comprised only a very small proportion of the total membership and enjoyed special privileges in attending conferences, it was equitable to propose cuts in this area rather than in other areas which would restrict services to the overall membership. Indeed, annual increases of approximately 10 per cent were proposed in the service expenditures.

The immediate economies recommended affected air fares for delegates, which would be based on excursion, as distinct from full economy, rates in future. The subventions to branches hosting the annual conference would be curtailed. A further increase in branch contributions would be unavoidable in two years, assuming that world inflation continued at the current rate. The Committee proposed also to review in depth the basis on which individual branch contributions were calculated and to recommend adjustments where necessary. Further, Allister Grosart explained, under the present constitution it was not possible to recommend any increase in branch contributions until 1978. An amendment to the constitution removing this restriction would, with the Council's agreement, be submitted to the General Meeting.

The Council approved all of the recommendations. In the course of the discussion three councillors effectively expressed the mood and approach of the meeting. Wilbert Winchester (Trinidad and Tobago) said that the CPA should be regarded as a very important forum for parliamentarians who should try to enhance its status. They could not do this by whittling down its activities, but must find ways to come to grips with the problem of financing the additional costs. They would have to think in terms of increased branch contributions. The Treasurer, Arthur Bottomley, expressed reluctance to ask governments for more funds immediately in view of the 20 per cent increase coming into effect in 1975.

Fred Daly (Australia) was of the view that the 1974 estimates were too conservative. The increases were too low in the light of current rates of inflation. He cited as an example the sum of £43,000 for salaries, national insurance and other items for the staff of the Secretariat, which he considered extremely low. He supported strongly the views expressed by Wilbert Winchester. He regretted that the Association had not asked for a 33⅓ per cent rather than a 20 per cent increase. A further increase in branch contributions should be made as soon as possible. Referring to the review of the basis on which branch contributions were calculated, he said that Australia could afford to pay a higher contribution in order to assist those countries which were not so well off.

Ripton Macpherson (Jamaica) was forthright in expressing his views. He was, he said, constantly amazed that so many countries represented at the conference continually paid lip-service to the principles of parliamentary democracy, but hesitated when it came to funding the money to ensure that the CPA continued. What was needed in the CPA, he emphasised, was expansion.

The Council considered a request of the Committee that it re-examine two changes to be made in the composition of the Committee. The first was that the UK and Mediterranean region should have only one regional representative, since it already provided the Treasurer; the second was that the immediate past Chairman should no longer be a member of the Committee. The Council agreed to reverse both changes.

The General Meeting of the Association, which took place in Colombo on 11 September 1974, approved the amendments to the constitution proposed by the Council. In the main they were matters of detail, described by the Chairman as part of a tidying-up operation. The amendment to Clause 37 was, however, crucial. It removed the restriction that branch contributions could be reviewed only at five-year intervals. Allister Grosart had described it as an intolerable constraint for any international organisation, and especially at a time of severe world inflation.

The 20th Commonwealth Parliamentary Conference was held in Colombo, Sri Lanka, from 1–15 September 1974.[3] It was attended by 169 delegates and 30 Secretaries to delegations, representing 84 branches of the Association. Two observers, John Wilson and Martin Finn, came from the kindred group in the Parliament of the Irish Republic. M. Xavier Deniau and M. Robert Moinet, were the observers from the AIPLF. The Commonwealth Secretariat was represented by R. Hunter Wade, Deputy Secretary-General.

The opening ceremony took place in the Bandaranaike Memorial International

Conference Hall, a gift from the People's Republic of China. The President of the Republic of Sri Lanka, H. E. William Gopallawa, arriving with a presidential escort of lancers, inspected the guard of honour. He was then received by the officers of the Association, who escorted him into the hall. The President of the Association, Stanley Tillekeratne, invited him to declare the conference open. The speech of the President was followed by those of the Deputy Prime Minister, Maithripala Senanyeke, and of Dr Henry Austin, leader of the Indian delegation.

The conference agenda, which included six parliamentary topics, was a very full one. Indeed, certain delegates complained at the General Meeting that it was overcrowded and allowed too little time for proper discussion of the major subjects. Another problem was that while the accommodation for the committee sessions was ideal, the main hall in which the plenary sessions were held was too vast. Delegations felt themselves distanced from each other. The tendency for plenary sessions to take the form of a series of prepared speeches, rather than a discussion and debate, was accentuated in these surroundings.

Dr N. M. Perera, leader of the Sri Lanka delegation, opened the first plenary session. The subject was 'The Indian Ocean as a Zone of Peace'. In an able speech he set out the political background that had led to this concept. It had found support at the UN General Assembly. Britain, the USA, the USSR and France had, however, abstained from voting on the relevant resolution. He appealed for full Commonwealth support. All who spoke after him endorsed the principle; only two delegates (Senator Allister Grosart (Canada) and Bryan Davies (United Kingdom)), mentioned the practical issues involved.

The second plenary session was on 'South-East Asia' and 'Problems of Peace and Neutrality in other Regions'. Puan Hajjah Aishah Ghani (Malaysia) opened and explained more fully the proposal for creating a South-East Asian zone of peace, freedom and neutrality. This concept gained wide support from delegates. But several called for greater realism.

Charles Fletcher-Cooke (United Kingdom) warned that 'If you are to be neutral, you must be strong'.[4] The capacity of small countries to achieve neutrality depended on their combining together for the purpose.

Senator Ramanlal Kapadia (Fiji) said, 'The question which we have to ask ourselves is whether the policy of neutrality has any relevance to the modern world. Neutrality must be vibrant, dynamic, forceful, constructive. Neutrality which is passive, timid, or cowardly, is meaningless and only fit to be buried.'[5] Sir Stephen McAdden (United Kingdom) and Lord Shepherd, leader of the United Kingdom delegation, both warned of the practical obstacles to maintaining neutrality. The Sri Lankans, Bernard Soysa and Felix Bandaranaike, strongly defended their concept of neutrality. The speech of another Sri Lankan, J. R. Jayewardene who was to become President of his country, was far more cautious. He outlined the problems and concluded: 'I am very doubtful whether one day the Indian Ocean will become a zone of peace. It can only become one if the whole world becomes a zone of peace.'[6]

The next two plenary sessions, one on the 'World Energy Crisis' and the other on 'The Law of the Sea', included a number of very informative contributions. Dr Henry Austin (India) opened on the subject of the energy crisis and Lord Shepherd (United Kingdom) on the law of the sea. Both spoke with authority and, supported by other delegates who spoke with direct knowledge, they awakened many delegates to the magnitude of the problems in each field. The fifth plenary session was opened by Fred Daly (Australia), who spoke with characteristic bluntness about the factors to be considered in any discussion of 'International Aid – Scope, Form, and Direction'. His speech set the realistic approach which most of the subsequent speakers adopted.

It was, however, in the six committee sessions that the conference was most successful. Sitting in rooms of an ideal size, delegates engaged in exchanges and debates. This applied especially in the discussions on 'World Population Year' on 'Control of Pollution and Protection of the Environment' and on 'Unrest among Youth: The Challenge to Educational Systems'.

Opening the committee session on 'The Problems of the Smaller Countries of the Commonwealth', Senator Derek Knight (Grenada) observed: 'Here in the Commonwealth Parliamentary Association we have perhaps the only forum in the world where the smaller countries spread over the entire globe, comprising different cultures, different levels of political development ... can meet and freely discuss their problems.'[7] He went on to speak about some of the common difficulties encountered by other delegates.

The most lively of the committee sessions were those concerned with parliamentary matters. The discussion on 'One Party and Multi-Party Parliaments' was especially stimulating as the protagonists of each system exchanged questions and arguments. In this as in all the other sessions, the conference was successful in educating, opening new horizons, and provoking thought among delegates from all regions of the Commonwealth.

On 30 June 1975 Arnold Smith, the first Commonwealth Secretary-General, retired. He had attended the conference in Ottawa in 1966 where, as recounted earlier, his address to delegates in a special meeting had drawn critical questioning. The Executive Committee then suggested to him that any future conference that he was able to attend he might prefer to submit a paper and answer questions rather than deliver a speech. At all subsequent conferences, except in Port-of-Spain in 1969 and London in 1973, he was represented by a deputy, which proved a satisfactory arrangement.

On his retirement the General Council recorded its recognition and appreciation of his services to the Commonwealth. His achievements during his ten years in office had indeed been significant. He had established the new Secretariat and had expanded it rapidly. Its budget in 1965–66, its first year, was £175,000 and its total staff was 41. In 1974–75, the budget was £1,411,340 and the staff numbered 279. The original purpose of the Secretariat was to foster consultation between Commonwealth countries. But Arnold Smith considered that it should provide special services which would contribute to the social and economic welfare of the developing countries, and in this he gained the support of the

Heads of Government. His outstanding achievement was the creation in 1971 of the Commonwealth Fund for Technical Cooperation which by 1975 had a staff of 63 and a budget of £3 million, separate from the staff and budget of the Secretariat, figures which rose to 98 staff and a budget of £8 million in the following year.

A Guyanese, Shridath Surendranath Ramphal, was appointed to succeed Arnold Smith. An astute, articulate and capable diplomat, he had served for some ten years in the government of Forbes Burnham in Guyana. With great verve he has carried on with the expansion of the Secretariat and its services.

Relations between the CPA Secretariat and the Commonwealth Secretariat have been informal, as specified by the Executive Committee, and cooperative, and between the two Secretaries-General, Robin Vanderfelt and Shridath Ramphal, they have been close and friendly.

The Executive Committee met next in Castle Rushen in Castledown, Isle of Man, from 26–30 May 1975. It carried out its customary task of reviewing the activities of the Association. It gave close attention to the arrangements for the 21st annual conference, to be held in India in October–November 1975. The President of the Association, Dr G. S. Dhillon, reported on the plans. By invitation Shyam Lal Shakdher, Secretary-General of the Lok Sabha, was present and explained matters of detail.

Receiving the report on publications and information services the Committee paid tribute to the Sri Lanka branch, which had printed a daily *Hansard* during the 1974 conference. The branch had also undertaken the printing and distribution of the official report of the conference. The Committee noted with approval a proposal for the Parliamentary Information and Reference Centre to produce a monograph on 'Conflicts of Interest of Ministers and Members', a topic which was under active review in many Commonwealth Parliaments. The Editor submitted that the Centre should produce more papers of this kind, providing comparative materials needed by members faced with these matters in their own legislatures.

The Library Support Fund had been affected by the 20 per cent cut in expenditure in the 1973 budget. A small sum had, however, been allocated from the CPA and Associated Purposes Trust to provide three donations of books. In all 16 branches had benefited from this scheme.[8] The Committee recorded its appreciation of this initiative and its hope that the fund could be continued.

The finances of the Association demanded special attention. The Treasurer presented the provisional estimates for 1975. Senator Allister Grosart then explained the recommendations of the Finance Subcommittee. He reported also on the broad policies and principles involved in producing a new constitution. His report and recommendations were approved by the Committee for submission to the Council and the General Meeting in New Delhi.

The General Council met in New Delhi on 27 October and 2 November 1975. Welcoming councillors on behalf of the Indian branch, Dr G. S. Dhillon recalled that India, together with Pakistan and Sri Lanka, had hosted the fifth conference in 1957. After the lapse of 18 years his branch was honoured to host the conference again. In 1957 there had been only 4 Indian state branches but now there were 19. This was an indication of India's support and of the Association's vitality.

Senator Allister Grosart presented the recommendations of the Finance Subcommittee. He recalled that its first report had been intended largely to contain inflation in the expenditures of the Association. Its proposals had resulted in a saving of some £20,000. But drastic measures were needed on the income side if the Association was to be solvent by 1 January 1977. He explained that the problems of the Association arose from its uniqueness among international organisations. The two main reasons were, first, that the Commonwealth was a world grouping with the largest ratio of developing to developed nations; and, secondly, that the CPA paid transportation costs of delegates to its annual conference. From the Finance Subcommittee's projection for the five years 1974–78 it had concluded that the deficit by 1978 would be £133,000, an impossible situation, especially as the Association had no assets.

After many days spent in examining the various alternatives, the Subcommittee had decided to recommend both a reclassification of branches and an overall increase in membership fees of 20 per cent. For the purpose of reclassification branches had been divided into three categories – those which paid more into the Association than they took out, those which paid their way, and those which paid less. Membership fees had been adjusted to provide that more branches would pay above the norm and would in effect subsidise the Association. Among other branches as few as possible would pay below the norm. If the membership fees as revised were accepted by branches, the additional income would be about £28,000. The overall increase of 20 per cent in membership fees would yield about £58,000. As from the beginning of 1977 branches would be paying something of the order of an extra £75,000 a year.

In the discussion on these proposals the councillor from Fiji, P. K. Bhindi, criticised the method of assessment. It was directly related to average expenditure. It should take into consideration population, GNP, size of legislature, number of delegates, and other relevant factors. This argument did not find support from other councillors. Tom Adams (Barbados) said that, while the criteria advanced by the Fiji councillor had been accepted by the United Nations, they could not apply to the CPA. Its principal expense was the fares of delegates, which could be readily calculated and met through membership fees. He did not consider the subcommittee's report to be perfect, but far greater imperfections would result if they sought to introduce UN practices.

The recommendations were adopted by the Council with Fiji abstaining. A third part of the motion, also approved, concerned the salaries of the senior staff of the Secretariat. They had been extremely low for many years and, notwithstanding this fact, it had even been proposed to the Executive Committee in Malawi in 1972, that they should be cut by 10 per cent as part of an overall economy. This had been strenuously opposed by the Australian branch, and especially by Fred Daly and Allister Grosart. The salaries were now increased to keep them broadly in line with grades in the UK civil service.

The constitution of the Association should, it was generally agreed, be reviewed further. The Executive Committee at its meeting in Sri Lanka had requested the Secretariat to produce a new draft constitution and to circulate it to all members of the Committee one month before its meeting in the Isle of Man. The new draft had been circulated on 25 March 1975. Senator Allister Grosart had, however, discussed the matter with the Secretariat when visiting London in January 1975. He was of the opinion that broad policies and principles should be decided before a revision of the constitution was attempted. He had produced a paper which the Committee decided to circulate to all branches. It decided also to formulate a series of questions to which branches would be asked to reply. The Council approved this procedure.

Among the last items on the Council's agenda was the election of officers and regional councillors. Sir Radhamohun Gujadhur, Deputy Speaker of the Legislative Assembly, Mauritius, was elected President and James Jerome, Speaker of the House of Commons, Canada, was elected Vice-President of the Association.

The General Meeting took place in New Delhi on 4 November 1975. It approved all of the recommendations of the Council. In particular, tributes were paid to Senator Allister Grosart for his financial report and proposals. Datuk Musa Hitam (Malaysia) spoke of his great command of the subject. The Chairman of the Executive Committee, Gerry Regan said, 'Senator Grosart has given very freely of his time to serve on the Subcommittee on finance, and has crossed the ocean from Canada to England for its meetings so many times that he should be given a pilot's licence, and he has done that at no expense to the CPA.'[9]

The 21st Commonwealth Parliamentary Conference was held in New Delhi from 26 October to 9 November 1975. It was attended by 188 delegates and 28 Secretaries to delegations, representing 86 branches. Two observers, Deputies Keiran Crotty and Michael Noonan, came from the kindred group in the Irish Republic. The AIPLF was represented by M. Xavier Deniau and M. Robert Moinet. S. S. Ramphal represented the Commonwealth Secretariat and addressed delegates in a separate meeting.

The opening ceremony was impressive. H. E. the President of India, Shri Fakhruddin Ali Ahmed, arrived by state coach at the Parliament Building, escorted by his bodyguards. The officers of the Association and members of the Executive Committee were presented to him. He was then conducted into the Central Hall. In inviting him to open the conference, Dr G. S. Dhillon, President of the Association, said: 'Political and parliamentary institutions all the world over are under tremendous pressure these days. The challenge which democracy faces at the present time is as to how far it can vindicate itself as an instrument of growth and social regeneration.'[10]

The President spoke of the continuing relevance and vitality of the Commonwealth. At the conclusion of his speech he formally released a new publication, entitled *Commonwealth Parliaments*. It contained contributions by many Presiding Officers and Clerks and had been edited and published by Shyam Lal Shakdher, the able Secretary-General of the Lok Sabha, to mark the holding of the conference in New Delhi.

The Prime Minister of India, Shrimati Indira Gandhi, spoke of India's commitment to parliamentary government. 'The involvement of so many millions in the national struggle made it inevitable that free India should shun any path reserved for a few,' she said.

> It had to be participatory democracy on the broadest base. We opted for this system not to emulate Britain or because the framers of the Indian constitution were unaware of other forms of democracy, but because it was best suited to the Indian reality. It was a deliberate choice and was determined by the non-violent nature of our fight, by our preference for peaceful and orderly change, and by our conviction that the people must have the deciding voice.[11]

She added: 'In the last 25 years we have withstood more than one military challenge, economic crisis and threat of secession. Our five general elections have demonstrated the value of a free vote and the maturity of our electorate, which in the 1971 parliamentary election numbered 274 million.'[12]

In thanking the President and the Prime Minister of India, Sir Radhamohun Gujadhur referred to the fact that the conference would be the first to be held in the Sansadiya Soudha, the newly completed Parliament House Annexe. He gave an assurance that all who attended next year's conference in Mauritius would be warmly welcomed.

The Sansadiya Soudha indeed provided admirable accommodation. The conference agenda was heavy.[13] Many of the topics had appeared in the agenda of previous conferences. But such subjects as world security, aid and economic issues, commodity prices, the environment and challenges to Parliament were continuing problems. Moreover, each conference brought together new delegates, who exchanged views, contributed and learnt.

The plenary sessions were somewhat formal. It was in the committee sessions that the discussions came to life. In the sessions on 'Multinational Corporations' and 'Commodity Prices, Terms of Trade and Indexation' Datuk Musa Hitam, leader of the Malaysian delegation, spoke with a broad knowledge and understanding. His contributions were stimulating and were acknowledged by all who took part in these sessions. Max Saltsman (Canada) and Roy Richardson (Trinidad and Tobago) were also outstanding. In the discussion on 'Producer or Consumer Country Cartels and Regional Economic Groupings', chaired by Senator Allister Grosart, the principal participants were again Datuk Musa Hitam and Max Saltsman, and also Tom Adams (Barbados). It was, in fact, a rewarding conference which benefited from having both a daily *Hansard* and a daily summary. It was fortunate, too, in that the Indian press and television gave it ample coverage.

On conclusion of the conference delegates were divided into four groups, which departed from New Delhi on different tours. Each tour was carefully planned to enable delegates to see as much as possible of at least part of the vast and fascinating subcontinent. The generous welcome and hospitality of governments and branches, like the effective organisation of the tours, were remarkable. For many delegates this experience made them recall the words of Shrimati Indira Gandhi at the opening ceremony, when she had said: 'Welcome to India, a strange land, strange not only to those who have come from abroad but even to many who have lived here all their lives. My father, steeped in India's history and culture, spent a life time discovering her. India is a world in herself – in space and time.'[14]

The mid-year meeting of the Executive Committee took place in Castries, St Lucia, on 26–29 April 1976. All members were present except the President and the South-East Asian regional councillor, Dr Mahathir bin Mohammed, who were detained by parliamentary duties. Senator Kamarul Ariffin attended as Dr Mahathir's alternate.

The opening ceremony in the Chamber of the House of Assembly was well attended. The Speaker, W. St Clair Daniel, welcomed the committee members, and then called on the Governor, Sir Allen Lewis, to declare the meeting open. The Premier of St Lucia, J. G. M. Compton, said that the great advances made since St Lucia became an Associated State had given it confidence to advance to full independence and in this, he hoped, St Lucia would enjoy the support of the Commonwealth. The Committee's Chairman, Gerry Regan, expressed the thanks of the Committee to Speaker St Clair Daniel and to the St Lucia branch.

At the first meeting the Chairman welcomed the new members – Senator Gordon Davidson (Australia), Sir Vijay Singh (Fiji), H. C. Kerruish (Isle of Man) and Harry Blank (Quebec). The Committee then reviewed the arrangements for the conference to take place in Mauritius in September 1976 and drafted the agenda.

In approving the accounts and balance sheet for 1975, the Committee noted that the position was better than expected, due mainly to the non-attendance of certain committee members and branch delegations at the Indian conference. The estimates for 1976 were to be reconsidered in Mauritius. The Committee expressed great appreciation of the Chairman's initiative in approaching the Canadian provincial branches with the suggestion that they double their membership fees in 1976. Six provinces had agreed and it was hoped that the others and the Canadian Federal branch would follow this generous example. The questionnaire on amendments to the constitution, circulated by the Secretariat in January 1976, had brought replies from only about a quarter of branches. It was decided to give them more time and to discuss the constitution in Mauritius.

A radical revision of the constitution was in mind. The management of the Association had become clumsy, inefficient and time-consuming. The Executive Committee of 19 members reported to the General Council of about 85 members, which in turn reported to the General Meeting of some 200 members. There was confusion over the authority of the Council and the General Meeting. The constitution vested in the Council full authority for the management of the affairs of the Association, but the General Meeting could, and on several occasions did, reverse decisions of the Council. For many years, indeed since about 1974, the abolition of the Council had been under discussion within the Secretariat and with certain branch Secretaries, such as Alan Turner (Australia) who gave close thought to the functioning of the CPA.

In Mauritius the Executive Committee appointed a Constitutional Subcommittee with Allister Grosart and Sir Vijay Singh (Fiji) as its members. Allister Grosart was the driving-force in this as he had been in the Finance Subcommittee. He himself now undertook the drafting of the constitution. In the course of the discussion by the General Council of the Executive Committee's initiative, a majority of councillors agreed that the Council should be abolished.

The Committee appointed also a new Finance Subcommittee which would in future be a standing committee of the Executive. Its members were Neil Marten (United Kingdom), H. C. Kerruish (Isle of Man) and Senator Kamarul Ariffin (Malaysia).

At its meeting in Mauritius on 25 September 1976 the Council elected the officers of the Association. James Jerome, Speaker of the Canadian House of Commons, was elected to succeed Sir Radhamohun Gujadhur as President for 1976–77. In thanking the Council the new President said that in his view the Association was in danger of becoming a Commonwealth Association rather than a Commonwealth Parliamentary Association. He did not want the Association to be charged with lacking the will or the capacity to discuss annually in conference the health and vigour of the parliamentary system which was the uniting bond between them all.

The Council then elected Ripton Macpherson, Speaker of the House of Representatives, Jamaica, to be Vice-President for 1976–77. The three-year term of office of the Treasurer, Arthur Bottomley had come to an end. In his place the Council elected Neil Marten (United Kingdom).

The Chairman of the Executive Committee, Gerry Regan, had also completed his term of office. All acknowledged that he had been an admirable Chairman and expressed warm appreciation of his services. Two members stood for election as his successor. One was Datuk Musa Hitam, Minister of Primary Industries, Malaysia, who was attending as alternate for Dr Mahathir bin Mohammed, the South-East Asian regional councillor. The other candidate was Bernard Soysa, Sri Lanka, the Asian regional councillor. In the ballot by 42 votes to 31 Datuk Musa Hitam was elected Chairman.

At the General Meeting of the Association, held in Mauritius on 29 September 1976, the third report of the Finance Subcommittee was presented by Arthur Bottomley who, as Treasurer, was its Chairman. He spoke of the tragic death of Senator Wilfred Krichefski (Jersey) in January 1975 and the appointment of H. C. Kerruish (Isle of Man) in St Lucia to fill the vacancy on the subcommittee.

Senator Allister Grosart explained to the General Meeting that, while the CPA would have a debit balance at the end of 1976, its future finances looked bright. The five-year projections, made by the subcommittee, indicated a surplus in 1977 and 1978. The projections had proved accurate for the years 1974–76, and he was confident that they would hold up in the coming years. In reply to a question from S. E. Calder (Australia), he said that the salaries of the Secretariat staff had been reviewed and were, he believed, now adequate.

The Finance Subcommittee had made a remarkable contribution. In 1973 the CPA had been heading for bankruptcy. The subcommittee's recommendations, involving an inevitable increase in membership fees and certain economies which did not damage the work of the Association, had amounted to a rescue operation. In Mauritius Arthur Bottomley and Allister Grosart retired from the Executive Committee. At the General Meeting and in the Council their services to the CPA were acknowledged. In this history, however, a special tribute to Allister Grosart should be recorded. He was responsible for the restructuring of the finances of the Association which averted insolvency. The CPA must always be indebted to him for the intensive work and imaginative approach which he devoted to its welfare.

The 22nd Commonwealth Parliamentary Conference took place in Mauritius from 18–30 September 1976.[15] It brought together 173 delegates and 30 Secretaries to delegations, representing 86 branches of the Association. M. Robert Moinet attended as the observer from the AIPLF. Shridath Ramphal, the Commonwealth Secretary-General, attended and was able to address delegates at a separate meeting.

The opening of the conference took place with full ceremony at the Mahatma Gandhi Institute, Reduit, Mauritius, on 22 September 1976. The President of the Association, Sir Radhamohun Gujadhur, recalled that Mauritius had in 1968 hosted the first meeting of the Executive Committee and in 1971 had been host to the African Regional Conference. His branch was honoured to be host to the plenary conference. He paid a special tribute to Dr G. S. Dhillon, his predecessor in office and a strong supporter of the CPA over many years. H. E. the Acting Governor-General of Mauritius, Sir Maurice Latour-Adrien, in a short speech then declared the conference open.

The Prime Minister of Mauritius, Sir Seewoosagur Ramgoolam, welcomed the delegates and expressed his support for the Commonwealth and the CPA. 'The Roman Empire disappeared', he said, 'because it could not suffer the changes dictated by progress, but the British Empire, being a flexible and adaptable institution, was able to face the changing conditions of life.'[16]

The conference extended over 14 sessions. The first four plenary sessions were concerned with aspects of 'The Commonwealth and World Security'. The policies of the super-powers, the neutrality of the Indian Ocean, and the problems of Southern Africa were discussed. While many of the arguments had been heard before, there was more frank talking at this conference. Senator D. B. Scott, leader of the Australian delegation, deplored the tendency of many delegates to criticise the US but not the USSR. Another Australian delegate, however, defended the Soviet naval presence in the Indian Ocean.

The Tanzanian, Zambian and Kenyan delegates among others condemned racialism in Rhodesia and South Africa, and criticised British policies. This brought a blunt reply from Robert Kilroy-Silk (United Kingdom). He condemned racialism whatever its source. It should be condemned in Uganda as in South Africa. He also deplored the element of hypocrisy of some countries, which criticised New Zealand's sporting links with South Africa, while they themselves freely traded with South Africa. He added,

> We have too much of a double standard, too much of a competition in our slogans to see who can be the most militant and the most outspoken. And our credibility, Mr Chairman, as a community of nations, as a Commonwealth, as individuals each with an individual conscience, is at stake, if we are prepared to tolerate double standards; if we are prepared to condemn one party and not another, if we are prepared to say one thing and to act in another manner.[17]

The eight panel sessions, two sitting concurrently in each session, again produced some of the highlights of the conference. The outstanding contributors in these sessions included C. L. Bolden (Barbados), Robert Kilroy-Silk (United Kingdom), Datuk Musa Hitam (Malaysia) and S. E. Calder (Australia). 'Parliament in the Modern World' was the subject of the two final plenary sessions. L. C. Schultz (New Zealand) and Neil Marten (United Kingdom) made notable speeches in opening the sessions. The final session was enlivened by an impassioned speech by A. W. Jones (Australia), condemning the action of the Australian Governor-General, Sir John Ker, in dismissing the Whitlam government, so that a general election would be held. The case presented by A. W. Jones was rebutted by Mark Carlisle (United Kingdom) and in greater detail by Senator D. B. Scott.

All of the conference sessions took place in the Dinarobin Pierre Desmarais Hotel in Le Morne, a beautiful site on the south coast of Mauritius. It provided a contrast to the conference in New Delhi, the densely populated and busy capital of the largest democracy in the Commonwealth. Each CPA conference has tended to have its own special character. The conference in India inspired a sense of grandeur and of history. The size and isolation of Le Morne instilled a sense of privacy and intimacy. The Mauritius conference was, indeed, a stimulating and enjoyable occasion.

Notes

1. Report of General Council (1973–74), p.21.
2. *Loc. cit.*
3. **Agenda and Opening Speakers, Sri Lanka, 1974**
   The Indian Ocean as a Zone of Peace – Dr N. M. Perera, Minister of Finance (Sri Lanka)
   South-East Asia and Problems of Peace and Neutrality in other Regions – Puan Hajjah Aishah, Ghani, Minister of Welfare Services (Malaysia)
   The World Energy Crisis – Dr Henry Austin (India)

Law of the Sea – Lord Shepherd, Lord Privy Seal and Leader of the House of Lords (United Kingdom)

International Aid – Scope, Form and Direction – Fred Daly, Leader of the House and Minister for Services and Property (Australia)

The Member and His Information – M. J. Lumina, Minister of State for Rural Development (Zambia)

Broadcasting and Televising Parliament – C. A. McLachlan (New Zealand)

World Population Year – panel session

The Problems of the Smaller Countries of the Commonwealth – Senator Derek Knight (Grenada)

Control of Pollution and Protection of the Environment – panel session

Unrest among Youth: The Challenge to Educational Systems – Ahmad Mattar, Parliamentary Secretary to the Minister of Education (Singapore)

One-Party and Multi-Party Parliaments – panel session

Electoral Systems and Referenda and their Impact on Parliamentary Democracy – panel session

Improving the Efficiency of Parliament – panel session

Commodity Prices and the Future Relationship between the Industrialised and Primary Producing Countries with Reference to the European Community and other Organisations – B. Ramsaroop, Minister of Parliamentary Affairs and Leader of the House (Guyana).

4. Conference Report (Sri Lanka, 1974), p.56.
5. Ibid., p.57.
6. Ibid., p.44.
7. Ibid., p.273.
8. The 16 branches were Bahamas, Belize, Bermuda, British Virgin Islands, British Solomon Islands, Cayman Islands, Cook Islands, Fiji, Himachal Pradesh, Malawi, Montserrat, Sarawak, Sierra Leone, St Helena, St Vincent, Western Samoa.
9. General Meeting (New Delhi, 4 November 1975), p.64.
10. Conference Report (New Delhi, 1975), p.4.
11. Ibid., p.9.
12. Ibid., p.10.
13. **Agenda and Opening Speakers, New Delhi, 1975**

    The Commonwealth and World Security – K. Raghuramaiah, Minister of Works, Housing, and Parliamentary Affairs (India); Datuk Musa Hitam, Minister of Primary Industries (Malaysia); J. B. A. Siyomunji, Minister for the Central Province (Zambia); Joseph Brincat (Malta)

    World Energy Crisis – Lord Shepherd, Lord Privy Seal and Leader of the House of Lords (United Kingdom)

    Building a New International Economic Order – panel sessions

    Multinational Corporations – panel sessions

    Social Problems – panel sessions

    Challenges to Parliament – William Whitelaw (United Kingdom); Bernard Soysa (Sri Lanka)

    The Commonwealth as an Instrument of Social, Political, and Economic Transformation – Maurice Dupras (Canada).

14. Conference Report (New Delhi, 1975), p.11.
15. **Agenda and Opening Speakers, Mauritius, 1976**

    The Commonwealth and World Security – K. Raghuramaiah, Minister of Works, Housing and Parliamentary Affairs (India); Satcam Boolell, Minister of Agriculture and Natural Resources, and the Environment (Mauritius); I. N. Elinewinga, Minister

of National Education, Tanzania; V. H. Courtenay (Belize)
Development Assistance – panel session
The Commonwealth and the Law of the Sea – panel session
Economic Problems and a New International Order – panel sessions
Social Problems – panel sessions
Parliament in the Modern World – L. C. Schultz, New Zealand; Neil Marten (United Kingdom).
16. Conference Report (Mauritius, 1976), pp.7–8.
17. Ibid., p.57.

19   The Working Capital Fund, 1977–79

The Association had survived a financial crisis. Its activities had come under frequent scrutiny and every possible economy made. Its constitution was being redrafted and streamlined for greater efficiency. It still maintained an impressive programme of plenary and regional conferences and parliamentary seminars as well as its publications and information services. But it needed to do more in pursuit of its objectives. By the mid-1970s, however, the CPA appeared to be stagnating or, in the words of Sir Charles Kerruish (Isle of Man), it was 'running out of steam'.[1]

At this time Parliaments were being overthrown or were in jeopardy in many countries of the Commonwealth. Dr Henry Austin (India), at the Executive Committee meeting in Sierra Leone in April 1977, expressed the view that the entire Afro-Asian world was at this time questioning the validity of parliamentary institutions.

In Ghana the government of Dr Busia had been overthrown in a military *coup* on 13 January 1972. A second military *coup*, this time led by Flight-Lieut Rawlings, was staged on 4 June 1979, who restored civilian rule and after elections, Dr Hilla Liman assumed office on 24 September 1979. But his government, too, was short-lived. In yet another military takeover on 31 December Rawlings again seized power.

In Nigeria civilian government was restored after elections in July/August 1979, ending nearly 14 years of military rule. The new constitution, drafted with great care to ensure stable democratic government, was to be abrogated on 31 December 1983. The elected President, Alhaji Shehu Shagari, and the Federal and state legislatures were overthrown by the army, led by Major-General Mohammed Buhari.

Bangladesh, admitted to the Commonwealth as a sovereign nation on 18 April 1972, came under military rule in November 1975. In Grenada the government of Eric Gairy was ousted on 13 March 1979 by the People's Revolutionary Party which dismissed the legislature.

In India a state of emergency was declared on 26 June 1975. In a general election in March 1977 the Congress Party lost to the Janata Front and there was a peaceful transfer of power. In a further general election in January 1980 the Congress Party, led by Mrs Indira Gandhi, was once more returned to office. Again India demonstrated the maturity and stability which are among the requisites for parliamentary rule.

Zimbabwe became an independent republic on 20 December 1979. Following the Heads of Government meeting in Lusaka in August 1979, negotiations began for the country to come under independent African rule. In a general election in February/March 1980 the ZANU party, led by Robert Mugabe, won a clear majority, and he became Prime Minister.

The CPA was affected by these events to the extent that branches were suspended or readmitted. But there was also within the Association a sense of concern that so many parliamentary regimes had been overthrown. For members of the Secretariat with commitment to the Association and its purpose, there was the feeling that the Association should be more active. The Executive Committee and the General Council seemed to be concerned less with new initiatives and expansion than with finance. The membership fees were to be kept to a minimum, although the fees were insignificant amounts in the budgets of most Commonwealth countries. Harold Holt had commented in 1959: 'It is quite absurd that an Association, having the potentialities that we know exist in this organisation, should be conducted on a sort of shoe-string basis ... I feel that what we are prepared to set aside for the work of this Association is almost absurdly small.'[2] His comment still applied in the 1970s.

Against this background a memorandum was produced by the Secretariat in 1976 entitled 'The CPA and the Future'. It reviewed the work of the Association over the ten years since the Executive Committee had been established and made proposals for the future. Certain of the proposals had been raised earlier, welcomed and then set aside for lack of finance: others were new. The major innovation proposed was establishment of a working capital fund. Branches were to be invited to contribute once for all the equivalent of double the amount of their annual membership fees or less to establish the fund. The monies would be invested and the income used to finance new ventures. It was a modest proposal, envisaging a fund of some £40,000. It was argued that this was a minimum figure to provide for the first stage of the growth urgently needed in the work of the Association.

The memorandum was submitted to the Executive Committee at its meeting in Freetown, Sierra Leone, on 26 April 1977. The fact that it was welcomed as 'timely and thought-provoking' and that it received positive consideration was due to the membership of the new Committee. The Chairman, Datuk Musa Hitam, was an executive chairman who believed in achieving results. The Vice-President, Ripton Macpherson (Jamaica), was a fervent champion of parliamentary government, who held that the CPA should be much more active in this field. The Treasurer, Neil Marten, who regarded his office as far more than a formality, was efficient and positive in his attitude to the CPA's interests. The Committee also included several other members with experience of the Association.

In the discussion on the memorandum, members were agreed that the CPA should do more to strengthen Parliaments, especially in the developing countries of the Commonwealth. Another matter of general agreement was the need to find a means of communicating effectively with the Heads of Government. A direct link might be established by the Chairman or another officer of the Association attending their meetings as an observer.

The Committee approved the idea of a working capital fund. Neil Marten considered that the capital sum of £40,000 was too low. He proposed a figure of £150,000. The Sri Lanka member, N. Wimalasene, argued that the figure should be £500,000. Marten said that he would speak to his Prime Minister and ask him to raise the matter with fellow Heads of Government.

The Committee appointed a subcommittee to pursue further the proposals in the memorandum. Its members were the Chairman and the Treasurer, Senator Derek Knight (Grenada), Dr Henry Austin (India), Senator Gordon Davidson (Australia) and Alhaji M. C. Cham (The Gambia). It was to meet in London in July 1977 and to submit a preliminary report to the Executive Committee in Canada in September 1977.

On one issue, emphasised in the memorandum, the Committee expressed strong agreement. This was the urgent need for additional office accommodation for the Headquarters Secretariat at Westminster.

The subcommittee on 'The CPA and the Future' met in Montreal and Toronto. It made an interim report to the Committee in Ottawa, and its final report was to be submitted in Penang in March 1978.

The General Meeting of the Association took place in Ottawa on 20 September 1977. The Vice-President, Ripton Macpherson, made a preliminary report on the views of the subcommittee, as endorsed by the Executive Committee. The prime purpose of the Association must, he asserted, continue to be the promotion of parliamentary institutions, but with a broader approach. He went on to outline the proposals considered. The annual seminars on parliamentary practice and procedure, hosted jointly by the Association and the United Kingdom branch at Westminster, had proved their value over the years. But it was now necessary to carry seminars into the regions and the branches. The basic purpose was to inculcate a greater appreciation and understanding of Parliament. Next, it was proposed that the CPA should organise study groups of experienced parliamentarians to consider in depth and report on important topics, such as parliamentary scrutiny of public finance, the special needs of legislatures in small countries, and parliamentary scrutiny of science policy.

The subcommittee considered that the CPA *Newsletter* served a useful purpose in informing members about the Association's activities. It proposed that a *Parliamentary Newsletter* would also be of value in keeping members in touch with parliamentary events in other countries of the Commonwealth. Further the Parliamentary Information and Reference Centre should be enabled to produce specialist studies and memoranda on aspects of parliamentary work. His report aroused wide interest and members agreed that these new ventures should be undertaken.

The report of the Treasurer showed how vulnerable the Association was to inflation, especially as it affected air fares. The estimates for 1977 were satisfactory, showing a surplus of some £23,000 at the end of the year. But the position deteriorated in 1978 and 1979. Indeed, by the end of 1979 the total estimated deficit would be some £73,000. This was accounted for by the high cost of delegates' travel expenses attending the conference in New Zealand. Such a deficit was unacceptable. It would be wrong in his view to attempt to cut down on the Association's activities. He had therefore recommended, and the Executive Committee had unanimously agreed, that membership fees should be increased by 20 per cent in 1979.

The General Meeting convened again on 23 September and approved the revised constitution. The work of preparing the new draft had extended over three years. The subcommittee appointed by the Executive Committee, had also considered subsequent amendments proposed by branches.

The principal changes effected by the new constitution were the abolition of the General Council, an increase in the powers and responsibilities of the Executive Committee, and the definition of the General Assembly, formerly the General Meeting, as the final authority with specific reserved powers. There was no dispute over the abolition of the General Council. The size, composition and powers of the Executive Committee as well as the powers to be reserved to the General Assembly were, however, closely debated. Certain of the larger branches were concerned about their representation on the small Committee. Paul Dean (United Kingdom) expressing his misgivings, said that there should be not two but four representatives from each region, making an Executive Committee of 30 members instead of 18. His proposal did not receive wide support.

Datuk Musa Hitam urged acceptance of a compromise which would allow flexibility. This compromise was that the size and composition of the Committee, and other matters, such as membership fees, the geographical regions, delegate eligibility, the relations of national, state, provincial and territorial branches with each other, should not be defined in the constitution. A schedule attached to but not part of the constitution would describe the current situation. Changes could then be made readily by the General Assembly without recourse to the more cumbersome procedure for amending the constitution. This was agreed. But Paul Dean obtained an assurance that his proposals for a larger Committee would be considered at the time of the conference in Jamaica in the following year. The other clauses of the draft constitution were discussed and finally approved.

At the end of this long meeting Datuk Musa Hitam, Chairman of the Executive Committee, moved a vote of appreciation to Allister Grosart, Sir Vijay Singh and Derek Knight for the time and work they had devoted to the constitution. The Association was indebted particularly to Allister Grosart who, after his review of the finances, had gone on to shoulder the burden of re-drafting the constitution. Tributes were paid to Betty May who had been closely involved in all amendments to the constitution and particularly in this latest revision.

The 23rd Commonwealth Parliamentary Conference took place in Ottawa from 19–25 September 1977. It brought together 179 delegates and 30 Secretaries to delegations, representing 88 branches. Senator Michel Chauty and Robert Moinet attended as observers from the AIPLF. The Commonwealth Secretary-General, Shridath Ramphal, attended and addressed delegates at a separate meeting. Delegates arrived in Montreal on 10 September and took part in a pre-conference tour from 12–18 September. During the tours they were the guests of the ten provinces of Canada.

The opening of the conference was performed by the Governor-General of Canada, H. E. the Rt Hon. Jules Leger, in the Senate Chamber of the Parliament Buildings. In welcoming the delegates and inviting the Governor-General to deliver the opening address, James Jerome, President of the Association, laid stress on its parliamentary character. The Governor-General spoke briefly. The Prime Minister of Canada, Rt Hon. Pierre-Elliott Trudeau, in his address to the delegates said: 'the world has changed with stunning speed in the eleven years since last the CPA met in this country'. He cited some of the changes in the midst of which they as parliamentarians must maintain their awareness and sense of balance and perspective which, he said, 'is characteristic of the Commonwealth Parliamentary Association and perhaps unique to it'.[3] The Vice-President of the Association, Ripton Macpherson, expressed on behalf of the delegates their thanks for the welcome and the generous hospitality extended to them since their arrival in Canada.

The 14 sessions of the conference, of which nine were panel or committee sessions, took place in the Government Conference Centre in Ottawa.[4] The vast hall in which the plenary sessions were held, together with the fact that delegates remained seated and spoke into microphones, tended to make the proceedings formal and little attempt was made to debate topics. The excellence of the accommodation for the committee sessions more than compensated, and provided the setting for valuable discussions.

The opening speaker of the first session, of which the subject was 'The Commonwealth and World Security', was Donald Jamieson, the Secretary of State for External Affairs, Canada. He suggested four basic themes for discussion – liberation in Southern Africa, the new international economic order, a more positive Commonwealth commitment to the world community, and a clearer engagement by the Commonwealth in finding solutions that would enhance the economic and social progress of its members.

In opening the session on 'Problems of Rhodesia, Namibia and South Africa', Dr H. K. Matipa, leader of the Zambian delegation, delivered a powerful speech. His condemnation of apartheid and of the minority government in Rhodesia was endorsed by most of the speakers. Alhaji M. C. Cham (The Gambia) and others renewed the call for Britain to send troops to put down the illegal regime of Ian Smith. Arthur Bottomley (United Kingdom) explained why the use of force had been rejected as a solution to the Rhodesian problem.

The panel sessions, in which a Chairman sat with two panel members, chosen for their special interest or expertise in the topics, were informative and stimulating. Indeed, many delegates took the view that they were more rewarding than the plenary sessions.

The mood throughout the conference and the tours was relaxed and friendly. Speaker James Jerome, President of the Association, was an active host and the Speaker of the Canadian Senate, Hon. Renaude Lapointe, could not have been more kind and concerned for the welfare of the delegates and members of the Secretariat. The organisation of a plenary conference demands careful planning and attention to protocol. The task is the more onerous when it takes place in the larger countries of the Commonwealth, like India, Australia and Canada, where the pre-conference tours are extensive. The Secretary of the Canadian branch, Ian Imrie, had begun planning well in advance and all praised his arrangements. The Association recorded its appreciation of his work. It placed on record also its indebtedness to Dr Maurice Foster, Chairman of the Canadian Federal branch, a former member of the Executive Committee, who over many years had been a strong supporter of the CPA.

The Executive Committee met in Penang, Malaysia, on 23–26 March 1978. The members arrived in Kuala Lumpur on 18 March. They were privileged to attend the Opening of Parliament by the Deputy Head of State, Duli Yang Maha Mulia Timbalan Yang di-Pertuan Agong. They later called on the Prime Minister, Rt Hon. Datuk Hussein Onn, and the Deputy Prime Minister, Rt Hon. Dato Seri Dr Mahathir Mohammed, who had himself served on the Executive Committee. They were also able to visit branches in Selangor, Kedah and Perak and, after the meetings in Penang, those in Malacca and Negri Sembilan. The Committee recorded its special appreciation of the excellent arrangements made for it by Datuk Azizul Rahman and Haji Ahmad Hasmuni.

The principal item on the Committee's agenda was the report of the subcommittee on 'The CPA and the Future'. Since three members had completed their terms as members of the Executive Committee, the subcommittee had been reconstituted. Its members now were Ripton Macpherson (Chairman), Maurice Dupras (Canada), K. S. Hegde (India), Derek Knight (Grenada) and Neil Marten (United Kingdom). It had met in Canada in September 1977 and again in London in January 1978. Its second report was now before the Committee in Penang. After discussing it closely and making some amendments, the Committee asked for a composite report for submission to the General Assembly in Jamaica in September 1978.

The Committee had, however, taken action on two of the proposals. The first concerned the *Parliamentary Newsletter*. This had been started in January 1978, its cost being met from the working capital fund. Four issues had been distributed and had been welcomed by members.

The other proposal concerned the working capital fund. The Chairman of the Executive Committee announced that Malaysia would make an initial contribution of £5000. The Treasurer, Neil Marten, then reported that he had spoken with the British Prime Minister, James Callaghan, about the fund. The outcome had been that the United Kingdom would contribute £100,000 subject to adequate pledges of support being given by other Commonwealth countries. The Treasurer said that he would now write to all branches, inviting them to contribute.

The General Assembly of the Association met in Jamaica on 29 September 1978. This was its first meeting under the new constitution, adopted in Canada in 1977. The General Council having been abolished, the Executive Committee now reported direct to the General Assembly. It was a lengthy report and each section was closely considered. Publications and information services were discussed fully and there was a clear consensus that they were valued and should be expanded.

Strong criticism was directed at the Grenada branch. This had first arisen at the regional conference in Trinidad and Tobago in June 1978, when no opposition member was included in the Grenada delegation. Now at the plenary conference in Jamaica, all three delegates from the branch were government members. K. Ramnath (Trinidad and Tobago) read from a letter, written by a member of the Grenada opposition as follows:

I wish to protest in the strongest possible manner the irregular composition of the Grenada delegation to the 24th conference of the Commonwealth Parliamentary Association.... This delegation is unrepresentative of the Parliament of Grenada and its composition violates the democratic principles, practices and traditions of the CPA with regard to the selection of members of delegations.[5]

The view of the Assembly was well expressed by R. D. Persaud (Guyana):

My own conviction, looking at the CPA, is that it must never develop into a Heads of Government institution or a total governmental organisation, but it must remain an organisation where there can be a reflection of the total parliamentary process within the Commonwealth. I think it is a duty ... to reach a consensus that representation means representation of Parliament.[6]

Lady Gairy, leader of the Grenada delegation, undertook to report to her branch the concern expressed by delegates.

Two matters aroused special interest in the General Assembly. The first was the report of the Treasurer on the working capital fund. The second was the report on 'The CPA and the Future'. The Treasurer said that he had written to branches and already £164,846 of the amount of £258,000 pledged had been received. The fund would be held in a trust and later in the meeting the Assembly passed a resolution authorising it. He then spoke on the purposes, as set out in a paper headed 'Support for Parliamentary Democracy: Setting up a Fund'. The income from the fund would enable the Association to expand its activities and specifically it would:

(i) send visiting teams of experienced parliamentarians to appropriate countries which agreed to hold seminars on parliamentary institutions;

(ii) send parliamentary lecturers to universities, schools and other educational institutions in appropriate locations, with particular emphasis on involving the younger generation;

(iii) finance the visits of parliamentarians to countries across the Commonwealth to study the variety of parliamentary institutions within the Commonwealth;

(iv) set up study groups of Commonwealth Parliamentarians on specific subjects and ensure that their findings and reports were placed before governments, Parliaments, and other relevant organizations;

(v) expand its publications programme and publicity.[7]

The President of the Association, Ripton Macpherson, who had chaired the recent meetings of the subcommittee on 'The CPA and the Future', then presented its report. The subcommittee had carried out a full review of the Association's activities. Specific proposals were that in future at least one-third of each conference agenda should be devoted to parliamentary subjects and that the reading of speeches should be discouraged. The Committee confirmed the principle, endorsed many times in the past, that there should be no resolutions at CPA conferences.

Proposals for expanding CPA activities included the holding of branch and regional seminars and study groups. The first study group would consider 'Parliament and the Scrutiny of Public Finance' and preparations for it were already in hand. The Committee also recommended expanded production of monographs and studies in the Parliamentary Information and Reference Centre. It commended the *Parliamentary Newsletter*. Continuing his report the President said, 'The other two matters that I think need to be looked at are, first, the recommendation for better accommodation and more staff. We have already heard this morning of the severe shortage both in terms of editorial staff and administrative staff. We feel that if the work of the CPA is to progress apace, it is necessary that we find additional staff and accommodation.'[8]

The discussion that followed the two reports was positive and lively. Members put forward further ideas for expanding the work in the parliamentary field. One proposal was for the production of a booklet on parliamentary democracy, an idea on which Howard d'Egville had been working at the time of his retirement. Gerald Ottenheimer (Newfoundland) suggested a workshop to examine and compare various forms of parliamentary government. Lord Lloyd of Kilgerran (United Kingdom) proposed a study group on 'Parliament and the Transfer of Technology'.

As important as the various ideas and proposals, raised by members, was the keen spirit of the discussion. It was as though they were responding to the injunction of the Executive Committee Chairman, Datuk Musa Hitam, that the CPA must never become static.

The 24th Commonwealth Parliamentary Conference took place in Kingston, Jamaica, from 25–30 September 1978. It was attended by 192 delegates and 28 Secretaries to delegations, representing 89 branches of the Association. The observers from the AIPLF were Xavier Deniau and Robert Moinet. The

Commonwealth Secretary-General, Shridath Ramphal, attended and addressed delegates at a separate meeting. Two special guests were Allister Grosart and Gerald Regan.

The conference was formally opened by H. E. the Governor-General of Jamaica, Florizel Glasspole, in the Pegasus Hotel, Kingston on 25 September. In his speech the President of the Association, Ripton Macpherson, referred to the Governor-General's distinguished parliamentary career extending over more than 25 years, during which he had always been a loyal and consistent friend of the CPA. He went on to express the earnest hope 'that this conference will focus attention in Jamaica on our parliamentary institutions and cause us to think through clearly their functions and their priority in the scheme of things, to re-emphasise the right of the freely elected representatives of the people to express their views and opinions and for Parliamentarians to recognise their responsibility to Parliament'.[9] He added that Jamaica had had its fair share of dedicated parliamentarians and he recalled the great contributions of Norman Manley, Sir Alexander Bustamente, N. N. Nethersole, Sir Donald Sangster and Edwin Allen. In his address the Governor-General laid emphasis on parliamentary government, adding that 'where democracy reigns Parliament is the hub around which a country revolves'.[10]

In his speech the Prime Minister of Jamaica, Michael Manley, said that he had become increasingly aware of the conflicting demands of constituency and ministerial duties. He explained that in a developing society an MP had at least two major constituency functions which could be of epic scale. First, he represented a veritable lifeline to survival for many of his constituents because of extreme poverty and inadequate social services. Second, if he is sincere about development and self-reliance he must be as much a mobiliser as a representative. He added, 'This is so because the Member of Parliament in this context is an important agent of change'.[11] The Vice-President of the Association, J. R. Harrison, Speaker of the House of Representatives, New Zealand, expressed the thanks of delegates to the Governor-General, the Prime Minister and the Jamaica branch.

The agenda of the conference differed in some ways from previous agendas.[12] On arrival delegates had been invited to suggest topics for one plenary session and the final choice had been made by ballot. Overall the agenda was more comprehensive.

Discussion in the first session came under the broad heading of 'The Current World Situation and Threats to Peace'. Some delegates spoke of the North–South dialogue and the new International Economic Order, but the principal topic was the situation in Southern Africa.

The session was suddenly galvanised by the speech of Senator G. Sheil (Australia). He stated that, noting the universal hostility towards the regimes in Rhodesia and South Africa, he had visited both countries to see for himself whether the charges made against them were true. He had found that conditions in both countries were far different from what their attackers alleged. Indeed, the standard of living of most blacks was far better than in other parts of Africa. He said that he described what he found. On his return to Australia he had told his government that it should reassess its policy towards Rhodesia and South Africa. He had been sacked from his Ministry as a result. He was, he stressed, speaking as an individual parliamentarian and certainly not for the Australian government or the delegation. Not surprisingly his speech aroused a fury and brought vehement denunciations.

The discussion on 'The Value of a Bicameral Legislature' was enlivened by conflicting views. Delegates from New Zealand and Queensland spoke strongly in favour of a unicameral Parliament. There was nevertheless a clear consensus in favour of retaining a Second Chamber.

The speeches in the third session, when the subject was 'The Effect of the EEC on the Commonwealth with Special Reference to Trade and the Lomé Convention' were well-informed. The value of the convention to the ACP countries was acknowledged, but delegates from non-ACP countries criticised it as discriminatory. The speeches of N. Mundia (Zambia), Subramanian Swamy (India), L. W. Athulathmudali (Sri Lanka), Paul Dean (United Kingdom), Puan Rafidah Aziz (Malaysia) and J. H. Falloon (New Zealand) were outstanding.

The standard of the contributions in the other sessions was high. The discussion on 'Unrest among Youth with Particular Reference to Unemployment and the Problem of Drugs' merits special mention. It was opened by Puan Rafidah Aziz (Malaysia) with a speech that was thoughtful and realistic. Other speakers, too, showed a keen awareness of the problem which was international in scale. As always the sessions on parliamentary topics were valuable occasions for the exchange of experience, bringing home to delegates the fact that most Parliaments faced similar difficulties and challenges.

Like the 1964 conference in Jamaica, this conference was remarkably successful. Each session lasted 3–3½ hours and was well attended; indeed, it was rare for delegates to be absent from their seats. As in the meeting of the General Assembly there was eager participation by all delegates. By some alchemy Jamaica seemed to have a special power to bring members closer together and to animate exchanges between them.

In 1964 Sir Donald Sangster had contributed notably to the success of the conference. Now in 1978 Ripton Macpherson proved to be a worthy successor. All delegates expressed appreciation of his chairmanship and affection for the man himself. Many tributes were paid to Edley Deans, Secretary of the Jamaica branch, not only for the excellent arrangements, but also for his friendly and helpful concern for delegates, Secretaries to delegations, and members of the Secretariat.

As part of its programme to celebrate the 150th anniversary of the founding of the state, the Western Australian branch invited the Executive Committee to hold its mid-year meeting in Perth. The meeting took place from 21–25 May 1979. The small and beautiful city was an ideal venue. The members were warmly welcomed and all facilities were provided.

The Committee's first item of business was to record the suspension of the Grenada branch, as a result of the recent *coup*. Derek Knight could therefore no longer serve on the Committee as a regional representative. Ripton Macpherson agreed to serve as acting regional representative in his place.

The suspended branches in Ghana, Nigeria, Bangladesh and Swaziland were expected to be revived in the near future after general elections. The Secretary-General reported that the Clerks-designate of all four countries had recently been in London. All were eager to establish branches in their restored legislatures. He suggested that they should be invited to attend the conference in New Zealand as observers. The Committee agreed, subject to the payment of all expenses by their governments.

The Committee received reports on ten regional conferences and seminars, already held or about to be held. The President of the Association, J. R. Harrison, Speaker of the New Zealand House of Representatives, accompanied by Mrs Harrison, had travelled extensively, visiting 36 branches. The Committee noted his report and expressed appreciation of the generosity of the New Zealand government in paying their expenses. The Committee considered finance, the working capital fund, and suggestions for new activities, and on these and other matters agreed its recommendations to be made to the General Assembly. It noted with pleasure that the plenary conference would take place in Zambia in 1980, in Fiji in 1981, and in the Bahamas in 1982.

In New Zealand the Executive Committee held meetings in Auckland on 16 and 17 November and in Wellington on 1 December 1979. Finance was a matter of urgent concern. The three-year projections showed an estimated debit balance of £102,605 by the end of 1982. Membership fees had been increased by 20 per cent in 1975, 1977 and 1979. The Committee agreed that a further 20 per cent increase in 1981 was unavoidable.

There was then a call for some compensating economies in the general administration and specifically in the publications and information services. Just one year had passed since in Jamaica the General Assembly had warmly approved the publications and information services and had called for their expansion. Moreover, the purposes to be served by the working capital fund included expansion in this work. Now the Committee was concentrating on making cuts The Chairman ruled, however, that the matter was not as simple as the discussion seemed to imply and that possible economies should be considered further at the mid-year meeting of the Committee to be held in Jersey in 1980.

Since this was the end of his term of office, Datuk Musa Hitam struck a valedictory note in presenting the report of the Executive Committee to the General Assembly meeting in Wellington on 30 November 1979. He expressed his personal thanks to all who had served with him. He had found the three years as Chairman a rewarding experience. 'On assuming office,' he continued,

I personally found it rather difficult to adapt myself to the body of distinguished names that made up the membership of the Association. I can safely and unashamedly say to you that there was an atmosphere of tension when I first assumed office because I followed the Malaysian practice of using the gavel rather indiscriminately and making decisions as Chairman which were considered at the time to be rather tough. It is of interest that some of my colleagues have taken note of the fact that I have somewhat mellowed since then.[13]

Datuk Musa Hitam went on to pay a warm tribute to the Secretary-General personally and to the Secretariat. Later in the meeting he congratulated Betty May on completing her 25th year in the service of the CPA. Many letters and cables of good wishes had been received from former officers, which he handed to her. He also spoke highly of the services of Susan Burchett who was leaving the Secretariat for health reasons. She had been promoted from Publications Secretary to Assistant Editor in recognition of her great abilities. The General Assembly formally recorded its appreciation of her services.

The report on the first study group of the Association was noted with interest. It had met in London from 10–13 September 1979 and had considered the basic problems of 'Parliament and the Scrutiny of Public Finance'. Under the chairmanship of Rt Hon. Edward du Cann (United Kingdom) the eight members, all with wide experience and of high calibre, from all regions of the Commonwealth, had discussed every aspect of the subject.[14] The Rapporteur was Peter Riddell, Economics Correspondent of the *Financial Times*. A guest with special knowledge of the subject was invited to attend each session and this further stimulated the discussions.[15]

Datin Paduka (formerly Puan) Rafidah Aziz, as Deputy Minister of Finance, Malaysia, had been a member of the group. She reported to the General Assembly that she had found the exchange of experience and views stimulating and valuable. She paid tribute to the group's Chairman, Edward du Cann and also to the Rapporteur, Peter Riddell. She concluded: 'As a member of the pioneer study group and on behalf of the other members, who unfortunately are not here today, I strongly recommend to the Executive Committee and to the Secretariat that similar study groups be set up in future years as an ongoing project of the CPA.'[16]

Datin Paduka Rafidah Aziz then referred to the decision of the Executive Committee at its meeting in Penang in 1978 that a second study group should consider the subject of 'Parliament and the Scrutiny of Science Policy'. The Canadian branch had agreed to host this group in Ottawa in autumn 1980. She said that this was a wide-ranging and important topic, but suggested that it might be narrowed down. 'Pollution and the Control of the Environment', for example, was a topic with which an MP could come to grips. Finally, she added that the consensus of the first study group had been that four days was not long enough to deliberate on such a matter as the scrutiny of public finance. She suggested that more time should be allowed for future study groups.

The report of the subcommittee on staff and accommodation, appointed by the Executive Committee, was presented to the General Assembly by Paul Dean (United Kingdom). The matter had been discussed by the Committee in Perth in

May 1979 and again in Auckland in November 1979. The subcommittee, comprising Paul Dean (United Kingdom), Neil Marten (United Kingdom) and Maurice Dupras (Canada), had been asked to review the staffing of the Secretariat in the light of the creation of the working capital fund and the expansion of CPA activities. The approach of the subcommittee, however, was, as stated by Paul Dean: 'We interpreted our terms of reference as being a need for economy and to ensure that our contributions to the CPA get the maximum value for money.'[17]

The subcommittee interviewed each member of the Secretariat. It noted that the Executive Committee had already approved the appointment of an Assistant Editor, in succession to Susan Burchett and a publications secretary. No other intake of staff was recommended. For special projects like the study groups, specialist appointments should be made on an *ad hoc* basis and only for the duration of the project.

Paul Dean expressed appreciation of the Parliamentary Information and Reference Centre which was doing valuable work. He then said:

> Having looked at the development over recent years, and the valuable service that it provides, we none the less felt that a period of consolidation rather than expansion would now be appropriate, particularly bearing in mind the additional work load undertaken at HQ relating to the new Working Capital Fund. We did recognise, however, that in recommending consolidation it would be important that the existing information should be kept up to date.[18]

The Executive Committee, in effect, rejected the subcommittee's report. Indeed, it authorised the immediate recruitment of an additional secretary. Further it proposed that the incoming Committee should appoint a new subcommittee so that 'a much more in-depth study could be carried out of the overall needs of the Secretariat'.[19] Shri K. S. Hegde, Speaker of the Lok Sabha, India, and Asian regional representative, added:

> Every organisation, if it is to function properly, requires not only an efficient staff but also the required strength. Despite the fact that we greatly appreciate the report submitted to the Executive Committee, because of changed circumstances we believe we should have a second look into that report. Therefore, we recommend that the next Executive Committee go into the matter and see whether there is a need to make further appointments to the staff.[20]

The working capital fund was growing impressively. The Treasurer informed the General Assembly that branches had to date pledged to pay £376,800 of which £322,500 had already been received. The income from the fund was expected to be about £35,000 in 1979. The trust deed for the fund had been examined by a subcommittee under the chairmanship of Shri K. S. Hegde. This was considered by the General Assembly and approved.

In discussing the use of this income the Assembly heard a report from Patrick Lawlor (Ontario). His branch had, he said, hosted the fifth Canadian regional seminar from 15–19 October 1979. The 80 members who took part included members from the Canadian region and guests from branches in Belize, Jamaica, St Kitts–Nevis–Anguilla, Trinidad and Tobago, and the United Kingdom. A special delegation of six members had come from the newly revived branch in Ghana. This had been made possible by a grant from the working capital fund.

The Chairman of the Executive Committee, Datuk Musa Hitam, then spoke on several projects under consideration. The study group on 'Parliament and the Scrutiny of Science Policy' would take place in Ottawa in the autumn of 1980. The scope of the study, its membership and the arrangements would be finalised by the Committee at its next mid-year meeting. Shri Ram Niwas Mirdha explained the plans of the Indian branch to hold an Asian seminar on parliamentary practice and procedure in New Delhi in January 1980. Two delegates would be invited from each of the branches in the Asian and South-East Asian regions. His branch would request financial assistance for this seminar.

The Secretary-General reported that requests for assistance from the fund had been received from the Solomon Islands and Kiribati, which planned to arrange seminars for their members. Swaziland and Botswana also wanted to hold local seminars. Other proposals, including publication of a history of the Commonwealth, were to be considered by the Committee at its mid-year meeting.

The election of officers of the Association was one of the last items on the agenda. Robinson M. Nabulyato, Speaker of the National Assembly, Zambia, a member who believed strongly in parliamentary institutions, was elected President for 1979–80. The Speaker of the Parliament of Fiji, Mosese Qionibaravi, was elected Vice-President.

Datuk Musa Hitam had been a firm and energetic Chairman of the Executive Committee. He had responded positively to the ideas put forward in the memorandum on 'The CPA and the Future'. Moreover, during his term of office he had gained the respect and friendship of the Committee's members and of the Secretariat. At the meeting warm tributes were paid to him personally and to his work for the CPA.

Malaysia had been a consistently strong supporter of the Association over the years. It had always appointed active and able members to serve on the Committee as was shown by the membership of Dr Mahathir bin Mohammed, soon afterwards to become the Prime Minister of Malaysia, of Datuk Musa Hitam, who later became Deputy Prime Minister, and Senator Kamarul Ariffin. It was noteworthy that the branch now nominated Datin Paduka Rafidah Aziz, Deputy Minister of Finance, to serve on the Committee as Asian Regional Representative.

Ripton Macpherson, Speaker of the House of Representatives, Jamaica, was unanimously elected Chairman of the Executive Committee in place of Datuk Musa Hitam. He had served on the Committee as Regional Representative, as Vice-President and President. The Association could not have had a keener friend and supporter.

The term of the Treasurer, Neil Marten, had come to an end. He had continued to give close attention to the finances even after becoming a Minister. In his place the United Kingdom branch nominated, and the General Assembly elected James Johnson, a backbench member of many years standing, who took an active interest in Commonwealth affairs.

The 25th Commonwealth Parliamentary Conference was held in New Zealand from 26 November to 1 December 1979. It was attended by 172 delegates and observers and 33 Secretaries to delegations. The two observers from the AIPLF were Xavier Deniau and Robert Moinet. The Commonwealth Secretariat was represented by C. A. Gunawardene, Director of the Information Division. Special guests who attended as former members of the Executive Committee were Senator Gordon Davidson (Australia), C. S. Dupré (Jersey), Sir Charles Kerruish (Isle of Man), Gerald Regan (Nova Scotia) and Sia Kah Hui (Singapore).

The formal opening of the conference by H. E. the Governor-General of New Zealand, Sir Keith Holyoake, took place on 26 November 1979 in the Chamber of the former Legislative Council. The President of the Association, J. R. Harrison, Speaker of the New Zealand House of Representatives, spoke of Sir Keith Holyoake's parliamentary career as a backbencher, Leader of the Opposition, Cabinet Minister, and Prime Minister, extending over nearly 40 years. Sir Keith Holyoake said that, while closely involved in Commonwealth affairs and in the work of the CPA during this long period, he had attended only one overseas meeting. This had been in Bermuda in 1946 and he cherished memories of the friendships forged then with Sir Anthony Eden, John Diefenbaker, and others who had been there.

The Prime Minister of New Zealand, R. D. Muldoon, then welcomed delegates. He said that all should address their thoughts to the ideals, expressed in the Declaration of Commonwealth Principles, agreed by the Heads of Government in Singapore in 1971. The disparities in wealth between different sections of mankind were, he said, too great to be tolerated. Nor could he take an optimistic view of the world economic situation. The accelerating price of oil was the major economic problem facing the world.

On behalf of the Vice-President, Robinson M. Nabulyato, who had been recalled urgently to Lusaka, R. V. Chota, Leader of the Zambian delegation, expressed the thanks of delegates to the Governor-General, the Prime Minister, and the New Zealand branch for their welcome and hospitality, especially during the pre-conference tours. The Zambia branch, he said, looked forward to hosting the conference the following year.

In the six plenary and six panel sessions the most pressing problems of the time were discussed.[21] 'The Energy Crisis' was the subject of the first plenary session. Shri Ram Niwas Mirdha (India) opened it with a masterly speech, dealing especially with the impact upon developing countries of the extraordinary rise in oil prices. Sir Arnott Cato (Barbados) explained how the OPEC price increases affected a small country and presented a major challenge to the recent economic resurgence in his island. Kenneth Baker (United Kingdom) cautioned, 'that we are going to enter a period of greater instability in world oil prices. The reason for that, of course, is that we are all so dependent on the Middle East which is inherently unstable.'[22] Several delegates stressed the need to cut down on oil consumption and to seek alternative sources of energy.

The session on 'The Refugee Problem', ably opened by Leo Moggie (Malaysia), brought home to many delegates the terrible plight of refugees not only in South-East Asia but also in Africa and Latin America. Peter Blaker (United Kingdom) spoke of Britain's involvement in Hong Kong which was at one time accepting 1000 Vietnamese boat-people a day. Referring to the refugees from Rhodesia, he said that the conference at Lancaster House in London was within an ace of success and gave real hope that these refugees would soon be able to return to their homes. The session on 'Africa South of the Sahara' brought expressions of hope that the Lancaster House negotiations would succeed and also expressions of the fears and mistrust harboured by many of the African delegates.

The panel sessions and those dealing with parliamentary topics were enlivened by valuable exchanges and discussions. Indeed, the conference benefited greatly from the presence of several strong delegations, among them the Indian delegation, led by Shri Ram Niwas Mirdha, the Jamaican delegation, led by Howard Cook, the Malaysian delegation, led by Leo Moggie, and the United Kingdom delegation, led by Peter Blaker.

Notes

1. Executive Committee Minutes, 26 April 1977.
2. Report of General Meeting (Canberra, 4 November 1959), p.11.
3. Conference Report (Ottawa, 1977), pp.4–5.
4. **Agenda and Opening Speakers, Ottawa, 1977**
   The Commonwealth and World Security – Don Jamieson, Secretary of State for External Affairs (Canada)
   Africa: Problems of Rhodesia, Namibia and South Africa – Dr Henry K. Matipa, Minister of State for Lands and Agriculture (Zambia)
   Parliament and the Preservation of Human Rights – K. S. Hegde, Speaker of the Lok Sabha (India)
   Commodity Prices and the Relations between Industrialised and Primary Producing Countries – panel session
   Racial Conflicts within the Commonwealth – panel session
   Challenges to Parliament by External Groups – panel session
   Assistance to Developing Countries of the Commonwealth – panel session
   Social Effects of Continuing Unemployment – panel session
   Parliament's Role in the Control of Government Expenditure – panel session
   Law of the Sea: Fish and Minerals – panel session
   Preservation of the Environment and Wildlife – panel session
   Relevance of Westminster-type Parliamentary System in Developing Countries – panel session
   The World Energy Crisis – Dr Maurice Foster (Canada)
   Conflicting Interests of Members between their Parliamentary Constituency, Party and

National Responsibilities – C. Robert Kelly (Australia).
5. Report of General Assembly (Jamaica, 1978), p.103.
6. Ibid., p.115.
7. Ibid., p.148.
8. Ibid., p.100.
9. Conference Report (Jamaica, 1978), p.xxiv.
10. Ibid., p.xxvi.
11. Ibid., p.xxvii.
12. **Agenda and Opening Speakers, Jamaica, 1978**
    The Current World Situation and Threats to Peace – P. J. Patterson, Deputy Prime Minister and Minister of Foreign Affairs (Jamaica)
    The Value of a Bicameral Legislature – Lakshman Singh, Speaker of the Legislative Assembly (Rajasthan)
    The Effect of the EEC on the Commonwealth with Special Reference to Trade and the Lomé Convention – N. Mundia, Cabinet Minister for North-Western Province (Zambia)
    Balloted subjects:
    The Need for Updating Medical Legislation on Abortion in the Commonwealth – Michael H. Beaubrun (Trinidad and Tobago)
    A New International Communication Order – Comrade Shirley Field-Ridley, Minister of Information (Guyana)
    The Role of the Opposition in a Parliamentary System – O. Gendoo (Mauritius)
    Conflict of Interests of MP's between their Parliamentary, Constituency, Party, and National Responsibilities – panel session
    The Fight Against International Terrorism – panel session
    The Smaller Countries of the Commonwealth – *Their Security and Future* – panel session
    Parliamentary Control and Scrutiny of Public Expenditure and Methods for Improving the Estimates Procedure – panel session
    The Problems of Ethnic Groups within the Commonwealth – panel session
    Unrest among Youth with Particular Reference to Unemployment and the Problem of Drugs – Datin Paduka Rafidah Aziz, Deputy Minister of Finance (Malaysia)
    Calling the Executive to Account by Parliament – Lord Drumalbyn (United Kingdom).
13. Report of General Assembly (New Zealand, 1979), p.82.
14. The Study Group on Parliament and the Scrutiny of Public Finance met in London in September 1979. The members of the group were:
    Chairman: Rt Hon. Edward du Cann, MP (UK) Chairman of 1922 Committee; former Chairman of Public Accounts Committee and former Economics Minister; currently Chairman of the Select Committee on the Treasury and Civil Service. Hon. David M. Connolly MP (Australia), Chairman of Public Accounts Committee. Rt Hon. Errol Barrow, MP (Barbados), Leader of the Opposition and Chairman of the Public Accounts Committee, former Prime Minister and Minister of Finance. Hon. Robert Andras, MP (Canada), former President of the Treasury Board. Hon. Shri Satish Agarwal, MP (India), former Minister of State for Finance. Hon. Datin Paduka Rafidah Aziz, MP (Malaysia), Deputy Minister of Finance. Hon. Francis X Nkhoma, MP (Zambia), Chairman of Public Accounts Committee. Rapporteur: Peter Riddell, *Financial Times.*
15. Guests of Study Group, London, September 1979:
    Among the guests who joined the group were Rt Hon. Joel Barnett, former Secretary to the Treasury and then Chairman of the Public Accounts Committee (United Kingdom), Sir Anthony Rawlinson, Second Permanent Secretary, HM Treasury

(United Kingdom), Sir Douglas Henley, Comptroller and Auditor-General (United Kingdom), George Cunningham, MP (United Kingdom) and Rt Hon. Terence Higgins, former Minister of State, HM Treasury (United Kingdom).
16. Report of General Assembly (New Zealand, 1979), p.93.
17. Ibid., p.95.
18. Ibid., p.96.
19. Ibid., p.97.
20. Ibid., p.103.
21. **Agenda and Opening Speakers, New Zealand, 1979**
    The Energy Crisis – Ram Niwas Mirdha (India)
    The Refugee Problem – Leo Moggie, Minister of Energy, Telecommunication and Post (Malaysia)
    The Security of the Smaller Countries of the Commonwealth – P. I. Wilkinson (New Zealand)
    Africa South of the Sahara – I. M. Kaduma (Tanzania)
    The Year of the Child – panel session
    Pollution and Protection of the Environment – panel session
    The Drug Traffic – panel session
    Population Growth and Economic Assistance to Developing Countries – panel session
    International Terrorism – panel session
    The MP – His Functions and Responsibilities – panel session
    Parliament, the Executive, and the Civil Service – J. Russell Ford (Bahamas)
    Freedom of the Individual, Human Rights, and the Authority of Government in a Parliamentary Democracy – J. Dickson Mabon (United Kingdom).
22. Conference Report (New Zealand, 1979), p.20.

At this time the major developments for the CPA were the restoration of parliamentary governments in Nigeria, Uganda, and in the newly independent state of Zimbabwe. Branches were promptly formed or reformed in those countries. The African branches had always been active in the Association and there now appeared to be promise of a broader participation. For the Zambia conference the agenda item 'Africa South of the Sahara' was sub-titled 'the beginning of a new era'. There was, indeed, a widespread belief that this was the beginning of a new era.

The mid-year meeting of the Executive Committee in 1980 took place from 19–21 April in Jersey. The opening ceremony was held in the Chamber of the States of Jersey on 21 April. The Bailiff, Sir Frank Ereaut, said, 'in authorising me to arrange this special sitting in honour of the visit to Jersey of the Executive Committee, the members of the Jersey branch of the Association have desired to pay to the Committee the highest tribute which it is in their power to do...'.[1] Ripton Macpherson, Chairman of the Committee, said in reply that the CPA owed a great debt to members of the states, both past and present, to former regional representatives, and to successive Greffiers. Indeed no branch had contributed more readily and generously. The branch was the first to host two mid-year meetings of the Committee and it had given promptly to the working capital fund.

As at previous meetings the Committee had a lengthy agenda and the amount of work done was impressive. Small subcommittees met, often in the evening, and their reports were closely discussed by the full Committee before it made its decisions or recommendations. New members, often without experience of the CPA, were usually somewhat restrained in the first year of their three-year term, but then, having grasped the purpose and functioning of the Association, they took an active part.

In these meetings, too, a strong sense of community and fellowship invariably developed. Members felt themselves to be part of a special team. When disagreements emerged in the course of discussions, they were quickly resolved; it was very rare for discord to erupt. At the end of their term members were usually reluctant to leave the Committee. They recognised, of course, that a regular influx of new members was essential and that all branches must have the right to representation at some stage. Many nevertheless deeply regretted that at a time when their commitment to the CPA had been strengthened and their enthusiasm kindled, the constitution required them to retire.

Feeling this strongly, Harry Blank (Quebec) put forward a proposal that members of the Committee in the five years following their retirement should receive invitations to attend conferences as unofficial observers, provided that in each case the branch or the member was responsible for all expenses. In presenting this proposal to the General Assembly in 1978, Datuk Musa Hitam said that members of the Committee 'feel that it is a waste of talent as well as of the interest of that particular [retiring] member ... to deprive him of direct association with the CPA in this manner'.[2] The proposal was approved.

Again reflecting this feeling, Datuk Musa Hitam initiated a new practice. This was the presentation of finely engraved plaques of Selangor pewter to retiring members of the Committee, thus commemorating their services to the CPA. The Malaysian branch has generously maintained this practice at its own expense, and it has been greatly appreciated.

Early in its meeting in Jersey the Committee learnt with regret that its Chairman might not serve his full term. Ripton Macpherson had said at the time of his nomination that the general election in Jamaica was expected in 1982. It now appeared likely that it would take place in 1980. He did not intend to stand for re-election. It was therefore probable that a new Chairman would have to be elected by the General Assembly in Zambia or in Fiji.

The Committee gave close attention to the further activities made possible by the working capital fund. Local seminars on parliamentary practice and procedure were approved for Kiribati, Solomon Islands, Fiji, Cook Islands, Malaysia, Botswana and Swaziland. An Australian proposal to hold a symposium on subordinate or delegated legislation in Canberra in October 1980 was reported by J. H. Brown, the regional representative from New South Wales. All branches in legislatures which had committees on this major subject would be invited to send a delegation and some 50 delegates were expected. The Australian branch requested a contribution from the fund towards the cost of this project, which was to prove one of considerable importance.

The Committee also discussed at length a proposal from the Jersey branch that there should be a separate conference of representatives of the smaller countries of the Commonwealth. It was argued that the annual plenary conference of the Association did not adequately serve the needs of the smaller countries. The Committee recognised that a separate conference was desirable, but there was concern that this might lead to polarisation or divisiveness. Subsequently it agreed to recommend that the first separate conference should take place in Fiji in 1981 two days prior to the plenary conference. The criterion for sending a representative was that the country's population should not exceed 250,000, but states, provinces and territories of federations were excluded. It was agreed also that a subvention from the working capital fund should be made to cover expenses of delegates during the two days of the conference and to meet 50 per cent of the travel costs of those who attended and were not delegates to the plenary conference.

The General Assembly of the Association convened in Lusaka on 3 October 1980. The President, Robinson M. Nabulyato, Speaker of the Zambian National Assembly, was in the chair. Reports on all of the regional conferences and seminars held during the past year were received and noted. The Chairman of the Executive Committee gave an account of the work and recommendations brought forward from its meetings in Jersey and Lusaka. Particular attention was paid to the report of the study group on 'Parliament and the Scrutiny of Public Finance' and the need to have it distributed as widely as possible. Preparations for the next study group on 'Parliament and the Scrutiny of Science Policy' were noted.

The General Assembly approved a grant of up to £5000 from the working capital fund to enable the Cook Islands branch to host the conference of the Australasian and Pacific region. But it was stressed that this was a special grant and not to be taken as creating a precedent. It also approved a proposal concerning the operation of branches of the Association. The effectiveness of each branch depended to a large degree on the strength of the support of its President, usually the Speaker, and also on the commitment and efficiency of the branch Secretary, usually the Clerk of the legislature. Many Clerks worked under severe pressure. In every region there were one or two branches which appeared to be dormant. The proposal was that the Assistant Secretary-General, Palitha Weerasinghe, should travel to each region, seeking to improve the operation of the branches and generally to promote the image of the CPA. It was considered that the fund could be used for this purpose.

The Treasurer spoke on the estimated income and expenditure account for 1980. A credit balance of some £25,000 would be carried forward. The projections for 1981–83 indicated, however, a deficit of some £50,000 by the end of 1983. This was primarily due to increases in conference fares. The Executive Committee recommended therefore an increase of 15 per cent in branch contributions as from 1 January 1982. After discussion, the General Assembly approved this increase.

Income from the working capital fund was expected to be some £75,000. The Secretary-General reminded members that in terms of the trust this could be used only to finance new ventures and the expansion of the Association's activities. He drew attention to the fact that a very large amount of the expenditure proposed under this heading would be on seminars and the study group.

Before adjourning the General Assembly elected the officers of the Association and regional representatives. The Speaker of the House of Representatives of Fiji, Mosese Qionibaravi, was elected President for 1980–81. Clement Maynard, Minister of Labour and Home Affairs, the Bahamas, was elected Vice-President. Five new regional representatives were elected and the retiring members were formally presented with plaques by Dr Ling Liong Sik, leader of the Malaysian delegation.

The 26th Commonwealth Parliamentary Conference was held in Lusaka, Zambia, from 27 September–4 October 1980. It was attended by 186 delegates and observers and 36 Secretaries to delegations. The AIPLF was again represented by Xavier Deniau and Robert Moinet. The Commonwealth Secretary-General, Shridath Ramphal, addressed delegates at a separate meeting. The special guests, attending as former members of the Executive Committee, were Senator Allister Grosart (Canada) and Maurice Dupras (Canada).

The formal opening of the conference took place in the Mulungushi Hall, Lusaka, on 27 September 1980. The arrival of the President of the Republic of Zambia, Dr K. D. Kaunda, was heralded by a traditional drummer. He was then greeted by the Secretary-General of the Party, M. M. Chona, who presented the Prime Minister, D. M. Lisulo, the President of the Association, Robinson M. Nabulyato, the Vice-President, Mosese Qionibaravi, and the Treasurer, James Johnson, who was welcomed as a special friend of Africa. Later the Chairman of the Executive Committee, Ripton Macpherson, presented the members of the Committee and the Secretary-General.

In his speech the President of the Association recalled that Zambia had been host to the first African regional conference in 1969, to the third conference of Commonwealth Speakers and Presiding Officers in 1973, and to the eleventh African regional conference in 1979. His branch was honoured now to be hosting the plenary conference of the Association. He continued:

Your Excellency, though no strongly worded resolutions will be moved and no formal decisions will be reached at this conference, the knowledge that the views we shall express here will be heard beyond the confines of the six continents and the five oceans of the world will give meaning and purpose to our deliberations. The problems facing the world today are a great challenge and trial for the Commonwealth. Our only hope lies in the strength born out of the fact that we in the Commonwealth represent more than one-third of the world's population. Our strength will give us confidence. In the same manner we shall be inspired by our faith in parliamentary democracy, in the rule of law, and the dignity and equality of man.[3]

President Kaunda in his speech declaring the conference open, said:

We cherish the memories of the meeting of Heads of State and Government which took place in this very Hall in August last year to deal, among other things, with a matter of grave concern to humanity, a matter which touched on principles dear to your Association, a matter which tested the political will and maturity of the Commonwealth. The capacity of the Commonwealth to solve its own problems was clearly demonstrated by the consensus reached over the fate of Rhodesia – happily Zimbabwe today.[4]

Dr Kaunda then spoke about the CPA.

Mr Chairman, reading the various conference reports that your Association has so ably published at the end of every conference, one is encouraged by the free exchange of views and the depth and strength of your principles of democracy. It is gratifying to observe that there are more similarities than dissimilarities in our parliamentary institutions. Credit must squarely go to the Commonwealth Parliamentary Association which has superbly provided a broad forum for the clinical analysis of all forms of parliamentary institutions. You have influenced each other and your various governments to appreciate the basic and central principles of parliamentary democracy.[5]

The Vice-President of the Association, Mosese Qionibaravi, in an eloquent speech paid tribute to Dr Kaunda and to Zambia for their part in the success of the Lusaka meeting. He also expressed warm agreement with him about the Commonwealth and the important role of the CPA in upholding parliamentary democracy. He said, too, that the CPA would be going from Zambia, the heart of Africa, in 1980, to Fiji the crossroads of the South Pacific, in 1981. He promised that Fiji would make the conference an event to be remembered.

The conference agenda, considered in seven plenary and six panel sessions, was broad and well balanced.[6] In the first plenary session, opened by Shri Bal Ram Jakhar, Speaker of the Lok Sabha, India, delegates spoke on the major danger areas in the world under the general heading 'Current Threats to International Peace and Security'. This was followed by a plenary and two panel sessions on 'A New Strategy for the Developing World: the *Brandt Report*'. The recommendations of the recently published *Brandt Report* were keenly supported by most of the delegates who spoke. All were agreed that the disparity in wealth between the developed and the developing world must be eliminated. The practical means for achieving this were often overlooked. Indeed, Neil Marten, leader of the United Kingdom delegation, warned, 'We should not be carried away in debating the Brandt Report on a wave of emotion and rhetoric. . . . But such rhetoric can arouse expectations beyond what is possible and then it ends in disappointment, frustration, and anger.'[7]

There were, however, several speakers, like T. H. H. Skeet (United Kingdom) and W. R. Baxter (Victoria) who talked of the practical obstacles to ensuring higher commodity prices and to adjusting the balance. Indeed, W. R. Baxter called for a halt to the attacks on donor countries, the United Kingdom and the United States in particular, which were generous in granting aid. In the two panel sessions delegates discussed various aspects of the Report in a mood of greater realism.

The third plenary session considered 'Africa South of the Sahara: The Beginning of a New Era'. The opening speaker, Mr Justice F. Chomba, leader of the Zambia delegation, developed the theme that ever since the white man set foot on African soil the indigenous Africans had suffered indignity and exploitation. The major part of the continent had now achieved freedom and self-determination, and only the problems of Namibia and South Africa remained to be solved. Other African delegates who spoke developed this theme and conveyed strongly the sense that a new era was beginning in Africa.

The plenary session on 'International Collaboration in Combating Drug Addiction and Trafficking', opened by Overand R. Padmore (Trinidad and Tobago) and on 'The Law of the Sea', opened by F. M. K. Sherani (Fiji) were notable for the many well-informed, indeed magisterial, contributions. On both subjects there were delegates who were able to speak with real and concerned authority. The sessions were impressive and educational for all present.

The panel session on 'Race Relations within the Commonwealth' started quietly. Several delegates spoke of the harmony within their own multi-racial societies. The discussion was enlivened, however, by Bob Collins (Northern Territory, Australia), who contributed positively throughout the conference. He bluntly contradicted the statement of the leader of the Australian delegation concerning the advances made in Australia in the treatment of the aboriginal people. He asserted that racism was still alive in Australia. Two Australian delegates rose to refute his charges.

The two plenary and three panel sessions on parliamentary topics were, as at previous conferences, valuable, especially for recently elected members and those in newly independent legislatures.

The conference was very successful. Both in the sessions and outside it had given opportunities for exchanges of views and experiences. For many delegates visiting Africa for the first time it had brought a closer understanding of the great continent and its peoples. Warm expressions of appreciation were made to the Association's President, Robinson M. Nabulyato, who had been a firm and dignified Chairman and a concerned host throughout the conferences and the tours. Special tributes were also paid to Mwelwa Chibesakunda, Clerk of the National Assembly, and the able Secretary of the Zambia branch and friend of the CPA.

The general election in Jamaica was held in October 1980. Ripton Macpherson did not stand and consequently vacated the office of Chairman. This was a great loss to the Association. An eloquent and witty speaker, a warm personality, and a strong champion of parliamentary institutions, he had been an excellent and well-qualified Chairman. The constitution provided that, pending the election of a new Chairman in such circumstances, the Vice-President should serve as Acting Chairman. Clement Maynard, the Vice-President, readily agreed to serve, although as a busy Minister the demands on his time were already heavy.

The mid-year meeting of the Executive Committee took place in Hong Kong from 2–6 May 1981. The formal opening was performed in the Legislative Council Chamber by the Secretary for Home Affairs, Mr Denis Campbell Bray, in the absence of the Governor. The Committee then met in a committee room of the Government Secretariat.

Receiving reports on six regional conferences and eleven seminars on parliamentary practice and procedure, the Committee noted that already a seminar had been held successfully in Zimbabwe. The idea of this seminar had arisen when the President of the Association and the Secretary-General visited

Harare after the conference in Zambia in 1980. For the seminar, the visiting members from Westminster were Arthur Bottomley and Paul Dean, together with John Sweetman, a senior Clerk; from India, Ram Niwas Mirdha, a former Deputy Chairman of the Rajya Sabha, and from Tanzania, I. N. Elinewinga. The Prime Minister, Robert Mugabe, opened the seminar and most of the members of the Zimbabwe Parliament attended. Its Presiding Officers had written to the President of the Association stating that the seminar had been of great value to their members and expressing the hope that the CPA would organise a regional seminar for the benefit of all African members.

Another African initiative came from the Clerk of the Zambian National Assembly, Mwelwa Chibesakunda. He suggested that a seminar of Clerks and certain parliamentary officials from West, Central and Southern Africa should be held. It would enable them to discuss matters peculiar to Parliaments in the African region, including procedures, the status and training of parliamentary staff, preparation of research papers for members, and kindred matters. He requested financial support from the working capital fund for this project. Subsequently the Committee approved a grant of £3500 towards the cost of the seminar.

The Committee noted with interest a report on the first Commonwealth Conference on Delegated Legislation Committees, which began in Canberra on 29 September 1980. A grant of £2500 had been made from the fund towards its cost. Sixteen Committees sent a total of 58 delegates who spent five days discussing the evolution of parliamentary controls over delegated legislation. The conference elected five members to form a committee 'to coordinate continued cooperation and exchange of views between participating Committees and to promote arrangements for future conferences'. The Committee was asked to publish a bulletin, documenting local Committee activities and procedural changes. It was also agreed that the next conference should be held in Canada in 1982.

In June 1981 Sri Lanka was host to a parliamentary visit and seminar. This formed part of an elaborate programme to commemorate 50 years of adult franchise. Every CPA branch was invited to send delegates and despite short notice 85 members, 5 members of the Executive Committee as well as 10 special invitees, including the Secretary-General, attended. The topics discussed in the seminar were 'The Presidential System and the Westminster Model: their Relevance and Applicability to Developing Nations', 'Universal Adult Suffrage and Proportional Representation', and 'Parliamentary Systems and Public Enterprises'.

At the Committee's meeting in Lusaka, on the initiative of Ripton Macpherson, it was noted that Philip Laundy's book, *The Office of Speaker*, published in 1964, was out of print. It was the only authoritative work on the Speakership in the Commonwealth and was constantly in demand by Speakers and members. It was, however, a specialist work which would be costly to produce and could expect only limited sales. For this reason the publishers were unwilling to undertake a new edition. It was suggested that a grant from the fund should be made to ensure publication. The Committee requested the Editor to discuss the matter with the author and to report to the next meeting with estimates. In Hong Kong the Committee noted that Philip Laundy was already working on a new book on the subject. It agreed that a grant of £6000 should be made from the fund, which included a subvention of £3000 to the publisher towards production costs.[8]

The Committee approved the production and publication of a cumulative index to *The Parliamentarian*, covering the first 15 volumes of the journal in its current form. This proposal had been made by Ripton Macpherson and first considered by the Committee in Jersey in 1980. He had said then that *The Parliamentarian* was invaluable to Speakers, members and Clerks, especially in the smaller legislatures which had no libraries or reference materials. An index would give them ready access to constitutional and procedural articles published during these years. It was agreed, too, that further indexes should be published at five-year intervals, the next one to appear in 1986.

Relations between the CPA and the AIPLF had always been cordial, but were restricted to exchanges of observers at conferences. Gerald Ottenheimer (Newfoundland) was the CPA's observer at the conference of the AIPLF in Gabon in September 1978. He reported that he had spoken there with representatives, whose legislatures also had branches of the CPA. 'In my opinion,' he said, 'they share my conviction that the friendly relationship between the two organizations should be valued and encouraged.'[9] He was unable to attend the AIPLF's 10th General Assembly in Geneva in July 1979. Senator R. R. Jeune (Jersey) went in his place. Addressing the Assembly, he said:

> Since the founding of the AIPLF some eleven years ago, a warm fraternal bond has, I believe, been forged between the two organisations. I hope this will long continue. At the same time it seems to me that there still remains a fundamental difference between them. A major purpose of the CPA is to promote the study and understanding of Parliament and in every way possible to strengthen parliamentary institutions. Parliament is seen as an essential part of the way of life of the countries of the Commonwealth. The activities of the CPA demonstrate this emphasis on parliamentary affairs. The seminars on parliamentary practice and procedure, the sessions in the Association's conferences, both plenary and regional, devoted to parliamentary subjects, and the publications of the CPA vividly demonstrate this concern for Parliament and for parliamentary democracy. I personally would like to see developing between the AIPLF and the CPA greater cooperation specifically in this field of parliamentary studies and activities. If this could be developed it would, I firmly believe, lead to a closer relationship between these two valuable organisations and this is something I would entirely welcome.[10]

At the CPA conference in New Zealand in 1979, Xavier Deniau by special permission addressed the delegates. He referred to Senator Jeune's speech in Geneva and said that his organisation was considering closely the need to make parliamentary affairs a major part of its activities. He went on to propose that the two Associations should set up a special Committee to cooperate in the parliamentary field.

In 1981 Senator Jeune reported to the Committee on further developments. Early in 1980 Robert Moinet and Mme M. F. Mercier of the AIPLF had met in Jersey with Edward Potter, Greffier of the States of Jersey, and R. S. Gray, Deputy Greffier, and himself. They had agreed on the composition of the special Committee and its purpose. This was to set up more systematic arrangements for the exchange of information on parliamentary matters and to provide advice and assistance to new parliamentary assemblies. The Executive Committee agreed to the proposed meeting of representatives of the two organisations, which Jersey would host.

In Hong Kong Senator Jeune informed the Executive Committee that this meeting had taken place in Jersey in January 1981. No permanent body had been set up, but one further meeting was proposed, probably in November 1981.

Following the success of the first study group held in London in September 1979, the Executive Committee had agreed that it was important to build up momentum and to establish study groups as part of the Association's permanent programme. It had approved plans for a second study group which met in Ottawa in November 1980. Its subject was 'Parliament and the Scrutiny of Science Policy'. Senator Maurice Lamontagne (Canada) was in the event unable to chair the meetings and at short notice Lord Sherfield, the United Kingdom member, took the chair. Its membership was distinguished and included Representative Brown from the US Congress, Chairman of the Congressional Subcommittee on Science and Technology.[11] The Rapporteur was Dean Clay, Head of the Science Section of the Research Department of the Canadian Parliamentary Library. The report of the study group was published in the October 1981 issue of *The Parliamentarian*.

It had been the intention of the Executive Committee to assess the value of the study group programme at its meeting in Hong Kong in 1981. At this meeting, however, the Committee took the view that it was too soon to evaluate the programme and that a third study group should not be postponed. This group was to meet in London in June 1982 to consider 'The Role of Second Chambers'.[12]

The General Assembly convened on 22 October in Suva, Fiji, which was, as was customary, towards the end of the conference itself. The President of the Association, Mosese Qionibaravi, Speaker of the House of Representatives, Fiji, was in the chair. He opened by welcoming delegates from new branches, which included Zimbabwe and seven Nigerian states.

The Treasurer reported on the estimated income and expenditure account for 1981 and said that the Association would start 1982 with a credit balance of £9100. Projections for 1982–84 showed, however, that the deficit by 1984 would be in the region of £183,250. In Hong Kong the Executive Committee had decided to recommend an increase of 10 per cent in membership fees. It now recommended an increase of 15 per cent. The General Assembly unanimously approved this increase.

The working capital fund amounted to £396,494 at the end of 1980. A balance of £29,484 brought forward from 1979 plus an excess of income in 1980 of

£40,093 gave the fund a credit balance of £69,577 at the end of 1980. Expenditure in 1981 was not likely to exceed £37,000. An estimated credit balance of £77,350 would be carried forward to 1982.

At the Committee's meeting in Hong Kong the Treasurer had pressed for economies in publications. The quarterly journal of the Association, *The Parliamentarian*, should, he proposed, be published only twice a year. This was rejected by the Committee. It agreed to recommend, however, that the official verbatim report of the conference should be discontinued. An expanded summary of proceedings should take its place.

At its meeting in Suva, however, the Committee reversed this recommendation. A number of factors, submitted to the meeting, led to the new decision. It was recognised that, as a most important international parliamentary organisation, the Association had a responsibility to publish a full report of the main event in its annual programme. Reports of proceedings of regional conferences were regularly published. Moreover, the official reports were historical records of the CPA and of the Commonwealth itself. They reflected the interests and moods of the time in all parts of the Commonwealth. They were essential documents for future historians. Furthermore, in most of the conferences there were sessions and individual contributions of outstanding interest and value (as indicated in many pages of this history) and they should be kept on record and readily available. The proposal that a set of corrected transcripts would be held in the Secretariat was an inadequate substitute for the printed report. The corrected transcripts were usually difficult to read and many hours of careful subediting were often needed before they could be sent to press. Also, the transcripts would be available only to historians and students in London. The proposed expanded summary would involve condensing into a few lines each of some 200 speeches by Speakers, Ministers, and members at every conference. This would be an exceedingly difficult, if not impossible, task for the publications staff. Finally the Committee had before it new printing estimates. In 1979 the cost of printing the report was £8000 and in 1980 it was £11,500. An estimate for printing the 1981 report, obtained from a reputable printing house in Hong Kong, was £4752. Taking into consideration all these factors, the Committee recommended acceptance of this estimate. The General Assembly approved the recommendation.

The first conference of representatives from branches in small countries of the Commonwealth had met on 8–9 October 1981 at the headquarters of SPEC, the South Pacific Economic Committee, in Suva. The venue was ideal for the purpose. Sir Robert Munro, President of the Senate of Fiji, was in the chair. Thirty-two representatives from 22 countries took part. Two observers from the Marshall Islands also attended. Sir Robert Munro tabled a report to the General Assembly. He spoke briefly, expressing the hope that such conferences would form part of the regular programme of the Association in future. He recommended that a verbatim report should be published. The General Assembly approved both recommendations. Clement Maynard, Vice-President of the Association and Acting Chairman of the Executive Committee, then moved that the next conference of representatives from small countries should be held prior to the plenary conference in the Bahamas in 1982.

The election of the officers of the Association and of regional representatives to serve on the Executive Committee was the next item on the agenda. Clement Maynard, Minister of Labour and Home Affairs in the Bahamas, was elected President for 1981–82. The Speaker of the National Assembly of Kenya, Frederick Mbiti Gideon Mati, was elected Vice-President. The office of Chairman of the Executive Committee was vacant. Three members were nominated – Gerald R. Ottenheimer, Minister of Justice and Attorney-General (Newfoundland), Dr Harry Jenkins (Australia) and Dr Bal Ram Jakhar, Speaker of the Lok Sabha (India). The result of the first ballot was Dr Jenkins 28 votes, Dr Jakhar 68 votes, and Gerald Ottenheimer 88 votes. In the second ballot Dr Jakhar gained 74 votes, while Gerald Ottenheimer gained 109 votes and was declared elected for a three-year term.

The 27th Commonwealth Parliamentary Conference, held in Fiji from 11–25 October 1981, must be recorded as one of the most successful conferences of the CPA. As noted earlier in this history, each conference has tended to have its own character. Many factors have played a part. The nature of the host country and its people, the President and the Secretary and staff of the branch are always important. Fiji has a compelling beauty and its people a warm friendliness. Mosese Qionibaravi, the President, as the able Chairman of the conference and the General Assembly, was always a genial and tireless host. Lavinia Ah Koy, Secretary of the branch and one of the most charming and efficient Secretaries in the Association, was with her assistants responsible for the excellent arrangements for the tours and the conference itself.

This was a special achievement, for the conference was the largest ever held. The overall number of visitors was 232 delegates, 37 Secretaries to delegations, 81 observers, and 75 spouses. The observers included M. Carlot, Speaker of the Vanuatu legislature in which a branch had just been formed. Xavier Deniau and Robert Moinet were again the observers from the AIPLF. Harry Blank (Quebec), a former member of the Executive Committee and Speaker Robinson M. Nabulyato (Zambia), the immediate past President, also attended. In recognition of the close relations between Fiji and Australia, Sir Condor Laucke, former President of Australia's Senate, and John Ferguson, Assistant Secretary of the Australian branch, were special guests.

H. E. the Governor-General, Ratu Sir George K. Cakobau, formally opened the conference on 19 October 1981. It was an occasion of traditional Fijian ceremonies of welcome to honoured guests, which with oratory, choral singing and dancing were colourful, dignified and for all present unforgettable. On the ending of these ceremonies the Governor-General and Adi, Lady Cakobau arrived. The President, Mosese Qionibaravi, welcomed them and invited the Governor-General to declare the conference open. The Prime Minister of Fiji, Ratu Sir Kamisese Mara, spoke and was followed by Vice-President Clement Maynard, who delivered an address of thanks.

The President in his speech said:

> One of the greatest benefits from our Association is the sense of fellowship and community it engenders amongst Commonwealth Parliamentarians.... Equally important among the objectives of the Association is the promotion of parliamentary institutions, the belief in which is one of the binding forces in the Commonwealth of Nations. It is heartening to note that this important facet of the Association's activities has been strengthened by the Working Capital Fund of the Association through the funding of local seminars, study groups, and publications.[13]

The Governor-General said that the Commonwealth stood for a moderate and constitutional approach to political problems and for the promotion of political, economic and social justice. He continued:

> In a world faced with constant flares of hostility, the Commonwealth should continue to be a force of moderation and reason. In this regard, your Association can play an important part for all of its members.... The Association has the equally important objective of promoting parliamentary democracy. In pursuit of these objectives the Association has recognized the different adaptations in member states to suit local conditions. But in devising appropriate parliamentary institutions I hope that we will always be responsive to the feelings and thinkings of our peoples and respect the right and freedoms of our citizens.[14]

The Prime Minister, Ratu Sir Kamisese Mara, welcomed all delegates on behalf of the people of Fiji. Then: 'We acknowledge the generosity of our developed nearby friend whose helping hand has assisted us in hosting this important meeting.'[15] This was a reference to a substantial grant made by the Australian branch towards the cost of the conference.

In six plenary and four panel sessions, delegates were able to discuss a wide range of topics.[16] In opening the first session, the Prime Minister of Fiji spoke of the chief matters of concern under the heading 'The Commonwealth and World Security'. 'The Commonwealth has a role,' he said, 'in the resolution of conflict not only in its own backyard but also in the world at large.'[17] He referred to the independence of Zimbabwe, to the situation in Namibia, and to the part the Commonwealth could play in pursuing the recommendations of the Brandt Commission. Other delegates also spoke on these topics.

L. G. Blake (Falkland Islands), in an impressive speech, brought up the basic rights of self-determination and territorial integrity, especially as they affected a small and remote territory. Neil Marten, leader of the United Kingdom delegation, speaking with characteristic directness, gave three examples of the Commonwealth's contribution to world security: Zimbabwe, Uganda and Belize. East–West relations were a source of concern. He warned that Soviet Russia was continuing to build up its military forces far in excess of its defence needs, while at the same time seeking to destabilise other countries. He did not, he said, ask

Commonwealth countries to take sides in the East–West issues, but he would urge those which chose to remain neutral to beware of attempts by the Eastern bloc to destabilise them. They should take to heart the lessons of the fate of Afghanistan and Cambodia. Several African delegates laid stress on the threat to world security posed by the situation in Southern Africa.

The plenary session on 'Control of Pollution and Protection of the Environment', ably opened by Dr Bal Ram Jakhar, revealed how the awareness of the need for action in this field had broadened and developed in many Parliaments. The panel session on 'Social Consequences of Continuing Inflation and Unemployment' was of special interest. Datin Paduka Rafidah Aziz (Malaysia) was in the chair. The panelists were Joel Barnett (United Kingdom) and J. S. G. Cullen (Canada). Errol Barrow (Barbados) also contributed actively to the discussions. A topic new to the agenda was 'The Year of the Disabled'. The discussions in this panel were informative as were those in the panel session on 'Population Growth and Control'. On both topics delegates, having heard the problems and action taken by other countries, were able to approach their own situations with a greater freshness and understanding.

The three sessions on parliamentary matters were, as in previous conferences, valuable in enabling delegates to compare systems of government and to learn of possible developments to promote greater efficiency in their own legislatures. The opening speakers in these three sessions were Keith Penner (Canada), Joel Barnett (United Kingdom) and Philip Smith (Bahamas), all of whom made outstanding contributions.

In the votes of thanks during the closing of the conference, Kenneth Comber, leader of the New Zealand delegation, suggested aptly that in the history of the Association this would be recorded as the 'friendly conference'. The President then called Lavinia Ah Koy and all her staff to the platform where they sang *Isa Lei* and other Fijian songs of farewell to their guests. The delegates found the occasion moving and, like the whole of the visit to Fiji, memorable.

In 1982 the mid-year meeting of the Executive Committee took place in Bermuda. In the Chamber of the House of Assembly in Hamilton on 10 May, the Speaker, F. J. Barritt, called upon H.E. the Governor of Bermuda, Sir Richard Posnett, to perform the opening ceremony. The Governor spoke of the long history of Bermuda's legislature, dating from 1620. 'Bermuda's parliamentarians', he said,

have built over the years a high degree of mutual trust and understanding with their constituents. This is appropriate for the oldest parliamentary system outside the British Isles. And just as Parliament is the beating heart of a country so the CPA is the beating heart of the Commonwealth. If the Commonwealth comprised countries with totalitarian forms of government these meetings would probably never take place. But in practice the CPA is a free association of freely elected people devoted to the service of their respective societies. This is one of the highest expressions of man's social aspirations and a vital component of world peace.[18]

In reply, the Chairman of the Executive Committee, Gerald Ottenheimer, praised Bermuda's contribution to the CPA and to the Commonwealth. It had hosted many CPA events as well as meetings of the British-American Parliamentary Group and recently the meeting of Commonwealth Finance Ministers. The durability and flexibility of the Parliament of Bermuda would encourage parliamentary institutions in other countries.

The Committee carried out its customary business, receiving reports on five regional conferences and eight seminars held since its last meeting, and on the other activities of the Association. It then reviewed relations between the CPA and the AIPLF. The Chairman reported on the 12th General Assembly of the AIPLF in Dakar, Senegal, in January 1982 at which he had represented the CPA. He had not, however, been able to attend the CPA/AIPLF meeting in Jersey on 6 April. George Cunningham (United Kingdom) and the Secretary-General had represented the Association. The Secretary-General said that the meeting in Jersey, chaired by Senator R. R. Jeune, had confirmed the standing arrangement whereby the two organisations exchanged observers to their respective conferences. The proposal for a joint conference, put forward by the AIPLF, proved impractical, however, because it would involve translation facilities, and difficulties over the agenda, the selection of delegates, and finance. Within the Executive Committee, moreover, there remained the feeling that the two Associations were not serving the same purposes and that the AIPLF was not basically a parliamentary association, but one concerned primarily with the French language and culture. Subsequently the CPA was invited to send an observer to a meeting in Paris and Toulouse on 'Espace et Télématique'. This was declined. The Committee agreed nevertheless that the very cordial relations between the two Associations should be encouraged and that exchanges of observers should be extended to include regional conferences.

In the absence of the Treasurer, James Johnson, through illness, the financial reports were presented by J. A. G. Smith (Jamaica). This was followed by discussion on the need to ensure that future Treasurers should have some financial expertise. It was suggested that the clause of the constitution, providing that the branch in the country in which the Headquarters Secretariat was situated would nominate the Treasurer, should be amended to provide that a member of any branch could be elected, subject to his having knowledge and experience in the financial field. It was finally agreed to hold over this issue for the time being. The Committee, however, requested W. E. Garrett, attending as alternate for Ernest Armstrong, to impress on the United Kingdom branch that it was a vital necessity that its nominee for the office of Treasurer should have financial qualifications.

The General Assembly convened in Nassau on 21 October 1982. The President of the Association, Clement Maynard, was in the chair. Early in the meeting the Chairman of the Executive Committee, Gerald Ottenheimer, submitted a recommendation that a study group should be appointed to carry out a comprehensive review of the structure, finances and procedures of the

Association. It would comprise one representative from each region and three members of the Executive Committee. The group would, it was envisaged, conduct its review in the same way as the working party fifteen years earlier. The group would have a strict schedule. It would meet in June or July 1983, make a preliminary report to the General Assembly in the autumn of 1983, and submit its final report at the time of the conference in 1984.

This recommendation arose from proposals, tabled by the Australian branch, which called on the General Assembly to make decisions at the meeting in Nassau. The two main proposals concerned the composition of the Executive Committee and the debating and voting on resolutions in the plenary conference. For some years the Australian branch had been seeking more regular representation on the Committee. It now submitted cogent arguments in support of increased representation of its region and the African region.

The Executive Committee, meeting a few days before the General Assembly, considered the proposals. It was reluctant, however, to have decisions made without more thorough examination. The appointment of the study group was intended to give the opportunity for such an examination. The Australian delegates welcomed the study group and accepted the compromise.

The General Assembly approved the proposed study group on 'The CPA and the Future'. It also agreed that it should submit recommendations on the composition of the Executive Committee to the meeting in Nairobi in 1983. It then considered the other Australian proposals.

The submission that the plenary conference should debate and vote on resolutions was discussed at some length. The Chairman of the meeting, Clement Maynard, recounted the past decisions on this subject. The working party in 1967 had unanimously decided that resolutions should not be allowed. This had been endorsed in 1978, 1979 and in 1980. The recommendation of the Committee to the General Assembly now upheld this position. It was agreed, however, that the study group could re-examine the matter.

The Cyprus delegate, Manolis Christofides, moved an amendment that resolutions be permitted, but only in exceptional cases where external aggression had been committed against a member state of the Commonwealth. F. H. Hunter (Belize) and J. T. Kolane (Lesotho) spoke in support of the amendment. Neil Marten (United Kingdom) cautioned against introducing resolutions. The Chairman put the question. The amendment was lost and the recommendation of the Executive Committee was adopted.

The Treasurer presented the estimated income and expenditure account for 1982. It was expected that a credit balance of some £26,283 would be carried forward to 1983. Projections showed nevertheless that there would be a deficit of £67,100 by the end of 1984. The Executive Committee recommended a 10 per cent increase in membership fees. This was approved.

Reporting on the working capital fund the Treasurer stated that of the 127 branches of the Association 60 per cent had contributed. The amount received was £466,560 and, as invested by the merchant bank handling the fund, it had a market value of £580,000. Grants from the fund had amounted to £86,000. Certain delegates expressed concern that the bank might invest funds in South Africa and were assured that all investment was in United Kingdom equities and government stock.

The General Assembly received reports on the study group on 'Parliament and the Scrutiny of Science Policy' and the study group on 'The Role of Second Chambers'. Senator Donald S. Jessop, leader of the Australian delegation, had been a member of the first of these two groups. He said that he had found its meetings valuable and enlightening. Senator Sir Arnott Cato (Barbados) reported that he and the other members of the second group had been unanimous in the view that the discussions had been very worthwhile. He looked forward to the reactions of members to the group's report which was to be published in the October 1982 issue of *The Parliamentarian*.

The second conference of representatives of small countries took place in Nassau on 11–12 October. The General Assembly took note of a report on its proceedings and agreed that a third conference should be held in 1983. The final business of the General Assembly was, as usual, the election of officers and regional representatives. The Speaker of the National Assembly of Kenya, F. M. G. Mati, was elected President for 1982–83. The Vice-President would be the nominee of the Isle of Man branch which would host the conference in 1984. In place of James Johnson whose term of office had expired, Mark Carlisle (United Kingdom) was elected Treasurer. The retiring members of the Executive Committee and the retiring Editor of Publications and Deputy Secretary-General, were then presented with commemorative plaques by Datuk Shahrir bin Abdul Samad, leader of the Malaysian delegation.

The 28th Commonwealth Parliamentary Conference took place in Nassau from 16–22 October 1982. It was attended by 190 delegates, 36 Secretaries to delegations, and 27 observers. Three special guests, all of whom addressed the delegates, were John Small, Deputy Secretary-General, Commonwealth Secretariat, Pio-Carlo Terenzio, Secretary-General of the Inter-Parliamentary Union, and Xavier Deniau, representing the AIPLF. The American National Conference of State Legislatures was represented by Assemblyman William Passannante, Speaker Pro Tem of the New York State Assembly and President of the National Conference, and Earl S. Mackay, the Executive Director.

The formal opening of the conference took place in the Brittania Beach–Paradise Island hotel and conference complex on 16 October 1982. The President of the Association, Clement Maynard, introduced H.E. the Governor-General, Sir Gerald Cash, and invited him to open the conference. In an impressive speech he underlined the commitment of the Bahamas to the Commonwealth parliamentary heritage and to the CPA. The Prime Minister, Lynden O. Pindling, then welcomed delegates on behalf of the government and people of the Bahamas.

The Bahamas is small but it has been and will remain, I trust, dauntless in its advocacy and defence of the parliamentary system. And although its resources are small and limited, it has endeavoured never to waver in its support of the Commonwealth Parliamentary Association.[19]

The first of the seven plenary and four panel sessions considered 'World Peace and Development'.[20] Several delegates took the view that this heading covered two subjects which, although linked, should be discussed separately. Opening the session, Shri Chandra Shekhar Singh, leader of the Indian delegation, spoke of global interdependence, embracing nations of the North and South, and he deplored the arms race. Military expenditure was mounting, but in 1980 western development assistance was only 0.37 per cent of GNP as against the target of 0.7 per cent laid down by the United Nations.

The leader of the United Kingdom delegation, Neil Marten, pointed out that without peace and stability development could not prosper. But they could not accept peace at any price and must be prepared to defend themselves. Dudley Thompson (Jamaica) expressed his fears that military preparedness for defence was a dangerous doctrine and a prescription for the arms race. Several delegates argued in favour of regional zones of peace.

Darrell E. Rolle, leader of the Bahamian delegation, opened the session on 'The Security and Future of the Small Countries of the Commonwealth'. The problems affecting the very fabric of Bahamian society were, he said, illegal immigration, poaching in Bahamian waters, and drug trafficking. Sir Arnott Cato (Barbados) described foreign mercenaries, insurrection, terrorism, claims to territory, and the international drug traffic as being the chief threats to the small states of the Caribbean. Other delegates spoke of the threats to their countries and of the need for them to band together where practicable.

The discussion on 'Approaches to Unemployment' in the third session brought out the magnitude of the problem as it affected almost all countries of the Commonwealth. Of the four panel sessions, the exchanges on 'Population Control' were perhaps the most stimulating. John W. S. Malecela (Tanzania), who contributed actively throughout the conference, spoke with great frankness on this subject. He suggested a wide range of social measures and also a CPA conference of women members on population control. Delegates from Hong Kong, Singapore and other countries made valuable contributions on sterilisation, abortion, the teachings of the Catholic Church, and on taxation and other incentives to limit the size of families.

The panel session on 'Preservation of the Environment with Special Reference to Wildlife' was chaired by M. P. K. Nwako (Botswana). A former member of the Executive Committee, he had prepared for this session a valuable paper on 'Wildlife as a Resource and its Impact on Utilisation of Other Natural Resources'. Poonam Chand Bishnoi (Rajasthan), one of the panelists, described the people of his state as 'aggressively conservationist'; this could be applied to the mood of the discussion in this session.

The five sessions on parliamentary topics were, as in previous conferences, of great practical value. The session on 'Parliamentary Privilege with Special Reference to Confidentiality' was especially notable for the contributions of Senator Donald S. Jessop (Australia), P. S. Mulema (Uganda), Geoffrey Palmer (New Zealand), Mark Carlisle (United Kingdom) and W. R. Baxter (Victoria).

The conference in the Bahamas in 1968 had been marked by a certain acerbity, arising in part from the Rhodesian crisis. In 1982 the conference was conducted in a mood of harmony. The standard of the discussions was high. Indeed, anyone interested in the topics on the agenda, and especially population growth, world wildlife and parliamentary privilege, would be well rewarded by reading the verbatim report of the proceedings.

Notes

1. Report of Executive Committee (1979–80), p.13.
2. Report of General Assembly (Jamaica, 1978), p.129.
3. Conference Report (Lusaka, 1980), pp.xix–xx.
4. Ibid., p.xxi.
5. Ibid., p.xxii.
6. **Agenda and Opening Speakers, Lusaka, 1980**
   Current Threats to International Peace and Security – Bal Ram Jakhar, Speaker of the Lok Sabha (India)
   A New Strategy for the Developing World: the Brandt Report – Keith Penner (Canada)
   A New Strategy for the Developing World: the Brandt Report – two panel sessions
   Africa South of the Sahara: the Beginning of a New Era – F. M. Chomba, Minister of Legal Affairs and Attorney-General (Zambia)
   International Collaboration in Combating Drug Addiction and Trafficking – O. R. Padmore, Minister of Government Construction and Maintenance, Minister in the Ministry of Finance (Trinidad and Tobago)
   The Law of the Sea – F. M. K. Sherani (Fiji)
   Race Relations within the Commonwealth – panel session
   The Role of Parliament in Relation to Public Enterprises – panel session
   One-Party and Multi-Party Parliaments: Relative Advantages and Disadvantages – G. M. Bryant (Australia)
   Parliament and the Scrutiny of Public Finance: Review of the Report of the Study Group – panel session
   Parliament and the Mass Media – panel session
   The MP: His Functions and Responsibilities – Laurie Pavitt (United Kingdom).
7. Conference Report (Lusaka, 1980), p.40.
8. *The Office of Speaker in the Parliaments of the Commonwealth* by Philip Laundy was published in London in 1984.
9. Report of Executive Committee (1980–81), p.39.
10. Report of Executive Committee (1978–79), p.56.
11. The Study Group on Parliament and the Scrutiny of Science Policy met in Ottawa in November 1980. The members of the group were:
    Chairman: Lord Sherfield, GCB, GCMG (United Kingdom), Deputy Chairman of the House of Lords Select Committee on Science and Technology and past President of the Parliamentary and Scientific Committee (United Kingdom). Senator Donald S.

Jessop (Australia), Chairman of the Senate Standing Committee on Science and the Environment. Dr Gary M. Gurbin, MP (Canada), Member of the House of Commons Special Committee on Alternative Energy and Oil Substitution. Dr M. S. Sanjeevi Rao, MP (India) Member of the Consultative Committee on Atomic Energy, Space and Electronics. Hon. Dr A. Mukasa Mango, MP (Kenya), Chairman of the Public Investments Committee. Prof. Ang Kok Peng, MP (Singapore), Department of Chemistry, National University of Singapore. Senator Dr Kusha Haraksingh (Trinidad & Tobago), Chairman of the Institute of African and Asian Studies, University of the West Indies. Hon. George E. Brown, Jr, Member of Congress (United States), Chairman of the Subcommittee on Science, Research and Technology, House of Representatives. Rapporteur: Dean N. Clay, Chief of the Science and Technology Division in the Canadian Library of Parliament's Research Branch.

Guests participant in the meetings of the Study Group were:

Rt Hon. Lord Shackleton, KG, OBE, Deputy Chairman of the House of Lords Select Committee on Science and Technology and past President of the Parliamentary and Scientific Committee (United Kingdom); Dr Walter Hahn, Senior Specialist in Science, Technology and Futures Research with the Congressional Research Service (United States); Dr Tom Moss, Staff Director of the Subcommittee on Science, Research and Technology, House of Representatives (United States); Dr Frank Maine, former Member of Parliament and former Parliamentary Secretary to the Minister of State for Science and Technology (Canada); Professor Colin Campbell, Department of Political Science at York University (Canada); and Dr Roger Voyer, Executive Director of the Canadian Institute for Economic Policy (Canada).

Dr Richard D. Brock, Counsellor (Scientific) at the Australian Embassy in Washington, attended as an observer.

12. The study group on the role of Second Chambers met in London in June 1982. The membership of the group was:

Chairman: Rt Hon. Lord Shackleton, KG, OBE, former Leader of the House of Lords and Minister in charge of civil service. Australia: Sir Condor Laucke, KCMG, former President of the Senate. Barbados: Senator the Hon. Sir Arnott Cato, President of the Senate. Canada: Senator Eugene Forsey, former Member of the Senate. India: Hon. Ram Niwas Mirdha, MP, former Deputy Chairman, Rajya Sabha. Malaysia: Y. A. B. Tun Omar Yoke-Lin Ong, former President of the Senate. Zimbabwe: Hon. N. C. Makombe, President of the Senate. Rapporteur: Mr George Clark, political correspondent, *The Times*, London.

13. Conference Report (Suva, Fiji, 1981), p.xxviii.
14. Ibid., p.xxv.
15. Ibid., p.xxvii.
16. **Agenda and Opening Speakers, Fiji, 1981**

The Commonwealth and World Security – Ratu Sir Kamisese Mara, Prime Minister (Fiji)

Control of Pollution and Protection of the Environment – Bal Ram Jakhar, Speaker of the Lok Sabha (India)

Social Consequences of Continuing Inflation and Unemployment – panel session

Promotion and Development of Tourism – panel session

Commodity Prices and the Relations between Industrialised and Primary Producing Countries – A. Rahim bin Datuk Tamby Chik, Deputy Minister of Home Affairs (Malaysia)

The Year of the Disabled – panel session

Population Growth and Control – panel session
Relevance of Westminster Parliamentary System in a Changing World – Keith Penner (Canada)
Parliament and the Scrutiny of the Executive – Joel Barnett (United Kingdom)
The MP – His Responsibilities to the Nation, to his Party, and to his Constituency – Philip Smith (Bahamas).

17. Conference Report (Fiji, 1981), p.1.
18. Report of Executive Committee (1981–82), pp.16–17.
19. Conference Report (Nassau, 1982), p.xxvii.
20. **Agenda and Opening Speakers, Nassau, 1982**
    World Peace and Development – Chandra Shekhar Singh (India)
    The Security and Future of Small Countries of the Commonwealth – Darrell F. Rolle, Minister of Education (Bahamas)
    Approaches to Unemployment – Keith Penner (Canada)
    The Freedom of the Individual, Human Rights and Responsibilities, and the Authority of Government in a Parliamentary Democracy – Sir Derek Walker-Smith (United Kingdom)
    Development of Alternative Sources of Energy – panel session
    Parliamentary Privilege with Special Reference to Confidentiality – panel session
    Population Control – panel session
    Preservation of the Environment with Special Reference to Wildlife – panel session
    Parliament and the Scrutiny of Public Finance – Shahrir bin Abdul Samad, Deputy Minister of Trade and Industry (Malaysia)
    The Role of the Opposition in a Parliamentary System – C. J. Hurford (Australia)
    Parliament and the Executive – F. Chuula, Minister of State for Decentralisation (Zambia).

The working party, set up in 1966, had carried out a thorough review of the Association's activities and administration. Its principal recommendation had been the creation of the Executive Committee. The subcommittee on 'The CPA and the Future', appointed in 1977, had also in effect conducted a review. Its main proposal was to establish the working capital fund. In both reviews emphasis was laid on the Association's basic purpose of promoting the study and understanding of parliamentary democracy. In each case the recommendations were adopted unanimously by the Association.

The working party, appointed in Nassau in October 1982, comprising nine members,[1] appeared to adopt a different approach. It decided that priority should be given to activities 'which promoted direct contact between members'.[2] Emphasis on parliamentary objectives was consequently diminished. The main concerns, as suggested by the working party's report, were the composition of the Executive Committee, improving conference discussions, the moving of resolutions, and economies. A New Zealand delegate commented in the meeting of the General Assembly in Nairobi that he did not consider 'that the report addressed in any significant intellectual way the future of the CPA'.[3]

This approach arose in large part from the provenance of the working party itself. The Federal Australian branch had been asserting for some years that it should have more regular representation on the Executive Committee. Within its region the branch had been unable to gain support for its claim. In Nassau the Australian case was pressed forcefully. It was then that the working party was set up and instructed to report in Nairobi in November 1983 specifically on the composition of the Executive Committee. It was also asked to carry out an extensive review of the Association's work and finances and to report to the General Assembly in the Isle of Man in 1984.

The Australian case was presented in Nairobi by Senator D. McClelland, President of the Australian Senate. He had been a member of the working party and would act as Vice-Chairman at its meeting in New Delhi in January 1984. He stated that all federations within the Commonwealth were regularly represented on the Committee with the exception of Australia and Nigeria. The African and the Australasia and Pacific regions were the largest contributors in fees to the Association and sent most delegates to the annual conferences. They were entitled to greater representation. Under the existing system his branch had to wait 24 years for its turn to have a member on the Committee. His branch proposed that the number of regional representatives be increased from two to three. Further, he stated, the four largest national groups in the region, namely Australia, Papua New Guinea, New Zealand and Fiji, would share the right to appoint the third regional representative. Each of the four groups would thus have representation every four years. He would propose that Papua New Guinea should provide the first of these representatives.

Several delegates, and the New Zealanders in particular, expressed opposition. D. C. McKinnon, speaking for the New Zealand branch, said, 'We feel that the extra representation on the Executive from our part of the world will not necessarily add to or benefit the CPA as a total entity. Those who serve on the Executive should be there to serve the CPA as a whole and not merely a region. We believe that a bigger CPA Executive is not necessarily a better CPA Executive.'[4]

Other delegates raised the question of the cost of increasing the size of the Committee from 18 to 25. Senator McClelland replied that this would be considered by the working party at its meeting in New Delhi in January 1984. The consensus of the General Assembly clearly favoured the Australian resolution, and it was approved. It remained to be seen whether the enlarged Committee would retain the sense of community, intimacy of discussion, and efficiency of the smaller Committee which had served the Association well over many years.

A major economy, designed in part to cover the extra cost of the enlarged Committee, concerned the printed verbatim report of the annual conference. The resolution, adopted in Nairobi, was as follows: 'The General Assembly approves the recommendation of the Executive Committee on the proposal of the Working Party that the verbatim reports of the Commonwealth Parliamentary Association conferences be discontinued and that the summary reports prepared in expanded form be published in *The Parliamentarian*.'[5]

The resolution had aroused strong opposition, but it came towards the end of two long sessions and the meeting was poorly attended. When put to the vote 28 members favoured adopting the resolution and 27 were against. The number of members entitled to attend and to vote was in the region of 200. On a point of order Tony Durant, a United Kingdom member of the Executive Committee and of the working party, said that, while a one vote majority was enough in a democratic system, he felt that such an important matter should be considered afresh. The Chairman, Sir Charles Kerruish, ruled that the resolution had been adopted.

The Executive Committee at its meeting in Malawi in May 1984 considered the recommendations in the working party's final report. It rejected some and approved others for submission to the General Assembly in the Isle of Man.

Further representations, critical of the enlarged Committee, had been received. There was concern that the increased membership would add £10,000 or more to the Association's annual expenditure, depending on the venue of the Committee's mid-year meeting. Thus, while the working party's final report dealt with the major activities of the Association, the emphasis was still on finance and exacting economies.

The General Assembly met in Douglas, Isle of Man, on 3–4 October 1984. The President of the Association, Sir Charles Kerruish, was in the chair. Early in the meeting several members proposed that the decision to discontinue publication of the verbatim report be rescinded. Shri Radha Nandan Jha, Speaker of the Legislative Assembly, Bihar, India, spoke strongly in favour of retaining the report. He was eager to move a resolution to that effect. The meeting, including Shri Jha, accepted the Chairman's proposal that the matter be discussed separately at a later stage.

Dr Bal Ram Jakhar, Speaker of the Lok Sabha, India, who had attended both meetings of the working party and, supported by Senator McClelland, had chaired the meeting in New Delhi, presented the report. The Chairman of the Executive Committee, Gerald Ottenheimer, said that the Committee had endorsed the recommendation that the conference should not debate or vote on formal resolutions. At the same time it had agreed that any consensus reached in conference sessions should be communicated more widely and promptly, and that guidelines on implementing this recommendation should be prepared. In particular it was felt that, when any member branch faced a threat to its territory or unity, the Association should accept the duty of providing a forum at either a regional or a plenary conference. This proviso had been added mainly on the instigation of the Cyprus branch which sought Commonwealth support in its dispute with Turkey.

Shri Jha was critical of the report as a whole: 'What we have seen from the recommendations is that the only consideration of the members of the working party was the finance of the CPA. Sir, we are not a commercial firm – We are parliamentarians of the world. Funds should not stand in our way...'.[6] In the resumed discussion on the verbatim conference report Shri Jha moved a resolution that the decision taken in Nairobi be rescinded. He declared that the report was an historical document, essential to future scholars and students of the Commonwealth and of parliamentary systems. Other delegates argued that the cost of transcribing, editing and publishing the report each year should be the prime consideration. They were disturbed, too, that the handling of this question, complicated not only by lapses of time but also by changes in the membership of the Executive Committee and especially of the General Assembly, had been so protracted and indecisive. Finally, Gerald Amerongen, Speaker of the Legislative Assembly, Alberta, moved an amendment to the resolution, referring the matter back to the Committee and instructing it to report to the General Assembly in September 1985. This amendment, imposing further delay, was approved by 63 votes to 13.

The Hon. Treasurer, Mark Carlisle, gave a lucid and comprehensive report on the Association's finances in 1983 and the estimates for 1984–85. A 15 per cent increase in branch fees, agreed in 1983, had added to the balance carried forward. Speaking on the estimates for 1984, he explained that the 10 per cent rise in branch fees for the year had in effect been reduced to 2 per cent. This was a result of the military takeover in Nigeria on 31 December 1983. The Federal and 17 state branches had gone into abeyance and the Association had lost branch fees amounting to £60,000. The mid-year meeting of the enlarged Executive Committee in Malawi had cost far more than the figure estimated on the basis of the old, smaller Committee. A final deficit for the year would reduce the balance carried forward to £25,555.

The estimates for 1985 presented a different picture. In accepting the Saskatchewan invitation to host the conference, the Association had agreed to pay £80,000 towards the cost. The appointment of the new Secretary-General would involve expenditure of some £15,000. At the same time the 15 per cent increase in branch fees, recommended by the Executive Committee, had in fact been reduced to 10 per cent by the General Assembly in Nairobi on the instigation of the United Kingdom branch. For this reason a deficit was expected in 1985.

In 1986 a deficit of £38,000 could be expected unless there was a further increase in branch fees. There was a strong argument for 10 per cent. A majority in the Executive felt, however, that in view of the pressures on smaller countries the increase should be kept as low as possible. He proposed 7½ per cent. On a total income of £700,000 the excess of income over expenditure would be £41,000 which meant that three years hence there would be only 2 per cent leeway in their estimates. The 7½ per cent increase was approved.

The working capital fund was, he reported, in good shape. The capital was £489,000 and the investment value £580,000. Only income from this trust fund could be used. Expenditure over income in 1984 would be £15,600, but a substantial balance had been brought forward. The working capital fund had been set up to finance new ventures and to expand the activities of the Association. The trustees of the fund have, however, been liberal in interpreting these terms. The working party and regional conferences, for example, have been considered eligible for grants from the fund. But its importance in providing for such new activities as study groups, regional parliamentary seminars, parliamentary newsletters, and the conferences of members from smaller countries has been recognised. Indeed, the impressive expansion in the work of the Association over the past decade has been almost wholly financed by the working capital fund.

The report of the working party and the reiterated demands for economies and for maintaining a tight budget might give the impression that in the years 1983–85 the Association was faltering and losing support among branches and members. In fact, the CPA was extremely active and continued to be strongly supported in this period. This is well illustrated by the invitations to host future conferences, extending to 1989.[7] Activities have included a full programme of plenary and regional conferences, seminars on parliamentary practice and procedure, publications, and conferences of members from small countries.

A project of special importance was a study group on 'The Security of Small States', which met in London on 19–21 September 1984. The background to this project was that the Heads of Government, meeting in New Delhi in November 1983, had called for a report on the subject. The Commonwealth Secretariat had appointed a consultative group to prepare the report. The CPA Executive Committee recognised that the Association was especially well placed to contribute on this major problem. Meeting shortly before the convening of the conference of members from small countries and the Association's plenary conference in the Isle of Man, the study group produced its report in time for consideration in both forums.

The ten members of the group, who were Ministers, Presiding Officers or backbenchers, from small countries, were able to speak with personal authority about threats to their security.[8] The group was particularly fortunate in having as its Co-Chairmen Sir Arnott Cato (Barbados), who has contributed richly to the work of the Association over many years, and Senator Wesley M. Barrett (Fiji). It was fortunate, too, in its Rapporteur, Dr John Henderson, the recently appointed Deputy Secretary-General, who, working under pressure, produced an admirably lucid and concise report. Copies were sent to the Commonwealth Heads of Government, to the Commonwealth Secretariat, to the United Nations, and to other organisations concerned with the welfare of small countries.

The report of the Commonwealth Secretariat's consultative group entitled *Vulnerability – Small States in the Global Society*, acknowledged the CPA report in the following terms:

> Although in the majority of states in our survey democracy is robust, there is much opportunity for improving stability by enhancing the democratic process nationally. For countries with an elected parliamentary system, the report of the recent Commonwealth Parliamentary Association study on the 'Security of Small States' is timely. We feel that its recommendations on enhancing public awareness of Parliament and active involvement in the democratic process, strengthening the technical support system available to Parliamentarians, expanding the role of parliamentary committees and adapting the parliamentary system to indigenous custom are very relevant. We believe that much improvement is needed in access to, and the quality of, information available to Parliaments. Research facilities for members of Parliament, including administrative assistance, should be upgraded, particularly in respect of information on foreign policy matters.[9]

Notes

1. **Membership of the Working Party**
   London Meeting, 18–22 July, Conference Room, 7 Old Palace Yard
   Chairman: Hon. J. A. G. Smith, MP, Minister of Labour and of the Public Service, Leader of the House, Jamaica (West Indies, Central and South American Mainland Region); Membership: Senator Dr Femi Ayantuga, Nigeria (African Region); Dr the

Hon. Bal Ram Jakhar, MP, Speaker of the Lok Sabha, India (Asian Region); Senator the Hon. Douglas McClelland, President of the Senate, Australia (Australasia and Pacific Region); Mr Keith Penner, MP, Canada (Canadian Region); Rt Hon. Mark Carlisle, QC, MP,* United Kingdom (Hon. Treasurer of the Association); Senator R. R. Jeune, OBE, President of the Education Committee, Jersey (British Islands and Mediterranean Region); Hon. G. R. Ottenheimer, QC, MHA, Minister of Justice and Attorney-General, Newfoundland (Chairman of the Executive Committee); Hon. Datuk Shahrirbin Abdul Samad, MP, Minister for the Federal Territory, Malaysia (South-East Asian Region).

New Delhi Meeting, 22–27 January 1984, Parliament House Annexe
Chairman: Dr the Hon. Bal Ram Jakhar, MP (elected in the absence of Mr Smith); Vice-Chairman: Senator the Hon. Douglas McClelland; Membership: Hon. Jenner B. M. Armour, MHA, Dominica (West Indies, Central and South American Mainland Region; attending as alternate for Mr Smith); Mr Tony Durant, MP, United Kingdom (British Islands and Mediterranean Region; attending as replacement for Sen. Jeune, who acted as Honorary Treasurer for the second meeting of the working party); Hon. L. Mulimba, MP, Minister of State for Decentralisation, Zambia (African Region; attending in place of Senator G. B. Hoomkwap, Nigeria, who had been appointed to succeed Senator Dr Femi Ayantuga); Hon. A. Donahoe, QC, MLA, Speaker of the Legislative Assembly, Nova Scotia (Canadian Region; attending as alternate for Mr Penner); Senator R. R. Jeune, OBE, (attending as acting Honorary Treasurer in the absence of Mr Carlisle,* Hon. Treasurer of the Association); Mr Ng Kah Ting, MP, Singapore (South-East Asian Region; attending as alternate for Hon. Dato Shahrir bin Abdul Samad); Hon. G. R. Ottenheimer, QC, MHA.
*Mr Carlisle was unable to attend due to illness.

2. Report of the Working Party of the CPA (March 1984), p.12.
3. Proceedings of the General Assembly of the CPA (Nairobi, Kenya, November 1983), p.140.
4. Ibid., p.139.
5. Ibid., p.176.
6. Typescript of the Proceedings of the General Assembly (Isle of Man, 1984), p.23.
7. The invitations to host the plenary conference are: Saskatchewan, 1985; United Kingdom, 1986; Malaysia, 1987; Australia, 1988; Barbados, 1989.
8. Membership of the study group on 'The Security of Small States': Co-Chairmen, Senator the Hon. Sir Arnott Cato, KCMG, President of the Senate, Barbados; Hon. Senator Wesley M. Barrett, President of the Senate, Fiji. Members: Hon. A. Loftus Roker, MP, Minister of Works and Utilities, Bahamas; Hon. F. H. Hunter, MHR, Minister of Works, Belize; Manolis Christofides, MP, Cyprus; L. G. Blake, MLC, Falkland Islands; Dr the Hon. R. G. Valarino, MHA, Minister for Labour and Social Security, Gibraltar; Hon. J. L. R. Kotsokoane, Minister of Education, Lesotho; Hon. Chief Fusitu's, Tonga; Hon. Willie Jimmy, MP, Vanuatu.
9. *Vulnerability: Small States in the Global Society,* Report of a Commonwealth Consultative Group (n.d.), pp.49, 50.

The 29th Commonwealth Parliamentary Conference took place in Nairobi from 31 October–5 November 1983. It was attended by 213 delegates and Secretaries to delegations, and by 42 observers. The official opening was performed by the President of the Republic of Kenya, H. E. Daniel T. arap Moi. He himself had taken part in CPA activities in the past, both as a delegate and as a member of a Westminster seminar on parliamentary practice and procedure.

The President of the Association, Hon. F. M. G. Mati, Speaker of the National Assembly of Kenya, said in his speech that the CPA 'exists to promote Commonwealth understanding and respect for parliamentary institutions which are so basic to our way of life. It is of special interest to note that, although we come from areas with different parliamentary systems and governments, we meet as Parliamentarians and equals.'[1]

The President of the Republic spoke of the evolution of the one-party system in Kenya. For a long time after independence there had been no constitutional barriers to the operation of various political parties. But it became clear, he said, 'that the people themselves have always felt happier and more secure, as part of the consolidation of our nationhood, with a one-party system'.[2] The four general elections in Kenya had been free, fair and democratic. Ministers, and up to 50 per cent of sitting Members, had at each election been replaced by the electorate. 'So what we have,' he said, 'is a freely chosen Parliament within a free society.'[3] He noted that the conference agenda would allow delegates to discuss the problem of Namibia and the abhorrent system of apartheid, which posed threats to international peace and security. He then declared the conference open. Sir Charles Kerruish, Vice-President of the Association, thanked him on behalf of the delegates.

Before discussion began in the first plenary session, the President of the Senate of Zimbabwe, Hon. N. C. Makombe, paid tribute to Humphrey Slade, who died on 13 August 1983. He had become a member of Kenya's Legislative Council in 1952 and Speaker in 1960. On Kenya's independence he was elected Speaker of the House of Representatives, and then, following constitutional changes, Speaker of the National Assembly. 'Mr Slade's reputation as a Speaker of great distinction was not confined to Kenya,' Mr Makombe said. 'He also made his mark among Presiding Officers throughout the Commonwealth. Today Presiding Officers meet frequently ... I believe there is real substance in the claim that all of these conferences owe something directly or indirectly to the action of Mr Slade in calling a conference of Presiding Officers of eastern, central, and southern African Parliaments in Nairobi in July 1964.'[4] The death of Mr Harry Nkumbula, a veteran Zambian politician, was also reported. Delegates stood in silence in memory of both men.

The conference agenda gave emphasis to parliamentary and economic and social matters in the six plenary and four panel sessions.[5] Towards the end of the conference two plenary sessions were concerned with international affairs. The opening session brought an exchange of information on the impact of oil prices, especially in developing countries, and on the search – productive in some countries – for alternative sources of energy.

The second session was opened by Dr Bal Ram Jakhar, who presented the subject of 'Poverty in the Third World' in global terms. He stressed that people living below the poverty-line numbered some 800 million, and explained what India had achieved by revolutionising the whole concept of agriculture in the subcontinent. People should, he said, exploit their own ways of survival before looking for assistance from other countries. He then listed ways in which developing countries might alleviate food problems. It was an impressive speech to which many other speakers paid tribute. The contributions in this session were of a high standard.

Over the years plenary sessions of CPA conferences have become occasions when delegates made statements about their national problems and practices. There has been little discussion or debate. It was for this reason that, first, committee and then panel sessions were introduced. A chairman and two or more panelists, usually chosen from among the delegates for their expertise or experience of the subject under discussion, opened and then stimulated exchanges with delegates. In Nairobi the four panel sessions were especially successful in providing lively and well-informed discussion. The panel session on 'The Civil Servant and his Relationship with Parliamentarians' in particular was notable. Its Chairman was Hon. Thakur Sen Negi, the independent Speaker of the Legislative Assembly of Himachal Pradesh, India. He had had a long and distinguished career as a civil servant and then as a politician. He had attended several CPA conferences and always participated actively as a thoughtful and devoted champion of parliamentary institutions. The discussion brought out several aspects of the subject, including differences in the position of civil servants in one-party and multi-party states. Hon. S. K. arap N'geny (Kenya) and Rt Hon. Merlyn Rees and Rt Hon. Jack Ashley (United Kingdom) were among those who made stimulating contributions. Indeed, anyone studying the role of the civil servant in Commonwealth countries would find the verbatim report of this panel session valuable.

In the plenary session on the effectiveness of international organisations, delegates concentrated mainly on the United Nations. There was general agreement that the UN had fallen far short of expectations. Opening the session, K. L. Fry, leader of the Australian delegation, spoke of the divergence of views in the Commonwealth on the Indonesian invasion of East Timor in 1975 and on the Falkland Islands war in 1982. A similar divergence was shown in references to American action in Grenada. The discussion revealed clearly that, while furthering international understanding, the Commonwealth could not play a major role in resolving international disputes.

'The Future of Parliamentary Democracy' was the subject of the fourth plenary session. All delegates asserted their determination to maintain the principles of the system as fundamental to the way of life of their countries. The problems of Namibia and South Africa, discussed in the fifth plenary session, brought unanimous condemnation of the policies of the South African government.

'The Dissemination of Information about Parliament', the subject of the final session, was considered by all who spoke to be a matter of vital importance. Louis Desmarais, the leader of the Canadian delegation, explained the methods, including televising of proceedings, used in Canada. He concluded, however, with a reference to a recent survey of national opinion, which had focused on the finding that 65 per cent of Canadians interviewed said that they had little or no interest in Parliament. The question raised by subsequent speakers was how to reach such people in their own countries. The responsibility of each Parliament and of its members to keep their electorates informed was of paramount importance. Most Parliaments made *Hansard* and other documents available to the public. All depended heavily on the news media which enjoyed special facilities. Several delegates, while denouncing censorship in all forms, spoke of the need for the media to show a greater sense of responsibility in reporting Parliament.

Peter Aringa, a Kenyan delegate, also made a plea for greater CPA participation in the dissemination of information:

The CPA has played a special role through its publications in explaining the legislatures of the Commonwealth and their contemporary roles. But the CPA should encourage bilateral and multilateral cooperation in strengthening research and publication departments in new legislatures for the better information of their own people, and for the exchange of information between legislative institutions.[6]

As has been noted earlier, each conference has developed its own character, reflecting the influence of the host country, the political and economic situation at the time, and also the evolving Commonwealth. The conference in Kenya differed greatly from the previous conferences held in Africa, namely in Kenya itself in 1954, in Uganda in 1967, in Malawi in 1972, and in Zambia in 1980. The strident threats of 'one man one gun', uttered by President Obote, had set the tone of most sessions in Uganda. The Malawi and Zambia conferences were marked by greater moderation in the discussion of the problems of Africa. The conference in Kenya appeared to have achieved a new maturity and depth. The principal concerns were not political but parliamentary and economic. The conference perhaps reflected a new stage in the evolution of the Commonwealth when the emphasis was on community of experience and cooperation rather than on partisan political issues.

The host branch contributed greatly to the mood of the delegates. The warm friendship and hospitality, extended by the President of the Republic, by the President of the CPA, by the members, and the staff were acknowledged by all delegates with gratitude. Tributes were paid also to Leonard Ngugi, Clerk of the National Assembly, and to H. B. Ndoria Gicheru, the conference director, who is well known to students of Parliament as the author of *Parliamentary Practice in Kenya*, the standard work on the subject.

Malta and the Seychelles were not represented at the Nairobi conference. Both countries had withdrawn from the Association. The Malta branch had been very active and its withdrawal was deeply regretted. The reason was a dispute with the United Kingdom. The Speaker of the Maltese House of Representatives had informed the Secretary-General that a resolution, presented by the government of Dom Mintoff, had been passed on 9 March 1983, threatening to leave the CPA unless the British government gave a satisfactory undertaking by 31 March that the remains of wartime wrecks and bombs in its ports would be removed. The Secretary-General replied that disputes between members within the Commonwealth should not affect membership of the Commonwealth or of the Association. By the same resolution Malta proposed to join the IPU. The Secretary-General pointed out that many Commonwealth Parliaments had membership of both the CPA and the IPU. The Malta branch was subsequently dissolved, but there was confidence that it would rejoin in due course.

The withdrawal of the Seychelles branch was of a different nature. The Seychelles has a one-party system in which no public discussion of political and constitutional matters is permitted. Members of the People's Assembly may not vote on any matter without instructions from their party branch committees. The President of the Seychelles told J. S. Malecela (Tanzania), a member of the CPA Executive Committee, that his legislature was so different from the parliamentary systems espoused by the CPA that he could not reconsider revival of his branch. The Executive noted the position and agreed that there was no further action to be taken.

The 30th Commonwealth Parliamentary Conference was held in the Isle of Man from 28 September–4 October 1984. The fourth conference of members from small countries took place there on 24–25 September. It was a bold undertaking for an island so small to host these conferences. It involved arrangements for delegates, Secretaries to delegations, observers, and spouses – a total of 339 visitors – as well as for the conferences themselves. All was done with the greatest efficiency, but the host branch achieved something more in enabling the visitors to meet the Manx people at every opportunity, and especially in their homes and at the *Mhelliah*, the farewell harvest supper. This helped to engender a sense of fellowship. H.M. the Queen Mother and H.R.H. the Princess Anne attended several functions, imparting to them further grace and dignity. The Prince of Wales met members of the CPA and Manx Executive Committees during a brief visit to the island.

The conference was officially opened by H.M. Queen Elizabeth the Queen Mother on 28 September. In inviting her to do so Sir Charles Kerruish, President of the Association and Speaker of the House of Keys, spoke of her tireless service to the Commonwealth. In her speech H.M. the Queen Mother said:

> In an ever-changing world, where circumstances sometimes seem to drive nations apart, the ties which unite the Commonwealth remain firm and immutable.... Your meeting here this week will, I am sure, show very clearly the CPA's success in fulfilling its aim to encourage understanding and cooperation between Commonwealth Parliamentarians and to promote the study of and respect for parliamentary institutions.[7]

The conference agenda again laid special emphasis on parliamentary subjects.[8] The sessions were reported to have reflected the same spirit that had been notable in Nairobi in the previous year. A summary of the discussions was published in *The Parliamentarian*;[9] a summary is, however, no substitute for a full verbatim report of the speeches of delegates. As has been noted often in this history, many conference sessions over the years have been outstanding and in the opinion of the present writer merit reprinting. Further, for those not present in the conference, the spirit and quality of delegates' contributions can only be understood and appreciated from reading the verbatim report. Regrettably, for the first time in the 74 years since the Association was founded, the conference in the Isle of Man has not been recorded in an official report. For historians and students of the Commonwealth and the CPA, it will be noted as the first unrecorded conference.[10]

All who took part in the conference and visit in the Isle of Man undoubtedly valued the experience. At the closing, warm tributes were paid to Sir Charles Kerruish and to his parliamentary colleagues who had been generous in their hospitality and assiduous in their concern for their guests. Robert Quayle, Clerk of the Tynwald and conference director, and the Tynwald staff received the highest praise for their efficient organisation and for their major contribution to the success of the conference.

The term of office of Gerald Ottenheimer as Chairman of the Executive Committee came to an end in the Isle of Man. He had served for three years as a Canadian regional representative before being elected Chairman. An indefatigable traveller, he visited many of the countries of the Commonwealth. His enthusiasm, impartiality and ability to find the consensus in meeting were appreciated by all members of the Committee. Dr Bal Ram Jakhar, Speaker of the Lok Sabha and an Indian Regional Representative, was elected to succeed him by the General Assembly.

It was regretted by all that Nigeria was unable to send delegates to this conference. Its branches went into abeyance in December 1983, following yet another military takeover. The hopes of many who had worked to establish a stable democratic system were destroyed. Soldiers are, however, ill-equipped to govern and their rule is unlikely to endure. Previously, when civilian government was re-established in Nigeria, branches of the Association were promptly revived. It is to be hoped that a democratic regime will be restored in the near future and that the Nigerian branches will again be part of the CPA.

Following the successful study group on the security of small states, the Executive Committee agreed that a new study group should be set up to consider electoral law and practice. This met in Halifax, Nova Scotia, on 25–27 September 1985. Shri J. P. Goyal (India) had proposed this study. Electoral law and practice were, he said, fundamental to the parliamentary system. A report by experienced MPs and electoral officers would contribute towards ensuring free and fair elections. After their meeting the members of the group travelled to Saskatchewan to attend the plenary conference, where their report was discussed.[11]

The Indian branches both through their delegates at conferences, participation of their members in seminars and study groups, and generally in promotion of the study of parliamentary affairs have made a major contribution to the work of the Association. A recent initiative has been the launch of an intensive programme on legislative drafting by the Bureau of Parliamentary Studies and Training in the Lok Sabha Secretariat, starting in November 1985. There has long been an urgent need in many legislatures for the training of legal or legislative draftsmen. Lacking funds and staff the CPA could do nothing, although the subject is central to the functioning of Parliament. The Commonwealth Secretariat has sought with some success to meet this need, but it continues to be pressing in smaller countries. The new Indian programme was intended primarily for Indian legislatures, but six places were allocated for participants from overseas.

The Grenada branch had been in abeyance since March 1979, when the elected government was overthrown by a revolutionary group. Following an invasion by US troops, elections were held on 5 December 1984 and a new government formed. The branch was promptly revived and welcomed again into the Association. At the request of the Prime Minister, Hon. H. A. Blaize, a seminar on parliamentary practice and procedure was held on 9–13 September 1985 for the benefit of the whole Parliament, most of the members of which lacked parliamentary experience. A strong group from other Parliaments took part in the seminar and contributed to its success.[12]

In July 1985, however, Uganda suffered another military *coup*. As in Nigeria, the Speaker and Clerk of the Parliament and others had endeavoured to establish a parliamentary regime. Tribal conflicts and other factors undermined their efforts. The branch was dissolved automatically on the suspension of the constitution.

The General Assembly, meeting in Saskatchewan on 10 October 1985, again discussed the official verbatim report of the plenary conference and whether or not it should be discontinued. Delegates had before them a paper on the subject, prepared by the new Editor, Andrew Imlach. The Hon. Treasurer, Mark Carlisle, recalled that the reasons which had led the working party and the Executive Committee to recommend discontinuance of the report were basically financial. The cost to the host branch in providing reporters and typescripts of speeches was heavy. The Executive Committee, in reviewing the recommendation, had been particularly concerned about the cost to the Association. The Editor had estimated that, using uncorrected tapes, thus sparing the host branch expense, a verbatim report could be produced at a cost of £7500–£8000. This represented an addition of about 1 per cent to the Association's annual expenditure.

In the following discussion, Lord Harmar-Nicholls maintained that the verbatim report was a luxury which the Association could no longer afford. The summary of the Isle of Man conference, published in *The Parliamentarian*, had been adequate. Delegates from India, New Zealand and Cyprus said that the report was essential for their branches and for posterity. Ms Annette King (New Zealand) said, 'We have one plenary conference a year. I believe that it is important to have a full and accurate report of that conference. If you have to rely on someone else's impression of that conference I do not believe you are reflecting history, how it actually happened and what was said.'[13] The motion to resume publication of the official verbatim report was finally rejected by 74 votes to 34. This decision applied only to the report of the Association's plenary conferences. Verbatim reports of the conferences of members from small countries continued to be published.

The Editor reported on the survey of members' views on the new format of *The Parliamentarian*. The response showed that they were overwhelmingly in favour of it. His brief report was received with applause.

The Hon. Treasurer, Mark Carlisle, whose term of office ended in Saskatoon, reviewed the finances in some detail. He observed that during the past three years the contingency reserves had been built up from nothing to its present figure of £75,000. It was vital to maintain the reserve at this level because both the income and the expenditure of the Association were subject to unpredictable vagaries. Next he explained the estimates for 1986–87. He then dwelt on the working capital fund, which had been a remarkable success. It had in 1985 passed £500,000 and, thanks to the work of the Association's merchant bankers, the market value of the fund on 3 August was £725,025. He had written to the Rt Hon. James Callaghan, who as Prime Minister had approved a grant of £100,000 from the United Kingdom government to start the fund. He had also written to Sir Neil Marten who had been Hon. Treasurer at the time when the fund was launched and had contributed greatly to its success. Both had replied expressing pleasure at this news and congratulations to the Association.

The 31st Commonwealth Parliamentary Conference took place in Saskatoon, Saskatchewan, from 7–11 October 1985. The conference of members from small countries was held in Regina on 1–2 October 1985. This was the first plenary conference of the Association to be hosted by a province/state of a Federation. As in the Isle of Man a relatively small branch undertook the major responsibilities of being host to some 368 visitors and of arranging hospitality, the conferences and the tours. The Saskatchewan branch earned the thanks of all. Special tributes were paid to Hon. Herbert J. Swan, the President of the Association and Speaker of the Legislative Assembly of Saskatchewan, and to Mrs Swan, as well as to members of the host branch. Gordon Barnhard, Clerk of the Legislative Assembly and conference officer, and his assistants were warmly commended for their efficient arrangements. A small branch acting as host can often achieve a greater sense of community and fellowship among delegates, especially if they are brought into contact with the local people. This was the experience in Saskatchewan as it had been in the Isle of Man.

The conference was formally opened by the Hon. Frederick W. Johnson, Lieut-Governor of the province on 3 October in the Legislative Chamber, Regina. The agenda was primarily concerned with economic and social problems.[14] Of the six plenary sessions, one was concerned with the United Nations and one of the six panel sessions considered the Gleneagles Agreement on sporting contacts with South Africa. Discussion of the report of the study group on electoral law and practice occupied one plenary session. It was notable that the media, both nationally and provincially, gave wider coverage to the conference – a welcome development, due largely to early briefing by the editor, himself formerly a Canadian journalist. A summary of the discussions was published in *The Parliamentarian*. There was no verbatim report.

Notes

1. Report of Proceedings of the 29th Commonwealth Parliamentary Conference (Kenya, 1983), p.xxi.
2. Ibid., p.xxiv.
3. *Loc. cit.*
4. Ibid., p.2.
5. **Agenda and Opening Speakers, Kenya, 1983**
   The Energy Crisis and Economic Cooperation within the Commonwealth – J. J. M. Nyagah, Minister of Water Developments (Kenya)
   Poverty of the Third World: The Challenge of Global Food Production and Distribution – Dr Bal Ram Jakhar, Speaker of the Lok Sabha (India)
   Housing and Human Settlements: What Role for the Elected Representative? – panel session
   Development Assistance with Particular Reference to the Transfer of Technology – panel session
   The Civil Servant and his Relationship with Parliamentarians – panel session
   The Problem of Unemployment in Commonwealth Countries with Particular Reference to School Leavers – panel session
   International Organisations – Their Effectiveness in Resolving International Disputes and Preserving Peace – Ken Fry (Australia)
   The Future of Parliamentary Democracy in the Commonwealth – Peter Hordern (United Kingdom)

International Peace and Security with Special Reference to Southern Africa – Namibia *and South Africa* – K. P. Morake, Minister of Education (Botswana)

The Dissemination of Information about Parliament – Louis Desmarais (Canada).

6. Report of Proceedings of the 29th Commonwealth Parliamentary Conference (Kenya, 1983), p.233.

7. Report of the Executive Committee of the CPA (1984–85), p.15.

8. **Agenda and Opening Speakers, Isle of Man, 1984**

The Commonwealth, the Arms Race and World Peace – Tim Renton, Parliamentary Under-Secretary, Foreign and Commonwealth Office (United Kingdom)

The Threat from Terrorism to Democratic Governments and to Parliamentary Institutions – Hon. E. L. Senanayake, Speaker (Sri Lanka)

The Cabinet System versus the Presidential System in Commonwealth Parliaments – panel session

Government by Regulation in a Parliamentary Democracy with Particular Reference to the Position of Delegated Legislation in Commonwealth Countries – panel session

Parliamentary Privilege with Special Reference to Confidentiality – panel session

The Role of Parliament and Parliamentarians in Influencing the Direction of the Economy – Erskine Sandiford (Barbados)

The Freedom of the Individual, Human Rights and Responsibilities, and the Authority of Government in a Parliamentary System – James Thrush (Zimbabwe)

Opinion Polls and the Political Process – panel session

Unemployment and its Social Consequences – panel session

Problems of Drought in Commonwealth Countries – panel session

The Security of Small States – Matthew Ramcharan, Speaker, House of Representatives (Trinidad & Tobago).

9. Vol. LXV, no. 4 (October 1984).

10. A taped record of the conference proceedings exists, but it has the disadvantage that delegates have not been able to correct their speeches as in the past. Bearing in mind that for many delegates English is not their native tongue, it has always been considered essential that each delegate should be able to correct and clarify his speech.

11. The members of the study group on 'Electoral Law and Practice' were: Chairman, Patrick Boyer (Canada); C. J. Butale (Botswana); Somnath Rath (India); Kenneth L. Shirley (New Zealand); W. St Clair-Daniel (St Lucia); Dr Lau Teik Soon (Singapore); Michael Colvin (United Kingdom). The Rapporteur was Jean-Marc Hamel, Chief Electoral Officer (Canada).

    Special guests were B. R. Nugent, Electoral Officer for New South Wales, and Carl Dundas, Special Legal Officer to the Technical Assistance Group of the Commonwealth Secretariat and former Electoral Commissioner in Jamaica.

    The meetings were also attended by the Chief Electoral Officer of Nova Scotia, D. William MacDonald, by the Chief Election Officer of Ontario, Warren R. Bailie, as well as by L. Gofetile (Botswana) and Colin Shepperd (United Kingdom).

12. The members and parliamentary officials who attended the seminar in Grenada were: Sir Paul Dean, Deputy Speaker, House of Commons (United Kingdom); Arthur Donahoe, Speaker, House of Assembly (Nova Scotia); W. St Clair-Daniel, Speaker, House of Assembly (St Lucia); Michael Ryle, Clerk of the Journals, House of Commons (United Kingdom); Philip Laundy, Clerk Assistant, House of Commons (Ottawa).

13. Transcript of Proceedings of the General Assembly (Saskatoon, 10 October 1985).

14. **Agenda and Opening Speakers, Saskatchewan, 1985**
    The United Nations: How can the United Nations be Strengthened to Enable it to Preserve Peace and Promote Disarmament? – Ted Lindsay (Australia)
    The Debt Crisis and International Currency Fluctuations: What Can be Done to Stabilise the Global Economy? – Lloyd Crouse (Canada); Lavi Mulimba (Zambia)
    Trade and Development Assistance: What Special Obligations Does Membership of the Commonwealth Imply? – Lloyd Crouse (Canada)
    International Year of Youth: What Can Tomorrow's Commonwealth Offer Today's Youth? – Lancelot Swan (Bermuda)
    Electoral Law and Practice; Discussion of the Recommendations of the CPA Study Group – Patrick Boyer (Canada)
    The Role of a Member of Parliament: Legislator or Social Worker? – Rt Hon. Ernest Armstrong, Deputy Speaker, House of Commons (United Kingdom)
    The Gleneagles Agreement on Sporting Contacts with South Africa: Can Gleneagles be Enforced without Violating Individual Rights? – panel session
    Agricultural Prices, Production and Distribution: What Must be Done to Relieve and Prevent Famine? – panel session
    Educational Mobility in the Commonwealth: What Can be Done to Enhance Educational Opportunities Throughout the Commonwealth? – panel session
    The Drug Problem: What Can the Commonwealth do to Curb Drug Abuse? – panel session
    The Decade for Women: Past Achievements and Future Challenges for Women in Public Life – panel session
    The Image of the Parliamentarian: What Can be Done to Improve the Standing of the Politician in the Eyes of the Public? – panel session.

15. Vol. LXVI, No. 4 (October 1985).

23 The Secretariat, 1983–85

The Headquarters Secretariat has always played an essential role in the working of the CPA and one which is not well understood. It is not merely an administrative centre. The Association was created by its first Secretary-General, Sir Howard d'Egville. He gave a dynamism and vision to its growth as an important international organisation. He was in complete charge of the Secretariat and the constant source of new ideas and developments. He briefed new members on the purpose and function of the Association. Indeed, the Secretariat has continued to exercise these functions. It informs new members of the Executive and the General Assembly and, most important, from within it have emanated the proposals for virtually all new developments such as the working capital fund, study groups, parliamentary newsletters, and the information centre.

D'Egville was, moreover, keenly aware of the need for continuity in the management of the Association. He sought, at times unwisely, to ensure that key members served for long periods on the General Council. At the same time he recognised that the Secretariat must be the chief source of continuity and consistency of policies and of management.

In an international organisation like the CPA all branches must have the right to provide officers and members of the Executive Committee from time to time and to regular representation on the General Assembly. For this and for other reasons short terms of service – usually three years – on the Committee are prescribed and immediate re-election is not allowed. Although unavoidable, such short terms of service inhibit continuity.

The General Assembly comprises all delegates appointed by the branches to attend the plenary conference. Many – indeed, often the majority – of the delegates are attending for the first time. They are nevertheless called on to approve and vote on matters put to them by the Executive Committee. From time to time branches have been asked to bear in mind, when electing or appointing their delegates, this need for continuity. Branches are, however, autonomous and must heed party allegiances and practices when choosing their delegates.

Another factor is the nature of the membership of the Association. All are Members of Parliament. Their priorities must be their constituencies, their parties, and the government of their countries, and, for those with drive and ability, the goal of ministerial office. Chairmen and members of the Executive Committee have usually been Speakers or Ministers. Their work for the CPA has been invaluable. As pressures of government increase inexorably, however, fewer younger members are coming forward to serve the Association.

In all of these circumstances the Secretary-General and the senior staff of the Secretariat alone can provide real continuity within the Association. They are professionally engaged and committed to the work. The Secretary-General should be in a position of authority to advise and guide the Executive and the General Assembly. Sir Robin Vanderfelt has striven conscientiously and with considerable success to perform this role. Moreover he has been strongly supported by the senior staff of the Secretariat. But his authority has been circumscribed.

On the retirement of Sir Howard d'Egville, the United Kingdom branch, which in effect dominated the General Council at that time, redefined the position of the Secretary-General. Moved by personal animus against d'Egville and by a resolve to bring the Association under the control of their branch, the then leading UK members, as recounted earlier, made it clear that d'Egville's successor should not be the director nor even the chief executive officer of the Association, but its servant. He should not act on his own initiative nor exercise authority, but must refer all proposals and decisions to the officers and the Council.

Although described in the constitution as the chief executive officer, the Secretary-General has been restricted in his responsibilities and closely overseen by his Executive and its subcommittees. This has applied particularly in the appointment and dismissal of the staff of the Secretariat. While himself appointed by the General Assembly on the recommendation of the Executive Committee, other senior staff in the Secretariat are chosen and appointed by the Executive. He may or may not be consulted, and he has no say in the decision.

The present procedure followed by the CPA in making senior appointments is time-consuming and costly. The posts are advertised throughout the Commonwealth. Selection boards in each region interview candidates and recommend one (or sometimes more) for further consideration. A final selection board meets in London, the fares and accommodation of the members of the board and the candidates being paid for by the Association. The board's recommendations are reported to the Executive Committee, which makes the appointments.

This procedure had not been invoked earlier. D'Egville had appointed all staff, and after his retirement, the senior staff had remained unchanged. All had served for more than 28 years. Indeed, Jack Fowler, to whom warm tributes were paid in the General Assembly for his work as Assistant Secretary-General and conference officer, and who retired in 1984, had served for 38 years. Betty May, to whom tributes were paid in Nairobi and who had received the honour of an MBE, had served for 29 years. Sir Robin Vanderfelt, who retired in July 1986, served the

CPA, first for 12 years in the UK branch and then for 25 years as Secretary-General.

In the period 1983–85 the Executive and its subcommittee on Staff and Accommodation devoted considerable attention to appointments to the Secretariat. The selection board which met in London on 19 January 1983 under the chairmanship of W. R. Baxter recommended the appointment of Dr John Henderson, who was experienced in the academic and parliamentary fields in New Zealand, as Deputy Secretary-General. The board also recommended that Andrew Imlach, who had been recruited from Canada in 1981 as Deputy Editor, be appointed as Editor of Publications. They took up their duties in July and June 1983, respectively, each for a two-year probationary period.

The editor at once sought to make *The Parliamentarian* more appealing by introducing bolder typography and including illustrations. He also expanded the contents so that it was no longer devoted exclusively to parliamentary matters. Although redesigned by the Editor quite independently, the journal became similar in style to the *Canadian Parliamentary Review*, the quarterly journal of the Canadian branches, which has been published since 1978 and is ably edited by Gary Levy. As recorded above, the new format of *The Parliamentarian* has been widely welcomed. Subsequently, Imlach's probationary period having expired, the Committee decided that his appointment should be permanent. At the same time it directed that he should have the assistance of an editorial board of four or five knowledgeable people, not necessarily Members of Parliament, but including the Chairman of the Executive Committee and the Secretary-General.

The Deputy Secretary-General, Dr John Henderson, withdrew as a candidate for the office of Secretary-General. He had, in fact, accepted the personal invitation of the New Zealand Prime Minister to be Director of a new advisory group in the Prime Minister's department. This was a great loss to the Secretariat and to the Association. John Henderson had, in his two years as a member of the Secretariat, worked with remarkable energy, ability and understanding of the purposes of the Association.

The important post of Deputy Secretary-General was thus vacant. After lengthy discussion the Executive Committee decided that it should remain vacant until its meeting in Saskatchewan. There the procedure agreed was that candidates should be invited through branches, interviewed and short-listed by the Secretary-General. It was hoped that the Deputy would be appointed by the Committee meeting in Newfoundland in May 1986.

In Malawi in May 1984 the Executive Committee had appointed a new subcommittee on Staff and Accommodation. Tony Durant was elected Chairman in place of W. R. Baxter, whose term of service on the Committee had ended. The subcommittee was enlarged to include a representative from each region. The reason was that it had the task of revising the terms of service of senior staff as well as the responsibility for the timetable and procedure for selecting the next Secretary-General. It would also serve as the final selection board. Under the chairmanship of Tony Durant, the subcommittee held a number of meetings and its recommendations were approved.

The final selection board met in London on 25–26 April 1985. Its Chairman reported to the Executive Committee in Cyprus on 29 April that the board had interviewed eight candidates, one from each region, apart from Canada and Asia which had each presented two candidates, and South-East Asia which had presented none. The board had decided to select the best candidate without considering regional factors. It was unanimous in recommending the appointment of Dr the Hon. David Tonkin, a former Premier of South Australia, an ophthalmologist and a consultant on health management.

Several members of the Committee expressed concern about the need for full Commonwealth representation in the staffing of the Headquarters Secretariat. The Committee reaffirmed the principle that the staff should be broadly representative of the regions of the Commonwealth.

At its meeting in Saskatoon, Saskatchewan on 10 October 1985 the General Assembly appointed Dr David Tonkin to be Secretary-General in succession to Sir Robin Vanderfelt, joining the staff of the Secretariat on 2 April 1986 and taking up his duties in July 1986.

All in Saskatchewan were aware that this was Sir Robin Vanderfelt's last conference as Secretary-General. Many warm tributes were paid to his integrity and dedication and to his unfailing courtesy and concern for individual parliamentarians. Lord Harmar-Nicholls, a United Kingdom delegate who had first been elected to the House of Commons in 1950 and elevated to the House of Lords in 1974, said that he had known Sir Robin throughout this long period. Of Sir Robin's contribution to the CPA and the Commonwealth he said:

> The transition from Empire to Commonwealth has been full of possible pitfalls with emotions and loyalties sometimes strained to the limit. The fact that the hazardous journey has been made with a minimum of setbacks is in no small measure due to the influence exerted by the CPA, that means by Sir Robin himself. That is why we are so genuinely grateful to him and why in 1973 the Queen honoured him with a knighthood.[1]

At the General Assembly in the Isle of Man the previous year Shri Radha Nandan Jha had paid a spontaneous tribute. Sir Robin, he said, 'is the soul of the conference. He is the soul of the CPA and he is due to retire in 1986. It is my view that the CPA is not in a position to dispense with his services. Some amendment must be made to our constitution so that he may, if given a new lease of life, continue to serve the CPA and the General Assembly.'[2] Addressing delegates in Saskatchewan, the Commonwealth Secretary-General, Shridath Ramphal, added his tribute: 'My own close and happy personal friendship with him goes back many years; but much more important, he has been a great friend to the whole Commonwealth and to literally generations of Commonwealth Parliamentarians.'[3]

The Chairman of the Executive Committee, Dr Bal Ram Jakhar, paid tribute to Sir Robin on behalf of the Association at the General Assembly in Saskatoon on 10 October 1985. He said to him: 'You deserve all our congratulations and all our appreciation for the work you have done for this organization, because this Association is not only an organization, it is a sort of family with branches all over the world.'[4] It was notable in this and other speeches that there was not only deep appreciation of his work but also a wealth of affection for the man himself. Indeed, it was decided by the Executive Committee that all branches should be invited to express their individual tributes by contributing to a fund to be formally presented to him at the conference in London in September 1986.

In responding to the speech of Dr Bal Ram Jakhar, Sir Robin said:

Whatever I have achieved I owe to the help, courtesy and kindness of countless Parliamentarians throughout the Commonwealth and to countless parliamentary officials as well as to all who have held office in the Association and to others. To have worked for nearly 36 years for the Association has been a challenge and a wonderfully unique privilege so much so that I cannot ever forget the CPA which I have grown to love and which is a great part of my life.[5]

Notes

1. Daily bulletin of Saskatchewan conference.
2. Transcript of Proceedings of the General Assembly (Isle of Man, 1984).
3. Transcript of Commonwealth Secretary-General's speech (Saskatchewan, 7 October 1985).
4. Transcript of Proceedings of the General Assembly (Saskatoon, 1985).
5. Ibid.

Epilogue

In the years since the CPA was founded, the Commonwealth has been transformed. It has grown in size and has developed new machinery of consultation and cooperation. It has, however, lost much of the sense of unity and devotion to high ideals which informed it in the 1920s and 1930s. In a number of countries the principles of the rule of law, human rights and parliamentary democracy have been sacrificed. By the end of the 1960s, in the view of a realistic observer, Professor Bruce Miller, it had become difficult to explain whether the Commonwealth stood for anything at all: it was best described as 'a concert of convenience'.

In the 1970s the Commonwealth Heads of Government endorsed declarations of principles. They were directed primarily at closing the gap between rich and poor nations, at racial prejudice and specifically apartheid. But they came at a time of world recession and of mounting racial, sectional and tribal conflict in many countries, and the Commonwealth has no power or authority to intervene in such conflicts. In fact, the Commonwealth remains a voluntary association of independent nations, each pursuing its own interests and closely guarding its own sovereignty.

The Commonwealth nevertheless survives and displays a real strength and cohesion. Its members see it as a forum in which they can press their policies and interests. They value the ease of communication, informality and flexibility which are not found in the United Nations nor in any other international organisation. This can have practical results as in the negotiations leading to the independence of Zimbabwe. Underlying this practical convenience have been shared experiences, a common language and a community of outlook which exert a binding force.

The CPA has reflected and influenced the evolution of the Commonwealth. It, too, has grown in size. In 1911 it had six branches; in 1985 there were 110 branches and a total membership of over 7500 MPs. Many hundreds of members of legislatures in every part of the Commonwealth have been involved in its activities. They have attended plenary and regional conferences and have taken part in parliamentary seminars, visits and study groups. They have regularly received the Association's journal, *The Parliamentarian*, newsletters and other publications. They have been able to call on the services of the information centre.

The CPA provides forums in which MPs from the largest and equally from the smallest countries of the Commonwealth can meet, argue and discuss. At the same time it engenders among them a sense of fellowship and community. It unites them in their belief in parliamentary government. In conferences and seminars they grow in knowledge and outlook. It promotes friendship and understanding. But it is the parliamentary bond which gives the Association its main strength.

The need for the CPA has never been greater than in the unsettled world of the late 1980s. Political instability, military *coups*, and scarcely veiled dictatorship have afflicted many countries of the Commonwealth. The CPA cannot intervene in their internal affairs, but it exerts a strong influence. It has done so because throughout the 75 years of its existence it has always represented the democratic principle and has promoted belief in the practical benefits of parliamentary government. This has been its major contribution to the Commonwealth and the world.

Appendix A: Dates of Formation of CPA Branches (in alphabetical order of branches)

Alderney, 1980 (effective 1 January 1981)
Antigua, 1953
Australia, 1912
  New South Wales, 1926
  Northern Territory, 1952 as subsidiary branch; affiliated, 1969
  Queensland, 1926
  South Australia, 1926
  Tasmania, 1930
  Victoria, 1926
  Western Australia, 1926
Bahamas, 1932
Bangladesh, 1973; in abeyance 1976–79; reformed, November 1979; in abeyance 1982
Barbados, 1933
Belize, 1950
Bermuda, 1928
Botswana 1962 as Bechuanaland; subsidiary branch; auxiliary branch & Botswana, 1966; main branch, 1968
British Virgin Islands, 1953
Canada, 1912
  Alberta, 1946
  British Columbia, 1928–33; reformed, 1934
  Manitoba, 1938
  New Brunswick, 1933
  Newfoundland, 1912–34; reformed, 1950
  Northwest Territories, 1974
  Nova Scotia, 1932
  Ontario, 1930
  Prince Edward Island, 1940–56; reformed, 1960
  Quebec, 1933
  Saskatchewan, 1937
  Yukon, 1975
Cayman Islands, 1964
Cook Islands, 1969 (formerly subsidiary branch)
Cyprus, 1978 (effective 1 January 1979)
Dominica, 1946
Falkland Islands, 1952 as subsidiary branch; auxiliary branch, 1975
Fiji, 1951 as subsidiary branch; affiliated branch, 1967; main branch, 1971
Gambia, 1949
Ghana, 1946 as Gold Coast until 1957; in abeyance 1966–69 and 1972–79; reformed, November 1979; in abeyance 1982–
Gibraltar, 1951 as subsidiary branch; affiliated branch, 1962
Grenada, 1946; auxiliary branch, 1967; main branch, 1974; in abeyance 1979–May 1985
Guernsey, 1952 as subsidiary branch; auxiliary branch, 1972
Guyana, 1939 as British Guiana; Guyana & main branch, 1966
Hong Kong, 1951 as subsidiary branch; auxiliary branch, 1972
India, 1927 (as British India to 1947); 1950

Andhra Pradesh, 1968
Assam, 1970
Bihar, 1973
Gujarat, 1961 (part of Bombay
   1952–61)
Haryana, 1969
Himachal Pradesh, 1971
Jammu & Kashmir, 1973
Karnataka, 1958 (Mysore 1958–73)
Kerala, 1973
Madhya Pradesh, 1955–60; reformed,
   1971
Maharashtra, 1952 (part of Bombay
   1952–61)
Manipur, 1976
Meghalaya, 1974
Nagaland, 1974; in abeyance 1976–77
Orissa, 1975
Punjab, 1958
Rajasthan, 1959
Sikkim, 1979
Tamil Nadu, 1955 (Madras until
   1969); in abeyance 1976–77
Uttar Pradesh, 1957–62; reformed,
   1971
West Bengal, 1952
Isle of Man, 1936
Jamaica, 1933
Jersey, 1952
Kenya, 1948
Kiribati, 1968 as Gilbert & Ellice
   Islands subsidiary branch; affiliated
   branch, 1971; Gilbert Islands, 1975;
   Kiribati, 1979
Lesotho, 1960 as Basutoland
   subsidiary branch; auxiliary and
   renamed Lesotho, 1966; main branch,
   1968; in abeyance 1970–72; reformed,
   1973
Malawi, 1951 as Nyasaland; main branch
   and renamed Malawi, 1964
Malaysia 1950 (as Federation of
   Malaya; Malaysia 1963)
   Johore, 1963
   Kedah, 1965
   Kelantan, 1978
   Malacca, 1973
   Negri Sembilan, 1963
   Pahang, 1963

Penang, 1971
Perak, 1963
Perlis, 1976
Sabah, 1951 as North Borneo
   subsidiary branch; affiliated branch,
   1961; state branch and renamed
   Sabah, 1963
Sarawak, 1951 as subsidiary branch;
   affiliated branch, 1959; state branch,
   1963
Selangor, 1963
Trengganu, 1963
Malta, 1925–31; reformed, 1948; in
   abeyance 1959–62; auxiliary branch,
   1962; main branch, 1964; withdrew
   March 1983
Mauritius, 1934; auxiliary branch, 1966;
   main branch, 1968
Montserrat, 1953
Nauru, subsidiary branch, 1968;
   main branch, 1969
Nevis Island, 1985; effective
   1 January 1986
New Zealand, 1912
Nigeria, 1948; main branch 1961; in
   abeyance 1966–80; reformed, 1980; in
   abeyance December 1983
   Anambra, 1980; effective 1 January
      1981; in abeyance December 1983
   Bauchi, 1983; effective 1 January 1983;
      in abeyance December 1983
   Bendel, 1980; effective 1 January 1981;
      in abeyance December 1983
   Benue 1982; effective 1 January 1983;
      in abeyance December 1983
   Borno 1981; effective 1 January 1982;
      in abeyance December 1983
   Cross River 1980; effective 1 January
      1981; in abeyance December 1983
   Gongola, 1981; effective 1 January
      1982; in abeyance December 1983
   Imo, 1981; effective 1 January 1982;
      in abeyance December 1983
   Kaduna, 1981; effective 1 January
      1982; in abeyance December 1983
   Kano, 1983; effective 1 January 1984;
      in abeyance December 1983
   Lagos, 1981; effective 1 January 1982;
      in abeyance December 1983

Niger, 1981; effective 1 January 1982; in abeyance December 1983

Ogun, 1980; effective 1 January 1981; in abeyance December 1983

Ondo, 1980; effective 1 January 1981; in abeyance December 1983

Oyo, 1980; effective 1 January 1981; in abeyance December 1983

Plateau, 1980; effective 1 January 1981; in abeyance December 1983

Sokoto, 1982; effective 1 January 1983; in abeyance December 1983

Niue, 1978; effective 1 January 1979

Norfolk Island, November 1979; effective 1 January 1980

Northern Ireland, 1924; in abeyance 1973-74; in abeyance 1975-

Papua New Guinea, 1952 as subsidiary branch; affiliated branch, 1970; main branch, 1976

St Christopher-Nevis-Anguilla, 1953

St Helena, 1970 as subsidiary branch; auxiliary branch, 1973

St Lucia, 1946; auxiliary branch, 1970

St Vincent, 1946

Seychelles, 1952 as subsidiary branch; affiliated branch, 1970; main branch, 1976; in abeyance 1977; reformed, 1980; withdrew 1982

Sierra Leone, 1952; main branch, 1961; in abeyance 1967-68

Singapore, 1949; main branch, 1965

Solomon Islands, 1962 as subsidiary branch; affiliated branch, 1970; (main) branch, 1978

Sri Lanka, 1927 as Ceylon; main branch, 1948; Sri Lanka, 1973

Swaziland, 1965 as subsidiary branch; main branch, 1969; in abeyance 1973-79; reformed, November 1979

Tanzania, 1951 as Tanganyika subsidiary branch; affiliated branch and Tanzania, 1961; main branch, 1962

Tonga, 1958 as subsidiary branch; main branch, 1970

Trinidad & Tobago, 1944; main branch, 1962

Turks and Caicos Islands, 1972

Tuvalu, 1968 as Gilbert & Ellice Islands subsidiary branch; affiliated branch, 1971; Tuvalu and auxiliary branch, 1976; (main) branch, 1978

Uganda, 1952 as subsidiary branch; affiliated branch, 1956; main branch, 1962; in abeyance 1971; reformed, 1981 (effective 1 January 1982); in abeyance July 1985

United Kingdom, 1911

Vanuatu, 1981; effective 1 January 1982

Western Samoa, 1953 as subsidiary branch; affiliated branch, 1960; main branch, 1970

Zambia, 1946 as Northern Rhodesia; Zambia and main branch, 1964

Zimbabwe, 1980; effective 1 January 1981

Appendix B: Former CPA Branches

1913 South Africa (dissolved 1961)

1925 Southern Rhodesia (dissolved 1965)

1925 Malta (in abeyance 1959–62; auxiliary branch, 1962; main branch, 1964; withdrew March 1983)

1926 Irish Free State (to 1934; but continued to pay token grant to 1948)

1937 Bengal (dissolved?)

1948 Pakistan (in abeyance 1958–63; in abeyance March 1969–February 1972 when Pakistan left the Commonwealth)

1951 Zanzibar (subsidiary branch; affiliated branch, 1961; dissolved 1962)

1952 Aden (subsidiary branch; affiliated branch, 1959; dissolved 1967)

1952 Seychelles (subsidiary branch; affiliated branch, 1970; main branch, 1976; in abeyance 1977–80; withdrew 1982)

1954 Federation of Rhodesia and Nyasaland (dissolved 1963)

1954 Punjab (Pakistan) (dissolved?)

1954 Madhya Bharat (dissolved?)

1955 Sark (subsidiary branch; lapsed early 1970s)

1956 East Pakistan ⎱ (in abeyance 1958–63; 1969–72 when
1956 West Pakistan ⎰ Pakistan left the Commonwealth)

1956 Eastern Nigeria ⎱
1956 Western Nigeria ⎰ (in abeyance since 1966)
1956 Northern Nigeria ⎰

1956 Southern Cameroons (dissolved?)

1957 British Somaliland (subsidiary branch; dissolved 1960)

1959 Federation of the West Indies (dissolved May 1962)

1964 Mid-Western Nigeria (in abeyance since 1966)

Index